The Elusive Phenomena

The Elusive

Edited by George F. F. Lombard

Published by Division of Research
Graduate School of Business Administration
Harvard University   Boston • 1977

Distributed by Harvard University Press
Cambridge, Massachusetts and London, England

Phenomena

An Autobiographical Account

of My Work in the Field of Organizational Behavior

at the Harvard Business School

F. J. Roethlisberger

Contents

Foreword by George F. F. Lombard   ix

1.   Introduction: What's the Point?   1

Book One   Finding a Focus for Myself and My Work

Part I: Choosing a Career: 1898-1942

2.   My Search for Certainty   11
3.   My Discovery of Life Space   29
4.   The Hawthorne and Related Researches   45
5.   Concrete Sociology   60
6.   Excursions in General Motors, Macy's, the Government, and Small Business   75
7.   A Period of Self-Renewal   90

Part II: Human Relations and Administration: 1938-1948

Introduction   105
8.   My Early Teaching Years   107
9.   Teaching by the Case Method   123
10.   Toward a Descriptive Theory of Behavior in Organizations   143
11.   The Administrator's Job   168

Part III: Human Relations as the Focus for Development, 1948-1957

Introduction   195
12.   Human Relations Practice   197
13.   Human Relations Training   217
14.   Human Relations Research   232

Part IV: Organizational Behavior as the Focus for Development, 1946-1967

    Introduction 253

15. The Social Organization of the Faculty 257
16. The Early Development of the Area of Organizational Behavior 273
17. The New Doctoral Program 287
18. Theories about Organizational Behavior 300
19. Learning to Count Sophisticatedly 323

Book Two   Restatements and Reflections

    Introduction: The Turbulent Sixties 343

Part V: Levels of the Knowledge Enterprise

20. Skill 349
21. Clinical Knowledge 368
22. Analytical Knowledge 383

Part VI: Revisiting My Subject Matter

23. Classes, Concrete Systems, and Spaces 401
24. The Battles of the Spaces 421

Part VII: Knowledge and Action in Modern Society

25. The Uneven Development of Knowledge and Action 435
26. Complementarity as a Way of Correcting the Imbalance 452

    References 475
    Index 485

Foreword

BY GEORGE F. F. LOMBARD

Louis E. Kirstein Professor of Human Relations Emeritus

The thought that he would write a book about his life and work was in Fritz Roethlisberger's mind for several years before his retirement. Though he spoke of it as his intellectual autobiography, what he wanted to say was not solely or even primarily about himself. He wanted to use the experiences of his life and work to clarify some intellectual and conceptual questions that he believed were neglected in business administration and the social sciences. He thought that confusions following from this neglect impeded the development of knowledge and the improvement of practice, especially in the fields with which he was most familiar, human relations and organizational behavior. He had in mind the last admonition of L. J. Henderson in his lectures on the methods of science (1970),* that the final task in scientific study is "the clear, explicit, and logical formulation of all relevant observations, analyses, and conclusions." Henderson went on to say, "*In scientific work the final task must be invariably performed. This is an induction from experience. It is a judgment from which there can be no appeal.*"

Much of what Fritz thought needed to be stated went against the conventional wisdom of our times. For this reason he felt that it would be necessary for him to make explicit his own views about the philosophical bases of science—the assumptions about the relation of science to the wider world that researchers usually take for granted when they report the findings of specific projects. His hope was that if he talked about his assumptions, others would be encouraged to think about theirs. He fully realized that exploration of these ideas would take him into questions of personal values and choices about which it was difficult to think clearly, let alone write clearly.

Fritz believed that if he wrote about his ideas too succinctly, in a didactic style of advocacy for them, any responses they elicited would

* See References, page 475.

be in adversary modes that would continue the arguments and controversies that diverted the energies of so many social scientists and teachers of business administration from productive research during his lifetime. He believed that he would have a better chance to clarify and communicate the ideas that he thought important if he described them in the context of his experiences.

Fritz was of two minds about the professional experiences of his life.

He knew that in one sense his career could be viewed as a "success." He was a major contributor to the Hawthorne Studies of the Western Electric Company, the best known researches about human problems in industry. His classes in Human Relations at the Harvard Business School could not accommodate the numbers of students who wanted to take them. He was much in demand as a speaker to business and academic audiences. He received Harvard University's Ledlie Prize, awarded to the person "who by research discovered or otherwise made the most valuable contribution to science or in any other way for the benefit of mankind."

At the same time, Fritz was dismayed over the confusions and controversies that sprang up around his studies and those of others in the same fields. He believed that these controversies prevented advancements of knowledge about management and the behavior of people in organizations that were within our grasp. Not to have made them was to him a professional failure, the sources of which required clarification.

Fritz sensed a recurring pattern in studies in these fields that affected others' work as well as his own. This pattern typically began when a researcher presented new findings that seemed like a breakthrough solidly based in research. The findings next became a popular success and were soon used as answers for problems in all kinds of situations, even in ones to which they had little relevance. Then the findings came generally to be regarded as having failed, except among a few die-hards who could not be argued out of their importance, as in a cult. Finally, the pattern started over again with someone else's breakthrough, as likely as not unrelated to earlier ones, so that progress was not achieved. An important reason why Fritz undertook to write *Counseling in an Organization* (1966) with Bill Dickson was that he thought he could use the story of the counseling organization at the Western Electric Company as a case study of this pattern. As he explained in the book, his initial hope was that other researchers would document similar experiences of their own, but that has not happened.

Fritz's ideas about how he could report his experiences to explain this pattern developed slowly, though systematically, as was his habit. He began before retirement by preparing a chronological outline of his work in some detail. *Man-in-Organization* (1968), a collection of his papers, resulted from this task and was published a year after he became emeritus. By this time he had in mind the general scope of the manuscript on which the present book is based, although not specifically how he would conclude it. That developed while he was writing.

From then on Fritz worked steadily on this manuscript, except as illness, occasional family obligations, and vacations interrupted. He and I met once a week for lunch. His progress—or lack of it—was our most frequent topic of conversation. He shared with me his excitements when he had found a way to state clearly some important point and his frustrations when he had not. Sometimes I could make a suggestion that he found helpful; more often, like any other writer, he had to work his problem out alone. I read each chapter as it came from the typewriter and gave him comments. He also talked frequently about his ideas with Anthony G. Athos, Louis B. Barnes, the colleagues who were closest to him personally at the time, and a few others. He made numerous revisions, even going back several times to the beginning of the book to try a fresh start.

When the first draft was completed, Fritz gave copies to Barnes and myself and also to Max R. Hall, then Editor for the Social Sciences at the Harvard University Press, who had helped him with *Man-in-Organization*, and asked for our comments. When he had received these, he began once more to go through the manuscript from the beginning. He had completed revisions through Chapter 11 and outlined further ones through Chapter 14 before his illness slowed down and finally stopped his work.

Fritz was not certain whether his manuscript should be published and, if it was, whether it should be as one book or two. If there were two books, he thought that one of them should be the account of his work, the other his thoughts after retirement. Alternatively, he thought that what are now the last seven chapters might make a series of articles.

Fritz's concern was whether his way of resolving the issues about science and organizational behavior that had fascinated and troubled him throughout his professional life was worth publishing. He knew very well that his resolution of the issues by means of a principle of complementarity had deep personal meaning for him in terms of the experiences of his life and work. His concern was whether this resolution was an act of faith and imagination entirely within himself or whether there was evidence for it outside himself at the phenomeno-logical level of behavior in organizations.

If his views were primarily personal and private, Fritz did not see why others should be expected to read about them, particularly in the guise of a contribution to science—the only context in which it inter-ested him to write about them. On the other hand, guided by Hender-son's admonition, he believed that he would not have fulfilled his role as a scientist unless he had made his ideas explicit.

When Fritz began to anticipate that he might not finish the revi-sions he had in mind, he asked me, if that time came, to decide what should be done with the manuscript. He wanted me to feel no urgen-cy about having it published. He said he would continue to rest in the peace he hoped to have, even if the manuscript was not published. In that circumstance he hoped that it would go into the archives of Baker Library, so that there would be a chance that in the future someone might read it and understand what he was trying to say.

Once I started work on the manuscript, I felt that the statement of his main ideas would be weakened if the parts were published sepa-rately. Consequently, I turned my attention, even in the early chap-ters, to highlighting his main themes. I added phrases, sentences, paragraphs, and in one place a page or two to clarify the structure of the book as a whole. In the process I may have made some of Fritz's sentences more declarative and definitive in tone than he would have wanted.

If I have done violence to Fritz's thoughts, though, it is more likely in Book II. Especially in the last four chapters I substantially rear-ranged the material, even moving some of it from one chapter to another. I also shortened it considerably.

Would that Fritz had lived to develop further the ideas that he expressed in those chapters! It has not seemed my role as editor to add my views about these ideas as substitutes for his, and I have not done so. Except for some minor editing and shortening and the addition of an excerpt from *Man-in-Organization*, the section at the end of the book on the skill and training of administrators is as he wrote it.

Fritz often said to me that he found it valuable in seeking a new synthesis of ideas to try first for a clear separation of the parts and only afterwards to attempt the statement of a new synthesis. I think that if his revisions of the manuscript had extended to the last chap-ter, he would have gone further with new suggestions for the design of the curriculum in schools of business administration. As it was, he could ask no more than that his clarification of the separate parts would give others a stepping stone from which to attempt a new synthesis. He died May 17, 1974, content that he had achieved that much.

For Fritz and for myself, I wish to express deep gratitude to the many people who over the years encouraged and supported the preparation and publication of this book. Fritz began the manuscript while George P. Baker was Dean of the School and Bertrand Fox was Director of Research. Later Lawrence E. Fouraker succeeded Professor Fox and still later became Dean of the School. In his administration first Richard E. Walton and then Richard S. Rosenbloom was Director of Research. Walter J. Salmon was Associate Dean for Educational Affairs. All of them were most generous with their support and encouragement, tangible and intangible.

Others' versions of some of the events in the history of the Business School as an institution and in the development of Human Relations and Organizational Behavior as fields of knowledge will differ from Fritz's view of them. This is unavoidable when persons with different perspectives and responsibilities participate in the same events. Neither Fritz nor I have attempted to present the "objective facts" about these situations; both of us have tried, rather, to present clearly his perceptions of them.

I received valuable comments from George C. Homans, Edmund P. Learned, Anthony G. Athos, Louis B. Barnes, C. Roland Christensen, Paul R. Lawrence, Jay W. Lorsch, Renato Tagiuri, Arthur N. Turner, and Abraham Zaleznik, and from Gerald B. Stratton and Jean Richon. Charles J. Christenson gave me generously of his time in my struggles with Fritz's statements about logic and scientific method. Though I did not accept all the suggestions I received, I am not the less grateful for the help given.

Fritz would have recognized with appreciation the many contributions to his ideas which he received throughout his teaching years from his students. He was especially grateful to his Doctoral students for the opportunity to discuss with them many of the ideas in Parts IV, V, VI, and VII. My work on the manuscript benefited from discussions with students in my seminars in 1976 and 1977 and in Eric Rhenman's in 1976. I am also grateful to Albert H. Gordon and to Dean Fouraker for the opportunity to discuss Fritz's work with The Directors of the Associates in September 1975.

I have no adequate way to thank Max R. Hall for his help. His conviction from the beginning that what Fritz wanted to say was important gave both of us the encouragement to go ahead on occasions when our own doubts and concerns held us back. His patient and persistent efforts to help us write clearly were without limit. No idea of Fritz's or of mine was too vague, no misplaced comma too small, that they failed to receive his careful attention.

Edward Anthony, Helen Cauchon, Rose Giacobbe, Elizabeth Karpati, Robert Lovett, and Barbard Rimbach helped at different stages. Gertrude O'Neil typed the original manuscript as Fritz wrote it. Her accuracy and dependability relieved him of many burdens. Eleanor M. Bradley, Roseanne Brady, Elizabeth Burr, Rachel Daitch, LuAnn Hahl, Jane Milner, and Gay Quimby typed the many later drafts. Eve Bamford made helpful editorial suggestions. Elizabeth Burr prepared the list of references.

Hilma Holton Gibb set aside important personal affairs to complete the copy-editing. Nancy Lou Hansen managed the publication process. The book was designed by David Ford. Susan Ackerman assisted ably in the proofreading; Nancy Donovan prepared the index.

Mary Esther Lombard and our family were most patient with my efforts and preoccupations during the months I worked on the manuscript. I am most grateful for their support.

Boston, April 1977

Chapter 1

Introduction: What's the Point?

For some of us there comes a time when we feel an urge to review our past in order to see where we have been. This time came for me in my late sixties, when I realized how closely my search for my subject matter and my search for my identity had been related. Often I had difficulty in separating out who I was from what my subject matter was. The two became tightly connected at an early stage in my life, and my later identity crises arose when I became perplexed with questions about my subject matter.

I seemed to be always wandering into as well as trying to extricate myself from someone else's bailiwick, and to have no bailiwick of my very own. This was not quite true. If I had not secretly cherished the idea that I did have one, I would not have been so conflicted. But whenever I tried to communicate it, I realized how personal it was, how it depended so heavily on hidden and unstated commitments.

For many years the question I found most embarrassing to answer was, "Tell me, Professor R., what are you teaching at the Harvard Business School?" In my early days I took this question seriously and tried to answer it. But this led so frequently to the next question— "Tell me, are you a nut and what kind of a nut are you?"—that I finally learned to answer the original question in a way that would not allow the second question to arise, at least not easily.

Yet, as I reflected upon my conflict, I realized how I had built my career upon it. I had become a professor without ever being able to state clearly what it was that I was professing. A professor without subject matter seemed a contradiction in terms, and yet, by golly, I had become—after much sweating, I confess—a professor at the Harvard Business School. But did this make me a professor of a subject matter among my peers at other universities? In institutional terms I was indubitably a professor; in subject matter things were and have continued to remain ambiguous. I wanted to be a professor who was well-established in both frames of reference, but I have never felt sure that I achieved this. I have never been quite willing to pay the price to realize it. To be a professor and to become a person have remained for me a difficult achievement.

I became interested in writing about my life and work in terms of this dilemma. I felt that the search for my subject matter and my identity among the elusive phenomena of human behavior in which I became involved, both as a person and as a professor, gave me a theme that would allow me to say some things that I have been wanting to say for some time and in a way that I wanted to say them. I felt there was a connection between my quandary and the quandaries of man in the modern world—not only of man in academia, but of every man and woman in the whole wide bloody modern world.

At the level of events my life has been fairly prosaic; only in relation to certain ideas does it take on any significance. This account of my life and work will be concerned chiefly with these ideas; how they developed; how they got nurtured and reinforced; how they led me into seemingly hopeless confusions and quandaries; how in spite of this I kept on chasing them. This focus, this search, determined the main parts into which I now divide my intellectual life. I say "intellectual life," even though it was very "personal" to me and contained many nonlogical elements.

1898–1942

During roughly my first 40 years I took a circuitous route to reach and finally settle down to make my career at the Harvard Business School. In this stage I became involved, both as a person and as a researcher, in the data of human behavior. I discovered what I will call "life space" and "social space." I will use the phrases "life space" and "social space," instead of the disciplines of psychology and sociology with which they are often identified, because what I discovered was not so much the disciplines as the phenomena with which these disciplines are concerned. Once this had happened, I could not keep my discoveries about these phenomena to myself. I felt the need to communicate them to others and particularly to managers in the modern world who, it seemed to me, were not giving these phenomena the attention they deserved.

1938–1948

With this attempt at communication I entered the next stage of my intellectual life journey, which overlapped a bit with the first. During this second period I became enamoured with two closely associated ideas, the idea of a professional manager and the idea of a management science, and how the two could be better realized if the theory and practice of administration could be better related. During this time I pursued these ideas in the classroom and communicated them to businessmen in speeches and articles.

In perusing these pieces now, I feel that the latent gist of my communication was to this effect: "Dear Mr. Manager, you dumb cluck, don't you see what an important guy you are? Why don't you 'wise up' to your distinctive competence and see that you have a higher function to perform than just making money and profits? Why have you so misrepresented yourself? Along with the scientist, you are one of the most important guys in the twentieth century"; and on and on I went. It could be said that I was trying to build up a professional identity for a reference group other than my own. Was the problem that without any professional counterpart in practice, I had no subject matter?

There is little doubt that my articles became popular. Many of them were given first as talks to a wide assortment of practitioners, from supervisors and foremen to middle and top managers and from personnel and industrial relations people to training directors, industrial engineers, and so on, in whose journals they were also published. Also, many of them were later republished in books of selected readings in personnel administration, human relations in industry, industrial psychology, industrial sociology, managerial sociology, applied anthropology, communications, organizational behavior, mental hygiene, counseling, general semantics, and so on. Curiously enough, the more popular these talks and articles became and the more my services for them were solicited, the more uneasy I became and the more I felt that my identity was threatened. Who was I that I could talk to so many different reference groups? I never got the satisfaction I was supposed to get from this popularity.

I will have little to say about these essays in this book. Most of them can be found in two volumes published by the Harvard University Press, the first under the title *Management and Morale* (1941); the second, *Man-in-Organization* (1968). The first collection expresses well my early excitement and optimism about the realization of a new role for the modern manager. It describes the ideas with which I entered the second phase of my intellectual journey. *Man-in-Organization* contains most of the pieces I wrote after 1941. I compiled this second volume as a companion piece to this autobiography. With this thought in mind I arranged the essays in chronological

3

order and wrote a headnote for each one, to say what I thought I was up to when I wrote it.

1948–1957

For the next ten years I continued to cultivate my own garden without being much concerned with the ominous thunderclouds that were slowly but surely gathering around me. During this third period I was concerned primarily with the human relations or communication skills required by persons desirous of improving their interpersonal behavior as individuals or as members or leaders of small groups.

By 1957 this primary focus on training in human relations skills had come to an end for me. By then—because of the so-called "knowledge explosion"—social scientists of all sorts were utilizing organizations as fruitful places in which to study the kind of behavior in which they were interested—individual, group, or organizational; rational, nonrational, or irrational; conflicted, cooperative, or power, etc. Even the applied mathematicians were getting into the act. As a result, what constituted business education was going through a revolutionary change. By 1957 I could no longer do my own thing in splendid isolation; I had to enter the existentially muddied water in order to clear things up a bit.

1957–1967

This part of my career, from 1957 until my retirement in 1967, is the most difficult for me to write about without becoming defensive and justificatory. I need to re-explore the two quarrels I had been having for some time: one with my colleagues at the Business School about the nature of administration and the other with my colleagues in the behavioral sciences about the nature of science.

To do this I will have to backtrack a bit in time. Both of these quarrels were highlighted during this period because I was engaged in what was then called the "new" Doctoral program. In this program the Faculty wanted to train teachers and researchers, not just practitioners of business. Although for a long time I had been having an internal chatter with myself about the phenomena of human behavior in relation to such questions as how they could be investigated, understood, and explained, as well as conceptualized in forms useful for practice, during this period these preoccupations increased. I felt that the roots of most of our arguments lay in the different ways in which we conceived these matters.

During this period I was instrumental in getting Organizational Behavior accepted as one of the formal areas of instruction and research at the School and as one of the special fields in the Doctoral program. Thus in these institutional terms I finally achieved a formal "subject matter." But no sooner had we separated ourselves in these ways than the same old questions reappeared within our group about the nature of the phenomena with which we were concerned and about the relations between theory and practice, science and administration, and knowledge and action.

I thought that we should not say that we had a common subject matter, if there was little agreement among us about what the phenomena were; or what the questions to ask about them were; or what the useful ways of classifying them for purposes of investigation and practice were; or how our findings could be understood or explained or applied and by whom. Instead it seemed to me that each of us had his own subject matter, his own ideas about what and for whom his knowledge was relevant. During this period of my life these individual subject matters seemed to multiply steadily. I became undecided whether this was a sign of healthy diversity or of chaos. I also came to realize that the situation had unfortunate consequences; for, whichever was the case, actions which might have had the potential to heal society's ills were not being taken.

Thus the absence of an agreed-upon subject matter, which seemed to me a characteristic of the behavioral sciences generally, not just of my own group, had consequences for society. One reason I am writing this book is to try to understand this lack. I want to explain why the problem persisted. I will try to do this by describing my encounters with it as I searched during my professional life for the phenomena with which my unsettled subject matter and personal identity were concerned.

1967–1974

I reached formal retirement age in 1965 but stayed on at half time for two more years at the School. By that time I had decided to write this account of my life and work in what I looked forward to as an atmosphere of peace and quiet away from the B-School, but that was not to be.

During this period revolution was in the air. It was all around me— the scientific revolution, the technological revolution, the managerial revolution, the educational revolution, the religious revolution, and the social revolution of the blacks, the young, the students, the white radicals, the New Left, the underprivileged, and the so-called economically underdeveloped countries. Everyone was for or against change in one form or another. The most vocal advocates of social change were in some state of protest and dissent against the old, the customary, and what was often referred to as "the establishment," whether it was political, business, educational, or religious. Conformity was out; rebellion or innovation was in. The liberals were no longer sure which was the real revolution, which the counterrevolution, and with which revolution they should identify and participate. One revolution was confronting or having a so-called dialogue with another revolution. Even computers were confronting and having dialogues with one another.

As can be imagined, it was difficult to write about administrative action when all this excitement about political and social action was going on. I felt at times like a dodo bird. All my ideas about how it might be possible to bring social change without violence and revolution seemed idealistic and old-fashioned.

Yet I felt that my ideas still had some relevance. So to the questions of "Where were you, Charlie, when all these storm clouds were gathering?" and "What did you do? What peace marches and protest movements did you join to bring peace and justice to this troubled land?" my answer has to be I was on no firing line but on some ivory-colored cloud—believe it or not—of all places at the B-School, trying to understand who, if anyone, was going to administer all these changes and revolutions that were going on. I shall try hard not to justify this position, but neither do I want it to be discounted. I felt that in my experience there might be some clues, if no solutions, for the future. That is why I continued to write while all hell seemed to be breaking loose around me and when on many occasions I was ready to take the hemlock.

Book One

FINDING A FOCUS FOR MYSELF
AND MY WORK

Part I

CHOOSING A CAREER, 1898–1942

Chapter 2

My Search For Certainty

I was born in an apartment house at 292 Central Park West in New York City, October 29, 1898. My father had been born in the Canton de Bern in the German part of Switzerland in a small town called Herzogenbuchsee, the ancestral home for some 300 years. He was seventh in a family of twelve children, the first of the second half dozen, as the family story is told. He came to this country in his early manhood to join his eldest brother, Robert, in order to import and sell wholesale to the American bourgeoisie the famous Roethlisberger cheese, which up to that time had been sold to and eaten exclusively by the crowned heads of Europe. Obviously I am reporting childhood impressions from stories told to me. They are a mixture of fact and fantasy which I make no attempt to unravel. The Roethlisbergers never retailed their cheese (perish the thought), and this is why most of my readers will be better acquainted with Kraft than with Roethlisberger cheese. By the economic laws with which my family was unacquainted, Kraft cheese survived, while theirs did not.

My mother was born in this country. Her father, Jules Richon, had been born in the Canton de Vaux in the French part of Switzerland against which the Canton de Bern had fought and won a mighty fight in some earlier period of Swiss history. Her mother, whose maiden name was Prudence Celestine Bodell, had been born in Paris, in a family which she claimed—but not too strongly—was descended from French royalty. At an early age my maternal grandfather and grandmother came to this country to seek a livelihood. They were befriended by Henri Mouquin, a well-known French restaurateur in New York City of that period. Under his auspices they soon married. They raised six children, of whom my mother was fourth. Hence, it may be said that both my mother and father occupied similar positions in their respective families. They were sort of in the middle, as I in time would be.

When my mother married, she was living on West 23rd Street,

where her parents ran a boarding house at which my father frequently ate. She was 16 years old; my father was about 20 years older. My mother had been brought up "strictly," in the French manner. My guess is that the marriage was arranged between her parents and my father.

My mother had two children very quickly, my sister Isa, first, and 14 months later, me. In my opinion now, my mother was not emotionally ready either for marriage or for the arrival of Isa, and even less for me. She had been, as I try to piece things together, a vivacious, good-looking, outgoing child, during adolescence both attractive to and attracted by the opposite sex. I suspect that her parents felt that marriage would keep her "out of trouble," so that she would not become whatever the "delinquents" of that period on West 23rd Street were called. Anyway, I doubt very much that she wanted to be saddled with two brawling brats at the age of 19.

"GOD COULD HAVE MADE A MORE BEAUTIFUL PLACE—BUT HE NEVER DID."

My parents moved to Staten Island when I was about five years old; a year later my father died, medically, it was said, from pneumonia. Alcoholism was also somewhat mysteriously associated with his going. My mother exacted a promise from me that I would not touch alcohol until after the age of 21, a promise which I kept but for which I have made up since. The story, often told me by my mother, was that all Roethlisbergers died from either overdrinking, overeating, or oversmoking, and that this fate, if I did not watch out, I would someday share. My guess now is that my mother's predictions will be about as good as what medical science will someday assign my death to.

The conscious memories of my life begin on Staten Island at the age of six when, after the death of my father, whose economic status had been slightly exaggerated, my mother, sister, and I moved from our high-social-status house on Central Avenue in St. George to our low-status, gas-lit quarters in the Baltimore flats on the wrong side of the railroad tracks, in Tompkinsville, Staten Island. Putting aside for the moment these social status differences, it was in these beautiful physical surroundings of Staten Island, about which George William Curtis is reputed to have said, "God could have made a more beautiful place—but he never did," and in the French bosom of my mother's family, her parents, brothers, and sisters, that I spent my childhood and adolescence.

The Roethlisbergers from my point of view were "finis" and "kaput." They remained for me for many years as a legend existing in part five miles across New York Harbor on Riverside Drive and Park Avenue and in part in Herzogenbuchsee, Switzerland, where in my childish imagination they went "a-go-go" in splendid carriages drawn by spirited Swiss horses to the applause of the local citizenry. At that time, however, because I was still unable to distinguish physical from social distance, I perceived both Herzogenbuchsee and Park Avenue as equidistant, that is, "far away."

Despite the difference in her surroundings, my mother did not have a bad time at the Baltimore flats, alongside which the Staten Island Rapid (a slight exaggeration) Transit Railroad ran its tracks. Here she was wooed by two men, a Monsieur Ferrand, a Frenchman, and Max Thaten, a German born in Bremen, who had come to this country at the age of 16 and was now an American citizen. Each morning, Monsieur Ferrand would throw a rose from the train to my mother as he wended his way leisurely to work in New York, while four times a day, Max Thaten, six feet, blond hair, blue eyes, with shirt sleeves rolled up and collar open, walked by to and from his place of employment, the American Dock Company at the foot of the road, on his way to work and lunch. Max Thaten was going places; Monsieur Ferrand was not.

I do not remember as a child having made any bets about which man would or should win. I nevertheless anxiously awaited the outcome, because I would be the loser on whichever side the fair coin of the mathematician fell. Perhaps this is not quite accurate. The German, who later became my stepfather, at least shared the American dream upon which my relation to him in future years was primarily based. The Frenchman, in my opinion, represented the old country, to which at an early age I became actively opposed.

My mother remarried about two years after my father's death. We moved shortly thereafter from the Baltimore flats to a house at 47 Frelingheuysen Road (after World War I, changed to Silver Lake Road) in Brighton Heights, a slight step up in the social community and approximately one hilly mile away from St. George and the Staten Island Ferry, which in turn were five cents or five miles from the Statue of Liberty and Bowling Green in downtown Manhattan.

My mother had three children by her second marriage: Max, Carl, and Wilma. Max died as a child, a shock from which, I now realize, my mother never completely recovered. Carl was 11 years my junior; Wilma or Dede, as she was called, came 11 years later, so, as the vegetable man used to say, my mother had three crops of children 11 years apart, my sister and me, Max and Carl, and Dede.

13

On holidays, birthdays, and anniversaries, my mother's family would often congregate to make "family whoopie." At all of these occasions, we sang The Marseillaise, with everyone standing at attention, including my stepfather. As 1914 approached, this ceremonial became more and more important. When my Uncle Francois (an uncle by marriage who had been brought up and educated in Alsace-Lorraine after the Franco-Prussian War and who still spoke French with a slight German accent) boomed forth "Allons, enfants de la patrie, le jour de gloire est arrivé," I became terrified. I feared he would break a blood vessel. Although his paroxysms disturbed me, they also brought me a bit closer to my stepfather. I did not see why he had to stand up for all this nonsense.

But let me finish with my father's family. When I was 14, they offered me a place in the cheese business on the condition that I would go to Europe to study French, German, and Italian. They felt that the economic success of the cheese business in America was dependent on the understanding of these languages. Mr. Kraft later thought otherwise and so did I at the time, but for other reasons.

The decision was reached at a solemn occasion in a small restaurant near Chambers Street in New York, where the "dusty" and "smelly" offices of the company were located and where the bookkeeper, who sat on a high stool with a green shade over his eyes, kept the company's accounts. At this restaurant, the menu was well established in advance (sauerbraten on Monday, hasenpfeffer on Tuesday, and so on). The wine which went with each meal was also well known by the waiter, so there was no need for anyone to speak. So for about an hour my uncle and cousins ate and drank in silence. There was really only one thing to say, and finally—I still don't know how I managed it—I said, "No. I want to be a civil engineer—to build bridges. The cheese business is not for me." Although at the time I did not realize it, I imagine now that there was a big sigh of relief from my relatives, even though on this momentous occasion a family tradition was broken. For the first time in 300 years, there was to be no Fritz Roethlisberger in the cheese business. I do not remember anyone getting weepy about it. I certainly did not.

To make a long story short, step by step I disinherited myself from my family: the Roethlisbergers, the Richons, and the Thatens. All this was not for me. I was an American—an isolationist by factors then unknown to me, but certainly not by any American foreign policy—who was not going to have anything to do with the mighty battles fought in Switzerland between the Canton de Bern and the Canton de Vaux or with the Franco-Prussian War. This was America, where race, color, creed, birth, heredity, nationality, family, and so forth, did not count and where individual merit, skill, competence, knowledge, liberty, freedom, and so on, did. I believed it with all my heart and in a crazy way, in spite of many subsequent experiences to the contrary, I still do. Even to this day, any "silly" Fourth of July oration and parade can bring tears to my eyes.

Despite our differences, Uncle Robert, my father's oldest brother, helped my mother finance my sister's and my education at the Staten Island Academy, a private school which I attended from 1905 to 1917. Although well-intentioned, his efforts turned out to have some unfortunate consequences as I experienced them. When we first went to the school, my sister and I could speak only French; this put us apart from the rest of the children. But also it soon became apparent that the parents of the children in my class moved in very different socioeconomic spaces than those of my parents. Indeed, I interacted with my classmates only at school; I hardly ever went to their homes.

As time went on, my stepfather's economic status steadily improved; he became rapidly Americanized and active in local community affairs. All this happened much later, after I had left the family. My mother and her brothers and sisters, except the youngest, all born in this country, always retained their French customs and manners and never mixed in the community. They lived and died as French families in the New World.

My chief complaint against the Staten Island Academy was not the social out-of-lineness I experienced there and for which surely the teachers had no responsibility. My complaint was that they kept my sister and me in the same class for 12 long years, when I felt I could have easily skipped a few grades. I was always at the top of the class. I always did my homework with, as well as often for, my sister because it was quicker that way. I was fascinated with the number patterns I found in arithmetic, algebra, geometry, and the sciences of physics and chemistry. These subjects were to me neat, orderly, true, certain, and real. They contrasted sharply with the higgledy-piggledyness of my personal and family life, where it seemed to me we were always getting into heated arguments involving the definition of words or matters I then called superstitions, or ideas about taste, manners, and modes of life derived from the old country.

Often these arguments started innocuously with a question such as, for example, was an amethyst a precious stone? It did not take long for the different members of the family to take sides on the question; either "Yes, it was" or "No, it wasn't." Neither the dictionary nor the *Book of Knowledge* was allowed to settle the question. This would have

15

been against the rules of the game as my family played it. I came to learn—but only much later—that this was one of the ways in which we expressed our concerns and affections for each other. All I saw happening at the time was that voices would get raised, the table would get thumped, dishes would rattle, silverware might get thrown, and sometimes my mother would leave in tears. I was always apprehensive about this outcome.

In this "nonscientific" family atmosphere where I spent my youth, my schoolwork became for me an escape from all this nonsense. In my opinion then, "science" knew and my family did not. There was no question about whose side I was on. It was as simple a choice as that. I was on the side of certainty. If my family wanted to remain uncertain about the status of an amethyst in the jewelry trade, that was their business; it was not going to be my business.

One further example may help to establish my attitude toward "science." In an elementary physics class which my sister and I both attended, the teacher performed an experiment on electromagnetism. He wrapped a wire coil around an iron bar, through which he ran an electrical current and by which he picked up some tacks from the table. The tacks happened to be of different colors. My sister was fascinated with the color of the tacks, so when she wrote up the experiment, which at that time we were required to do, she spent most of her exposition upon the cute colored tacks that went hippity-hoppity on the bar when the current was turned on and then hippity-hoppity back again onto the table when the current was turned off.

When I tried to explain to her that the color of the tacks had nothing to do with the point of the experiment, she remained unconvinced. For me then her case was hopeless. Yet who knows which of us was the better observer? Perhaps the kind of paint on some of the tacks had affected their magnetic properties with the result that some were more hippity-hoppity than others. Who knows? But whether or not my sister observed this, I will never know. I never asked. I got the point, and she did not; so I went to college, and she did not.

While at the Academy I walked from one end of Staten Island to the other—a distance of 14 miles—in order to become a first-class Boy Scout, but with this accomplishment my activities in that direction ceased. I never earned any merit badges, and during my last two years at the Academy I discontinued my affiliation with the Boy Scouts entirely. Although I enjoyed their outdoor activities—playing "Jack, Jack, show the light" among the tombstones at night in the Moravian cemetery adjacent to a log cabin we built in the woods—I suffered acute self-consciousness about wearing the uniform. I would walk miles rather than take a streetcar with my uniform on.

During this period I read books avidly, but not what would be called "good books." My family had no library; the school had none that I remember. I went to a small Carnegie library in St. George, where the sociologists will relish to hear I read the hundred or so Horatio Alger stories about going from rags to riches. It was my first exposure to the "Protestant ethic" in its most primitive form of sink or swim, do or die, succeed or fail, and so on. I do not remember having any difficulty in absorbing the values of individual competence and hard work of the Protestant ethic; these seemed to have already become my values too. How could this be? Anyhow, I did not equate success with money. Even at an early age I identified with scientists and engineers more than with captains of industry inside or outside the cheese business.

Although as a baby I was baptized at the Eglise Evangélique Suisse-Française de New York, my religious indoctrination and training thereafter were practically nonexistent. After the ceremony took place, my parents and maternal grandparents placed a drop of wine—of the appropriate kind and vintage, of course—on my tongue in order to see if I would make the proper grimaces. This would establish without doubt whether or not I was an accredited member of the Roethlisberger-Richon combination. Believe it or not, I passed the test. My family felt, I assume, that the good Lord would see matters likewise and take good care of me. And in a way He did, but in a roundabout manner.

My stepfather, before marrying my mother, attended the Presbyterian church in Staten Island. My mother, sister, and I occasionally went there, but not often, because this interfered with the preparation of the midday Sunday meal. This was a matter of great importance to my mother. In time none of us went to church.

During my adolescence I cannot remember worrying too much about theological questions. I fell quite naturally into what seems to me now a state of passive agnosticism. Crude as it may sound, it was my existence and not God's that had me bothered. I remember tussling with the question of my death and nonexistence. How could this be? Around this question I had many nightmares.

But in the daytime science and its concrete achievements would come into the foreground of my consciousness, and I was reassured. I could see the steam engine on the tracks below me, the steamboats in the harbor, and on clear days Brooklyn Bridge in the distance. Electric lights, the telephone, and the automobile as commonplace extensions of technology were just coming into existence, at least for our family at the Baltimore flats. Even at that time I could distinguish slightly between words that produced useful things and words that seemed to produce mostly hurts, fights, and paroxysms like those of my Uncle Francois. Exactly what constituted the difference it took me many years to learn.

So both at the Staten Island Academy and later at Columbia I concentrated upon mathematics and the physical sciences. When I graduated from the Academy in 1917, I spoke at the commencement exercises upon "The Romance of Dirt." For me at the time dirt meant coal tar, a by-product from the destructive distillation of coal, from which the German chemists had developed synthetic dyes. I was all set to become a chemist or chemical engineer and with these career plans, speaking euphemistically, I entered Columbia College.

I had two illnesses during my last two years at the Academy, which I mention briefly because of the social rather than the physical significance that they had for me. In 1915 my appendix burst and peritonitis set in. I was in the hospital eight weeks and operated on three times to remove pus pockets that formed in my abdomen. During this period I fell in love with my nurse, who was some years older and about whom I wrote my only love poem. In 1917 I had a case of mastoiditis, for which I also had an operation. Both these illnesses occured at a period when my interactions with my own age group were of importance and needed reinforcement. I had made two close friends, but one of them had died. Both these illnesses, however, turned me inward toward my own reflections as a source of satisfaction. This private world of hopes and fears I shared with no one, and in an important sense I was not in touch with it myself. It was leading me more by the nose than I was directing it. But I was not aware of this at the time; I discovered it only later.

COLUMBIA AND M.I.T.

The transition from the Staten Island Academy to Columbia College was a much bigger one than I then realized. The three years that I spent there from 1917 to 1920 were lonely ones. The classes were large, and I never got to know my professors. Because of my preoccupation with the sciences and with preparing myself for my career, no new vistas opened up. Three courses, one in contemporary civilization, another in philosophy, and another in comparative literature, intrigued me; but I felt they should not divert me from my major "career objective."

Probably World War I helped to make my educational experience at Columbia disjointed. The excitement was elsewhere, but I do not remember having any strong desire to enter the fray. I enlisted—or should I say was drafted—into the army in September 1918, at the beginning of my sophomore year; but the only engagement I encountered was "The Battle of Morningside Heights" at Broadway and 116th Street in the newly founded Student Army Training Corps. I still remember our first engagement with wooden guns at Baker Field. Somehow the statisticians in the Army headquarters in Washington (whatever the Pentagon of that period was) must have failed to correct their estimates of the nationwide distribution of uniform sizes for the New York City population. So with hats flopping over our ears, sleeves dangling over our hands, and legs wrapped in too many extra yards of cloth puttees, we paraded around Baker Field while the drill sergeant barked out his commands. The one we welcomed most and which always created a slight twitter in the ranks was "As you *was*." We were a formidable sight and had the Germans seen us, I always suspected, the war might have lasted longer. But the news never leaked out, and I was given an honorable discharge from the United States Army shortly after Armistice Day on November 11, 1918.

The other nonacademic skirmish in which I engaged while at Columbia was of a slightly different character. It was with the local chapter of my fraternity, Beta Theta Pi. The behavior of my fraternity brothers, when they sang, "Oh, you must be a Beta Theta Pi, or you won't go to heaven when you die," it seemed to me, bore a resemblance to the behavior of my Uncle Francois, when he sang "The Marseillaise," and it disturbed me in the same way. At the time I did not have a label for this kind of behavior, so in this sense I did not really know what was disturbing me.

One incident will illustrate what I mean. I signed a letter to the president of the fraternity, in which I complained about something for which I felt I had been unjustly accused, "Yours in sackcloth and ashes." The official closing signature from one Beta to another was supposed to be "Yours, in—Kai—," where the blanks stood for two secret words, which luckily I cannot reveal because I do not remember them. Anyway they stood for two values one could not have enough of, such as, for example, courage and loyalty.

The president thought that by substituting sackcloth and ashes for these blanks, I was poking fun at these sacred words. I protested my innocence, because at that time I had not heard about the unconscious. How the president, who I have every reason to believe was as illiterate about Freud as I was, could read my unconscious presents a mystery. Anyway my letter created a hullabaloo of such proportions that I was nearly but not quite excommunicated from the fraternity. They forgave me, but being uncharitable at the time, I did not forgive them. As a result of this incident and others of a similar character, I excommunicated myself from Beta Theta Pi, just as I had already disinherited myself from my family.

Had I stayed at Columbia to finish my work in engineering, it would have taken me three more years at the School of Mines, Engineering, and Chemistry after my junior year at college, from which at the end of the fourth year I would have obtained an A.B. degree. I decided to leave Columbia to enter the Massachusetts Institute of Technology. About this time M.I.T. had started a new course called Engineering Administration (Course XV). It was to be a combination of economics and engineering. I thought that this combination represented my career interests better than the courses at Columbia. Consequently I finished my last two years in engineering at M.I.T.; took a summer course in 1921 at Columbia to complete my requirements for the A.B. degree from there; and received my A.B. from Columbia in 1921 and my B.S. from M.I.T. in 1922.

How I rationalized my decision to go to M.I.T. is clear, but how I reached the decision is vague to me. It looks to me as if I was running away from something more than I was running toward something. I may have been beginning to have doubts about my qualifications for engineering. I had not done very well academically at Columbia, that is, not as well as I wanted to. Commuting from Staten Island to Columbia, one and a half hours each way, was becoming irksome, but the alternative of living at the fraternity house was equally unsatisfactory. I had become slightly interested in economics. All in all, a change was indicated and Course XV seemed to be "it."

Very fortunately my economic situation allowed me to make the change. Shortly after my father's death, my sister and I were each left $10,000 from the estate of our Uncle Ulrich in Switzerland, a person I had never met nor even knew existed. My mother held this capital in trust for me until I reached the age of 21; I financed the rest of my education from the interest derived from it. Although I had to spend some of the capital, I never spent it all and have some left to this day. There is little question that this money allowed me to do many things in a not strictly Horatio Alger fashion, for which at times I felt guilty—but not much.

My two years at M.I.T. from 1920 to 1922 were a steady disillusionment from beginning to end. Course XV—at least the so-called economics part—was really a course in "scientific management" and "Frederick Taylorism" and was aimed at the newly emerging occupational group called at the time efficiency engineers and later industrial engineers. Most of the courses had little to do with economics, as I thought of that discipline both then and now. Two stories will illustrate what I mean.

In one of my classes the professor advocated keeping the toilets hot in the summer and cold in the winter, so that employees would not congregate there. He also asserted that a shower bath was more efficient than a bath in a tub, because one could wash his hair at the same time. I was infuriated with these examples of efficient practice. This was not the kind of knowledge for which I had come to M.I.T. Behind these practices I saw no theory of the kind I found in physics and chemistry. To me they were pure, unadulterated nonsense. I am using strong language, because it expresses the strong feelings I had at the time. For many years thereafter, I took great delight in collecting such "horror stories" about Course XV. By telling them with embellishments in certain quarters I was able to become the life of the party. Had anyone at the time asked me just what I was so upset about, I probably would have been able only to stammer, "It's obvious, isn't it?"

Without question, Course XV had a profound effect upon me but in directions entirely different from those that the designers of the course intended. When I was to meet unscientific scientific management in the flesh much later on, as we will see, I was loaded for bear. As a reaction at the time, I became an ardent socialist, which I remained for the next five years of my life. During my two years at M.I.T. I read Karl Marx, Thorstein Veblen, and Upton Sinclair much more avidly than Adam Smith, Alfred Marshall, and David Ricardo, or whatever the standard text in economics was in Course XV at the time. (I think it was Taussig.)

While I was at M.I.T., my interest in engineering also waned. In this case it was not the underlying theories of physics and chemistry that bothered me; it was that I had no skill in applying them. The laws of thermodynamics were one thing; the steam engine was something else again. Any machine, whether it be an electric motor, dynamo, gasoline engine, blast furnace, or what not, at the level of skill baffled me. The principles behind these machines I thought I understood, but when I had to deal with them concretely, even under laboratory conditions, I felt I was in another world.

The link between theory and practice I never made, nor was I sufficiently interested in the nature of the physical universe itself to continue with the disciplines of physics or chemistry for their own sakes. Thus two avenues of development gradually evaporated for me. And, to boot, my introduction to the economic and social world through Course XV was so disillusioning that I began to question seriously whether I had chosen the right field for my career. One thing was clear, it was not scientific management. This extension of technology into social space was repugnant to me. But neither was becoming a socialist a career for me. I suffered acutely from a sense of frustration and a sense of felt injustice. With all my carefully laid out career plans, how could this have happened to me? I had done all the right things, but the rewards for doing them were not forthcoming. How could this be? I needed many more years of experience before I could answer these questions.

A TWO-YEAR INTERLUDE

I spent the two years from 1922 to 1924 ruminating at a low-grade level about this conflict and developing a new set of career plans. Because I felt I had made a heavy investment in an engineering education, I decided to give its practice at least a try. I sought employment as an engineer from several different firms (about whose employment practices I could cite a number of interesting cases) and finally landed a job as a chemist with the American Smelting and Refining Company in El Paso, Texas. .

My job was to act as an umpire between the mines and the smelters, whenever a serious discrepancy existed between the two about the amount of metal in the ores delivered from the mines to the smelters. Each of them made independent analyses of these ores. Obviously the smelters could not extract from the ores more metals (copper, lead, gold, silver, etc.) than the ores contained, and the efficiency ratings of the smelters (in terms of metal yields) would be affected by analyses which showed that a batch of ore contained more or less metal of a particular kind than was actually present in it.

Because I was not interested then in matters of organization and because of my socialist leanings, I could not take this umpiring seriously. Since both the mines and the smelters were owned by the same company, it seemed to me these disputes, which had some resemblance to the disputes in my family, were just matters of bookkeeping and transferring money from one pocket to another. These rationalizations, I am afraid now, only helped me to assuage my feelings of inadequacy on the job.

At M.I.T. I had analyzed only one ore in an afternoon, about two or three hours; on this job I had 40 to 50 analyses to do in a day. To make matters worse, the gold and silver determinations occurred at the end of the day, when I had to put my batch of 40 or 50 samples in a furnace for cupellation and without a pyrometer with which to judge its heat. If the furnace was too hot, I evaporated some of the silver; if it was too cold, I froze the cupellation. In either case the whole day's work was ruined, and I had to begin over again. My senior chemist colleagues, old-timers, could judge the heat of the furnace by the color of the flame, whereas I could not. This was my first experience (outside a book) with the difference between *knowledge of acquaintance* and *knowledge about*—a distinction about which I will have more to say later. At this time the distinction did not help my feelings of inadequacy. Each weekend I crossed the bridge to Juarez, Mexico (there was Prohibition in the U.S.A. then), and drowned my sorrows in 10 barrooms in a night. In less than six months, before the company could act, I quit the job.

I spent the next three months in Mexico. I visited a friend from M.I.T. in Aguacalientes. He was a chemist at one of the smelters whose ore analyses I had been umpiring. I went with him each evening to the plaza, where the girls walked around in one direction and the boys in the other, the object being to entice a particular girl, with whom one wished more intimacy, outside the circle. Even at this, as I remember it, I was not too successful. My heart, I explained to myself then, was not in it. I was like an Horatio Alger reader, a first-class Boy Scout, an A.B. and a B.S. degree holder who had lost his radar set, and I could not enjoy this absence of direction and uncertainty with or without women. I finally wound up in Vera Cruz, where I took a boat for home.

The next year I worked as a sales correspondent for the American Book Company, located then at Washington Square in New York City. This job was not my major occupation or preoccupation. I lived in the Village, read a great deal, and went to the theater on and off Broadway. In my own mind I was a "Bohemian," preparing myself, as one might suspect, to write the great American novel. During this period I discovered the contemporary American literature that was beginning to emerge. Unlike the classics I had read before, this literature was addressed to my generation, the lost generation, with which I identified. I read avidly such writers as Sinclair Lewis, Theodore Dreiser, Sherwood Anderson, Eugene O'Neill, H. L. Mencken, James Branch Cabell, George Jean Nathan, John Dos Passos, the feature writers of the *New York World*, the so-called Algonquin Group such as Heywood Broun, Franklin P. Adams, and Christopher Morley, some writers overseas such as Somerset Maugham, H. G. Wells, John Galsworthy, and Thomas Mann. I will add to this list Ernest Hemingway and F. Scott Fitzgerald. Although they may have come later, in my memory they all merge together.

This literature spoke to my sentiments as no literature had spoken to them before. These writers opened up vistas that my previous courses and readings had not touched. I began to read a much wider range of authors than I had previously known. I even read over again some of the classics I had been instructed to read before. Through this literature I shared vicariously in the "life spaces" of others. I found that others shared many of my questions, doubts, and anxieties, and I imagine this comforted me. These writers put in words things about which I felt strongly, but which I had not been able to articulate. Although they reinforced my pessimisms and tarnished my Horatio Alger picture of the American dream, this disenchantment fitted well into my continuing interest with socialism as a cure for the ills of the modern world. Man's human condition and his social condition were for me at the time unseparated.

HARVARD UNIVERSITY

Although this literature appealed to many of my sentiments, it did not satisfy my passion or search (or should I say compulsion or obsession?) for knowledge and certainty. Thus my life as a Bohemian and writer was short-lived. This was still not really "me." I felt that behind all the uncertainty I was experiencing, there must reside something more substantial—some wisdom—that I was missing. I thought it might reside in that part of academia I had not yet fully experienced, the community of scholars in the humanities. I entered the Department of Philosophy in the Graduate School of Arts and Sciences at Harvard University in the fall of 1924. I had read some William James, George Santayana, and Josiah Royce, and although I knew they were no longer at Harvard, their intellectual successors, I thought, would be.

It is difficult for me to write about my three-year period as a graduate student at Harvard, because such a gap exists between my evaluations of it then and now. I will speak only of my disillusionment, because it fits well into the theme which characterized my life up to 1927 and with which I want to end this chapter. Later I shall turn to its more positive effects, when a new chapter in my life emerged and I discovered who I was and not just who I was *not*.

Over the portals of Emerson Hall, where the Department of Philosophy is housed, there exists the inscription, "What is man that thou art mindful of him?" The story goes that President Eliot substituted this inscription during the summer vacation for "Man is the measure of all things," the inscription for which the philosophy faculty had voted before they went to the mountains or seashore for their holidays. (At this time men of affairs were not seeking their wisdom.)

Anyway, when I entered Harvard, realism was back in the saddle. Alfred North Whitehead had just come from the University of Cambridge, in England. He had introduced the new analytical philosophy, which he and Bertrand Russell had developed while writing the *Principia Mathematica* to restore the crumbling foundations of arithmetic.

With my background and search for certainty, this seemed to be the school of philosophy for me. I sat at Whitehead's feet while he wrote *Science and the Modern World*. I took a course with H. M. Sheffer in "Mathematical Logic." I learned to talk about the noneuclidean geometries and Boolean algebra. I saw how all of arithmetic could be derived from "and," "or," and "not" (set theory). I learned to build toy mathematical systems with given axioms and deduced theorems from a class of finite entities, such as "chairs," and the relationship "to the left of." I got brave enough so that I did not have to give names to the entities or the relationships. After a bit, I learned how to talk "about something and anything but nothing in particular" (Whitehead); that is, I learned to speak the language of mathematics, where "you never know what you are talking about or whether what you are talking about is true" (Russell).

This logical austerity was like a breath of fresh air; I was enthralled even though I was also chilled to the bone. At the time more than the foundations of mathematics were crumbling for me. I too needed something firm upon which to stand—something a bit more tangible than I felt "and," "or," and "not" to be. I did not realize how close to the "truth" I was and how I might have been able to state my problem, at least intellectually, in these terms. At that time I was specializing only in "not." I did not become acquainted with "either-or" and "and-or" until much later.

Because I had come to Harvard to prepare myself for accreditation to "the community of scholars," I could not major only in Whitehead and Sheffer. So I took courses from the other members of the Department of Philosophy; they instructed me in the other absolutes, about which these scholarly gentlemen knew from their readings of Plato, Aristotle, Descartes, Leibniz, Spinoza, Locke, Berkeley, Hume, Kant, Hegel, and so forth. Many of these absolutes seemed to me to be lacking in red corpuscles. In particular the various metaphysical proofs for the existence of God also seemed to me to be travesties of reason. They had for me about as much validity as the principles of efficient behavior that I had been given in Course XV at M.I.T. I could not dance gracefully in the "ballet of bloodless categories" of metaphysics any better than I could dance to the tune of the concrete "nuts and bolts" of technology or of the dehumanized "time and motion" of scientific management. I was getting to feel that everyone was out of step but me.

Although Professor Sheffer reassured me that someday with the aid of mathematical logic I could reduce these different philosophical systems to a form in which I could see what was sense (logic) and what was nonsense (semantics), I felt that I could not wait this long. I was still an eager beaver in search of the truth in the "here and now" and not at some place and time in the "there and then." I could not see how the study of ancient history or how becoming a philosopher's philosopher was going to help my plight. It seemed to me that 90 percent of philosophy was unmitigated nonsense, though I did not dare say so even to myself. The consequences of such an admission would have been too terrifying.

Somehow—I don't now remember how it happened—I elected to do my dissertation on Descartes under Etienne Gilson, a visiting professor from the University of Louvain in Belgium and a distinguished medieval scholar. Why I chose Gilson and not Whitehead is something I cannot understand now, unless it was as a symptom of my mounting anxieties, over which I had by then little control. Anyway, Professor Gilson felt, as any good scholar should, that it would be impossible for me to write my thesis on Descartes without reading all of his letters in medieval French bound in a set of volumes that took up, I felt at the time, mountains of shelves in Widener Library.

By this time not only the flesh but also the spirit was weak. I never finished my thesis, and I never got my Ph.D. degree. This was for me the end of the world. I felt deserted, forsaken, and alone. Slowly and steadily but surely I had reduced my life "to dust and ashes." Something for me had come to an end. I had carried a certain set of assumptions about career development to their bitter and inevitable conclusions.

It was no joking matter. I could not laugh. I did not realize until many years later what a lucky guy I was. Yet at this fateful moment a glimmer of the possibility occurred. It turned the whole direction of my life.

Someone—I don't remember who it was—suggested that I talk to Elton Mayo, who had just joined the Harvard Business School Faculty in order to conduct some researches on the motivation of workers. I did not see the connection, but anyway I made the appointment. When I saw Mayo, I told him of my plight. I expected that he would be as horrified as I and that he too would banish me to Dante's ninth circle of purgatory. Instead he seemed curious and amused. His amusement bothered me a little, but when, after the second interview, he offered me a job, it put a different complexion on the matter. If he could resurrect the unholy and the damned for something useful, then I was all for him. I could allow him to laugh, even though at the time I could not laugh.

With this event I will end this chapter. A miracle had occurred, the nature of which I did not then understand. Why, when I was at the end of my rope and in utter despair, anyone should have wanted to throw me a lifesaver, I will never know. That is Mayo's story, not mine. But for his helping hand, I was to be ever grateful. For many years thereafter I felt I could never cease to repay him.

Mayo turned my attention to all those matters from which I wanted to escape: my Swiss heritage, my father, my mother, my childhood, the cheese business, my Uncle Francois, my stepfather, Beta Theta Pi, the machine, scientific management, and even "the community of scholars." With this new look at the adult world of which I could make no sense and from whose nonsenses I was desperately trying to run, a new Fritz was born. What had been something from which to escape became now a new source of intense curiosity.

My life contains only two miracles: I will mention the second one now, even though it occurred two years later and belongs chronologically in the next chapter. It was Margaret Dixon, the girl—she was then twenty-two—who became my wife in November 1929. The day of the month I do not remember, but it was Thanksgiving eve. It was this day with all its symbolic meaning for me that we celebrated, even during the Roosevelt Thanksgivings, for the next 34 years until she died. Although Margaret will appear only infrequently from now on in the matters I will write about, this does not mean that she did not play a major role in my development. But her part is something about which I cannot even yet talk quite sensibly, and it is upon my intellectual life that I am trying to concentrate, difficult as that may be. Anyway, when I found my Margaret, my quest for certainty in its exaggerated form was over. This is why symbolically my marriage belongs at the end of this chapter, when for me something had come to an end and something new was being born. This did not happen all at once; even human miracles, I was still to learn, have limits or "boundary conditions," as we would say now.

Chapter 3

My Discovery of Life Space

"Sicklied o'er with the pale cast of thought," I joined the Harvard Business School in September 1927 as an instructor, at an annual salary of $1500. It would be more accurate to say I joined Mayo, who was there. My knowledge of business as business was practically nil; I did not know the difference between a stock and a bond. At this time, the country was in a period of economic prosperity, the depression being still two years in the future. Since the price of stocks was a popular subject of discourse in the Business School Faculty Club, my ignorance placed me in great jeopardy, and I did not interact much with my colleagues for fear they would find it out.

MAYO'S IMPACT UPON ME

For the next few years I sat at Mayo's feet, spellbound by his knowledgeability, creative imagination, and clinical insights. He knew the great philosophers and the classical economists much better than I. He also knew about two areas with which up to this point I had had some acquaintance but little knowledge—psychopathology and social or functional anthropology.

Sigmund Freud, on the one hand, and Bronislaw Malinowski and A. R. Radcliffe-Brown, the anthropologists, on the other, were making a stir in intellectual circles. They were having as great an impact on social science as Alfred North Whitehead and Bertrand Russell were on mathematics. The difference was that, whereas Whitehead and Russell were trying to provide a better underpinning for a knowledge that already existed, Freud and the social anthropologists were seeking uniformities in the phenomena of human-social behavior about which no knowledge existed.

A few facts about Elton Mayo are in order here. He was born in Australia in 1880. He acquired his education and studied medicine there and in England, but never received his medical degree. In

29

Australia he taught at both the Universities of Adelaide and Melbourne. During World War I he became interested in what was then called "shell shock" among soldiers. His work and studies brought him international recognition, and he came to this country under the auspices of the Rockefeller Foundation. His first appointment was at the University of Pennsylvania. Here his industrial studies attracted the attention of Wallace B. Donham, then Dean of the Harvard Business School. Donham invited him to come to Harvard, and Mayo joined the School in 1926 at the age of 46.

I cannot begin to estimate the number of hours I spent with Mayo. We discussed topics ranging from the humanities to the social and physical sciences to the scientific enterprise and finally to miserable old me. During the next five years these hours could easily have totaled into four figures. Up and down the abstraction ladder we went; but no matter how high up we went, Mayo always brought me back to the lowest rung—to what all these ideas meant "here and now" in the concrete. We read many books together—Janet, Freud, Jung, Adler, Piaget, and Durkheim, for example. I asked questions and he commented upon them. Never had I read this way before; never before had I had this kind of relation to a teacher and to an older man to whom I could state freely not only my intellectual questions but also my personal doubts, anxieties, and concerns.

Mayo's impact upon me was great, not so much in terms of the knowledge he imparted as in terms of pointing me in the direction by which it could be gained. Under his tutelage I became a phenomenologist. I use the word phenomenologist instead of empiricist or positivist because Mayo was neither of the latter. He was saying, "Keep your eyes on the phenomena. That is where knowledge begins, as well as where it has to return, if the cookie isn't going to crumble."

For Mayo this was more than a platitude; it meant a dedication to a *hard, persistent, intelligent, responsible, unremitting* labor with the phenomena in the concrete and not in the library. This was one of the first elements, never to be forgotten, in the acquisition of knowledge—an *intimate, habitual, intuitive familiarity* with the phenomena, from which in time systematic knowledge about them could be gained.

The words I have just emphasized did not come from Mayo, but from Lawrence J. Henderson, with whom he was associated and about whom I shall talk later. They saw eye to eye about this inescapable first element in the acquisition of knowledge. They also saw that intuitive familiarity with the phenomena alone was not enough and that to it a logic had to be added, if it was to develop into something more than clichés about the phenomena. For Mayo and Henderson, however, there were two kinds of logic: one kind which *overdetermined, overconceptualized, overlogicized,* and *oversystematized* things, and another which opened them up for investigation. It took me some years to tell the difference between the two.

To the first kind of logic Mayo said "rubbish." This was like music to my ears. For some time I had suspected there was much rubbish in academia. Course XV at M.I.T. and my readings in philosophy at Harvard had clinched this for me, but I had never been able to say rubbish with the gusto that Mayo did. Mayo released me from my inhibitions. With this release, for me a good portion of academia, particularly the German philosophers, went down the drain. I was freed to look at and listen to the world in which I lived with the aid of the second kind of logic, which did not make premature closures and wrap things up in pink ribbons and say *finis.*

I had reached, as Carlyle said in *Sartor Resartus*, the point of the *Everlasting No* when *"Das ewige Nein* pealed through all the recesses of my *Me* and when my whole *Me* stood up and recorded its protest. I am not fatherless, an outcast. I am a man, I am free." This protest of indignation and defiance against the universe, society, academia, God, or the devil (at that time I was not sure which) was my first step into manhood. In terms of my background this negation had to precede my affirmation of life. But before I was to reach the *Everlasting Yea* and become fully productive, I had to go, as Carlyle predicted, through the *center of indifference*. This took me another 15 years.

Let me return to Mayo. What stimulated my imagination was his capacity to synthesize the insights coming from the sources I have mentioned—Janet, Freud, Durkheim, Malinowski, and so on—into a diagnosis of the ills of the modern industrial world in *The Human Problems of an Industrial Civilization* (1933) and his other books and articles. Here was no dry and dusty scholarship for its own sake. This was bringing knowledge to bear on practice or what practice in the social sciences could be, if, as Mayo put it, "they would give up their Cinderella complex and don the crystal slippers, and walk into adventure." This idea had me lit up like a Roman candle, but its terrors as well as its delights I learned about only much later. At this point in my life there existed a hiatus between Mayo's ideas and what in particular I could do about applying them.

THE COMMITTEE ON INDUSTRIAL PHYSIOLOGY

When Mayo came to the Business School, his work was financed from a grant of $100,000 a year for a period of five years from the Laura Spelman Rockefeller Foundation to the Committee on Industrial Physiology of Harvard University. The members of this committee were Wallace B. Donham, then Dean of the Business School; Elton Mayo, a psychopathologist; Lawrence J. Henderson, a biological chemist; William Morton Wheeler, a biologist; and David L. Edsall, then Dean of the Medical School. Each member of the committee had an appointment at the University, but only Dean Donham's and Mayo's were at the Business School.

This committee set up shop with the division of labor as follows. Under the assumption that there existed too many opinions and too few facts about man at work (a reasonable assumption at the time), it was thought that it might be well to begin by examining empirically what actually happened to man at work, not only from a physiological but also from a human-social point of view. Henderson was the logical choice to head up investigations of the first kind and Mayo of the second. Consequently, the Fatigue Laboratory was set up under the direction of Henderson, and the Department of Industrial Research (whose goals were somewhat vague) under the direction of Mayo. Both were housed in Morgan Hall, the faculty office building at the Business School. It was to be an interdisciplinary enterprise, although that word was not in common usage at the time.

Even to my then organizationally and scientifically untutored eyes, what Henderson and the Fatigue Laboratory would do Monday morning at 9 a.m. was clearer to me than what Mayo would be up to. Henderson and his colleagues, Bruce Dill and Arlie Bock, could set up their treadmills, and they could measure the physiological effects (on dogs and men) of different simulated conditions of work. Mayo, on the other hand, seemed to be sitting in his office and practicing his charisma or doing his research on me. Although when I joined him I suffered from a fatigue that did not come from any excess of lactic acid in my blood, I did not feel that I and the peculiar psychosocial fatigue from which I suffered should become the sole subject of Mayo's investigation. Such a study by the greatest stretch of my imagination could not justify the annual expenditure of fifty thousand bucks. (I did not then conceive of my association with Mayo as an in-service scientific development training program.)

COUNSELING STUDENTS AND WHAT IT MEANT TO ME

Hence, while Mayo was contemplating how he was going to apply his ideas to industry, I started interviewing students who were in some kind of quandary that was not strictly medical. In the spring of 1927, before I met Mayo and came to the Business School, I had started this kind of work informally among the undergraduate and graduate students at the University under the auspices of Dr. Alfred Worcester and Dr. Clifford Shaw. Dr. Worcester was then in charge of medical services for all students at Harvard; he was reported to have performed the first appendectomy in the United States. Dr. Shaw, if you can believe it now, was the one and only psychiatrist for students in the whole University.

In the spring of 1927 Dr. Worcester, a kindly and at that time quite elderly gentleman, set up what he called Hostess House (later named Lyman House for its donor). This was for students who, as he put it, were not ill enough to go to Stillman Infirmary and yet needed some attention. He put a motherly woman in charge of the House. I lived there for two years from 1927 until 1929, until I was married. I think Dr. Worcester felt there should be a man in the house, and I at that time was grateful to be that man, even speaking euphemistically. Students would stay there for a period ranging from a day to a couple of weeks. Many of them would come for tea, which was served every afternoon.

Although my activities in relation to counseling students developed slowly and informally, in time they took up the major portion of my day-to-day work. During the next five years I must have counseled well over 200 students on both "this side" and "the other side" of the Charles River.

As the distinction between "this side"and and "the other side" of the Charles River will come up again, let me digress a moment. Harvard College, the Graduate School of Arts and Sciences, the Law School, the School of Public Administration, in fact, the principal departments or schools of the University except the Medical School and the Business School, are in Cambridge on the left bank of the Charles River. The Business School is in Boston, on its right bank; but unlike the Medical School, it is geographically close to the College. At this point of the Charles, one can walk across a bridge from one side to the other in a matter of minutes. In spite of this physical closeness, in the early days there was little two-way traffic, intellectually speaking, across the bridge. If asked how to get to the Business

School from Harvard Square in Cambridge, an imaginative resident of the left bank might reply, "Just across the River and a thousand miles to the right." Likewise a resident of the right bank, on being asked how to get to the Law School from the Business School, might reply, "Just across the River and a thousand miles to the left."

The difference between the two sides was often expressed in terms of theory and practice. The inhabitants of the left bank were supposed to be concerned only with theory, truth, and knowledge for its own sake, whereas the inhabitants of the right bank were supposed to be concerned only with matters of practice and the application of knowledge toward materialistic ends. These stereotypes linger to this day, but not nearly as strongly as they did during the period about which I am writing. At that time before the days of the atom bomb, the computer, the missile, going to the moon, and the military-industrial-educational complex, the distinction between *pure* and *applied* knowledge and research was easier to maintain.

To return to my counseling of students: my services were sought for this kind of activity more and more. In time I had a full-time job counseling students on the right bank of the Charles. Assistant deans, professors, and even the local physician at the Business School, Dr. Fabyan Packard, referred to me "problem cases" of one kind or another for whom at that time there were no clear medical labels for whatever was biting them. Many were students who were worried because they were not doing as well scholastically as they or somebody else thought they should be doing. One of the things that interested me was the number, particularly at the Business School, who were in no scholastic trouble at all but who nevertheless worried about failing. My most visible success was with a student who was on the verge of being asked to withdraw for scholastic reasons. I do not remember now how many hours I counseled him, but I saw him quite often. Anyhow, when he graduated with distinction, Dean Donham heard about it and thought there might be something significant about what I was doing.

It can be seen that I had stumbled accidentally into a pasture that I found rewarding. Like one of B. F. Skinner's pigeons, every time I listened to the problems of a student, I was fed a piece of grain by him (i.e., rewarded by "thank you's"); I began listening like crazy. As listening to students was virgin territory at Harvard, I could easily have built up my activities into a job requiring the full time of more than one person. For this counseling activity I received great help from Mayo. As time went on, more and more of the discussions I had with him were about the situations of the students with whom I was working.

But was this what I wanted to do or was supposed to be doing? Who was rewarding me and was this the reward I wanted? Obviously I was getting satisfaction from the students who felt I had helped them and I was getting some recognition from the Business School. After three years, the School increased my annual salary to $3600 and I was made an Assistant Professor. But what was I a professor of? What was my subject matter? Should I go to medical school and study to become a psychiatrist, or should I go to the Graduate School of Arts and Sciences and study to become a psychologist? What did these professions think I was up to? And without the proper credentials what recognition would I receive from them? What was my reference group? To what group was I aspiring to belong? Whose recognition did I value? Why did Mayo not tell me what I should be doing? In this connection, let me say that I have no recollection of Mayo ever giving me an order or telling me what I was supposed to be doing. So long as I was following my interests, he seemed satisfied.

The internal chatter I had with myself about these questions steadily mounted. It looked as if the pattern of my life thus far (i.e., changing career objectives) was beginning to repeat itself. But this time I changed my job description without changing my formal job status; that is, I stayed at the Business School as an assistant professor. I did not change my concern with the phenomena in which I had become interested; instead I changed the place where I studied them. A number of factors helped me in this transition, the most important one being that I became involved in the Hawthorne researches. I shall write about them in the next chapter; here I will speak of the other factors.

From my counseling activities I was learning about myself as well as about my students. It would have been difficult to look at the character of their preoccupations without looking at my own; the similarities were embarrassingly apparent. But slowly a difference began to emerge. Up to then I had been reacting passively to my preoccupations; I had no real transactions or dialogue with them; I never talked back to them; I just stewed about or was stampeded by them. Slowly I learned to gain some control over them, and my preoccupations became more closely related to what I was attending to and doing. I learned to reflect upon instead of stew about my experiences.

As I thus regained control of my preoccupations, neither going back to graduate school to study psychology nor to medical school to become a psychiatrist seemed particularly attractive. At that time—at least at Harvard—psychology was psycho-physics and heavily influenced by Wundt and Titchener. Clinical psychology under Henry Murray was just beginning to emerge but was far from having arrived. At the Medical School there was only one course in psychiatry, and it was not the brand of psychiatry which interested me. In short, to choose either alternative would have meant foregoing for years my contact with the phenomena of human behavior about which I had become curious.

Reflecting on these matters I decided to stick with the phenomena and not with the traditional labels by which at that time they were carved up. It looked to me as if life had played me a queer trick in landing me at the Business School, in a setting which seemed incongruous for the development of my emerging interests. Nevertheless, this time I was going to accept and live with the incongruity and the anxieties it generated. I was going to follow my own interests in the job I was in. This was one of the most important personal decisions I reached, and it was one I constantly reaffirmed. With each reaffirmation it became easier to stick with the decision, but the settlement did not become a comfortable one overnight.

IDEAS, FACTS, KNOWLEDGE, AND TRUTH

Now I want to return to the phenomena about which, partly by chance and partly through Mayo, I had become curious and with which, partly by reinforcement and partly by choice, I decided to stick. I call this episode my discovery of life space.

When I was in philosophy, I was more interested in the "true" than in the "real," the "good," or the "beautiful." To use traditional subdivisions of philosophy, I was more interested in epistemology (what makes knowledge knowledge) than in metaphysics (what makes the real real), or ethics (what makes the good good), or aesthetics (what makes the beautiful beautiful). These sixty-four dollar questions I decided to consider no longer—at least not until I retired. Mayo told me that philosophy was a good subject to engage in at the beginning and end of one's life. In the middle years, he said, one should live it.

One epistemological distinction still meant a great deal to me. This was the one David Hume made between two kinds of knowledge: one that referred to "relations of ideas" and the other to "matters of fact." Analytical propositions, as they were called in philosophy, such as "The sage is wise," belonged to the first kind. In such propositions, the predicate (wise) was contained in the subect (sage), so that nothing new had been added; they were true apart from experience and thus constituted *a priori* knowledge. Synthetic propositions, on the other hand, such as "The rose is red," belonged to the second kind of knowledge. In such propositions the predicate (red) was not contained in the subject (rose). Their truth was contingent upon experience and could not be known apart from experience; they constituted *a posteriori* knowledge.

Although it was this distinction that had led to Hume's skepticism about knowledge and Kant's resolution of it, I felt it was important to maintain this distinction without having to accept wholly either Hume's or Kant's epistemological conclusions. The distinction, it seemed to me, neither cast a giant shadow on the status of *a posteriori* synthetic propositions, as Hume thought, nor did it require the possibility of *a priori* propositions in order to get out of this dilemna, as Kant thought.

Hence, in the best fashion of the day, that is, in terms of the newly emerging analytic philosophy of Whitehead and Russell, I put the propositions of both logic and mathematics in the class of *a priori* analytic knowledge and the proposition of common sense and science in the class of *a posteriori* synthetic knowledge. The criterion for the truth of propositions in the first class was logical consistency; the criterion for the truth of propositions in the second class was some correspondence with the phenomena, a matter which could not be settled apart from verification by observation.

However, I did not keep these two kinds of propositions—analytical and synthetic—totally unrelated. It seemed to me that the development of scientific knowledge required both kinds of propositions, so long as they were differentiated from and related to each other. At the time, I was not too clear what this relationship was. It seemed to me that the question was going to be settled by experience, not philosophical dogma. In this case, experience seemed to me to mean having something to do with convenience and utility as well as observation.

Thus, I had three different notions of the truth in the back of my mind: (1) the notion of consistency, (2) the notion of correspondence to the phenomena, and (3) the notion of convenience and utility. In matters about truth I was a bit of a logician, a bit of a positivist, and a bit of a pragmatist, and so I have remained for the rest of my life. For to me now the question no longer was which one of these truths was absolute; it was how these different notions about truth worked together to produce knowledge.

As the search for an answer to this question lurked behind the scenes throughout my career, I want to describe how it began in my counseling activities with students. When I started interviewing students, I conceived of my mission partly as a research project and partly as a counseling service to them. Helping them was important to me but not my sole objective. I was also interested in the preoccupations of the students and the uniformities I felt I saw in them. These became the phenomena about which I became curious and which I wanted to understand.

The readings that I have previously mentioned helped me. Both Pierre Janet and Sigmund Freud had influenced Mayo. In talking about obsession or compulsion neurosis (Mayo, following Janet, used the word obsession), Mayo contrasted and related the two men's approaches to psychopathology. He felt that Janet described the phenomena better, whereas Freud showed their historical determination. That is to say, Freud was more concerned with how the obsessive's thinking got that way, whereas Janet was concerned with its present form. The researches of Janet on mental illness are of course much less well known in this country than those of Freud. Janet's most important books (1909, 1919, and 1921) have not been translated into English, although *Psychological Healing* (1925) has been. Mayo wrote a book in 1948 about Janet's work.

As a result, I was somewhat of a maverick in interviewing students; that is, I used the most general ideas underlying the conceptual schemes of both Janet and Freud. I concentrated first on the nature of a student's preoccupations here and now; only if I thought it necessary did I explore his personal history to see what may have influenced him in his present direction. This seemed to me the natural course that most interviews took anyway. Many times I would state the form of the student's preoccupations in Janet's terms; I hardly ever stated the dynamics in Freudian terms. Here I felt I was following the principle of doing the least harm—a principle upon which, as Mayo and Henderson told me again and again, the practice of medicine was based.

I also found Janet's concepts more congenial than Freud's, because during this period I was anti-metaphysical. Freud's way of thinking seemed to me to have too many metaphysical entities circling around in it. I felt that I could study a person's preoccupations and concerns without having to posit an unconscious. Moreover, much of the "wild" psychoanalytical talk that certain circles indulged in at that time I found distasteful. I was going to stay as close to the phenomena as I could and become well acquainted with them before seeking too quickly for any explanation of them.

In constantly comparing Janet and Freud, Mayo performed an inestimable service for me. Although annoying at times—because of course I was still bothered about who was right—the comparison prevented me from going off half cocked. I had to try to make sense out of both positions. It could be said that I experimented with Freud's ideas more upon myself than upon my students. I underwent psychoanalysis for a period of six months, after which my analyst died; he had been analyzed by both Freud and Jung (and at this period in Boston they were tops). I did not continue with anyone else. This may have been unfortunate, but by this time I had become interested in relating preoccupations to another class of phenomena which I thought also needed to be studied and about which I will talk in the next chapter.

THE UNIFORMITIES I OBSERVED

Let me state here five uniformities I observed in the students' preoccupations, how I thought these uniformities were related, and how they constituted a basis for the exploration of "life space."

(1) *Preoccupation and Attention.* The first observation was the lack of any effective relation between what a student was preoccupied with and what he was or was supposed to be attending to. Instead of his processes of preoccupation and attention reinforcing one another, they were working against each other. The student's moments of attention provided little substance for his reflections, and his reflections provided little illumination for his experiences when at attention. His preoccupations thus prevented him from fixing and sustaining his attention upon his work; and his inability to fix and sustain his attention upon his work reinforced his preoccupation about his inadequacies in dealing with external surroundings.

(2) *The Form of Thinking: the False Dichotomy.* When I looked at the form of the thinking underlying these preoccupations and not at their content, I could make a second observation. The preoccupations of most students took the form of an overelaboration in logic of an oversimplification in fact. Instead of treating the world of fact as complex and keeping his thinking about it simple, the student tended to treat the world of fact as simple and to complicate his

39

thinking about it. As a result he was "complicating" his life not in relation to the complexity of relations that existed in "matters of fact" but in relation to an oversimplified logicization (relation of ideas) of them.

The products of this kind of thinking I call "false dichotomies." Some common ones I found among the students were (1) safety-danger, (2) success-failure, (3) superiority-inferiority, (4) good-bad, (5) independence-dependence, and (6) obedience-rebellion. The underlying logical form of these dichotomies was, for example, "Everything that is not safe is dangerous"; or "Everything that is not successful is failure"; or "Everything that is not good is bad", and so on.

At that time, I wrote a paper on the "false dichotomies" I found among students; I called it "The Nature of Obsessive Thinking." I did not publish this paper, but it circulated among persons who were interested in student problems. Forty years later I included it in the collection of essays I previously mentioned, *Man-in-Organization*.

Since the paper is available, I shall not here expand my conception of the false dichotomy as a manifestation of obsessive thinking except for one further remark. Although this was my first encounter with the false dichotomy, it was not my last. Neither was it my last experience in differentiating the conditions under which two processes can reinforce each other from the conditions under which they become antagonistic. On the one hand, preoccupation and attention can develop fruitfully together, in which case there is an increased capacity to attend to, learn from, and make proper evaluation of and decisions about one's external surroundings; or, on the other hand, they can become bifurcated, in which case there is a diminished capacity to attend to, learn from, and make proper evaluation of and decisions about one's external surroundings.

Although I did not do so then, I will call these two possibilities the "going around in circles" and "the figure eight maneuver" and diagram them for the case of the relation of preoccupation to attention as follows:

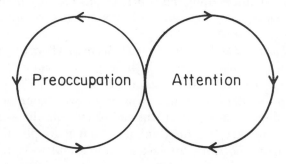

As depicted by the arrows and the point of interaction of the two circles, these two processes could develop either separately or together by a figure eight maneuver. I was to meet this dual possibility again and again in relation to many other processes of human and social development. I call attention to this particular manifestation now so that I can refer to it later.

As can be seen from my study of obsession, I was entering peripherally into matters which later became more central to my concern—the learning, problem-solving, and decision-making processes. But instead of looking at how persons do or should learn, do or should make decisions, and do or should solve problems, I was looking at what prevented them from doing so. It seemed to me that study of the latter lent itself better than the former to empirical investigation; i.e., it had more to do with "matters of fact" than with "relations of ideas." This experience was invaluable to me. It was one which many years later I wished my friends in operations research and decision theory had had.

(3) *Preoccupations and Personal History.* It was much easier to specify the dysfunctional consequences of obsessive thinking for attention, learning, and reaching decisions than to specify their determinants. In this respect Freud was more illuminating than Janet, but with Freud's insights and their conceptualization I only went part way—or perhaps I should say—I "stayed loose."

I assumed that man's past history was carried forward into the present in terms of meanings and that sometimes the present meanings had become divorced from the events from which they had originally been derived. The events were buried in memories, some of which could be brought back to consciousness and some of which could not, and so were lying, in a manner of speaking, in the unconscious. But the meanings remained and still operated here and now in the present, often as misevaluations of present situations. These misevaluations were what got man's obsessive thinking into trouble with his external social surroundings. It made sense to me to suppose, as Freud illustrated so well clinically, that many of these misevaluations had their origins in a person's childhood before he was able to evaluate these relationships properly, and that psychoanalysis, as a form of psychotherapy, might allow him to do that.

In no sense was I anti-Freud. The statements I have made so far, plus others I shall make later, are about what were to me Freud's great contributions not only to abnormal but also to normal psychology. What I mean by "staying loose" is just that I did not populate what I call preoccupations with high-level constructs, such as the id, the ego, and the superego; I did not want to have the unconscious id and the unconscious superego whacking each other around while the battered ego stood in fear and trembling between them. For the time being I wanted to stay at a lower level of abstraction.

(4) *Preoccupations and the Future*. It seemed to me that the preoccupations of students could not be reduced completely to interactions between the past and the present. The expectations of the future seemed also to reside in these preoccupations. (Perhaps here I was affected by Jung.) It seemed to me that students' expectations of the future affected the present. Some personal future goals seemed to enhance the present and give it significance whereas others seemed to do just the opposite, to make the *here and now* enervating and to deprive it of meaning. Many of the false dichotomies I observed seemed to do just that. So in life space I conceived of the future as a means instead of an end and the present as an end instead of a means. We live in the present, not the future; when the future comes along, as it has a way of doing, it becomes the present. It seemed obvious to me that if we developed future goals that tended to make the present enervating, we would be living a miserable life. It seemed to me that this was what I had been doing during the early period of my life. This was the fourth uniformity I observed. I elaborated on it in a talk I gave later called "The Secret of Success," published as Chapter 5 in *Man-in-Organization*.

(5) *The Dyadic Relation*. A fifth uniformity that I observed in my interviews with students had me still more intrigued. In order to tap a student's preoccupations, that is, in order to get him to tell me about matters of importance to him and to express his negative as well as his positive feelings, I had to develop a certain kind of behavior or method of interviewing. Under certain kinds of behavior on my part, students' preoccupations tended to become shy and not to reveal themselves. When I used other approaches, preoccupations came out of hiding, as it were, and expressed themselves. In this uniformity I felt I was getting closer to the meat of the coconut. I wrote a paper on the interviewing method which I developed to get these mental creatures out in the fresh air. Again I did not publish it right away, but later with revisions it became Chapter XIII in *Management and the Worker*.

In this chapter I have tried to describe my own personal discovery of life space and the entities and relations with which I populated it. Many other people had discovered it before, but once I did, it became my own. I was often surprised, though, to find persons, some of whom were called psychologists, who, it seemed to me, had not discovered it.

In the center of life space I put the entities I call preoccupations. They were fraught with sentiments, feelings, and emotions. Although not as visible or tangible as the entities of physical space, under certain conditions they could be tapped and verbalized. Although they had an ideational aspect, they could be treated as "matters of fact" and not as "relations of ideas." The "ands," "ors," and "nots" which they contained were not as clear and precise as those of logicians; instead, logical distinctions were all jumbled up in them. Nevertheless, they had rules of their own and could be empirically investigated.

For me these preoccupations were not only the stuff that dreams are made of; they also played an important role in a person's relations to his present surroundings. They affected his capacity to attend, to learn, and to reach decisions. In these preoccupations the past, present, and future were all bound together in a living, moving, dynamic reality. They contained man's doubts and anxieties and his feelings of guilt and shame about things he may or may not have done in the past, as well as his hopes and aspirations for the future. They could be the source of his bondage to and determination by the past, as well as the source of his creativity and freedom in the present. They could be treated as rubbish, or they could be mined for gold. Moreover, they went during the 24-hour day, according to the language of different investigators, from *dreams, autistic thinking, reveries, preoccupations, or syncretistic thinking* to skilled *reflections* about the world in which the person lived and his relations to it.

In these preoccupations, at whatever level they were manifested, I put all of a person's values—what was important to him—in terms of which he ordered his preferences and gave meaning to the reality about him. I conceived of these preoccupations as a nonrandom accumulation of matter-energy existing in life space which, when a person knew how, could be released for productive work instead of for commiserating about "little old me."

Whenever I refer in later chapters to things that are individual instead of social, I will be speaking about these preoccupations and their subject matter, that is, about the perpetual internal chatter we have with ourselves. This is the closest I can get to the individual. Although these phenomena are contaminated by the social, their particular concrete manifestation for each of us in the end is individual; they bear the stamp of our own individual embroidery.

For me then preoccupations were as close to the phenomena of life space as I could get. I felt that so long as I was in touch with these phenomena, I could leave verbal constructs about them to philosophers and psychologists. They had the words; I was in touch with the territory. This for me was more than a fair exchange. How smug could I get? But at least this way of thinking gave me time to stay loose about life space, until I could take a look around at the other spaces with which it got entangled.

As we shall see more clearly later, I had a curious way of backing into my colleagues' bailiwicks at the Business School. One of them I have mentioned already, namely, decision making; another was related to problems of control, with which executives were also supposed to be concerned. In both cases I approached these problems from their subjective rather than their objective side. I feared that my colleagues viewed me as approaching these problems "ass-end-to." From my point of view I approached them with the "right end up." Between these differences of perception, a confrontation was to occur someday. At this time I was oblivious of the eventuality. I just sat at the periphery of the Business School's activities, while Mayo performed his magic, with Dean Donham at the center.

Chapter 4

The Hawthorne and Related Researches

The period of my life about which I now want to talk, 1932–1942, covers the depth of the Great Depression, the slow economic recovery of the country, the rise of Hitler and the birth of the Third Reich in 1933, the beginning of World War II in 1939, up to and including Pearl Harbor in December 1941. It was a turbulent period filled with action and reaction and not many constructive interactions. Perhaps this is not entirely accurate; in this country there was the New Deal.

What *preoccupations* came to mean to me during the previous period, *interactions* came to mean to me during this period. They became the new element that needed to be researched. The unit for investigation was no longer the monad but the dyad and the triad, that is, relations between persons. For me these became the molecules which needed to be understood and cracked, if a whole storehouse of frozen energy was to be released for constructive purposes. I call this period my discovery of social space, and I will be concerned with it in this and the next two chapters.

Perhaps I should say that the titles and dates I assign to these periods do not specify literally my actual activities. They designate rather the dominant intellectual motifs of my life during each of these periods. As a matter of fact, I continued to counsel students from 1932 to 1941, but I no longer gave that activity my full time. I began to phase it out gradually, and it terminated with the entrance of this country into World War II in 1941. Likewise my interest in social space began during the years 1927–1932, but this was not the dominant motif of my attention during that period.

THE HAWTHORNE RESEARCHES

My curiosity about social space started when I became connected with the Hawthorne researches. These researches were begun and conducted by executives of the Hawthorne plant (on the outskirts of Chicago) of the Western Electric Company, which is the manufacturing arm of the Bell System, the American Telephone & Telegraph Company.

Although these researches have been fully reported, let me state briefly from my point of view what they were about. Essentially these researches were concerned with the productivity, satisfaction, and motivation of workers. They went roughly through four phases: from an almost exclusive concern with employee productivity, to a concern with employee satisfaction, to a concern with employee motivation, and finally to a growing realization that the productivity, satisfaction, and motivation of workers were all interrelated.

The early illumination experiments from 1924 to 1927, before either Mayo or I were connected with them, dealt with the effect of the quality and quantity of illumination on the efficiency of workers. The results of these experiments were not only inconclusive but also rather curious. In one experiment, for example, the workers were divided into two groups: the test group, where the workers were submitted to intensities of illumination of increasing magnitude, and a control group, where they worked under a constant intensity of illumination. Contrary to expectations, production increased in both the test group and the control group, and the rise of output in both cases was roughly of the same magnitude. Several further experiments of this character exhibited similar curious outcomes. It looked as if the workers were reacting more to the positive concern of the experimenters about their working conditions than to the actual physical changes in illumination. This response later came to be called the "Hawthorne effect." But also it could be argued that the inconclusive findings resulted from the difficulty of testing for the effect of a single variable in a situation where there were so many uncontrolled variables.

To correct for the latter difficulty, the experimenters set up the Relay Assembly Test Room in 1927. Five women assembling telephone relays, made up of approximately 40 parts, were segregated in a room where their conditions of work could be carefully controlled, their output carefully measured, and their behavior closely observed. Under these conditions they were submitted to 13 different experimental periods which varied in the number and duration of rest pauses and in the length of the working day and week. During the first year and a half of the experiment, when the conditions of work—in terms of rest pauses, etc.—steadily improved, the output rate also steadily rose. Here was strong evidence in favor of the experimenters' hypothesis that fatigue was the major factor limiting output. But then in Period XII when the experimenters decided to return to the original conditions of a full 48-hour week without rest pauses, coffee breaks, and what not, productivity, instead of taking the expected nose dive, maintained its high level. Here again it looked as if the workers were responding more to the positive concern of the experimenters for their welfare than to the experimental conditions as such. In short, the experimenters were not behaving as typical supervisors, a fact that escaped their attention in their zeal to set up a controlled experiment. Could it be that it was to this altered behavior of the concerned experimenters that the workers were responding positively?

This possible interpretation launched the researchers in a new direction; it was called the Interviewing Program, a search for what was determining the satisfactions of the workers and possibly affecting their production. In this shift the former experimenters became clinicians, in which role they had to learn how to get the workers to talk about matters that were important to them. Not only did this attempt to listen sympathetically but intelligently to what the workers had to say produce in many instances what was now coming to be recognized as the positive Hawthorne effect, it also revealed the difference the behavior of their supervisors made to the workers. For if you can believe this now, the supervisors were neither listening sympathetically to their subordinates nor trying to understand intelligently what their subordinates were telling them.

It looked as if the Hawthorne researches were regressing slowly, step by step, to the obvious and were not discovering any new gimmicks to make the workers more productive and contented. There was still one more obvious discovery to be made. It occurred in the Bank Wiring Observation Room, which the investigators set up in order to find out what was going on in a work group without making changes in its situation.

This room contained 14 workmen representing 3 occupational groups—wiremen, soldermen, and inspectors. These men were paid a group piecework: the more the group turned out the more they earned. Thus, one might expect that they would have been interested in maintaining total output, and that the faster workers would have put pressure on the slower workers to improve their efficiency. This was not the case. Among the workers in the room there was an output norm about what constituted a fair day's work. Workers who violated this norm by either producing too much or too little were punished by the workers themselves. Each worker's level of output depended more on his position in the informal organization of the group than upon his intelligence, dexterity, or economic motivation per se.

From then on, the researchers became more and more interested in the informal organization of small work groups, how the workers' behavior was being controlled within the group, and how this behavior related to the formal control procedures set up by management. At times it looked as if the workers' informal organization and management's formal procedures were working in opposition to each other.

MAYO'S RELATION TO THE HAWTHORNE RESEARCHES

Mayo' participation in the Hawthorne researches was unusual from the point of view of orthodox scientific methodology—so unusual that it aroused the curiosity of many social scientists. Some of them felt that some kind of skullduggery was going on. Let me try to correct this misunderstanding by stating the facts as I perceived them. I have also written about Mayo's part in the researches in the papers published as Chapters 19 and 20 in *Man-in-Organization.*

Mayo had nothing to do with the design of or conduct of the original illumination experiments or of the Relay Assembly Test Room. Dr. C. E. Turner, Professor of Biology and Public Health at M.I.T., was one of the chief advisers of the investigators in the early period. Most of the early statistical studies were made under his direction.

Mayo came into the picture—I cannot specify the exact date— sometime around Period XII in the Relay Assembly Test Room, when the persons in charge of these experiments were having trouble interpreting their findings. I believe that Mr. Pennock, then superintendent of the inspection branch of the company and greatly concerned with these studies and their findings, was the person who initiated the first contact with Mayo. From this beginning a relationship gradually developed between Mayo and the executives of the company, which all of them found rewarding. The relationship never became a highly planned collaboration, but always remained a spontaneous one among interested and concerned parties. There were no formal contracts or agreements of any kind, as far as I know.

In this manner Mayo became informally the chief adviser to these researches during their later periods. He helped in the training of the interviewers for the Interview Program, as I did. W. Lloyd

Warner, about whom I shall speak later, also influenced the design of the Bank Wiring Observation Room study.

In the later days of the researches Mayo made many visits to Chicago for periods of about two weeks at a time. Just how many I have no records to determine. I also visited the plant, but less often than Mayo.

The division of labor between Mayo and me was roughly this. He interacted with the top executives of the company more than I did. I interacted with the lower levels of supervision more than he did. The three persons whom I saw most were William J. Dickson, Harold A. Wright, and Mark L. Putnam. At that time they were section chief, department chief, and division chief, respectively: that is, Bill Dickson reported to Hal Wright and Hal Wright to "Put" Putnam. As long as they remained in the company, even though their titles changed, Bill, Hal, and Put always occupied the same relative positions in the supervisory hierarchy. In time they all became very good friends of mine. I count them among the most pleasant working associates I ever had.

Mayo himself never collected any of the data for the Hawthorne researches. I did, but only to a limited extent. I spent the summer of 1931 interviewing supervisors in the Operating Branch. These data are reported in Chapters XV and XVI of *Management and the Worker* under the titles "Attitudes Within the Supervisory Organization" and "Complaints and Social Equilibrium." The latter chapter illustrates well my emerging interest in social space. ·

There is little question that this informal collaboration between Mayo and the Hawthorne researches was unusual. It tended, I believe, to make some people suspicious about what was going on. Granted that something unusual was happening, in what sense was it unusual? In no sense did Mayo keep secret any of the facts I mentioned above, nor did he ever claim credit for the researches; he always bent over backward to give the company and the persons who had been involved in the research their full share of credit. (See his preface to *Management and the Worker*.) In no sense did he distort the data for his own personal advantage. He brought in other persons to look at them, including T. North Whitehead, W. Lloyd Warner, George C. Homans, myself, and others. No body of data, so far as I know, was ever scrutinized with such care and from so many different points of view.

To understand the developing relationship between Mayo and these researches and his contribution to them requires the understanding of why Mayo was Mayo. As I tried to indicate in the last chapter, Mayo was an adventurer in the realm of ideas. The Hawthorne researches provided him with an unusual opportunity to test his ideas in the industrial arena. Executives of the company came to him because they could not interpret their findings. He gave them an interpretation which later achieved recognition by having not *his* name, but the company's name—"the Hawthorne effect"—given to it.

Again and again Mayo performed this function of interpretation. The data were not his; the results were not his; the original hypotheses and questions were not his; but as the researches continued, the interpretations of what the results meant and the new questions and hypotheses that emerged from them were his. Also, the way of thinking which he brought to the researches and which finally gave them a sense of direction and purpose was his.

Let us see how this happened. Mayo's interpretations were never premature closures to the effect "Well, we've buttoned this up; now let's talk about something else." They were always of the character "What do these results mean for future research and action? What new questions do they raise?" Instead of telling the executives this, he tried to help them see these potentialities for themselves.

In other respects Mayo's behavior was also unusual. Instead of arriving for work at the company at 9 a.m., he would often arrive around 10 a.m. or later. Instead of eating lunch with the top executives at the country club, he would take them for lunch to some joint on Cicero Avenue where the workers ate and where he could get the onion soup he was fond of. He did not conform to the mores of the industrial world; he never played up to the preconceptions of the executive; he treated them as intelligent men.

As a result, the executives of the company could not fit Mayo easily into either the world of business or the world of academia. He was neither a stereotypical businessman nor a stereotypical long-haired academic. Again and again in his talks with them, Mayo could take some simple employee situation from an interview—the case of Hank, for example—and before one was aware of what was happening, Hank no longer was only a direct cost, a set of motions, a seeker of security, a coffee-breaker, a rate-buster, a feather-bedder, a trouble-maker, an apathetic worker, and so on and on. Instead, as Mayo wove his spell, Hank became a person with motivations which the executives could share and identify. Many of these executives who had risen from the ranks had lost contact with the concrete, because their heads or minds were now supposed to be in the clouds of economic abstractions. They welcomed this return back home and felt rejuvenated.

The executives became once again curious about human motivation, especially in relation to some of their oversimplified logics of control, wage incentive systems, for example. Mayo never advocated that the toilets be hot in the summer and cold in the winter to keep Hank from staying there so long. He was interested in why Hank went to the toilet so often and stayed there so long—a question Course XV had not raised.

Besides showing the Hawthorne investigators the significance of the results for future research and providing them with a sense of direction, Mayo also opened up for them the opportunity to participate in the enterprise of science, not in the sense of its conventional rules and hardware but in the sense of adventure and curiosity. Most of the Hawthorne investigators were not scientists in the conventional definition of the term. They did not possess the proper credentials. Nevertheless, he provided them with a new world for development.

Yes, Mayo's contributions to the Hawthorne researches were unusual—in fact so peculiar and so rare that one cannot easily attach labels to them. They were the contributions of a blithe spirit and a creative mind. Let's bow our heads in silence for a moment, because without Mayo's contributions the results of the Hawthorne researches would still be in the archives of the company in their green files collecting dust. Nobody would have known what they meant.

More than this, without Mayo's support and encouragement, the Hawthorne researches would never have continued to the stage they did. They would have died in their tracks. By his behavior, Mayo escalated the positive Hawthorne effect. To his concern, interest, and curiosity, the Hawthorne researchers responded with increasing vigor, just as the employees had responded with increased output to the concern, interest, and curiosity of their researchers. At the time, I called this the "double-whammy Hawthorne effect." Today the condition is called synergy, that is, when $2 + 2 = 5$.

WRITING *MANAGEMENT AND THE WORKER*

I have dwelt at some length on Mayo's relation to the Hawthorne researches both to correct misunderstandings about it and also to provide examples of my growing interest in the importance of interpersonal relations and how they might be researched. My own participation in these researches became more active in September 1932, when the data from the various studies at Hawthorne were shipped to the Harvard Business School for the purpose of further study, analysis, and final recording. The result was two publications: one two-volume book, *The Industrial Worker*, by T. North Whitehead, in which he re-analyzed all the data of the Relay Assembly Test Room; and a book, *Management and the Worker*, by Bill Dickson and me, in which we reported the chronology and direction of the various Hawthorne studies and analyzed what they meant as they developed from one stage to another.

When Bill Dickson and Hal Wright arrived at Morgan Hall with their truckload of data, the country was deep in the depression. Hal remained for about six months and then was called back to Hawthorne for another job; Bill remained with me for the next three and a half years, until February 1936, when *Management and the Worker*, except for the concluding chapters, was completed. During this period, although he worked six days a week, Bill was on the company's payroll on a two-to-three-days-a-week basis. He received additional funds from Mayo's Rockefeller Foundation grant to help him out. Had Bill remained at Hawthorne, he would have risked being laid off because of his relatively short service with the company; but because he remained at Harvard somewhat invisible from the company, the hand of the complete layoff never descended.

My motivation for writing *Management and the Worker*, as I reflect upon it now, had some features worth mentioning. At that time, this was the last book I ever expected or wished to write. It was not my dream book; for me it was a labor of duty and a way of paying back my debt to Mayo. (One good turn deserves another.) I felt that sufficient publicity had been given to these important studies for them to be fully recorded and documented. Doing so was not Mayo's forte. He had publicized them in speeches from one corner of the land to the other, as well as in France and England, where he often went on vacations during the summers. But with my obsessive background this was not enough.

Although I admired Mayo's blithe spirit, I was never able to achieve it—certainly not then. I worried that the Rockefeller Foundation might find out someday that it was sinking its money into a bottemless pit from which there would be no tangible return. Mayo, it seemed to me, treated the Rockefeller executives in the same way he treated the executives of the Western Electric Company. So far as I knew, he never made any official reports of his activities to them; he dined and wined them once each year and told them about Hank and Suzie and Period XII in the Relay Assembly Test Room.

So I too was among the persons who worried about Mayo's behavior, because it did not fulfill my lingering Horatio Alger notions about how to succeed. My job, it seemed to me, was just too much fun and not enough work, and this was neither right nor the road to success. To right this wrong, to keep my job—which any day I thought might vanish—and to repay my debt of gratitude to Mayo, I buckled down and sweated through a voluminous body of data which held for me at that time as much attraction as Descartes' letters in Widener Library. So help me, except for what God and the psychoanalysts know, this is the whole truth about how I got involved in writing *Management and the Worker*. I had to get a visible tangible product—a book—that Mayo could show for his labors, whether anyone read it or not.

In spite of this motivation, this sweating through of a body of data was what I needed; for the first time I realized what research—not in the library—was about. I learned a great deal that was to stand me in good stead for the future. I place this work at the very top of the experience which I have had. I have come to believe that for the seekers of knowledge there is no substitute. Engage in it at least once or forever hold your tongue. The consumer of knowledge can never know what a dicky thing knowledge is until he has tried to produce it.

After we had put in three and a half years of hard labor with these data, the manuscript went to the company for factual review. It stayed on the desks of various executives at the company's central headquarters for three years, until May 1939. I thought it might have gotten lost there, although I had occasional reports of progress. One report I heard was that the public relations department did not like the word hierarchy, because, after all, there were no angels at the Western Electric Company.

After three years of not being able to find anything more damaging to the company's public image than that, in May 1939, Clarence Stoll, the president of the company, gave the go-ahead signal to publish. At this point Bill and I wrote the concluding three chapters and the manuscript went to the Harvard University Press with a subsidy of $3,800 from Mayo's grant. The subsidy was necessary because, obviously, the book would not pay for itself; no one was going to read it. This did not bother me. What did matter was that the next time the Rockefeller people came to be wined and dined, there would be not only the proper wines and foods on the table; there would also be a book.

Contrary to my expectations, *Management and the Worker* became a best seller for a book of its kind. It went through 15 or more printings. No personnel manager could afford not to have it on his shelf, even though he may not have read it. In time he did not need to, for the findings of the Hawthorne researches were restated and misstated in hundreds of books on personnel management.

Management and the Worker became not only a status symbol; it stimulated a great deal of a new kind of research in industry. This to me was its important contribution. It also provoked a great deal of criticism among the social scientists in academia, about which I will write later. In the period about which I am writing, this criticism was not one of my major concerns.

LLOYD WARNER AND THE YANKEE CITY STUDIES

Although by temperament, skill, training, and interest Mayo was primarily a clinical psychopathologist, this orientation was never the aspect to which he pointed when he talked about the need for research. Here he kept pointing to the social lacunae which had developed from the rise of science and technology and which he thought nourished neuroses and obsessions. This to him was the direction in which Freud's findings, as well as those of Durkheim's about *anomie*, were pointing and where the big payoff in understanding and practice might be. He felt that from psychopathology we knew more about the nature of the adapting individual than the nature of what he was adapting to. In the lingo of today, he felt that the new psychopathology had provided a better model of man than a model of society. Hence, although Mayo talked about individuals from a background of rich personal experiences with them in the concrete, he talked about many societies whose description existed only in books.

For Mayo these books were limited to those which had been based on some empirical investigation, such as the studies of the social anthropologists—Malinowski and Radcliffe-Brown. These latter studies were based on extensive field investigation, and he felt they were promising. Consequently, shortly after he joined Harvard, he added a social anthropologist to his staff—W. Lloyd Warner. Warner held a joint appointment, that is, one half of his time and salary were allocated to the Department of Anthropology across the River and the other half to the Business School.

Warner, a student of Malinowski's, had studied primitive communities; now he wished to study a modern community by using the same methods that a social anthropologist would use to study a primitive one. This was a daring idea because, at the time, in the universities anthropology was anthropology and sociology was sociology, two distinct and separate disciplines. Although at Harvard no river separated them, no bridge connected them either. They just lived side by side in a state of hands-off coexistence on the same side of the river.

Warner, like Mayo, was also an adventurer in the realm of ideas. Both had a bit of charisma about them. Whereas I complemented Mayo, so that it took a long time before our differences became overtly exposed, Lloyd Warner and Mayo tended to draw sparks quickly from each other. But they were fruitful sparks—functional is the technical term—and so from them for awhile useful products emerged. Lloyd chose a town 40 miles north of Boston as his site for study. Its disguised name is Yankee City, which I will still use, even though many persons now know its real one.

For five years Lloyd and his colleagues collected as much data about Yankee City as the Western Electric Company had collected about its employees—literally tons. Assisting him Lloyd had three brilliant young men—Conrad Arensberg, Eliot Chapple, and Burleigh Gardner. All three were younger than I; their relations to Lloyd in the early days were similar to mine to Mayo; that is, they were his disciples, although each broke his "positive transference" with Lloyd much sooner than I worked through mine with Mayo.

Although I never had anything directly to do with the Yankee City study, I felt I participated vicariously in the field work experience there. I was an interested spectator in many of their discussions. They also felt that they had a "bear by the tail." It could be truthfully said that all the social anthropology I learned came from Lloyd, Eliot, Connie, and Burleigh. They all became good friends of mine and they stimulated my thinking to no end. When I was with them, there was never a dull moment and to them I owe a great deal of my discovery of social space. They were the first ones who stuck my intellectual nose in it. (My predispositional nose—because of my background—was already well acquainted with it.)

After they discovered the social structure of Yankee City with its six classes—the upper uppers, the lower uppers, the upper middles, the lower middles, the upper lowers, and the lower lowers—I felt I could also "class angle" individuals in society. In intellectual circles at this period, social class was talked about less freely than sex. That is to say, it had become more acceptable to state a person's sexual identifications—i.e., what sexual objects or aims he had succeeded or failed to identify with—than to state his class identifications—that is, what social class he belonged to or aspired to belong to. To state my own case as an example, I now suffered not only from castration anxiety but also from social status anxiety. I was a lower middle aspiring to become an upper middle or even a lower upper who had not as yet achieved the grade. At this period this diagnosis was tough to take. Reference group theory and identity crises had not been born.

Lloyd Warner and Elton Mayo never saw eye to eye over the question of functionality and dysfunctionality. Lloyd felt that Mayo saw dysfunctionality too readily and overlooked the functional aspects of modern institutional life. For example, Lloyd got excited by seeing how an association, such as the Knights of Pythias, helped its members to relate to the class structure. This left Mayo cold; he was more concerned with what the Knights of Pythias was doing for Hank, one of its members, to become a more adaptive person in the modern world.

When the books about Yankee City came to be written, part of the voluminous data went to Chicago, where Lloyd had become a professor at the University of Chicago, and part of them stayed for a while in Morgan Hall at the Business School with Eliot Chapple. In time a set of illustrious volumes—the Yankee City Series—appeared. For the interim and under Eliot's charge at Morgan Hall, things took a different turn. As Eliot's and my offices were adjacent, I became involved in the shift of direction. At this time both Eliot and Conrad Arensberg were moving in the direction of positivism. By that I mean they felt that *interactions* not only *could be studied* but also *should be studied* apart from their content or meaning. According to them, the failure to do this was what prevented anthropology—and for that matter most of the social sciences—from becoming truly scientific. From their point of view the frequency and duration of interactions could be observed and objectively measured. Moreover, the initiator and the terminus of the interaction, although more difficult to determine, could also be observed and counted. For them these were the hard data by which matters of organizational behavior were to be explained and dealt with.

Eliot became enamored with this idea. He succumbed to what Abraham Kaplan calls "the law of the instrument"; that is, "Give a small boy a hammer, and he will find that everything he encounters needs pounding." This is just what Eliot did; he pounded everthing and everyone in sight, including Lloyd, his colleagues, and his best friends with his ideas. This did not make for either harmony or constructive conflict.

Finally, Eliot gave up working with the contaminated data of Yankee City to follow his own interests. In time he developed his "interaction chronograph," a machine with which he could measure the frequency and duration of a person's interactions under controlled conditions. With its aid, he continued his researches and applied his results by trying to facilitate the fit between persons with certain measurable interaction patterns and jobs requiring such interaction patterns. After leaving Harvard, he never accepted another academic appointment. Many of us who were troubled by him then feel now that be has not received the academic recognition he deserves.

As I look back at my relations to these younger men, I do not remember ever thinking of them as rivals except perhaps for Eliot. Even with him, "rival" does not express correctly the relationship that existed between us. Eliot's "breakthrough" seemed to me a "break with" a more needed pedestrian approach. The development of the social sciences, it seemed to me, would require for a long time just ordinary "tillers of the soil" (clinicians and field workers), not fancy "new models." In this sense Eliot was a threat to the development of the area as I thought it should take place at the Business School. I could buy his concepts readily enough as tools for research in one element of social space. In fact, as will be seen, I used them constantly. But I felt that discarding sentiments, symbols, and meaning as unnecessary for investigation was like throwing out the baby with the bath water. This risk I was neither emotionally nor intellectually ready to take; intellectually it does not make sense to me now. So Eliot had me disturbed plenty; my emerging career at the Business School, as I then envisaged it, was at stake.

THE COUNSELING PROGRAM AT WESTERN

When Bill Dickson went back to the Hawthorne plant in 1936, he collaborated with Hal Wright and Mark Putnam in developing a counseling program for employees. This was the company's first attempt to apply the findings from the Hawthorne researches. I spent the summer of 1938 at the plant to help train the counselors. For the next three years I also helped to develop understanding of this approach to employee relations throughout the company and in the Bell System itself. At that time the Western Electric Company had two other plants in addition to Hawthorne: one at Kearny, New Jersey, and the other at Point Breeze, Baltimore, Maryland. This was my first experience in consulting; it came about very informally.

First Hal Wright went to the New York headquarters of the Western Electric Company; later Mark Putnam went to the headquarters of the American Telephone and Telegraph Company with a similar assignment. In my consulting capacity I worked mostly with these two men. As I have said, both of them were my very good friends. I enjoyed the assignment, even though I was never sure what I was accomplishing.

This assignment was my first experience with a large staff organization and the kind of work its members did. They seemed to be involved in a great deal of paper work; the language on their papers for a while had me stumped. In some respects it bore a resemblance to the language of academia, but in other respects it was different. Although both languages were dealing with abstractions, the language of these staff executives seemed to stay at a dead level, devoid of any relation to the concrete or to any ideas which made the blood circulate.

As most of these staff people in their earlier jobs had been very much in touch with concrete things and people, this level of discourse surprised me. Their heads were neither in the clouds nor their feet on the ground; they seemed to be out of touch with both the tops and the bottoms of the organization. Many of them seemed to me to be unhappy and in a state of suspended animation indulging in a monotonic mumbo-jumbo which I found neither informative nor inspiring. I had met this ballet of bloodless categories in philosophy; to meet it again in industry was a surprise to me. It was deadly; in time I gave a name to these phenomena. I called them "the logics of management." I populated "organizational space" with them as one of the major categories which existed there. Actually I thought these logics were nonlogics; by calling them "logics" I created a confusion about which I will say more later on.

At the time, I thought these staff executives needed a dose of applied epistemology. They needed to know the difference between matters of fact and relations of ideas; between words and the things words stood for; between the symbol and the phenomena being symbolized; between the logical and the nonlogical; and so on. All my communications, as I look back at them now, were pretty highbrow. I wrote memoranda, gave lectures, and conducted discussions concerning the functions of a conceptual scheme, the difference between the abstract and the concrete, between theory and practice, and between knowledge and skill and how they could be usefully related. I wanted to turn the nonlogico-experimental language of organizations into the logico-experimental language of science. What a silly ass I was!

Although the counseling program at Hawthorne continued until 1956, when it was discontinued, my active connection with it came to a close in 1941. Intellectually other things had begun to interest me more; also the external environment had begun to change. I was traveling back from Chicago by train when I first heard about Pearl Harbor. I still remember that awful feeling in the pit of my stomach. This could not be, but it was; and for me something came to an end. Speculation was no longer the order of the day; action was needed. Although I always continued to be interested in the counseling program, my active connection with it ceased. I was not to pick it up again for 25 years, when with Bill Dickson I wrote a history of the counseling program, *Counseling in an Organization* (1966), at a period of my life when one gets the yen to try to understand what, if anything, he has been up to—a well-known syndrome of approaching old age.

Chapter 5
Concrete Sociology

A few other persons, in addition to Mayo and the social anthropologists, influenced me greatly between 1932 and 1942. During that period there was one school of thought at Harvard which for a while seemed to me to contain only two members. One was the originator of the school, Vilfredo Pareto, an Italian sociologist, who died in 1923, but whose thoughts existed in French in an exciting—some say Machiavellian—book called *Sociologie Générale*, of which there were just a few copies in Widener Library. To be exact the book first appeared in 1916. It was translated into French a year later and into English in 1935. The other member was Lawrence J. Henderson, very much alive, in an office close to mine in Morgan Hall, the director of the Fatigue Laboratory, and Pareto's most ardent advocate, whose mission in life seemed to be at the time to populate this school of thought with more members. Henderson provided for me another role model besides Mayo's during this period.

L.J. HENDERSON

Whereas Mayo was more vigorous in his thinking, Henderson was more rigorous. From Mayo I got my insights and inspirations; from Henderson I received the invigoration that one gets from a dash of cold water. It can be said that in Mayo I found my intellectual mother and in Henderson my intellectual father. The functions that each provided were needed to round out my intellectual and emotional development.

When Henderson joined Mayo at the Business School in 1927, he had already received international acclaim for his work in blood chemistry; he was the authority at Harvard on the scientific method; and he was also a good friend of President Lowell. When he crossed the River from its theoretical to its practical side, his scientific colleagues and friends viewed the passage with dismay and thought that his mind had begun to fail him. As I came to understand it, he was not really changing his job, but only his job description. In his work on blood chemistry, he had reached one of those dead ends where, unless one can make an intellectual leap forward, a creative act of the highest order, one just continues to go around in circles and keeps rediscovering America. This is a disease from which those of us in the pursuit of knowledge sometimes suffer, something I was to learn much later when I began to suffer from the disease myself.

In his study of the blood, Henderson had discovered a system of many mutually dependent variables with which at the time he did not have the mathematics to cope. While he was ruminating about this problem, he discovered Pareto, whom he found had been concerned theoretically with the same problem, although in a different subject matter, sociology. Up to this time Henderson had shared the disdain that most members of the harder sciences have for the softer ones. In fact, he would have called sociology not a science but a branch of philosophy, which, as a subdivision of the Department of Philosophy called social ethics, it had been at Harvard in an institutional sense until 1931. However, when Henderson discovered Pareto, he became a one-book sociologist.

Henderson was an M.D. who had never practiced medicine; he had gone immediately from medical school into research, but he had a secret admiration for clinicians. It was their skill that he admired in Mayo. He also had an admiration for those he referred to as "men of affairs." In this category he put Mr. Donham, Dean of the Business School. These three—Mayo, Henderson, and Donham—formed a triumvirate who, in the opinion of others as well as myself, had a terrific impact upon the School. From their association were forged the links for what was to become the School's distinctive competence for the next two decades. Whatever the conceptual and intellectual underpinning was for what the School was up to, they provided it. Although this statement may sound disparaging of my then colleagues at the Business School, I do not mean it this way, as I shall try to make clear later.

As I look back now at our situation in terms of a "role constellation," I can see that the Department of Industrial Research was sitting pretty. On our side we had Donham, the Dean of the School—a first-rate man of affairs; we had Henderson, the arch exponent at Harvard of what made science science—"Jesus Christ" or "Pink Whiskers," as the students called him; and we had Mayo, a clinical adventurer of the first order. When each of these men performed his respective role, the constellation worked extraordinarily well. But when Henderson tried to make like a man of affairs and Donham like a social scientist, it did not. But then we had Mayo, who had the skills, even if not the accepted labels, to pick up the pieces. What more could we want or need?

HENDERSON AND PARETO

But I still worried. As time went on, Henderson became more interested in Mayo's work than in his own Fatigue Laboratory. Henderson organized a seminar on Pareto in the Faculty of Arts and Sciences. This seminar in time became famous, because it was attended by many distinguished professors from most of the disciplines in the University as well as by some distinguished men of affairs from outside. It almost looked to me as though Henderson had organized the seminar to tell his colleagues and friends what's what.

At the seminar in its early period Henderson would read the *Sociologie* slowly in French, because it had not yet been translated into English; he elaborated on the significance of each point Pareto made and then invited discussion. If anyone by this time had not "gotten the point" (as my sister had not about the cute, colored tacks I described in Chapter 2), Henderson would rise from his chair by the fireside in Winthrop House and deliver a lecture to the effect of "How stupid can you get!" This behavior did not stimulate much discusson, at least not among the few graduate students and younger faculty members who were present.

Only one time do I remember Henderson stumped. That was when Pitirim Sorokin, the then newly appointed Professor of Sociology at Harvard, broke forth after Henderson (a la Pareto) had dealt cavalierly with Kant's categorical imperative. At the close of this seminar, Sorokin rose in full wrath and delivered, as I remember it, a half hour's oration, saying in effect, "You can't do this to me and the values I represent." The hour was getting late; the happy hour, cocktail hour, or dining hour for most of us had arrived. Whether this had anything to do with it, I do not know. All I remember, without the aid of Eliot Chapple's interaction chronograph but with the aid of his insight, is that Henderson kept his mouth shut. There was no dialogue; there had been only two monologues; and as I remember it, Sorokin never appeared again.

As one can see, I am portraying Henderson as a man not very skillful at interpersonal relations. This was so; and I can provide anecdote after anecdote to illustrate it. For example, I can cite the case when my wife and I drove him to the Worcester State Hospital, a mental hospital, to deliver a lecture on Pareto. The psychiatrists there thought my wife was his wife and Pareto had something to do with "paretics." I can also remember the occasion during Harvard's Tercentenary in 1936, when the Fatigue Laboratory had pictures in Morgan Hall illustrating the sites of their work in the Andes (under high altitude conditions) and at Boulder Dam (under extreme heat conditions). Miss Cotter, a member of the financial office, because she was flustered and didn't know quite what to say to Henderson, who was also looking at these pictures, blurted out, "It pays to advertise." Henderson responded, "My dear Miss Cotter, that is an empirical proposition which requires facts to substantiate it."

Incidents such as these two stay in my mind because of the incongruity between what Henderson was trying to show, the importance of sentiments in social life (i.e., nonlogical behavior), and his inability to practice this insight personally. When Miss Cotter, for example, in order to make conversation said, "It pays to advertise," he did not treat her statement as an expression of friendliness, which it was. Rather he turned it into a logico-experimental proposition which required verification, and with that misevaluation he lowered the boom on poor Miss Cotter. He did this to everyone. At that time in the Business School many nonlogico-experimental propositions about business were in the air—hot air, I should say—so that Henderson never lacked opportunities to exercise the double whammy I described on members of the Faculty, especially at the Business School Faculty Club on this side of the River, where he often ate lunch. To this day, one comes across echoes of the scars of these interpersonal encounters, which have now become funny stories. But in spite of his limitations in interpersonal relations, I admired and respected Henderson tremendously. Henderson knew what the functions of a great university were and why they tended to breed a certain kind of eccentricity. I felt that he was as seriously concerned as I was about what made knowledge knowledge. This was serious business and nothing to joke about. If it ever came to a showdown, there was no question about where I stood. I was behind Henderson one hundred percent.

The distinction between logical and nonlogical behavior became very important to me. I used it over and over again. To me, within limits it was a useful distinction to maintain. In some senses the logical and nonlogical seemed to be disjointed sets of phenomena, although in other senses they were not. All the human relations problems in which I became interested seemed to me to lie where the logical and nonlogical intersected. I was annoyed by those who blurred the distinction in order to reduce one to the other.

Social relations to me were not logical relations, and they differed from technological relations. Where man could be logico-experimental, in the Paretian sense, was in the world of technology. Here there could be a logical relation between means and ends. In social relations this simple relation between means and ends became more complex. That I had to cross the river in order to get on the other side I put in the world of physical and technological space. But to establish social relations with persons across the river required more than merely crossing the physical river. Putting a hat on my head to protect it from the rain or sun seemed to me an action which should be differentiated from taking off my hat when I passed a woman acquaintance on the street. These actions addressed themselves to different relations.

Pareto had been trained as an engineer, so this distinction perhaps meant something to me in view of my own training that it may not have meant to some of my colleagues. When Pareto talked about the logico-experimental, I translated it into the world of technological space; when he talked about the nonlogico-experimental, I translated it into what I call social space. These spaces were populated with different entities and relations; I concurred completely with Pareto and Henderson that they should not be confused.

For some persons the words logical and nonlogical were more important than the distinction Pareto and Henderson were trying to make by using them. To say man's behavior most of the time was nonlogical, that is, motivated by matters of sentiment and feeling more than by matters of fact and logic, was considered unflattering. But to me that was what made man essentially human. That some men were willing to die for the values they stood for did not make them to me particularly logical in an instrumental, sequential sense; but it did make them attractive and human in an end-in-itself sense.

In spite of the arguments the distinction between logical and nonlogical provoked, I felt this distinction should be maintained. It could be misused and made into a false dichotomy. It could be blurred by specious attempts to reduce one to the other. It could be difficult to practice. But when all was said and done, I thought it was important to maintain the distinction at the level of phenomena before making any "quickie" integration verbally. To reduce technological space to social space or vice versa was, I felt, one of the big confusions in the world in which I was living. These confusions created no solutions or resolutions; but they did create arguments, and they also created strikes and wars. Only through the notion of a system could the logical and nonlogical become integrated. Only as components of a system could the two be made rational. About this I shall have much more to say later.

SOCIOLOGY 23

Thus slowly, step by step, I became a concrete sociologist, that is, a person who was interested in observable interactions between persons, involving feelings and sentiments at a microscopic level. I was aided in this process by Henderson, who had now begun systematically to formulate his thinking about concrete social phenomena.

This Hendersonian-Paretian synthesis emerged in a course on concrete sociology (Sociology 23, as it was listed in the Harvard catalog), which Henderson introduced across the River in the Department of Sociology. This invasion of spaces raised some dissonant questions: for instance, what was a biological chemist housed at the Business School doing across the River in Sociology; and what, if any, was the difference—with no value judgements implied—between concrete and abstract sociology? I will let the reader imagine the various nonlogical forms in which these questions were answered, depending upon which space one occupied on this side or on the other side of the River.

Henderson organized his course on concrete sociology in the following manner. In three introductory lectures he stated what he thought was a useful way of thinking (what he called a conceptual scheme) for persons who were investigating concrete social phenomena as well as for professional persons and men of affairs who were responsibly involved in dealing with those phenomena. A series of illustrative cases, given by scientists, professionals, and responsible men of affairs, demonstrating the usefulness of Henderson's conceptual scheme, followed the lectures.

The lectures said in effect that the conceptual scheme was useful when the interactions between persons in a particular situation could not be conveniently disregarded. In such cases the interactions could be the most important elements determining the situation which you were attempting to diagnose objectively or in which you were personally involved. If, for example, you were in a situation where the ceiling fell on a man's head and he was rendered unconscious, then you could ignore for a while the interaction between persons and concentrate upon the interaction between the plaster and the man's head. But suppose, on the other hand, you are a doctor examining a patient in a state of coma which resembles a particular neurological syndrome. A man wearing a derby hat, which he does not take off, and smoking a cigar, which be does not take out of his mouth, walks to the bedside of your patient and speaks gruffly to her. You ask the attending nurse, "Who is this man?" and she answers, "This is the patient's husband." Then a new piece of information (involving interactions and associated sentiments) has been introduced, which you, in making your diagnosis as a responsible doctor, cannot conveniently disregard; that is, you had better reconsider your diagnosis and treatment.

For his case lecturers, Henderson chose a wide assortment of persons, including Lawrence Lowell, Crane Brinton, Chester Barnard, Elton Mayo, George Homans, Bernard De Voto, and me; but it was not a random selection. Although the assortment covered a wide range of disciplinary, professional, and men of affairs identifications, the property which determined who was included in this set of persons was "Did you get the point of Henderson's seminar on Pareto?" If you had, you were in; if you had not, you were out. There is no question I wanted to belong to this set, even if at the time it had no institutional or disciplinary sanction but, in the opinion of some, was just an aggregate of Hendersonian-Paretian nuts.

Although the course on concrete sociology had only one-half of a part-time student enrolled in its first round, the course was held and the individual lecturers gave their cases to the other lecturers in the course and their respective wives, who were urged to attend. In time more students attended; and in each round Henderson refined his introductory lectures. As Henderson never used two words where one word would do as well, these lectures became the most pithy pieces of pure "Hendersoniana" in existence. Although mimeographed, these lectures were not published until 1970. I have reread them many times and each time I have found something that I had previously missed. For many of us, these lectures on concrete sociology remained for years the most quoted unpublished material we knew of. Although it had been Henderson's plan to publish a book of his lectures with illustrative cases, he died at the age of 64 in 1942 before the book was completed. After his death, efforts were made to have these lectures published with annotations, and Chester Barnard was chosen to do this job. But, for reasons I am not privy to, the project fell through.

How Chester Barnard, then president of the New Jersey Bell Telephone Company, became acquainted with Henderson I do not know. But I do know that in time Henderson brought him into association with a number of influential people at Harvard, including Donham, Whitehead, and President A. Lawrence Lowell. For them Barnard became the one and only executive in captivity who not only could run a successful organization but could also talk intelligently about what he was up to in the process. This so captivated academia that he became its darling. The above-mentioned men urged him to put down his thoughts about organizations, and *The Functions of the Executive* (1938) resulted. It was then and is now in my opinion a great book, and it has become a classic. One can see the influence of Henderson and Pareto throughout the book, which in turn greatly influenced my thinking about organizations.

From 1931 to 1933 and again in 1935, Barnard served as state director of the New Jersey Relief Administration, a role which allowed him to taste organizational life outside the Bell System. The experiences which he analyzed and wrote up in the form of a case for Henderson's course on concrete sociology, inspired his only piece of formal research as a participant-observer. Later he included it as Chapter III in his own book of papers on matters of organization entitled *Organization and Management* (1948).

HENDERSON'S CONCEPTUAL SCHEME OF A SOCIAL SYSTEM

Let me return to Henderson and his three lectures on concrete sociology. According to Henderson, concrete sociology had to do with interactions between persons. These interactions often took the form of mutual adaptation and skill and often involved strong sentiments. For the understanding of such complex phenomena, Henderson said, both theory and practice were necessary conditions and the method of Hippocrates was the only method that had ever succeeded widely and generally:

> The first element of that method is hard, persistent, intelligent, responsible, unremitting labor in the sick room, not in the library: the all-round adaptation of the doctor to his task, an adaptation that is far from being merely intellectual. The second element of that method is accurate observations of things and events, selection, guided by judgment born of familiarity and experience, of the salient and the recurrent phenomena, and their classification and methodical exploitation. The third element of that method is the judicious construction of a theory—not a philosophical theory, nor a grand effort of the imagination, nor a quasi-religious dogma, but a modest pedestrian affair or perhaps I had better say, a

useful walking stick to help on the way—and the use thereof. All this may be summed up in a word: *The physician must have first, intimate, habitual, intuitive familiarity with things; secondly, systematic knowledge of things; and thirdly, an effective way of thinking about things.* (Henderson, 1970, page 67; the italics are mine, FJR.)

The conceptual scheme, effective way of thinking, or simple walking stick that Henderson proposed for the study of interactions between persons was Pareto's idea of a "social system." He thought this conceptual scheme was the most convenient then available; it was relatively simple and clear. Like Willard Gibbs' physico-chemical system it had the psychological, though not logical, advantage of consisting of *things* which had *properties* (or attributes) and *relations*. The *things* or components of this social system were persons. They had properties and relations that varied from person to person. Their *properties* consisted of attributes that were both logical (e.g., economic interests) and nonlogical (e.g., sentiments and their verbal manifestations). Their *relations* developed into a second order of things, such as families, labor unions, religious bodies, professional associations, business organizations, etc. Moreover, Henderson went on to say:

> The properties and relations of persons exist not in a changeless state, but in a state of flux. However, the instantaneous states and the changes are not chaotic or random states and changes. On the contrary, they are in general subject to connections and constraints of a kind that may be referred to, or considered as in a measure determined by, the conditions of equilibrium ... defined by Pareto as "a state such that if a small [not too great] modification different from that which will otherwise occur is impressed upon a system, a reaction will at once appear tending toward the conditions that would have existed if the modification had not been impressed." (Pages 88–89.)

To many readers this conceptual scheme of a social system may not sound as simple and clear as Henderson said it was. In time huge debates were to occur about it; not only about the components of the system, those bloody *persons*, but also about their properties and relations as well as that mysterious condition of equilibrium which was supposed to exist among them. But let me not rush my hurdles; at the time, I was willing to accept this "simple walking stick," because Henderson never forced it down my throat. Over and over again he said about this (or any other) conceptual scheme things so obvious that they are likely to be dismissed as platitudes. As in the scrimmage of intellectual warfare they are likely to be forgotten, so let me repeat them.

(1) *The Need of a Conceptual Scheme for Purposes of Investigation.* Henderson said that in the acquisition of knowledge a conceptual scheme (that is, a useful way of thinking) was a necessary piece of equipment. To put it bluntly, "no conceptual scheme, no knowledge." This I could easily accept. I was no follower of Locke, who believed in the *tabula rasa* theory of knowledge, that is, that the mind was a blank tablet upon which experience wrote its record. The mind was not just a passive glob of recorded experiences but an active, selective, discriminatory instrument. With Kant I believed that experience without concepts was blind and that concepts without experience were empty. I had seen this illustrated by Mayo in the Hawthorne researches.

(2) *A Matter of Convenience and Utility and Not of Truth or Falsity.* But Henderson also said that the test of a conceptual scheme, unlike that of a proposition, was not whether it was true or false, but whether it was useful and convenient. This also I could easily accept. I was a pragmatist. I could see that the uniformities in the phenomena that a conceptual scheme helped to unearth were what needed to be verified and not the conceptual scheme itself. The conceptual scheme was just a useful instrument toward this end. If it did its job, more power to it. If Kurt Lewin's statement "There is nothing more practical than a good theory"—a statement which persons in group dynamics quote because Lewin and not Henderson is their hero— means the same as what Henderson meant when he spoke of the utility of a conceptual scheme, then I accepted it also as a similar insight.

(3) *A Way of Thinking to be Practiced.* Henderson also said that you could not find out if a conceptual scheme was useful unless you practiced it. The proof of the pudding was the eating thereof. This was one of those obvious remarks I now want to underscore. Its implications were tremendous, but I don't think I realized them fully at the time. It meant that someday and sometime—for better or for worse—the seeker of knowledge had to become committed. Abstract debates about whether or not a conceptual scheme was useful, by persons who refused to test its utility by using it, caused a disease from which some academics suffered. Mayo called the disease obsession. There was no test for the utility of a conceptual scheme except what could be learned from trying to use it. A conceptual scheme was something to be used—not just talked about.

(4) *To Be Practiced in Relation to a Class of Phenomena*. Henderson said a conceptual scheme was not a multipurpose tool; it was useful only in relation to a certain class of phenomena. The conceptual scheme of a social system, for example, could be used in situations in which human interactions could not be conveniently disregarded. It could be used by persons in positions of responsibility to gain intuitive familiarity with the way events happened through an involvement with them that was not purely intellectual. This made a lot of sense to me; it meant to me that Henderson's conceptual scheme was a peewee man-made tool that he had constructed for the specific purpose of searching for uniformities in interactions between persons—no more, no less.

(5) *To Be Used So Long as It Remained Useful*. Henderson stated very carefully, "Beware, young man—in your conceptual scheme you may think you are in touch with some ultimate reality—you may think you have a real bear by a real tail. Nothing could be further from the truth. You have just a simple walking stick to assist you *here and now*. This walking stick will return someday to that glorious graveyard of abandoned working hypotheses of which Henri Poincare spoke so eloquently."

How inspiring were these words! They had me agog. But did I really understand them? When that date for abandonment became for me many years later a living present, would I bury the walking stick in which I had invested so much and say, "Dear walking stick, my faithful servant, you have served me well, but now into Poincaré's highly populated but venerated graveyard you go?" Would I gallantly and cavalierly just toss it away and perhaps shed a few tears? Or would I resist and say, "You have some utility still."

But way back in the dark ages of 1938 before the computer, I did not hear that Henderson was talking about the difficult problems in the search for knowledge that reside in the space between no ideas and preconceived ideas, between a present focus and a future fixation, and between some commitment here and now and a possible overcommitment in the future and that awful line of demarcation in between. No, I was too interested in myself and in my own doubts and perplexities to hear that.

(6) *Be Prepared for That Day When Another Way of Thinking May Be More Useful*. Henderson warned "Commit yourself to a point of view, young man. Without such a commitment, nothing useful results. But," he also said, "someday, young man, your commitment (your

conceptual scheme) will have done its job. Be prepared for that day. Be thankful for what it has done. But when that day comes, be of stout heart—rejoice and abandon it with hallelujahs." How true but how difficult! Between how easy it is for a young man with no investment and no commitment to do this and how difficult it is for an old man with a heavy investment and perhaps overcommitment to do it lies the problem of the social sciences. In a way this is the problem about which I am writing this book.

Did I not do to my older generation what the younger generation is doing to me now? In all honesty what is the difference? Let's not waste any more words on this point; there is no difference. The life and social spaces I had discovered had been discovered by man again and again. They were entombed in history, in art, in literature, in poetry, in religion, and in ideologies. Perhaps there was a slight difference. Perhaps I and my notion of "science" had the effrontery to believe that we could release knowledge from this entombment. We could smash the human molecule and release it for its creative destiny. Megalomania?

Yes and no, because Henderson said even though your conceptual scheme was not an ultimate, your belief in it as such was functional. If you did not believe you had a bear by the tail, you just would not hang on. So in the last analysis the science enterprise was also nonlogical. It had to do not only with nonlogical matters of fact as well as reconstructed logics (relations of ideas) by means of which uniformities among the facts could be arranged in some elegant axiomatic fashion, but also in the end it rested on some nonlogical beliefs and assumptions about an orderly world which existed in the uniformities residing in the facts and not just in some consistency in the ideas about them.

KORZYBSKI AND GENERAL SEMANTICS

During this period there was one living non-Harvard man who also influenced me—Count Alfred Korzybski. His book on *Science and Sanity* (1933), although difficult to read, seemed to me to be saying something important. What I think attracted my interest was the way he put epistemology to work, so to speak. Boiled down, his approach seemed to me to be *applied epistemology*.

At this time there was considerable interest in comparing the way a child thinks (Piaget) with the way a primitive thinks (Levy-Bruhl) and with the way a neurotic thinks (Freud). Only a genius or a nut

71

would have tried to compare the way a mathematician thinks (Russell and Whitehead) and the way a neurotic thinks (psychiatry). Korzybski was such a man.

Because he took such an extreme position, which at that time did not fit well into any discipline, Korzybski never gained any academic post or much recognition. His field was neither strictly philosophy, mathematics, linguistics, semantics, psychiatry, nor mental health. It was a brilliant one-man synthesis of all these things which he called general semantics to differentiate it from ordinary semantics (e.g., Ogden and Richards, *The Meaning of Meaning*). In time he gained disciples, the most well-known being S. I. Hayakawa, Wendell Johnson, and Irving Lee. Irving Lee is the one I got to know best. He was a brilliant person who unfortunately died young.

In 1937, before these men appeared on the scene, I took a seminar with the Count, as he liked to be called. There was no question he was a bit of a "weirdie." He had Henderson backed off the map in seeing to it that you got the point. He did this with the help of a cane, which he would use not only to point to his scribblings on the blackboard, but also to point to each member of the seminar. When this happened, the student (or disciple) was supposed to say, "Yes, dear Count (or Master), I got the point," and repeat literally word by word the point the Count had made. The Count accepted nothing less as confirmation. He would not proceed with the next point until each member had said, "Yes, my dear Count, the map is not the territory; it can never be the territory; it can never include all the territory; this is true now and forevermore." As this was a teaching technique quite different from the lecture method at Harvard across the River or the case method at the Business School, about which I will speak later, I was fascinated. Little did I realize then that I was to meet the Count's technique again many years later with the learning machine. As one can see, Korzybski was ahead of his time, both in his subject matter and in his pedagogical methods.

But in spite of what then seemed to me eccentricities of behavior, I felt that Korzybski's points were so simple and obvious, when one stopped to think about them, that they should be exploited. After all, you could see that many people often responded to words instead of to the things that the words stood for, and because there was not just one word for one thing but often different words for the same thing, sometimes the same word for different things, and sometimes words that referred to no things, as well as some things for which there were no words, one could see how these words unattached to anything in particular might get anyone into a bit of a semantic muddle.

For example, a man might confuse the word "woman" with the particular woman he married; and when she did not conform to the word "woman" (i.e., the man's conception of what physiologically, psychologically, or sociologically he thought made a woman a woman), he would get angry. That is, he got angry when he found out he had married a particular woman instead of the word "woman." To Korzybski, this was a serious confusion; that is, to get angry at such an obvious misevaluation. The particular woman he married was not a word, or was she? (Do you get the point, dear reader, or do you want to argue it? My cane is pointing right at you.)

Korzybski thought that the villian of these semantic reactions (i.e., reacting to words instead of to what words stood for) was my good old friend, Aristotle—the founder of the logic which had gone down through the ages from the time of the Greeks until the time I entered Harvard in 1924 without having one "and," "or," or "not" changed. It was this logic that Whitehead and Russell were trying to clean up—a process which resulted in their finding that logic and mathematics were the same; that is, they both dealt with *relations of ideas* rather than with *matters of fact*.

But whereas Whitehead and Russell were concerned with the crumbling foundations of arithmetic, Korzybski was concerned with the crumbling foundations of society, that is, for example, with the increasing number of cases in the divorce courts because a man had found that he had married a particular woman instead of a word. Korzybski thought that something should be done about this.

How could the ordinary man (not gifted persons like Russell and Whitehead) clean up his language so that his world of words would bear some structural resemblance to the world of non-words in which he as a person (not a word) in relation to other persons (not words) lived? This was the intriguing idea which I felt Korzybski addressed and which I too thought needed some attention. In spite of his eccentricities, I felt he had hold of something important. We could not have people jumping around and responding to a world of words which had no correspondence with the world of non-words in which people lived. Such a hiatus might lead not only to an economically productive social jungle but also to a looney bin.

So Korzybski decided to offer to the comman man what he called "semantic devices"—devices used by the mathematicians—to keep the world of words structurally related to the world of non-words.

For example, he said that when you talked about the woman you married (1) *you should index her*; you should say, for example, "I married woman$_1$," (i.e., a particular woman) instead of "I married a 'woman'" (i.e., a word). Or to put it more precisely, you first should change the word "woman" to the mathematical symbol W_i (any woman) and then you should give "i" a number from the set of positive integers, 1, 2, 3, 4, etc.

Then (2) *you should "date" her*, not in the imprecise layman's sense, but in the more precise sense of mathematics; that is, you should realize "I married woman$_1$ (1966)," not "woman$_1$ (1954)." She was 12 years older in 1966 than she was in 1954.

Then (3) *you should hyphenate her* instead of bifurcating her. Instead of saying "Gee whizz, I married a beautiful body with no brains" or vice versa, you should say "I married a mind-body" or "an emotion-intellect," not one or the other but both.

Only after you had "extensionalized" her (i.e., made your references to her more specific) in this manner should you now (4) *put her in quotes*. By so doing you meant that at one level of abstraction she might be a "nitwit," but at another level of abstraction she was also "lovable"; that is, you loved her all the same. She was for you now a "lovable-nitwit," despite what Aristotle said about the law of the excluded middle.

So while Russell and Whitehead were trying to clean up logic (the world of words) so as not to get confused by what is meant when one says that A implies B, Korzybski, through his semantic devices of indexing, dating, hyphenating, quoting, and so on, was trying to get the world of words and logic to have some correspondence to the world of non-words, that is, to the world of interactions; that is, to what Pareto called the nonlogical. With my background I fell for this idea like a ton of bricks.

But in spite of all these semantic devices, let us remember, as Korzybski did, that no matter how well you index, date, hyphenate, and so on your words so that they correspond structurally to and do not distort the living (nonverbal) reality which confronts you, they (the words) can never be identical with the territory they represent. That living holy delicious terror—your wife—can never be reduced to words. She is a nonverbal reality of terror and delight you have to learn to live with. A good set of words can help you to relate to her better, but they never can exhaust or substitute for the nonverbal terrors and delights she can give you.

Chapter 6
Excursions in General Motors, Macy's, the Government, and Small Business

Up to 1938 my industrial experience had been limited to the Bell System, especially its manufacturing arm, the Western Electric Company. To many of my colleagues at the Business School, it seemed as if I were generalizing from a very narrow base. In one sense I was, but in another sense it seemed to me unlikely that the social phenomena we found at Western Electric resided there and only there. In the Relay Assembly Test Room and in the Bank Wiring Observation Room we discovered patterns of behavior that were not peculiar to one company. They were the outcome of mass production, task specialization, and "scientific management" processes. Surely these processes were going on elsewhere; from my point of view, many of the criticisms that were being made of the work were not relevant. Still I thought I ought to look and see before reaching this conclusion. Two experiences helped me in this direction. One was at General Motors in 1938 and 1939, the second at Macy's in 1939 and 1940.

GENERAL MOTORS

The first of these studies came about because John C. Baker, who was then at the Business School as an Assistant Dean (he later became President of Ohio University), was studying compensation plans for a book he was writing on the subject. In this connection he learned that General Motors was having problems with its executive bonus plan, which did not seem to be working motivationally in the manner General Motors hoped for. The expectation was that the bigger the bonus, the greater the productivity of the executive. Yet in some instances, the correlation was inverse. So the company felt that a study should be made in which personal data would be obtained in contrast to the statistical data that John's previous studies about bonus plans were based on. As he put it, he and the company wanted to get "behind the figures."

Because of my then known skills in interviewing, my aid was solicited. Obviously I could not interview top executives at General Motors, it was said, in the way that I had interviewed workers at the Western Electric Company, so I would have to modify my procedures. I told them to leave this to me. We organized a team of four young men: William Day, later President of the Michigan Bell Telephone Company; Sargent Kennedy, later Secretary of the Corporation at Harvard University; George Lombard, later Associate Dean for Educational Affairs at the Business School; and John Fox, later an Assistant Dean at the School and for some time in charge of its foreign operations.

I mention the later developments of these young men not only because they are impressive but also to emphasize that all four had much more inclination for, interest in, and "savvy" about matters of administration than I had. Besides this, they were all about six feet tall, more or less (I am about five and a half feet) and from my point of view they were as stalwart, intelligent, vigorous, energetic, and interpersonally capable young men as could be found anywhere. When I led this troop of four men to charge the citadel, that is, the headquarters of General Motors, then at 1775 Broadway, New York, I felt I was well supported from the bottom.

I was also well supported from the top. In this study I was a kind of working supervisor; but we also had two generals. John Baker, the generalissimo supreme, I have already mentioned. After the initial arrangements, he left us to do our work and gave us occasional words of encouragement. Our second commander-in-chief was Philip Cabot, then Professor at the Business School, elderly, and close to retirement. Philip Cabot was Professor of Public Utilities; he was a Cabot who could speak to businessmen as well as to Lowell, who a few years earlier had retired as President of the University. Since my association with Mr. Cabot, as I always called him, was my first close relation with an "upper-upper," as Warner would say, and with another "role model" with which to identify, as some other kind of -ologists would say, I had better say a few words about how I saw him myself.

If we had arranged Henderson, Mayo, and Cabot on a continuum from less to more action-oriented, they would appear in just that order with Cabot the most eager to get things done. They would also appear in the same order if we arranged them in terms of from more to less "disciplined minds" in the academic sense. In Mr. Cabot

I met one of the most challenging and refreshing minds I ever encountered in academia. He darted in and out of a discussion with pungent and caustic but highly pertinent remarks. In him I saw the forthrightness of expression (i.e., saying and doing what one damned pleased) that tended to be associated, as I had learned from Warner, with men whose social position was secure by birth and family.

About Richard Cabot, his brother, who had been Chairman of the Social Ethics Department across the River, Philip Cabot would say, for example, "There are fools, goddamned fools, and my brother Richard." Richard in turn would say of Philip, "One never knows where Phil begins and nervous prostration leaves off." As these were quite different forms of expressing concern and affection for each other than those in which my family had engaged, I was perplexed; but as Warner told me, these forms varied with social class, which put me, as well as the Cabots, back in their proper places in social space again.

Anyhow in this study, Bill Day, Sargent Kennedy, George Lombard, and John Fox were in the front lines; I was in the second line; and Phil Cabot and John Baker were in the rear lines, to be brought into the fray if and when the situation required their services. The strategy (worked out primarily by General Motors) was that we would make our first preliminary skirmishes (pilot studies) in four divisions of the company in New York and its vicinity before going to Detroit for the major engagement.

Attached to our team, acting as liaison officer between us and the G.M. executives, was Merle Hale, about whom I could recount many colorful stories, but I won't, because it would lead me astray. However, Merle did know the preferences of the top executives of the company for all sorts of matters down to their minutest details; for example, whether so and so—some big shot—preferred short or long words, sentences, paragraphs, or reports; red or black ink, white or yellow or green paper, and so on and on. He was invaluable to us in setting up the interviews, but he was not so helpful in telling us after an interview how the executive had liked us and liked being interviewed. At times I feared that we might have a self-fulfilling pipeline in operation.

As can be seen, with my four stalwart young men and with Philip Cabot, John Baker, and Merle Hale, I was as protected as anyone could have possibly been from making an ass of himself. If I did, there is no one to blame but myself. But at the time I was not interested in getting either acceptable or respectable information. I wanted to know what motivated these executives or, as was said at the time, "what made them really tick." However, in focusing our research on matters of compensation, I felt I had tied an albatross around my neck. The data did not come alive to me this way. As I look back on it now, I think I was hunting for the "executive syndrome" similar to the "worker syndrome" we had found in the Bank Wiring Observation Room. Not until I found this, could I understand what the data meant. I was all around the edges of this syndrome, as I learned later, but at that time I could not get my fingers on it. Let me summarize briefly some of the separate observations we made that did not jell for me then into a meaningful pattern.

In interviewing an executive we used what would now be called a nondirective interviewing method. We allowed him to talk about matters which concerned him, hoping that he would talk about his salary, bonus, etc., in this context. Only if he did not, would we ask direct questions about these matters at the end of the interview. Our stickiest interviews were always those in which the executive talked about what he thought we were interested in and hence what he ought to talk to us about, namely, matters of compensation, and as a result he would make only respectable clichés about them.

There were quite a number of interviews—some of our most interesting—where, contrary to the predictions, the executives talked as freely as the workers at Western had about matters of concern to them. Often, as was true of the workers, what they said had little to do with matters of compensation as such. When it did, as was true of the workers, justice in the distribution of these rewards was more important than the absolute amounts. Also, as was true of the workers, the executives welcomed being intelligently and sympathetically listened to; this was for some of them a unique experience, as it had been for the workers at Western. Moreover, it did not seem to matter to them that they were being listened to by men much younger, earning much less, in some cases one-tenth as much, and this pays a high tribute to the four young men and their skills of listening.

The content of the interviews, however, differed from the workers' in important respects. Whereas a worker might have talked about losing his home during the depression, an executive might talk about how he lost his yacht or Cadillac. I could not get concerned about the latter. Eliot Chapple would say that I was paying too much attention to or reacting too much to the symbols "home" and "yacht" and that this is what threw me off. There is a half truth to this. There is little question that I identified more with the workers than with the executives. It has always been easier for me to see things from a worker's point of view than from an executive's. Even when I looked at the problems of leadership, I looked at them from the worker's or subordinate's point of view. A diagram will help to clarify this point, because this distortion ran through a good portion of this period of my life and I corrected it only later. (Some of my critics would say I never did.)

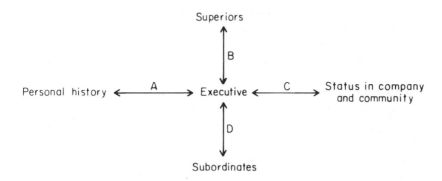

I can express the similarities and differences I saw between the executives at General Motors' headquarters and the workers at Western in terms of the above four relations. Relation A is, of course, life space, as discussed in Chapter 3. In reference to it, the executives, like the workers, had once been children; they had had fathers, mothers, brothers, and sisters. Also as life went on, many of them had accumulated wives and children. Some of them had suffered emotional and social deprivations and losses just as heartrending as those of the workers. In terms of man's fundamental human condition I saw little difference between them and the workers. When an interview reached this level, I could easily identify with the executives.

In reference to relation B, we heard many sentiments so similar to those of the workers that at first I could not believe my ears. The executives also wanted a kind, considerate, understanding boss who would not breathe down the back of their neck and who would not misevaluate the contributions they made and thereby affect the share of the bonus they got. Here also because of my background, I could emotionally identify with their fears of the big, bad wolf who might castrate them.

In reference to relation C, the executives, like the workers, wanted their rewards to be proportional to their investments; that is, they also wanted age, service, experience, know-how, loyalty, etc., to count. Furthermore, they did not want anyone to change the symbols, other than compensation, by means of which their high status in the structure was made visible. With these concerns I could not identify easily. Yet I was aware, particularly in one division, how nontransferable the skills and knowledge of some of the executives were. They were like computers with only one built-in decision-making program. Had they lost their jobs, they would have had difficulty getting others outside the company with equivalent salary and status, let alone bonus.

Nor could I identify with many of the sentiments they expressed in relation D, which, of course, was absent in the case of the worker. An executive who referred to one of his subordinates down the line as a $10,000-a-year clerk [remember, this was in 1938] is an example of what I mean. In this relation, as I said before, I think I concentrated more on the executive's lack of understanding of his subordinate than upon the difficult problems of evaluation and decision he faced from his point of view. I thereby missed an important part of the syndrome for which I was hunting.

In the General Motors study I also had my first one-shot experience in trying to communicate research findings to top management. Our feedback session, as it would be called now, was held under very formal conditions in the Board of Directors' room on the umpty-umpth floor (I will let the reader guess its ordinal position) of 1775 Broadway, with almost all the top executives present, including Alfred P. Sloan, Chairman of the Board, but not William Knudsen, President. As was the custom at General Motors in such presentations, all materials—not only charts and diagrams but also the text material itself—were flashed on a screen and read aloud. So I, who made this presentation, read slowly the sentences that everyone else could also read, trying hard, like Henderson, to underscore each point so that no one including you-know-who would fail to get it.

We organized our materials in terms of the four divisions we studied. We did this to preserve the anonymity of the individual executives and also because we felt that the four divisions were four quite different social systems apart from which matters of compensation and the bonus, in particular, could not be intelligently understood. We also did it because we wanted to look at the divisions in Detroit, where we understood that the major battle of the bonus was fought and where as brave soldiers we wanted to go. So the gist of my blow-by-blow presentation led to one big point, namely, "Dear

Mr. General Motors (or as John Fox would have said, 'My dear Generous Motors'), you see now that we've been good boys; we can be trusted, with Merle Hale's help, not to rock the boat. Please let us go to Detroit, where we can see some real line executives and where (as would be said today) 'the action is.'" At the end of the presentation we felt that Mr. Sloan "got the point." He asked some very intelligent questions and seemed to be interested. As we thought that he was the source of light, heat, and power in the company, we thought we were in. Even Merle Hale, which surprises me now, thought the same. Anyway, that night we had a big victory celebration in New York in some night club at which John Fox led the band, a kind of behavior in which he was prone to indulge when he had a few too many martinis.

But alas, in a few days we got the news that because Mr. Knudsen had not been present at our presentation, we would have to make it over again for him personally, because his approval was mandatory before we could go to Detroit, where it was said he was "Czar." We had missed a node somewhere in the company's decision tree.

In Mr. Knudsen I met for the first time the kind of executive of whom I was to meet a great many more later and for whom I gained in time a great deal of respect. But the first meeting was a shock to my academic nervous system. Not only was Mr. Knudsen a man of few words; he also liked words with the fewest letters in them, and of the two-letter word "no," he was particularly fond. His reputation for taciturnity—his dislike for the world of words, the abstract, and the invisible, and his love for the world of the concrete, the mechanical, and for what could be seen and touched—was well known and was the source of innumerable stories and legends in the company. Merle Hale could recite them by the hundreds.

The one I remember best, because I was able to use it many times later to "make a point," occurred at the time when Bill Knudsen was a foreman in a plant of Henry Ford's. When Mr. Ford visited him at his place of work, the conversation between them went something like this (a Scandinavian accent for Bill Knudsen's part of the conversation helps to make the story realistic):

H. F. What are you doing with a spittoon at your desk, Bill?

B. K. I spit, Mr. Ford.

H. F. Why do you spit, Bill?

B. K. I chew tobacco, Mr. Ford.

H. F. Why do you chew tobacco, Bill?

B. K. It helps me to keep my goddamned mouth shut, Mr. Ford.

A few days later Bill Knudsen was called to Henry Ford's office, where he went with some trepidation because he thought he was going to be fired. Instead Mr. Ford said, "How would you like to be superintendent of the maintenance shop? I like people who know how to keep their mouths shut."

So we made our second presentation in the same place and under the same conditions as before to an audience of one—Mr. Knudsen—who never blinked an eye or twitched a muscle while I recited, without too much pep, I am afraid, points one to twelve of why he should be eager to have us go to Detroit. At the end of the presentation there was one of those embarrassing silences which are difficult for some of us to handle. Anyhow, Mr. Cabot could not take it, and he told one of the stories for which he was famous. He must have felt he also had a point to make. I remember his story well, because I had heard it many times before. I have not the slightest idea now what the relation was between my presentation and the point of Mr. Cabot's story. Perhaps there was none.

The point of Mr. Cabot's story was that, when Mr. Donham became a top executive of the Old Colony Trust Company, he improved the morale of the bank by letting go his top executives and getting better jobs for them in other organizations, thereby creating promotions for many men down the line in his own organization. I think Mr. Cabot might have said that the story showed that, although businessmen had accepted the principle of the elimination of the unfit and the superannuated, they had not yet seen the importance of the elimination of the fit. Mr. Donham's success illustrated this latter principle. As can be seen, it is a tricky story to tell and one that can be easily misconstrued. One has to play with the idea a bit before getting the underlying half-truth it contains. Mr. Cabot, unlike Mr. Knudsen, gesticulated a great deal when he talked, so his arms were going around like windmills when he wound up to the point, if any, he was trying to make.

There was another long pause and then Mr. Knudsen said, "Vat happened to de bank?" With this, as I remember, the meeting broke up. The Harvard troops were completely routed. The commander-in-chief, the noncommissioned officer, and the four stalwart soldiers beat a hasty retreat to Boston, where we licked our wounds. We never got to Detroit. The data we had collected were never written up, but I personally learned a lot.

MACY'S

In our next study we went back to looking at workers, but in this case, workers on the selling floor of a large department store in New York. This study was initiated by Dr. Temple Burling, then the psychiatrist at Macy's and later a professor at Cornell University in its School of Industrial and Labor Relations. Dr. Burling wished to conduct studies of work groups similar to those that had been made at Western.

In this study I was assisted by George Lombard and John Fox. We chose to study two contrasting departments selling two quite different kinds of merchandise: little girls' dresses on the fifth floor and a motley array of merchandise, from screwdrivers to canaries, in the basement, to which the salesclerks referred as the "dust bowl" and in which they called themselves "Okies." George Lombard gave his attention to the first department, and the data he collected there became the source of his doctoral thesis, later published as *Behavior in a Selling Group* (1955). The data from John Fox's department, the basement, were never organized beyond what was required for purposes of communication to Dr. Burling and some executives who were interested in our general findings about the store as exemplified in these two departments.

In these studies we were particularly interested in the salesclerk-customer relation—a relationship which was absent in the case of the factory worker—and the difference that this relation made, if any, to the productivity and satisfaction of salesclerks. We were also interested in what difference the kind of merchandise sold made to this relationship. As these findings have in part been published, I will comment only on some general observations we made.

By this time in my career I had become interested in studying what I called the social structure of organizations. I meant by this not just studies of small work groups, although they were a good place at which to begin. I meant that the whole organization of a business needed to be looked at from the point of view of social structure. The social structure of the three organizations, parts of which I had had an opportunity to look at—the Western Electric Company, General Motors, and now Macy's—were very different. These differences could be explained in part by the different environmental conditions (economic, technological, etc.) from which they had emerged. They also had an inner integrity of their own; each had developed its own social system which needed to be understood as an integrated totality before its relation to its economic environment could be understood.

Two points seemed important to me. First, the mainsprings of motivation and cooperation resided in this living dynamic totality—this social space—and second, the principles of scientific management kept missing and ignoring it. By this time I equated scientific management not only with cost reduction but also with the reduction of these social spaces to technological spaces. Thereby I believed that proponents of these principles inadvertently (because this was not their malicious intent) "messed up the show." This tendency I found common to all three of the organizations I had studied, but it was manifested to a lesser degree at Macy's. To me the relation with customers, which pervaded the organization from top to bottom—and not only in a narrow economic sense—accounted for this difference, and so it was to this relationship that I glued my eyes and ears.

Everywhere I looked, Macy's was a different show from the other organizations I had seen. The top executives were a different breed of cats. They were part of the cultural life of New York; they read books; they went to symphonies and the theater. They were aware of the melting pot of ethnic groups of which Manhattan was composed. Although they had no pyrometers to measure the heat of this bubbling cauldron, they knew these things in the way that the old-timers at the American Smelting and Refining Company knew how to judge the amount of heat from the color of the flame; that is, they knew intuitively what Lloyd Warner had stated more explicitly about social classes. In fact they would have felt that this was so obvious that only an academic would have bothered his head to state it.

The buyers knew not only that their customers belonged to social groups; they also knew that the merchandise was teeming with social values and relationships. A customer buying a screwdriver or a can of paint was not the same as a customer buying a little girl's dress. So different kinds of relationships were evaluated for the salesclerks, and I began dividing merchandise into logical and nonlogical merchandise. In the former I put such merchandise as screwdrivers and cans of paint; in the latter I put canaries and little girls' dresses. Selling nonlogical merchandise involved more social relationships. I felt still more sure of this when John Fox told me that he heard a salesgirl saying "I'm not just selling canaries; I'm selling canaries to people whose children have flown away." John observed that this salesgirl seemed to sell more canaries than her fellow clerks.

As Eliot Chapple will be glad to hear, the duration of the interaction between salesclerk and customer in the case of nonlogical merchandise seemed to me longer than in the case of logical merchandise. Also, the color of a little girl's dress seemed to make more of a difference to the customer than the color of a screwdriver. Besides, a little girl's dress might be sold to the aunt, sister, or grandmother, as well as to the mother of the little girl. And the awareness of these differences of relationship seemed to me to make a difference not only to the salesclerk's productivity, but also to the satisfactions she got from the job as well as the satisfactions the customer got from her purchase of the merchandise.

Macy's was selling a great deal of merchandise to many different kinds of people in the middle and lower classes, where more people resided, as the pollsters much to their surprise found out when Franklin Delano Roosevelt was reelected in 1936 with a whacking majority. For although I did not mention it earlier, I should say now that the social classes in terms of cardinal numbers took the shape of a pyramid; that is, there were more people at the bottom than in the middle and more people in the middle than at the top. During the depression this made a big difference, because at this time the associations (in which Warner was interested) which linked the top and bottom of the class structure were not operating very well.

What General Motors was to learn later when the automobile became more of a nonlogical consumer item than it was in the thirties and what the associated Bell Telephone companies were to learn still later when they found that the color of the telephone made a difference to customers, Macy's knew intuitively in 1940. This was not because executives at Macy's were any brighter; rather, the system of relationships of which they were a part was different. The mass market to which they were relating in New York City was not a homogenized, undifferentiated, economic entity. It was teeming with socially differentiated customers, who from my point of view were often not logical but who from Macy's point of view were always right. If they preferred pink to blue or blue to pink, the argument ceased. But when this nonlogical consumer became a worker, the rules changed. What he (or she, for that matter) wanted was no longer automatically right. He had to be told what he hadn't ought to want in terms of fact and logic. He hadn't ought to want to be secure, to belong, and to be loved. He was told that he lived in a competitive jungle that was highly productive. All the high priests of economics agreed upon this fact. "What a jungle, but how productive!"

That at Macy's, the top management, the buyers, and the salesclerks were more people-oriented than the respective segments of

the other organizations at which I had looked was not exactly newsworthy. But at the time I equated science with the exploitation of the
obvious. What made the obvious obvious was a better place to begin
than what made the extraordinary extraordinary. And if the social
space I was looking at and thought important was so obvious, why
was this obviousness being ignored in employee, supervisory, and
executive relations?

At that time I felt I could capture the flavor and the richness of
the three social systems I looked at by means of a novel better than
by a case study or by any propositions expressing the relations of x
to y. And yet if progress was to be made, something more than
anecdotes were needed. How could I bring Society with a capital "S"
or Organization with a capital "O" down to the microscopic level?
How could I make clear at the microscopic process level, for example, what Jack Straus, President of Macy's; Walter Gifford, President
of the American Telephone and Telegraph Company; Clarence
Stoll, President of the Western Electric Company; Alfred P. Sloan
and William Knudsen, Chairman of the Board and President respectively of General Motors, meant at the symbolic level to me and I
think to many other persons in their respective organizations? They
were leaders with quite different leadership styles, symbolizing the
values of their respective intricate social systems. These social systems were not random accumulations of matter-energy; they had
not developed by chance. What were the more microscopic social
processes from which these organizations and their leaders had
developed?

PHILIP CABOT'S EXECUTIVE DISCUSSION GROUPS AND
MANAGEMENT AND MORALE

Toward the latter part of the thirties, when all the signals told of an
approaching war, Philip Cabot organized a group of executives who
would meet two or three times a year at the Business School over
long weekends to discuss their common problems. At this time Philip
Cabot's hourglass was running low: he knew his years were numbered. The oncoming war and his precarious existence touched off a
spark. It was as if he said, "Let's not talk trivia; let's talk about
matters that are of importance to us." To those who attended these
sessions who are still living, the sparks linger. Phil Cabot at this
moment of suffering reached his most creative heights.

How I got involved in these groups is again one of those fortu-
itous combinations of time, place, and circumstance. Cabot at this

time must have felt that Mayo's diagnosis of the ills of modern industrial civilization wanted an audience of responsible businessmen. He brought together some of the outstanding business leaders of the time and fed them Mayo in person in small doses interlarded with homely stories about his own boyhood and experiences in business which he felt helped to make the point. The gist of many of his stories was that from boyhood on he had gone from being a member of a majority group (Yankee) to being a member of a minority group in Boston. These stories were always told with humor; they may have had a touch of nostalgia, but they never contained a note of bitterness. They were always pointing to the coming of the new and not the passing of the old. This was also true of his stories about business. He never talked about the capitalistic system and its preservation but rather about the new forms into which it might develop—in fact, had to develop, if it was to survive.

At these meetings I presented a number of papers. As can be expected, they were about the social structure of business and its importance for the problems of leadership. I always wrote out my papers in advance, because frankly at that time I still thought businessmen were the big bad wolves of society and I was terrified by them. To my amazement even now, these papers were well received. Copies of them were requested. Cabot personally published some, and others were published in the *Harvard Business Review* and other journals. In time I collected them all, added three new chapters, and published them in a book called *Management and Morale* (1941), which like *Management and the Worker* went through umpty-umpth printings. From *Management and Morale*, unlike *Management and the Worker*, I received royalties which dribble in to this day. It became one of the Harvard University Press's best sellers—the kind of business they usually do not go in for. Both these books were sold more by word of mouth than by any promotional activities of the Press. I dedicated this small book to Philip Cabot, because he had provided a forum for Mayo and me. Interesting to me as I look at it now, the dedication reads, "To Philip Cabot, whose interest in thinking scientifically has not diminished his capacity for acting intelligently."

TRAINING WITHIN INDUSTRY

During the latter part of 1941 and the early part of 1942, I spent considerable time in and out of Washington, D.C., with the Office of Production management (OPM), later to become the War Production Board (WPB), in one of its activities called Training Within

Industry (TWI). This activity was headed up by Channing Dooley, on leave from the Socony-Vacuum Company, and Walter Dietz, on leave from the Western Electric Company. They brought together a host of experts on supervisory training who produced what in time became three famous packaged training courses: Job Instruction Training (JIT), Job Methods Training (JMT), and Job Relations Training (JRT). Of the three, JIT was by far the most popular and successful.

I had nothing to do with the development of JIT or even JMT; my contribution, if any, was to JRT. But JRT was not—I would not have anyone believe it—my baby. It was the product of a committee of which I was only about one-hundreth of a part. This was my first experience in producing things in a committee, an experience for which I had not been emotionally or educationally prepared.

I have always been lucky in having very understanding bosses and this was true of Chan Dooley and Walter Dietz. They knew not only how to get things done in a bureaucracy; they also knew me. I was finally sent on a trip to visit small machine plants in New England which because of the war were on the verge of expansion. With the aid of John Fox, I visited some dozen plants to see what problems they would encounter in feeding the increasingly devouring jaws of war with the products that would be required.

This was also my first experience with small businesses. Up to this time I had been preaching about the functionality of informal organization. Now I saw the reverse side of the coin. After an organization had reached a size of about 500 people, it seemed to me the decision rules had to become more formalized. At this size the implicit understandings of people who had worked together over long periods of time were not enough. With the introduction of new people, more explicit rules were needed. I wrote a report to this effect, but it was not exactly hot news; this had been assumed in all bureaucracies long before I discovered it.

My period (of about six months) in Washington—let's face it—was not effective. The phenomena in which I was interested were in Washington all right—oh boy, were they!—but they were contained by a wall of paper as thick as the Maginot Line, and I had not as yet learned the trick of going around it. Moreover at that time I did not think this was cricket. Let me end this short chapter of my life by paying my respects again to Chan and Walter. They were wonderful guys; at the time they had far more important problems than my hang-ups to worry about, but they did worry about them, and for this I am grateful. We said goodbye, but I felt that they always remained my friends.

Now this chapter of my life comes to a close. I had reached a certain amount of success by a route to which Horatio Alger may have subscribed, even though it did not look that way to me then. But Horatio let me down badly, because when the "success" that had been in the future became a living present, it was not anything like he had promised it would be. It was not the same animal at all. He had told me only about its sweet delights; he had not told me about its unholy terrors. This was what I now had to learn about.

The learning process did not start with a bang or with bombs bursting in air; it started ingloriously with what, for want of a better word, I will call a nervous breakdown.

Chapter 7
A Period of Self-Renewal

In the year 1942 something came to an end for me. In retrospect I think four events helped to touch it off: Pearl Harbor on December 7, 1941; Mr. Cabot's death on December 25, 1941; Dr. Henderson's death on February 10, 1942; and Mr. Donham's retirement as Dean in June 1942. The mantle of responsibility was slowly descending upon me. I had always taken the responsibility given to me—in fact I had always been very serious in this respect—but I had never assumed it by myself cheerfully.

Also, in 1942, my relationship with Mayo was at a low level. At that time I felt (incorrectly, as I see it now) that he was giving me little or no support for the direction in which I wished to go at the Business School and in which I thought he also should go. Mayo was satisfied to remain a fringe member of the Business School Faculty and I was not. Yet his approval and support were important to me, in fact far more important than that of my other colleagues; and so my old anxieties about my identity and subject matter, which had been submerged but never completely liquidated, reared their ugly heads again. My unrewarding experience in Washington also aided in provoking self-doubts about what, if anything, I could contribute to the war effort.

These anxieties became so acute that I finally consulted Dr. Arlie Bock, a former member of the Fatigue Laboratory, who had now succeeded Dr. Worcester, about whom I spoke earlier, as head of all the health services at Harvard University. When I told Arlie about my anxieties, he suggested that I spend a period of time at a place in Vermont called Spring Lake Ranch, an "extended farm family," whose owner—Wayne Sarcka—Arlie said was a delightful and interesting chap with ideas about mental health in which I might even become interested. Regardless of that, Arlie said the Ranch was a place where, for the time being, I could pitch hay, do farm chores, and in this manner enjoy the period of self-renewal which he thought I needed.

Although I went there with some reluctance and got back to nature and away from books, Mayo, and the B-School for a while, I also became involved in the purposes of this extended farm family, of which I, together with some 20 or more other persons, became a paying "guest." Besides being an extended farm family, Spring Lake Ranch, as conceived by its layman owners and managers, was a halfway house for mentally ill persons who either were not ill enough to go to a mental hospital or who had been in a mental hospital but now needed an experience with more freedom, as well as loving care, to prepare them for re-entering the "normal world" as fully participating members.

Although I enjoyed doing my farm chores and exercising my muscles according to the program in which Wayne Sarcka believed, with my background and interests I could not remain without being concerned about the people who were there. Nor could I be unobservant of the interactions they had with one another and with Wayne and Elizabeth Sarcka, the husband and wife owners, managers, administrators, and healers of the place. I could not be unconcerned with how Wayne and Elizabeth met the needs of their "guests" and also kept the farm activities going; that is, the cows milked, the beef cattle coralled, the chickens fed, the grass cut, the hay mown, the garden weeded, the snow plowed, the maple sap sugared, the roads passable, the woodlands cleared, the buildings repaired, the water flowing, the plumbing running, the lamps lit (because there was no electricity), and so on and on.

Right before my eyes was an organization of an entirely different kind from those that we studied and wrote cases about at the Business School. Although the Ranch's purpose or primary task was the rehabilitation of people, it could also be conceived of as a farm in which the employees were emotionally disturbed persons who paid instead of were paid to do the work of the farm. The farm was administered by the Sarckas, who also helped the workers (guests or patients) to help themselves to get better, so that they could cope with a less sheltered and more normal environment. Thus, here was my administrator-helper in the flesh; but his employees were nonunionized, negatively paid, and somewhat disorganized.

It looked as if Providence was being kind to me again by providing me with a laboratory in which all the elements of social behavior in which I had become interested—namely, matters of organization, administration, cooperation, communication, and leadership—were present, but in such a new mix that it took me a good while to sort them out. In the process of trying to find out what was going on at Spring Lake Ranch, not only did I become "cured," but also my role slowly changed from that of guest to that of participant-observer to that of consultant to that of trustee and even to that of manager, because one summer, when the Sarckas took a holiday, my wife and I were in charge.

To make a long story short, I spent about six months (April to September, 1942) at Spring Lake Ranch. I tore down an old barn and with its manure-stained black ash (now extinct) lumber and the aid of my wife Margaret and daughter Jean and a local carpenter, I built a small house on the premises (costing about $2,000) where during the next 10 years we spent many of our holidays.

I shall not try to explain why, after having become well enough to return to the "normal" environment of the Business School, I should have chosen to spend my holidays with a bunch of nuts at the top of a magic mountain in Vermont. I will only say that I always found these stays rewarding experiences, both emotionally and intellectually. Wayne and Elizabeth, as well as many of the guests, became our warm friends. Also the operation of Spring Lake Ranch fascinated me intellectually. Many of my notions about mental health, as well as matters of administration and organization, were being challenged, and this concerned me. I want to tell this part of my story next; I will start with the guests.

THE ORGANIZATION OF SPRING LAKE RANCH

Among the guests there was a wide assortment of mental patients from alcoholics to drug addicts, agitated and burnt-out schizophrenics, psychopathic personalities, epileptics, and neurotics of all descriptions. (These are not my labels; they were the labels given by the referring psychiatrists or physicians. Once these patients became "guests" at the Ranch, these labels were not used.) Most of the guests were more seriously ill than the "normal" obsessive students I talked about in Chapter 3 or than I thought myself to be. Many of them had been in mental hospitals, where they had had electric or insulin shock treatments or lobotomies, which were very popular at the time. This was in the days before the discovery of tranquilizers. Some of them had suicidal or homicidal tendencies.

Never before had I seen such a range of "abnormal behavior" put together under one such uncompartmentalized roof. At times it seemed to me as if the referring psychiatrists from the New York and Boston areas sent some of their most difficult cases there. But Wayne never turned anyone down because of either the seriousness of his illness or his inability to pay.

Although I often raised questions with Wayne about the need for a more careful screening of the guests before they arrived, my suggestions fell on deaf ears. Wayne had an almost compulsive urge to show up the psychiatrists and their fancy theories about mental disease and health. To some extent, but far less, I shared some of his beliefs about these matters. As a result, after the day's work had been done in some fashion and before tomorrow's God-awful work had to be done, Wayne and I would frequently go to Rutland (about 10 miles away) and over a glass of beer (or should I say two, three, or more, because no alcohol was allowed "on the hill") we would discuss the problems of the guests and their relation to him and to each other. And the services I offered, as I hope will be no great surprise to the reader, were mostly in the direction of listening and of raising questions for Wayne, not me, to answer. This is how my role as consultant really began.

What had me both disturbed and intrigued was how one could run a profitable and efficient farm and also rehabilitate people at the same time. From a strictly business point of view, Wayne's venture was not profitable; his operations were mainly in the red and provided him and his wife at the most with a bare livelihood. That they even did this was something I often wondered about. The facts were difficult to determine, because Wayne kept few financial records of his operations. He made little or no separation between the accounts of the Ranch and his personal accounts. For Wayne, he and the Ranch were one and indivisible.

Wayne often said that producing a quart of milk cost about the same as producing a quart of champagne, but there were no hard figures to check this. There were no historical standards which allowed him to say that his losses this year were greater or less than the year before. There were no cost standards which allowed him to say what his costs should be (for example, the cost of producing a quart of milk) at the level of business (for example, the number of guests) at which he was operating, because there were no standard methods of operation. In short, there were no standards at all. In this respect Spring Lake Ranch was atypical of the organizations I had looked at, such as the Western Electric Company and General Motors. One of the major ingredients of these organizations was absent. No fooling!

From the point of view of his guests, Wayne's lack of interest in his financial situation and in efficient farm operations had some positive consequences. Not having any good standards by which to evaluate the effectiveness of the organization from a cost point of view, he was free to give his attention (although never entirely) to his guests and their recovery. Sometimes this lack of concern for his financial situation got him into trouble. For example, when Wayne drew a check for an amount for which he did not have sufficient funds in the bank and the check bounced, Wayne looked upon the event as an ordinary one in the process of doing his kind of business; it was not a matter of any great importance. If this were to happen to me, I would have been horrified. But when I finally realized that what was serious to me was just a peccadillo to him and that if at first you did not succeed in getting from him the money he owed you, you just tried again, I learned to accept it. In the wider community, of which the Ranch was a part, though, some of the members were sometimes not so understanding.

Wayne would have given me the shirt off his back, if I needed it, and he expected that I would do the same for him. Thus, when I say there were no standards at the Ranch, I mean there were no technical standards. At another level there were standards of what human relationships were and should be. The place was filled with these standards and they were closely associated with Wayne and his life style and had their roots in his early family history.

Like me, Wayne was a first-generation American; his father had come from Finland as a marble cutter, had settled in the town of Proctor, Vermont, the headquarters of the Vermont Marble Company, and had worked there until he was injured and laid off. In this company town, Wayne, the eldest of four children, was brought up; he even worked for the company when he was young. But just as the cheese business was not for me, so cutting small marble angels for tombstones or door stops (Wayne's first job) was not for him. As soon as he could manage it, he left Proctor, never to return, as did his brothers and sisters also. All that was left in Proctor now was his father's grave where, amidst the surrounding marble statues and tombstones, there stood one big hunk of natural unfinished granite which Wayne personally had lugged and put there. When I saw this grave for the first time, I felt I did not need to embellish with words where Wayne stood in relation to Proctor and his family; I felt I knew.

I shall not go into the details of Wayne's life after he left Proctor and finally settled down with Elizabeth, his wife, at Spring Lake

Ranch. Although of great human interest, the details do not alter the essential drift of the story I want to tell. Briefly, his life during this period was that of a high-grade roustabout (my evaluation) with adventures in this country as well as in the Near East. During this time he developed the philosophy of life which he brought to the Ranch.

This philosophy of life, as I saw it, included some of the following elements: a strong belief in hard work, in the simple country life, out-of-door living, fresh air, and exercise of the muscles; a great respect for and trust in the unique individual and in his capacity for growth under the above conditions; an extreme distaste for the trappings of urban civilization, competitive living, and book knowledge; a vision of a self-contained cooperative community to which each would contribute according to his ability and be given according to his needs; and a stubborn determination to make his dreams about such a community come true.

Operating on each guest, then, were two sets of forces: one which said "You have a place here and always will have, if you will help me to make my dreams come true," and another which said "After a period of self-renewal here, you will be better prepared to go out and face this lousy, competitive, dog-eat-dog world." It was the first voice I heard the most. Wayne never ceased to tell me about his plans for the Ranch, which included not only his dreams about the kind of human relations that would exist there, but also the concrete things, such as new buildings, tennis courts, golf links, ski runs and tows, and so forth, that would materialize in time from such a cooperative endeavor.

On my first visit, for example, he showed me where the new buildings, tennis court, golf links, and ski tow would be, but for Wayne, as he talked, the time required for their realization vanished. He saw and talked about these things as if they were right there before his eyes, whereas what my eyes saw were only uncleared woodlands, big boulders, and swamp lands. These sites were always referred to by Wayne and gradually by the guests in terms of what would appear in time. Where the tennis court was to be *was* the tennis court. From a reading of his brochures about the Ranch, the referring psychiatrist or a guest's relatives who had never visited the Ranch could have thought that these things were already there. To Wayne this was not deception, because also implicitly described in the brochure were the hard labor and the muscles his guests were to exercise for their own good and recovery and by means of which these things were to be realized.

During the ten-year period I was involved with the Ranch, some of the plans did materialize. What I saw with my unimaginative eyes first as a piece of swampy land and for the following 10 years as just a bigger and bigger rock pile to which hundreds of guests had contributed at least one rock finally did become a tennis court and a good one at that. Although Wayne was a dreamer, he was willing to work hard and long hours for the realization of his dreams. His superabundance of physical energy and vitality was one of his most marked characteristics. In my first days at the Ranch I became tired just looking at him, and I think many of his guests did also.

Wayne not only had a philosophy about the good life and dreams about the concrete things that would materialize from its practice; he also had some skills of a high order in relating himself to people and particularly to the rather sick people I have mentioned. He practiced his magic or therapy within a task role and seldom as a professional healer who saw his patients only in a highly structured interview.

Many of his interactions with guests were in small work groups which engaged in chopping down trees, digging fence holes, pitching hay, and so forth. And what I saw happening on these occasions was something like this. Wayne would take a small group of guests to the site where someday a ski run and tow might be. After painting a glowing picture of this eventuality, he would provide them with axes, show them how axes were to be used for the purposes for which they were intended (because some of the guests had never swung an axe before and some had homicidal and suicidal tendencies), and then he would begin chopping a tree himself. As more and more began to engage in this activity, he would spend time with each one, giving him pointers on how to improve his skill. He rewarded them not only for how efficiently they handled the axe in relation to the tree, but also for trying. I never once saw Wayne engage in a power struggle with anyone who refused to engage in this activity and thought Wayne and his enthusiasms a bit silly. Wayne knew where the locus of power was. Any guest at any time could have defied Wayne and told him to jump in the lake; sometimes one did. When this happened, Wayne might point out the consequences that would follow in time from a refusal to cooperate, but the choice of whether or not the guest wished to cooperate was up to him and argument about it did not occur.

I have said the Sarckas often referred to the Ranch as an extended farm family; this label was more than a euphemism. In many respects Wayne and Elizabeth were papa and mamma and the guests were their children. The latter frequently referred to Wayne as the "great white father." As can be imagined, the guests often projected upon him their hostilities toward their own parents. All the active and passive mechanisms for gaining attention from, getting power over, getting even with, or withdrawing from these new authority figures were always present. The skill with which Wayne dealt with these mechanisms never ceased to astonish me. He never denied the authority he had nor tried to escape his current involvement; he accepted the images projected upon him. I never heard him express any feelings of self-pity nor stew very long nor entertain guilt feelings about some difficult or wrong decisions he had made. He seemed to be able to take these matters in his stride and to accept the ambiguities of the situation in which he found himself as leader. In this setting I saw some miraculous changes take place on the part of some—but not by any means all—of the guests.

Although I often had the urge to research the Ranch, I could never bring myself to do it. Wayne and Elizabeth and the guests were too close to me; it would have been like researching one's own family. Moreover, in the process the magic might disappear. What I have said so far is only a small part of what I observed. During the next ten years, I had ample opportunity for further observations which I would like to summarize at a higher level of generalization. In doing so I am jumping ahead of my story. Some of these generalizations I could not have stated in 1942. However, since I do not want to come back to the story of the Ranch, I will state them in a form which will allow me to relate them to experiences which I shall discuss in later chapters.

PROBLEMS OF ADMINISTRATION, LEADERSHIP, AND THERAPY

Although I thought that securing the services of the members of an organization for the purposes of that organization was an essential function of *any* administrator in *any* organization, the importance of this process was highlighted at the Ranch. Here it could not be easily overlooked and disregarded. It was of the essence.

The purpose of the Ranch was the rehabilitation of its guests and was related to Wayne's visions for the Ranch and his ideas about mental health. Nevertheless, the daily running of the Ranch required that the farm activities be carried out in some fashion. Wayne needed a farm in order to rehabilitate his guests and he wanted his guests to run it; he did not want it run by outside help. Thus although the primary task or purpose of the Ranch was the rehabilitation of its guests, another side to the coin—the task functions of running a farm—was also present and could not be overlooked or disregarded by its administrators.

Whereas at the Western Electric Company or General Motors, the securing of the cooperation of the employees often was subordinated to the efficient operation of the plants, at the Ranch the opposite was true: the efficient operation of the farm was subordinated to getting the cooperation of the guests to perform tasks that were necessary if there was to be any farm to run.

As a result the Ranch, as a farm, was not very efficient; as a farm household it had few conveniences. To see this did not require an efficiency expert. Any guest, no matter how ill, could see it after being there only one day, and it was often the chief source of his gripes. Whereas the guests at the mental hospitals from which they had come had been provided with many of the services they expected, such as warm rooms and hot water, at the Ranch the guests often had to get off their fannies before they could get such services.

To put it somewhat extremely, they had to stoke the furnace before they could get a warm room; they had to repair a chair before they could sit down; they had to pick the vegetables if they were to have them for dinner; they had to build a tennis court if they wanted to play tennis; and so on. No matter how inefficiently these activities were done, the guests at least had to get off their fannies in order to do them. Once a guest got this point—and it was a hard one at times for almost any guest to disregard, because it appeared at a very elementary level—Wayne had him on the hook and the first step towards his rehabilitation had been taken. Thus it could be said that although the Ranch was not efficient as a farm or as a farm household, this inefficiency was not entirely dysfunctional from the point of view of the rehabilitation of some of the guests.

Thus, when I once told a group of Boston and New York psychiatrists that a part of Wayne's magic or therapy was the inefficiency of his operations, because that required the patient to take an active posture toward his environment and to try to do something to improve it instead of griping about it, I was not entirely joking. In some respects I thought the workers at General Motors, for example, who had the "best" policies, the "best" methods, the "best" tools, and the "best" machines handed to them without having anything to say about them, were suffering from somewhat the same kind of disease from which many of Wayne's guests suffered who had previously been at mental hospitals.

In both cases the mainsprings of action had not been touched. I did not elaborate this point because it did not follow that I thought that General Motors had to become more inefficient in order to secure the participation of its workers. Nor did I think that Wayne should run his farm and household inefficiently in order to cure his guests. I just thought that Wayne had a more difficult job than General Motors to get the cooperation of his "workers."

For what rewards did Wayne have to offer? Unlike "Generous Motors," he could offer no monetary rewards in terms of wages or bonuses. Although he did pay a small amount of wages to, or reduce the charges for, some of the guests who performed their work regularly and faithfully, these rewards, although not negligible, were inoperative for many of the other guests, some of whom had wealthy families. The one big reward he held out, as I saw it, was to the effect that if you started working and latched on to the purposes of the Ranch, you would get better and so be able to cope better with life here or anywhere else for that matter; and if you did not, you would not. So Wayne built up his guests' expectant trust in the efficacy of his methods of healing, and he made no bones about it.

He did it quite directly and I must confess this had me bothered, because it smacked of "If you do what papa says, you'll get better and if you don't, you won't." This kind of influence I had tried to avoid—at least in theory—in the counseling-helping relationship I had practiced with my students. It would be incorrect to believe that my approach was completely value free. Whereas Wayne appealed to the values of an active, strenuous, physically healthy, and democratic way of life for individual development, I appealed to the values of curiosity, science, and learning about oneself in relation to others (as well as a democratic world view) as the bases for such development. Even at that time, however, I saw that Wayne's approach had more appeal than mine for many of the guests at the Ranch in terms of their particular backgrounds and illnesses. For many of them my counseling approach would have been somewhat anemic; they needed something with more oomph to it.

Although Wayne worked more directly on the external than the internal environments of his guests, he did not entirely overlook or disregard the internal. If the referring psychiatrist, for example, recommended professional psychotherapeutic treatment for his patient, Wayne would take him to a psychiatrist in Rutland. But he had no psychiatrist "on the hill." There Wayne was the chief medicine man. The medicine he practiced was not pure but eclectic; that is, it combined a number of elements that some specialists in healing would have thought incompatible, but which to Wayne formed an organic whole.

It could be said that Wayne's "magic mountain" resembled to some extent a "cultural island"—a term which became popular later—in which each guest could earn a place by the way he behaved here and now, regardless of his status in terms of age, sex, occupation, marital status, class, education, color, creed, ethnicity, or kind of mental illness. There were few visible signs of status on the hill. The staff—the little there was of it—could not be differentiated from the guests; everyone, including Wayne and Elizabeth, was on a first-name basis. But here the resemblance to other cultural islands ended. Whereas the members of many cultural islands were rewarded for practicing human relations and the democratic way of life in discussion groups, the members of Wayne's magic mountain were rewarded for practicing these things in relation to getting something accomplished. The task dimension was ever present, and it is this that had me interested.

To boil these observations down still further, what fascinated me were the ambiguities which Wayne faced in trying to combine the administrative and healing roles. Yet the attempt itself seemed to me to have therapeutic elements. For example, either of these statements could have been made and supported: (1) that Wayne was trying to run a farm; or (2) that he was trying to cure people under the most difficult and impossible of conditions. In both cases he faced so many cats and dogs (independent, dependent, intervening, and interacting variables) that it was difficult to determine which one to concentrate upon, except to say, "Do what the immediate situation demands as well as you can." For example, if the beef cattle strayed out of their corral and were doing damage to the garden of a neighboring farmer some five miles away and the farmer was mad about it, the rule said "Don't just stand there, go and bring them back. And get going right away!"

This injunction to do what the immediate situation demanded made it difficult for both Wayne and the guests to play any fixed roles, because the ever-changing situation required different roles at different times. Was Wayne permissive, autocratic, person-oriented, farm-oriented? To use terms familiar today but not in use at the time, was he practicing theory X or theory Y? At different times he was more one than the other. It was difficult to ascribe to him any one style of leadership.

From the point of view of the guests, was Spring Lake Ranch a more sheltered environment than the environments to which the guests hoped to return? One could have as easily said the opposite. At the Ranch, except for the rule I mentioned above, there were fewer rules and prescribed roles to guide the guests than in the outside world. It was far less structured than most situations in which the guests would find themselves later.

For what type of mental illness was Wayne's therapy most helpful? It was hard to say. What had me curious was how difficult I found it to predict the recovery of any guest from the initial conditions and symptoms he presented when he arrived at the Ranch. Among those who seemed to me to be the most seriously ill, some got better and some got worse; and among those I thought less ill, some got worse and some got better. The difference, it seemed to me, resided more often in the ongoing interactional situation than in the initial condition of the guest. One small intervention at the right time and place could make a big difference. At that moment some useless cycle was broken and some more constructive and useful cycle emerged.

The conclusion I reached from my experiences at the Ranch was that there was no one best therapeutic method or leadership style. Stating it extremely, there were no principles of therapy or leadership; there were only *uniformities* in the processes of individual growth and learning, and individual and group cooperation. How the therapist or leader latched onto these uniformities could vary widely. There was not just one right way. These observations about life and work at the Ranch were to me matters of fact which persons working on ideas about organizations, purposes, therapy, leadership, and the needs of people had to take into account. I had not found many who did.

I would be remiss if I ended the story of this period of my life with what I learned at the Ranch about matters of therapy and leadership in general and failed to say anything about what I learned about myself more particularly. I went to the Ranch, as will be remembered, not as a failure, but after having achieved a certain amount of success. It was a curious state of affairs about which for a while I could make neither head nor tail. How could this be? Although there are different interpretations for the new anxieties that success brings, let me state my version of my own case as I then saw it.

There is no question that Mayo, Henderson, Donham, and Cabot opened up new worlds for me. But as each of them died, retired, or was about to retire, I had to face this new world alone without his support. This was frightening to the small child who, metaphorically speaking, still lingered within me in my preoccupations and with whom or with which I had still not learned to cope successfully. This small child was still looking for the certainty and security which I had not found when I was chronologically younger. Neither the new world I was facing nor the success I had achieved so far in dealing with it was satisfying the small child who was still in me. But they never could.

Although intellectually I saw this, it took me some time to learn how to deal with this small child. At first I tried to eliminate him and legislate him out of existence. The more I tried to kill him off, the more he would taunt me with the thought "So you think you are emotionally mature. Stop kidding yourself."

I finally decided to take another tack. Still speaking metaphorically, instead of hating him, I decided to love him more. After all, he was the source of both my creativity and my anxiety. With a bit more love, instead of being fenced in with hate, he might learn to grow up (the Hawthorne effect?).

So much for my inner life in metaphorical terms; in more conventional terms it was obvious that the new world I was about to face without the support of Mayo and the others would bring new responsibilities, new choices, and new commitments for me. It promised no security or certainty. I had to decide for myself who I was and where I wanted to go. The conventional trappings of success in Washington were not for me. But I could go back to the School and attempt to become a competent teacher. This is what I did.

Part II

Human Relations and Administration
1938–1948

INTRODUCTION

The next period of my life covers the war years from 1938 to 1948. It includes the Munich parley in 1938, the declaration of war in 1939, the evacuation of Dunkirk in 1940, our entrance into the war in 1941, and so on until the discovery and use of the atomic bomb on Hiroshima and VJ day in September 1945. It includes the aftermath of the war with the Nuremberg trials of major German war criminals during 1945–1946, the return of the war veterans to peacetime activities, the strike at General Motors by the United Automobile Workers in 1945–1946, the strike in 1946 of the United Steel Workers involving some 750,000 workers, and the beginning of the trial of Alger Hiss in 1948. This period also marks the end of colonialism, the formation of the United Nations, and the beginning of our rise to leadership of the Western world with the Marshall Plan in 1947. Franklin D. Roosevelt died and Harry Truman became President of the United States in 1945.

During this period of great turbulence I became a teacher instead of a soldier, an educator instead of a social reformer. I was through with the heroic posture, the quick and easy answer. The solution for the world's ills became for me the slow processes of education and re-education for that stick-in-the-mud, the administrator.

During these war years I gave joint courses with my colleagues and became an integrated member of the Business School Faculty. I was promoted to full professor in 1946. Had it not been for these war courses, I doubt if I would ever have become interested in matters of administration. I would more likely have remained a specialist than a generalist. These joint courses whetted my appetite about what Mr. Donham had said the School was all about, namely, *administration*.

However, during the aftermath of the war, something else happened—something extraneous perhaps but nonetheless real—which affected my relation to the School. Through my writings up to then—*Management and the Worker* in 1939 and *Management and Morale* in 1941—my reputation and influence outside the School was greater than within it. However, toward the end of this period this out-of-lineness began to rectify itself. It happened in the following way.

Following the war, when productivity teams from all parts of the globe came to the U. S. A. in order to learn from us how to become more productive, some of them visited Harvard. Instead of asking to see the big chieftains in production, marketing, finance, and control, they asked to see me. They would say to the Dean, then Donald K. David, "We want to see Professor Roethlisberger and hear about the Hawthorne effect. What is this Hawthorne effect anyway? If it is as good as he says it is, we want the Hawthorne effect also." These requests helped no end in building up my reputation at the School. The trouble was I had no machine with which to produce the Hawthorne effect; it depended upon a way of thinking about matters of productivity.

But Don David, who was marketing oriented and felt, like Macy's, that the customer was always right, said, "For goodness sake, Fritz, I don't know just what these people want, but you seem to have the magic medicine. Please package it in words of one syllable." This I tried to do, albeit with some difficulty. That's how I became a "bigger shot" at the Business School, though still not a very big one. There was a vital ingredient missing, and that was not Mr. David's fault; he was always most considerate of me. It was me and my screwy motivation, when the small child, whom I mentioned earlier, would still peer occasionally over my shoulder and say, "Come on, my dear boy, give up this silly fight"; and I would stick out my now ulcer-coated tongue, the badge of success, and ask him, "Says who?"

Let me leave these higher levels of symbolic abstraction and get down to the level of the events from which they are abstracted. I want to show how I went from what seemed like a peripheral activity at the School to the holy-of-holies of the School's concern about what makes *administration administration*. This is the story of how I began to tie together for myself the ideas I had gained from my research years with Mayo and Henderson and the purposes of the School concerning the education of administrators. To do this I will have to turn the clock back to 1938 and discuss some events which occurred during the previous period. I will do so, though, from the point of view of teaching, not research.

Chapter 8
My Early Teaching Years

The first formal course given at the Business School by the so-called Mayo group was called Human Problems of Administration. It was introduced in 1938, eleven years after the Department of Industrial Research had been formed under the Committee of Industrial Physiology. In that year Thomas North Whitehead (North, as he was called, was the son of Alfred North Whitehead) and I organized a one-semester elective in the second year of the School's two-year program for the degree of Master in Business Administration (MBA). We gave it until the spring semester of 1943, when the School began to phase out its civilian activities for the remainder of the war.

In these early days the course was addressed to the staff personnel officer rather than the line executive. Benjamin Selekman, a man of great experience in labor arbitration, joined us in giving the course, and it grew to be a two-term course. At this period Ben was keen on integrating labor relations and human relations. A clue to the kind of person he was can be gained from a rumor that circulated in 1936 to the effect that he and I were the only two Faculty members who voted for Franklin Delano Roosevelt.

We conducted this course by the case method. Mayo never took a great interest in this development; for him a case was a case history. What the Business School called a teaching case was as foreign to him as it was to me at the time. Moreover, Mayo was not interested in matters of classroom pedagogy. Wherever he gave a course, he lectured and answered questions.

In 1937, the year before we began our course at the Business School, North and I introduced a course with the same name, "Human Problems of Administration," at Radcliffe College in its newly established one-year graduate program in personnel administration. This was a new departure in education for Radcliffe. Its most enthusiastic sponsor was Edith Steadman, a bold, courageous, and outspoken woman, of whom in time I became more fond than terrified.

I taught in the program at Radcliffe for ten years. During that period the program had no official connection with the Harvard Business School. Beginning in 1954 it became co-sponsored and was called the Harvard-Radcliffe Program in Business Administration. North Whitehead became its director and Mrs. Ragnhild J. Roberts its co-director. Five years later its curriculum was considerably changed, so that its graduates would be eligible to apply, if they wished, as second-year students to the M. B. A. program at the Business School; for a while they were the only women accepted there. In 1964, when any qualified woman was permitted to apply to the Business School, the Harvard-Radcliffe program was discontinued.

In the early days the Harvard Business School, organizationally speaking, was still for men only. During the years when I taught in the Radcliffe program, its emphasis was more on training women for personnel work than for the other functions of business. Its first class contained five women, all of whom in time made outstanding reputations in their fields. By the time I left the Program, it had about 40 students.

I will never forget my first classroom meeting with those five women in 1937. They had been placed in a circle in the center of the room with a spotlight shining on them. I think both North Whitehead and I ran the discussion. There was a large, shadowy audience composed of officials from Radcliffe—even the President might have been there, although I'm not entirely sure of this—to watch Radcliffe's first daring experiment in "practical education" for women.

It was not exactly in my opinion an ideal setting either for intellectual or cozy group discussions about matters of human relations between the sexes. For the most part we faced each other in terror but as I said, these were five very unusual young women. In time they put both North and me at ease.

Although I do not remember the case we discussed at this first meeting, I do not think I would go too far astray if I said that I told them about another remarkable group of five working women in a big factory in Chicago who had been segregated in a nice, small, cozy room—just as we were—had been fed lollipops at their rest periods, first one in the morning, then one in the afternoon, then one both in the morning and afternoon, and then one more to take home with them for bedtime, and how during all this time, for one-and-one-half years, output steadily rose. And then how the mean old managers took all their lollipops away and output still went up. Now wasn't this strange? How could they explain this? (If the reader needs a reference for my facetious remarks, see the account of the Relay Assembly Test Room experiment in *Management and the Worker*, pp. 19–186.)

Well, believe it or not, the discussion went fast and furious. All sorts of hypotheses were put forth and entertained in which, as I remember, even the shadow audience participated. I wound up the evening by giving them the correct answer. I said, "This is due to the Hawthorne effect. Now that you have a name for it, I hope we will be able to progress more rapidly at our second meeting at which you will not get such special treatment." With that dramatic closure, I picked up my papers and strode out of the room. Thus my practical education in teaching women began and practical education for women started at Radcliffe.

As I began to interact more with my colleagues at the Business School, one thing became clear to me. In spite of all their wisecracks about "inhuman relations," theorists, and so on, they wanted "in." They felt excluded from something that Dean Donham himself supported and thought important. Although they felt we were an exclusive club with our own private jargon—obsession, nonlogical behavior, anomie, and so on—still they wanted to be included in this development. This should not have been a big surprise to me, but it was.

As the war approached, the School organized a course called Management Controls. When I returned from Spring Lake Ranch in the fall of 1942, I taught in this course with a group of professors who at the time were a much more integral part of the School than I was: Richard S. Meriam, Edmund P. Learned, Ross G. Walker, and Franklin E. Folts. They were all much more knowledgeable than I about business and economics. The point of the course was to try to make a fruitful marriage (not a shotgun one) between control in the accounting sense and control in the human-social sense. In my fantasy thinking, Dick, Ed, Ross, and Frank were to provide the more serious masculine and logical part of what made control control, whereas I was to add the more monkey business, nonlogical, and feelings side of the control phenomena. Anyway, cases were collected to illustrate the possible fruitful marriage of the two. I think we all had fun giving this course and also learned something. I certainly did.

Although I had had about six years of teaching experience by 1943, it was not until then that I began to take teaching seriously as a career. Interestingly enough, it was in two off-beat courses—in the Radcliffe program I have just mentioned and in a retraining program for war production, about which I will speak in a moment—that I found myself as a teacher. In them I came to realize all of a sudden I could let go, be myself, and express myself in a way I was unable to do in other kinds of social or work groups.

I had had a similar experience in my counseling interviews, when I found myself saying things in that context that I hesitated to say under ordinary social conditions. I found teaching also highly rewarding and rewarded. In fact, a uniformity that runs through my life is that in those situations in which I could be congruent with myself, I was successful. These situations happened to be, of all places, (1) in the counseling interview, (2) in the classroom, (3) in the field observing, and (4) at my desk writing with the devil (or small child) nudging my pencil.

THE WAR INDUSTRY RETRAINING PROGRAM

The War Industry Retraining program sponsored by the government in 1943 was the School's first major experience with adult education. In its first rounds it was not populated, as it later came to be, with top executives, that is, with presidents, vice presidents, would-be presidents, and other such influential persons. This only happened after the war when it became our Advanced Management Program. In the beginning it had only an assortment of middle-aged men—many of them my age or older—who had lost their jobs in finance or marketing because of the war and who wished to do their bit for the war effort in a civilian activity closely related to it. At that time this area was production. In this program I taught a course called Personnel and Management Controls.

Probably what helped me in the early sessions of this program was that the participants were obviously persons in the first place and executives in the second or third places. Hence, in these classes there was no stereotype about what made an executive an executive to interfere with what I wanted to teach. I remember one student who would take his shoes off and fall asleep in class. When he explained this behavior to me, he said sheepishly it was not because he was uninterested in my or his colleagues' comments in class, but because all his previous jobs had been standing-up ones with the result that he had come to equate sitting down and going to sleep.

Then there was the question of grading. The School first thought that executives would want to know where they stood and grades would help them find out. One of us had to explain to them the intricacies of the Business School's grading system. At that time, the words that went with the numerical grades were as follows:

Distinction	High	93
	Middle	88
	Low	85
High Pass	High	83
	Middle	81
	Low	79
Pass	High	77
	Middle	75
	Low	72
Low Pass	High	70
	Middle	68
	Low	65
Unsatisfactory	High	60
	Middle	55
	Low	50

As I remember it, we had difficulty in explaining the difference between a high low pass and a low high pass. For the rest of the session the question was never cleared up. At the drop of a hat, the discussion would be renewed, until the Faculty decided to give up grading these men, a practice that continues to the present time.

Besides this grading problem, there was also the problem of responsibility. Up to this time many Faculty members at the School believed that responsibility was a property of an executive in the same sense that wisdom was a property of a sage. That is to say, an irresponsible executive was a contradiction in terms; he could not exist.

When the participants in this program started acting like irresponsible schoolboys instead of responsible executives and came to class unprepared and slightly the worse for wear from their previous evening's alcoholic discussions about the differences between a high low pass and a low high pass, some Faculty members were reduced to a state of cognitive dissonance. They had to reappraise the situation and consider the possibility that if a person is treated as a schoolboy, he may respond by acting like one. This helped me no end in explaining to my students and colleagues why workers were often viewed by management as irresponsible.

Some of the cases we used helped me to relate to these men. There was one case in particular I remember, which involved an executive called Mr. Brewster (disguised name) who carried home each evening and weekend a bulging briefcase of his company's reports. The case was about the company's report system; it showed all the reports that came to Mr. Brewster's desk by means of which, it said in the case, he managed the company.

Well, to these men there was something fishy about this case. They took an extreme dislike to Mr. Brewster. I would just mention his name, and there would be boos, catcalls, and howls of derision or laughter. All this was grist for my mill, because I also thought that there might be a slight discrepancy between the real Mr. Brewster and the Mr. Brewster that had been represented in the case, as indeed I later found out there was when a team of researchers, Hugh Cabot, Harriet Ronken, and David Ulrich—trained by George Lombard and me—studied the company. The study resulted in a series of cases that became celebrated. The cases can be found under the title of the Marshall Company (disguised name) in *The Administrator, Cases on Human Relations in Business*, edited by Jack Glover and Ralph Hower, the first case book published for the course called Administrative Practices, about which I will write below.

As I said, I taught in this retraining program throughout the remainder of the war before it became the School's plush Advanced Management Program. I also taught in it for a while after the transformation took place in 1945. The first session broke the ice for me. Many of the participants became friends of mine; one in particular, Gerald B. Stratton, became one of my best. When Gerry joined the program in its first round, he had just come north from Memphis, Tennessee, where he had been engaged in politics, fighting the Crump machine. Because of these activities he had lost his job. He called himself a carpetbagger from the South. Confronted by another person, he was at ease—in fact charming; but confronted by a column of figures he wilted away into confusion.

At this time I decided that my goal was not to make persons into better executives but instead to make executives into better persons and if in particular cases this was not possible, just to make persons into better persons in whatever occupational role they chose. I was convinced that this was for each of us the road to success. Otherwise one would be cutting the phenomena against the grain. I must have had in mind some notions about what later came to be called individual development.

Anyway, after the program, Gerry did not go into production; he served the remainder of the war in the Merchant Marine and then went into sales. I have followed his career and individual development with great interest. To me, and I think to him also, both have been highly successful and I do not mean financially. He never became an executive officially; he remained a salesman. But in this role he performed services I would have called executive, even though the company he worked for never saw it this way.

ADMINISTRATIVE PRACTICES

When the School returned to civilian operations in 1946, it revised its first-year curriculum in the M.B.A. program. It introduced for the first time for first-year M.B.A. students a required course relating to people. This course came to be named Administrative Practices, often called "Ad Prac." Heretofore matters relating to the motivations, productivity, and satisfaction of people had not been taught as a separate course in the first year; they had been the responsibility of each professor in whatever function of business he taught. Thus every professor was an expert about human beings, in the same sense that Freud once said jokingly that everyone was an expert in child psychology, having once been a child himself. By 1946 this truism had begun to wear a bit thin, so the Faculty finally decided to introduce this new course concerned with "how to get things done through people."

In spite of its name and crude form of conceptualization, by introducing the new course the Faculty finally acknowledged that *people* along with *finance, production, marketing,* and *control* (cost accounting) were one of the important elements of administration. How I wish now we had kept the old title, Human Problems of Administration, but there were then strong forces in operation that dictated otherwise and to me the name was not of chief importance.

The new course was originally patterned after the Management Controls course I have mentioned. As it was now a required first-year course, it was taught by the case method in seven one-hundred-man sections and was staffed by a Faculty group of four or five, including me. Professor Edmund P. Learned was in charge. In the early years of the course many of the School's great case teachers were connected with it: Jack Glover, Ralph Hower, Kenneth Andrews, Chuck Gragg, Joe Bailey, and others.

At the time, I think I recognized the importance of the course for the development of my area of concern, but also I accepted the fact that other influential members of the faculty wanted to have a say in regard to what the course was to be about. This I realized in a vague sort of way was the price I had to pay for the integration with the School which I also wanted. But nothing could be further from the truth than the notion that I appraised the situation realistically at that time.

Although I taught in Administrative Practices for only two years, from 1946 to 1948, I kept in close touch with its development. About the history of this course (now many years later it is called Human Behavior in Organizations), I will have more to say later. The problems which in time the course presented about what was to be taught, how it was to be taught, and by whom it was to be taught raised all the big issues about the School's training of generalists and administrators. Although these conflicts were latent in the situation and I was dimly aware of them at the time, I was in the mood to let sleeping dogs lie. A few words about the organization of the School, though, are relevant at this point.

THE POLICY OF INTERCHANGEABLE PARTS

From its inception the School was anti-departmental. The departmental system, as practiced "across the River" and in most universities, Dean Donham felt, created artificial boundaries which were more dysfunctional than functional. Dean Donham's great dream was to create a new atmosphere of interrelated subject matters under the concept of administration. Under this concept at the School there were no department heads; each professor reported directly to the Dean. There were teaching groups, such as marketing, production, finance, control, and now administrative practices, but these teaching groups had their identity only in the required courses of the first year of the M.B.A. program. They were not departments but groups of professors brought together for the purpose of teaching the large first-year required courses. From this concept a philosophy of professors as interchangeable parts gradually developed.

This philosophy reached its peak during the period when Donald K. David was Dean (1942–1955). Essentially, it was the logical continuation of Dean Donham's idea. We were all generalists training generalists and doing this in terms of either *production* or *marketing* or *finance* or *control* and now also of *people*. All courses were taught by the case method from the point of view of an administrator. In these terms we were all interchangeable and competent to teach any of the elements of administration. We were all teaching the same thing—administration—and teaching it by the same method—the case method. In time, as we grew older, we all became automatically competent to teach policy as well as anything having to do with people.

I was both attracted and repelled by this conception. To understand my ambivalence, one has to look at my background and my growing concern about my area or subject matter. In one sense I was a specialist; I was concentrating upon a class of phenomena—the interactions between persons—that I have called social space. Yet I also saw that the understanding of these phenomena was critical to the executive's job, particularly when he was implementing a policy or decision. In fact I could not see how the administrative point of view could be conceived fruitfully apart from such phenomena. Nevertheless, I felt that my growing area of concern could be developed in the direction both of a specialization (a science) and of a generalized point of view for a responsible actor in an organized human activity (an administrator). I did not see why I had to choose exclusively either one development or the other. But inasmuch as at the time neither was I ready nor was the situation propitious for me to do both, I started with the second.

Moreover, by 1946 my total situation had changed considerably. By this time the Mayo grant from the Rockefeller Foundation had run out. Mayo was to retire in the following year. There was no longer this anomalous entity, the Department of Industrial Research, of which I had been a member. I was now on the School's payroll in the full sense of the word, and I was now fully liable to the interchangeable-part concept. Ouch! Still my success with the "retreads," as the first participants in the Advanced Management Program called themselves, had convinced the senior Faculty and Dean David that I was headed in the right direction, so I obtained my promotion to full professor.

SOCIAL RELATIONS AND GENERAL EDUCATION ACROSS THE RIVER

Following the war, in 1946, many other exciting developments in addition to the course in Administrative Practices were taking place in my area of concern. Interdisciplinary integration and research and general education were part of the social climate at Harvard, as they were also at other universities. At no period of my life before or

115

since was the social climate more propitious for the development in so many different directions of my own growing concerns and interests. In fact, it was so lush that again I experienced some difficulty in deciding which particular jungle to cultivate.

In the Graduate School of Arts and Sciences a new combination was being formed among the social sciences, to be called in time Social Relations. Talcott Parsons from Sociology, Harry Murray from Clinical Psychology, Gordon Allport from Social Psychology, and Clyde Kluckhohn from Social Anthropology spearheaded this new combination. In many of their discussions I was an interested spectator. At that time, although not professional unknowns, they had not achieved the full professional eminence that they all later attained. They were then, relatively speaking, young men. That I was included in their discussions pleased me; I was all for what they were for, namely, the breaking down of the barriers that existed among certain aspects of anthropology, sociology, and psychology. For a more fruitful development, a synthesis among the four disciplines of sociology, social anthropology, social psychology, and clinical psychology was needed. But what was this new combination to be called? Human Relations, as some thought? "No, no," said Mr. Donham. "Human Relations is being taught on the Business School side of the Charles River." This was enough to damn the title. We could not have both sides of the River teaching the same thing, could we now? So the label Social Relations was chosen for the development "across the River." Later (1950) the Ford Foundation called the new area the behavioral sciences. Anyway, it should be noted that this new combination excluded Economics, Political Science, and History for many reasons which I cannot go into here.

There was another umbrella under which these social sciences could congregate across the River: General Education. With this development I had little to do except indirectly through Dean Donham, who, on retiring as Dean of the Business School in 1942, had joined the Human Relations group, as we were now called. Though the name originated with others, it soon became so widely used to refer to our work that we decided to adopt it too. Mr. Donham became interested in introducing a course at the College in its new General Education program. George Lombard assisted him, particularly with the collection of case and reading materials. The course, started in 1946, was called Social Science 112: Human Relations. This time Mr. Donham had no objection to the name being used "across the River," in part because it helped to denote the connection of the course with work at the Business School. It is interesting to note that, even though we were referred to as the Human Relations group at this time, there was no course at the School with the title Human Relations until 1948, when I used the name for a new course I introduced in the second year of the M. B. A. program (see Chapter 12).

In connection with the course at the College, Mr. Donham conducted what came to be called the Visiting Firemen Program. Under this program professors from other universities who were interested in general education, the case method, or human relations spent half a year or a year observing the teaching at the course at the College. They saw how cases were collected, disguised, written up, and taught. Discussions were held prior to and after each class. I held a seminar for these professors in which we read and discussed the literature of the field. The seminar, which I adapted from Mayo's, was thus a forerunner of the one I gave years later for Doctoral students in Organizational Behavior (Chapter 18).

The three universities which participated the most in this program were Colgate, University of Kansas, and Ohio University. The presidents of these universities at the time—respectively, Everett Case, Deane Malott, and John Baker—had all been Assistant Deans under Mr. Donham during his tenure as Dean of the Business School. The program created considerable interest among these participants. As their numbers grew, annual conferences were held, usually at one of the three other universities in which interested members of the faculty of arts and sciences of the host university participated. The topics discussed centered on the three interests I mentioned above, general education, the case method, and human relations. As can be imagined, there were some faculty members present who were skeptical not only of the teaching method of the new course at Harvard but also of its substantive content or lack of it.

Although I had known Mr. Donham as Dean, it was during this period I got to know him best. To me he will always be the Dean who gave the School its distinctive competence. It was he who never tired of saying that business was more than applied economics, that the important word in the School's title, *Graduate School of Business Administration*, was administration; that the training of the generalist—not the specialist—was the School's essential and major job; and that the case method was the essential tool for training the generalist. As I have said before, in the conceptualization of this basic posture, Donham received much aid from Henderson and Mayo.

Probably very few deans at other universities have been able to exercise the amount of influence on their faculties that Mr. Donham did on his about what was to be taught and how it was to be taught. I doubt very much if any future dean of the School ever will. To understand his influence, one must remember that when Mr. Donham became Dean in 1919, the School was small, and what made a graduate business school a graduate business school was an open question. Mr. Donham had strong ideas and convictions about this, and he tended to collect persons for his Faculty who shared his vision and conviction. They were mostly economists who had received the light and were willing to renounce their disciplinary allegiances for a higher end, the training of generalists. As I have mentioned earlier, with no departments and no strong subject matter allegiances on the part of the Faculty, Mr. Donham welded an organization that I think was atypical of most universities. The primary reference group for each professor at this period became the institution—the Harvard Business School—and not his discipline. This created a loyalty and an esprit de corps that was phenomenal.

As I look back on it, I think this orientation was functional for the School during this period of its history. However, in time the institution tended to become ingrown. No one could teach in it who had not gone through its processes of indoctrination. The atmosphere became intellectually more stifling than innovative. I shall have more to say about these matters later, because they became crucial to my growing concern about my subject matter and its relation to the School's aims.

Mr. Donham, in my opinion, was a great person and leader in spite of the authoritarian overtones of his leadership style. With me he was always understanding; he never demanded of me more loyalty to the institution than I was willing to give. I remember only one occasion when I was very upset about something, the particulars of which I don't remember, when I went to him and said in essence, "If this is what you want me to do, you can go to hell." Much to my surprise, his response was, "Fritz, I've been waiting for you to say this to me for a long time." After that we got along much better.

Yet when upon his retirement in 1942, Mr. Donham decided to join our group, I viewed it with mixed feelings. No kidding, his personality was much stronger than mine. Up to this time Mr. Donham had been the University's greatest money raiser—not only for the Business School, but also for other departments of the University. In my eyes, he had had a very successful career. As I got to know him better, I realized that being the University's biggest money raiser was not enough for him. There was another kind of contribution he wished to make and somehow and in some way that I did not understand, it was connected with the area of human relations. In conversations with me about the Faculty he had brought together and developed, he sometimes expressed dissatisfactions that I could not understand. I have never been closely involved in School politics, and I certainly was not then. But I can imagine now that Mr. Donham may have been doing then what I am doing now—reevaluating what he had been up to.

As I reflect upon it now, I do not think I was very understanding about Mr. Donham and his course in Human Relations at the College. What I saw was that Mr. Donham was taking us on a new jaunt—an interesting one, to be sure—at a time when I thought there was a big job to be done at the School. With a shortage of personnel, we were scattering our shots over a wide territory instead of concentrating intensively upon the developments needed right here at the School. As I see it now, had he joined forces with the development I wished to make, he would have come into conflict with the new Dean, Don David, and the School. By playing "across the River" in a new ballpark, he insulated himself from any direct influence upon the School's development and vice versa.

I never put my whole heart behind Mr. Donham's venture across the River. To me it was an organizational anachronism. Trying to run a college course from the Business School, I felt, was ultimately doomed to fail. So I let George do it. Moreover, I resented trying to "sell" to faculty members at other universities the point of view of human relations and the case method for their courses in the social sciences and the humanities. I realize that with the word "sell" I am using an emotionally laden word, but this is the way I perceived many of our conferences with the participating universities. I had too many doubts and qualms of my own about what we were teaching and how we were teaching it to sell anyone anything, and I resented strongly being put in the position of doing so. And certainly the case method, human relations, and general education were not for me one big undifferentiated ball of wax, even though for Mr. Donham they seemed to have this property.

I have not said anything about the students in Mr. Donham's Human Relations course across the River. To state it briefly, I think the undergraduates enjoyed being listened to instead of talked to, although some of them wondered, as we all did, just what they were learning. Certainly their discussions of cases—at least those not involving too much of the logics of management—seemed to be as intelligent as those of graduate students.

The Visiting Firemen included some extraordinarily gifted people both in matters of teaching and matters of administration. There were so many that I am reluctant to mention names, but I will name two. One mathematician who attended the program, George Starcher, later became President of the University of North Dakota; and I guess, although I do not know for sure, that the Harvard experience had something to do with the change in the development of his career. The other, Hilden Gibson, from the University of Kansas, was one of the most gifted teachers I ever knew. He became the leading light at our reunions and, had he lived, would undoubtedly have developed this collaboration among universities beyond the limitations of my own imagination. But after Mr. Donham's death in 1954 and Hilden's death in 1955, I confess I could not see this as our main line of country. I feel like a criminal for saying this, but to the extent that I had any influence I let the effort die.

There are just two other names I want to mention in connection with Mr. Donham's venture across the River. Because of the shortage of men when his course was introduced in 1946, two women were hired as research assistants—the then Misses Frances Mulhearn and Harriet Ronken, of whom one was an attractive extroverted brunette and the other an attractive and more introverted blonde. Both of them, in addition to their physical charms, had brains. One was a Boston Irish Radcliffe product; the other a Minnesota Protestant Bryn Mawr–Radcliffe product.

Although George Lombard was more directly in charge of their training than I, I was able to play in the background, which I have always found to be a preferable position. Had both these young women been men, their promotion at the School would have been assured. But this was not the case.

Harriet Ronken later married Rolf Lynton, a student of mine in the Human Relations Clinic about which I shall speak later. Afterwards they went to India, where they became involved in developing training programs for dealing with the interrelated problems of individual, community, and economic development. I count them among my most successful second-level practitioners. Frances Mulhearn married Stephen Fuller, and both of them, like the Lyntons, also became concerned for a while with developmental problems, but in the Philippines instead of in India.

In this chapter I have tried to show how my early teaching experiences were mostly in what were considered by the School off-beat courses in off-beat programs, such as the Radcliffe program, the

War Industry Retraining Program, and the Visiting Firemen Program. Not until 1946 did I become associated with a required course in the School's top-drawer M. B. A. program—the course called Administrative Practices. This course in time brought what I thought I was up to in teaching administration into sharp confrontation with what the School thought that *it* was up to. But in 1946 this was not a problem.

As I reflect upon it now, the year 1946 seems to me to mark a sharp turning point in the development of the social sciences that I have referred to as "Human Relations" and "Social Relations." For a while thereafter the foundations, particularly the Ford Foundation, newly constituted in 1950, made large grants for research in these areas, many of which went to the business schools in the United States and later overseas.

In reflecting upon the early courses in which I taught, I am impressed with how little difference the sex, education, age, or management level of my students made to me in what I thought I was teaching. Whether they were men or women; high school graduates, college undergraduates or graduates; in their twenties, forties, or sixties; foremen, middle, or top management, I do not remember that I changed my tune very much, and I used the same cases.

Nor do I remember thinking that one group was smarter or had better judgment than another. The only differences I noticed were that I had to spend less time building up a rationale for what I was up to with the women than with the men and with the experienced than with the inexperienced. When the men returned from the war, I had some of my most enthusiastic students. At no period in the School's history were there more students preparing for personnel work.

Even in the Trade Union Program, which started in 1942 and in which I taught for a while, I did not feel I had to change either my teaching style or what I was teaching. From 1943 to 1946 many of these union men were in the same class that I was teaching in the Advanced Management Program. Their presence with management men certainly livened up the discussion, but in these discussions I was amused to find how often the union men were arguing like management men and vice versa.

As the effects of the age, sex, and education of the students upon the classroom process were interminable topics of discussion among my colleagues, I wondered why I thought they made so little difference. Were these questions unimportant to me because of my "subject matter," or because I lacked one? Among these experiences and observations, it seemed to me there lurked matters which needed explanation.

The trouble with raising questions is that you have to answer them; at least that seemed to me what I intended to do when I accepted responsibility for developing this field by committing my life and work to it. I will need the next three chapters to describe the answers I came to.

Chapter 9

Teaching by the Case Method

I start this chapter with qualms, because I do not wish to rehash what have become for me tired and outworn controversies. Yet since I spent many years cultivating the case method of teaching, I want to say a few things about what it meant to me when I was teaching actively.

Although I would like to believe that when I decided to become a teacher, I made a list of the different teaching methods available to me and estimated the payoffs for student learning that I could gain from each one and that I chose the combination that would yield the largest return, this is not the way it happened. I was at the Harvard Business School, celebrated for its teaching method. When I began to teach, I chose the method which was most readily available to me and which I could use and modify, if necessary, for my purposes. Given the time and place, this happened to be the "case method."

Although the case method at the Harvard Business School refers primarily to a teaching method, it also has research implications. In addition, for some people, it has overtones approaching a mystique which cannot be easily conceptualized and overtones that have to be seen in operation to be understood. This is why I will have to watch my step carefully as I talk about it.

According to legend, Mr. Donham, a graduate of the Harvard Law School, brought the case method, as practiced at the Law School, to the Business School when he became Dean. If by case method is meant a discussion method instead of a lecture method in which the professor lectures on a case, this could easily be true. Here the similarity ceases, because a business case differs from a law case. It also differs from a case history as used in medicine and social work. This difference is largely due to the fact that there exists a so-called body of substantive knowledge in law and medicine which does not exist in business. Perhaps to appease some, I should say such a body of knowledge did not exist in business at the time I am writing about; it resembled more a body of opinions.

Thus in most general terms a case at the Harvard Business School meant a description of an administrative problem in business about which it was felt someone in charge should do something. The case could not be "arm-chaired." It had to be a statement of a real problem in a real company and about real people, although the real names of the company and people were generally disguised. To get such a case meant that someone (at the B-School, called a case writer) had to go out in the field and talk to someone in some organization; he just could not or should not sit on his fanny and make it up. (This is where the research I mentioned above came in.) Furthermore, the case did not have to illustrate the right or wrong way of doing something. As the footnote added to each case written at the School points out, "This case was prepared as a basis for classroom discussion rather than to illustrate either an effective or ineffective handling of an administrative situation."

So far I do not think I have said anything about the case method with which my colleagues would seriously disagree. Now I want to say some things about the way classroom discussions of cases were conducted by my colleagues and by me in order to reach certain objectives.

THE OBJECTIVES OF THE CASE METHOD (AS I HEARD THEM)

Many features of the case method of teaching were attractive to me. Let me cite some of them.

(1) Seeking the active participation of students in reaching a solution to a problem.

(2) Providing students with a description of a problem situation from which to draw conclusions and propose actions in regard to what to do about them.

(3) Helping students to seek for *relations among the facts* in a case and drawing conclusions about what to do from them, instead of deducing actions from principles (opinions, clichés) about what should be done.

(4) Fostering discussions among students about the problem and its solution instead of restricting the discussions to interactions between individual students and the instructor.

(5) Fostering independence of thought and judgment on the part of students.

(6) Helping students to see the difference between making decisions under the burden of responsibility and just talking about what should be done in situations where this constraint is absent.

I have cited these objectives because they were the ones I heard most often from my colleagues, not only in their few written statements about the method, but also in their many discussions about it at Faculty, committee, and staff meetings as well as at informal meetings at lunch.

But I also had qualms about the ways in which these objectives were often rationalized and implemented and about the kinds of data the cases did and did not contain.

(1) Around the case method there was an aura of anti-intellectualism. Its rationale was often stated in opposition to theory instead of in relation to it.

(2) Its concentration on the "facts of the case" at times obscured to me the most important fact of all, namely, that facts do not speak for themselves and that they need to be interpreted if they are to be understood.

(3) In all of the early cases the "facts" were exclusively economic facts or formal organizational facts. There were hardly any human, social, informal organizational, or small group facts. As a result, many of the cases contained very little raw data; the data in them were highly interpreted to begin with. Many of them were written in the impersonal third person. As a consequence, evaluative statements were often included without stating who had made them. These unidentified evaluations were often treated as facts. Problems were often stated without describing for whom they were problems. Often the source of information about a problem was just one executive in the company.

(4) Also, as I observed the behavior of my colleagues in the classroom, I often could not reconcile it with our intent to foster independence of thought and judgment. Many instructors had call lists; that is, they had a preselected list of students upon whom they would call for recitations. What resulted seemed to me more like individual recitations than group discussions. The instructor kept attendance records and graded each recitation. Unexcused absences and tardiness in coming to class were treated as serious offenses and could affect the students' grades. Some professors refused to let students who were tardy attend their classes.

(5) All these practices were rationalized in terms of reinforcing responsible behavior on the part of the students. The responsible

executive, it was said, met his appointments promptly and punctually and if he could not, he had good reason for not doing so. So a student, it was argued, should begin to act like an executive in class. The responsible executive (a) was always punctual; (b) was never absent except if ill; (c) was decisive and not "sicklied o'er by the pale cast of thought"; (d) looked at the facts and eschewed theory; and (e) weighed the alternatives "realistically" and "tough-mindedly" in terms of the economic reality; and (f) wore a jacket and tie, preferably a suit, vest, and tie.

Frankly this mumbo-jumbo appalled me. It was not that I questioned the reality of the phenomena my colleagues were pointing to. It was their attitude toward these phenomena that appalled me—their utter seriousness, lack of humor, and lack of curiosity about them. How could they not see that the absences and tardinesses of their students might bear some relation to their own behavior as teachers in the classroom? How could they not see that there might exist a discrepancy between the independence of thought and judgment they were supposed to be fostering in students, on the one hand, and the conformity of behavior in terms of their own cultural preconceptions of responsible behavior that they were demanding of students on the other? But none of this seemed to make problems for some of my colleagues. They could debate endlessly the pros and cons of call lists and rewarding and punishing students for punctuality and tardiness or attendance and non-attendance at classes.

For me at the time, the case method, if it was to be the celebrated teaching method it claimed to be, had to be justified in terms of the learning process. Instead of using it to reinforce certain institutional norms and values about the way businessmen should behave, it seemed to me it could and should be developed in terms of the way persons learned about themselves and others in the process of attaining their own personal goals as well as the goals of the organization. Therefore, I went in this direction in all the courses I taught. I had no call lists, made no attendance checks, locked no doors, and conducted the class on a volunteer basis. I was permissive and, as time went on, I became more "nondirective." What I meant by nondirective I shall explain in a moment. It could not be deduced from the dictionary meaning of the word, as some of my colleagues tried to do.

I did not grade directly an individual student's contribution to the classroom discussion. My attitude, as I told my students, in effect was, "You, the student, can help yourself by participating in the classroom discussion; you can't hurt yourself by so doing. Your final grade will be your written examination grade, which you can improve but not lower by talking in class. If you get a high pass in your examination, for example, you will get a high pass as your final grade, even though you did not open your mouth in class or seemed to me to be off-beat in all the remarks you made in class. However, if you get a low pass in your examination but also have made in my opinion helpful and intelligent contributions to the discussion in class, I will raise your final grade accordingly. By my behavior in the classroom itself I undoubtedly will be rewarding you or witholding my reward from you by the kind of attention I give to your contribution. Your fellow students I assume will be doing the same. Let's see if we can get some insight into this process as the course develops."

Thus I tried to allocate my rewards to students in the manner B. F. Skinner fed his pigeons pellets of grain for doing what he wanted them to do. But I did not know about Skinner then. As I look back, I can see more clearly than I did then the kind of behavior I rewarded. As would be said now, I discouraged zero-sum games between myself and the students and among them. I encouraged more cooperative than competitive games between and among us. I encouraged frankness of expression—what today would be called leveling. I tried to make expressions of feelings as legitimate for discussion as statements of facts. All these things I hoped the student would find rewarding—not because I, the teacher, said so but because the phenomena said so.

THOSE AWFUL "PERFECT" SOLUTIONS

My mission can also be stated in more intellectual terms. For example, it bothered me that the discussion of a case frequently went in the following way:

(1) The identification of a problem as a deviation from a company standard; which reduced itself
(2) To someone who was not doing what he was supposed to be doing; which resulted
(3) In a search for the villain or villains who were responsible for this state of affairs; and who, if found,
(4) Was to be told, "We can't have this happening any more or else you know what"; and if so,
(5) Introducing new persons who would do what they were supposed to do; and furthermore,
(6) Introducing *new* rules, *new* regulations, *new* control systems, or *new* policies, which in many cases involved the complete reorganization of the company, so that this deviation would not happen any more.

This ring-around-a-rosey kind of verbal solution had me completely unnerved. It was as if all the behavioral phenomena in which I was interested were just not there. At the drop of a hat the students would reorganize the company and provide it with all the standards and controls it needed. If management did not know its costs, for example, it should install a cost-control system; if management did not know what the consumer wanted, then it should do consumer research; if foremen were not supervising well, foreman training should be introduced; and so on and on. The textbooks provided all the answers, and I was left high and dry.

Not only were the students well equipped to make an organization into a perfect organization, they were well equipped to change people's attitudes, motivations, and personalities into the proper ones. With a stroke of their verbal wands, they could change deviant employees into conforming ones; untactful supervisors into tactful ones; autocratic supervisors into democratic ones; apathetic workers into highly motivated ones; rate busters and job killers into regular ones; and so on and on. It was a sight to behold! But not for my sore eyes or ears. Again and again the students had me behind the eight ball. But by the questions I asked them it looked as though I was against all of the good things in this best of all possible worlds.

So after a few weeks of "perfect solutions," I introduced two constraints into our discussions. I outlawed as solutions to the problem under discussion all company reorganizations and changes in a person's motivation or personality. I said in effect, "Let's treat the policies of the company as given and the kinds of people working for it as given. Let's see what can be done within this framework before we introduce new rules, new regulations, new policies, or new persons with new personalities and before we discharge old persons with old personalities or change their old personalities into new ones. Let's accept the fact that the policies of the company and the behavior of all the people in them from managers to workers fall far short of perfection. Let's try acting in this imperfect world and see what this feels like. Let's consider what we might be able to do in this second best of all possible worlds."

In this way I hoped to get the students not only to see why things were the way they were before they introduced a change; I also hoped to get them to focus on their own motivations as well as the motivational and interactional elements in the problem situations they were diagnosing. These were the elements with which they would ultimately have to deal when they had to implement the perfect solutions they had reached. It was not easy. For many students it was like searching in a dark cellar for a black cat that was not there.

BLIND SPOTS

These perfect solutions seemed to me to result from the fact that students assumed that only logical and strictly economic behavior should be present in the problem situations they were discussing. All other forms of behavior were either not recognized or ignored or outlawed. For many students the phenomena of human behavior that should not be there were not there because by definition they should not be there; or if, by God, they had sneaked in, then they should be eliminated at once. With Korzybski I felt that these were serious misevaluations. I called them "blind spots" and will illustrate them by the following two lists.

BLIND SPOTS

Those kinds of behavior that were acceptable and supposed to be present.	Those kinds of behavior that were not supposed to be present and so in a logical sense were either "not there," or, if so, were to be eliminated.
1. Logical actions	1. Social interactions
2. Behavior based upon facts	2. Behavior based upon feelings, sentiments, or evaluations associated with the above interactions
3. Formal organization	3. Informal organization
4. Technological organization	4. Social organization
5. Planned behavior	5. Emergent behavior
6. Intended consequences of behavior	6. Unanticipated and undesired consequences of behavior
7. Operational relations of how to get from state A to state B most efficiently	7. Exchange relations between person A and person B when they interacted with each other
8. Efficient relations	8. Situationally satisfying relations
9. Logical conflicts	9. Nonlogical conflicts
10. Organizational goals and decisions	10. Personal goals and decisions
11. Optimal decisions to minimize costs or maximize profits	11. Decisions about what might make the outcomes more satisfying to persons
12. Economic assessments of expected monetary return	12. Personal involvements and commitments

How was I to get students to address themselves to their blind spots? By teaching them the concepts of the psychologists and sociologists? Of what utility was it to provide a concept for my students, if the phenomena of which the concept was a property did not exist for them? This technique, giving a student a word and hoping that this would produce the phenomena that the word stood for, seemed to me like producing a map for a nonexistent territory. It not only went against my epistemological and phenomenological leanings, in which phenomena came before words; it also went against my understanding of the case method of learning.

While I was pondering these dilemmas, it occurred to me to ask why these phenomena were not there for my students. Of course I saw that they were not there because they were not supposed to be there. But who said they were not supposed to be there? Well, believe it or not, it was no personal villain; it was a set of cultural assumptions and beliefs. These societal and cultural factors had ruled them "out of existence."

For example, our democratic society said we were all equals; hence, there were *no social classes*. Our Western European civilization (Aristotle?) said we were all rational; hence, there was *no nonlogical behavior*, except in penal and mental institutions. The economists said we were motivated primarily by economic interests; hence, there were no other kinds of motivation. Classical academic psychology only paid attention to man's conscious processes; hence, there were no *unconscious processes*. Our credo said we were all tough-minded individualists; hence, there were no *soft-minded conformists*. There were no people who wanted to keep a job, to have job security, to have friends, to belong, to be identified with something other than themselves. We were all individualists seeking our own individual successes, regardless of what happened to our fellow men.

None of my researches to date had given credence to any of these beliefs as simple causal determinants of the behavior I had observed. These beliefs were there, of course, in the verbal behavior of many persons I had interviewed; but they were there in relation to other determinants of their behavior and frequently they were there as derivations from them. And these derivations in turn were sometimes functional and sometimes dysfunctional for action in a given situation. But whether they were one or the other was an empirical question; it could not be answered by *logic*, but only by *observation*.

As the sociologically knowledgeable reader will see, I had in mind the Paretian triangle, as illustrated below.

The Mutually Dependent Relations Among
Sentiments, Beliefs, and Action

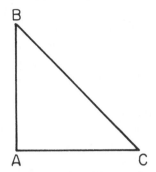

A = nonverbal residues (sentiments)
B = verbal derivations (rationalizations, beliefs, assumptions)
C = overt behavior (action)

The words "residue" and "derivation" are technical terms which Pareto invented in order to escape the tricks that old terms play. A residue is a manifestation of a sentiment. A derivation is an assertion, argument, or explanation whose credence comes more from the residue which supports it than from anything logico-experimental. Both residues and derivations are found in the verbal utterances and actions of people. Both are obtained by analysis and abstraction from concrete social phenomena. The residues are the more constant part, the derivations the more variable part, of social phenomena. A rationalization in the Freudian sense is one kind of derivation.

For Pareto, residues were one of the important elements in social systems that are in relations of mutual dependence with other elements, e.g., derivations. Hence, to treat derivations or beliefs as the cause of the observed social behavior was a common but serious error. According to Pareto, outside of pure mathematics, a person can seldom talk more than 30 seconds without expressing a sentiment; in this sense the residue or manifestation of sentiments, or sentiments for short, are the mainsprings of social action.

Many of the above statements I have taken from L. J. Henderson's three lectures on *Concrete Sociology*. Although I shall keep in mind the distinction between residues and derivations, I shall not employ these terms again. For residues I shall use the word sentiments and even sometimes feelings; for derivations I shall use such words as rationalizations, beliefs, assumptions, or evaluations.

To return to the diagram, according to this way of thinking C did not follow from B as logical conclusions from given premises or as given effects from given causes. Both B and C were often expressions of A; in this sense B and C were related to each other. But this was far from being a logical relation (relations of ideas); it was an empirical relation (matters of fact). But how could I get my students to see this relation of B to C via A, when B (a derivation) said A (a residue) was not supposed to be there? As you can see, I had the magician's problem in reverse. Instead of pulling a rabbit out of a hat, where the rabbit wasn't in the first place, I had to put the rabbit back in the hat, where it was in fact in the first place.

THE POINTING FINGER AND WHAT WAS BEING POINTED TO

How was I to perform this trick of the week? Well, if you can believe this now, A was right there in front of my nose! What was not there *in the cases* was there *in my students' discussions of them*, but I was looking for it in the wrong direction. I was looking for it in what they were pointing to instead of paying attention to the fingers with which they were pointing. I remember that this tendency, inculcated at an early age by our educational system, was why the magician could deceive an educated adult more easily than a child who had not yet learned the lesson. Thus, like a Simple Simon, the child would look at the finger where the magic was being performed instead of being diverted by what the magician was pointing to when he performed the trick. I was flabbergasted but excited by my naiveté.

Gradually I tried to divest myself of the bad habits I had learned as a student at Columbia, M. I. T., and Harvard—that is, of trying to make sense of or to integrate all the different things people were pointing to instead of focusing upon their pointing fingers. In the latent assumptions (logical and nonlogical) of the pointing finger I might find the uniformities for which I was seeking. I should have remembered from my days in philosophy that if I kept chasing and trying to integrate all the bloody things people were pointing to, I would be involved in a hopeless mish-mash. But if as Freud, Mayo, and Pareto told me to do, I kept my eye on the pointing finger, a uniformity might emerge.

The method I developed in the classroom was addressed to this problem. The method could be used at different levels, but the thrust was always the same. It asked in effect: "What are the underlying schemas of assimilation of one sort or another—assumptions, values, feelings, sentiments, residues, derivations, needs, norms, collective beliefs, perceptions, and so on—by which you (the student) are evaluating X (the problem) and deciding what is to be done? Unless we get these schemas and the problem from the right end up, confusion will result."

I tried to make explicit the assumptions and values that were in our discussions, all the things which made X (what was being evaluated) real, true, valid, important, significant, relevant, and salient for the students. In this way I tried to unfreeze the hard bullets that the students called facts into their process components. The schema I used is illustrated in the following diagram. For this analysis of the process of evaluation, I am indebted to Irving J. Lee, a student of Korzybski, who spent a year at the School observing the case method. He reported some of his observations about the method in *How to Talk with People* (1952) and in *Customs and Crises in Communication* (1954).

The Related Components of the Evaluations That Students Called Facts

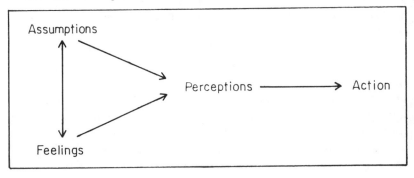

This schema said, for example:

(A) If student X tends to come late to my classes and I *assume* he does this because he thinks my course stinks,

(B) I will *feel* angry at X who is threatening my conception of myself as a good teacher who is giving a good course; and

(C) Hence, I will *perceive* him as disrespectful; and

(D) I will punish him by locking the doors, so that he cannot do this to me.

On the other hand it also said, for example:

(A) If student X tends to arrive late to my classes and I *assume* that this may be due to the fact that the professor in his preceding course tends to run his classes beyond the closing hour,

(B) I will not get annoyed with the student. (I may be annoyed with the professor who feels the need to make a brilliant closure to a disorganized case-discussion one minute before the closing hour.) Instead I will *feel* sorry for the student caught in this predicament; and

(C) Hence, I will not *perceive* student X as disrespectful to me; and

(D) I will let him attend the class, even if he is late.

My communication to students went something like this. "So long as you are willing to decompose your evaluations this way, I will accept them. But when you present me with these unanalyzed evaluations as pure 'facts,' I will blink my eyes. I will not accept them. I will reflect them back to you."

Because for me there is no more important distinction in the realm of human behavior than the one I am now trying to make, let me go around it again. At the time Irving visited the School, he was working on an evaluation quotient, a way of measuring proper evaluation and misevaluation. In 1952 I wrote a paper utilizing the distinction (Chapter 10 in *Man-in-Organization*).

By proper evaluation neither Irving nor I meant that an evaluation was necessarily correct, and by misevaluation we did not mean that it was necessarily incorrect. By the first we meant only that a person was aware that he was evaluating, so that should his evaluation be wrong, it could be corrected. By misevaluation we meant that the person was not aware that he was evaluating, so that if his evaluation was wrong, it could not be corrected. For persons who were unaware in this way, facts were facts and could not be altered.

For example, if a student made his decision in part from strong feelings and recognized this, even though he might not know the source of his strong feelings and might be unwilling to change them, I could accept this. But if he rationalized, disguised, or denied his feelings and, so to speak, said they were not there in the action he recommended, I remained skeptical and continued to explore his views. I did not browbeat him into an admission by saying, "See here, you dumb jerk, these feelings are motivating you, but you will not admit it." If I did this, I would be *assuming* that the student was willfully doing this; I would get angry; I would *perceive* him as dumb and I would give him a verbal tongue-lashing because he did not recognize his assumptions, feelings, and perceptions.

If I did this, obviously I would not be practicing what I preached. From the point of view of the student, his feelings in a certain sense were honestly not there. I could not assume they were there for him without becoming seriously incongruent with my own theoretical position. The method I used to address this problem has been called nondirective. I did not coin this word. It does not mean being indirect, circuitous, oblique, deceitful, not proceeding in a straight line, going roundabout, or any of the other synonyms one can find for "indirection" in the dictionary. "Nondirective" means reflecting and restating as *directly* as possible, in a way which describes both the pointing finger and what is being pointed to, the complete statement of which the student had given me only half.

So far as I know, Carl R. Rogers used the word nondirective first in relation to his counseling method as he described in *Counseling and Psychotherapy* (1942). For Rogers it meant addressing the feelings underlying the content of the discourse. Here I have given it a somewhat wider meaning and a more cognitive twist. But the underlying thrust of looking at the pointing finger is the same.

My nondirective stance was as innocuous—and also as directive—as some of the following questions:

(1) Am I correct in believing that you *feel* [after the student had used the word *think*] this way about so-and-so's behavior?

(2) Do I understand you to say that "from your point of view or from where you sit" [which the student did not say] that so-and-so looks (feels) to you this way?

(3) From what you said I am not sure whether you *assumed* that so-and-so is lazy because he is not motivated or because he is not motivated in the way you are or think he should be. Would you clarify this for me?

(4) Is there any way you might be able to check these assumptions which it seems to me you are making about X (the problem)?

(5) Is it possible that A judges B to be a disagreeable fellow (where A and B are characters in the case), because A finds B's behavior threatening to him in some way?

(6) I gather that you feel that when supervisor A gave employee B the heave-ho, he was not being very tactful. Please tell me what the tactful remark in this situation would be. What would you say?

(7) What should A *say* and *do* in this problem situation if B is A's boss, subordinate, friend, an older man, a younger woman? Would or should these differences of relationship make any difference in what A says or does? How? Why? Why not? (In many early cases this kind of information was not always provided. Employees were just employees with no sex, age, seniority, marital status, education, or background. They were just neuters who did or did not do what they were told.)

(8) I am not clear if you are telling me what A would do or should do if you were A with his personality; if A were you with your personality; if A were A in his role in the company in the case; or if you are A in your student role here in the classroom. Would you clarify this for me?

(9) I am not clear whether you mean that A *can* communicate with B; A *does* communicate with B; or A *should* communicate with B; and whether in this particular situation all three propositions hold; or only two; or one; or none. I'm confused. Perhaps you can clarify this for me. Is it important to straighten this out before we act?

(10) In your opinion, is the statement you made a descriptive statement or a normative one?

(11) In your opinion, is what you said a fact or an inference?

(12) I gather you feel that A's behavior is a deviation from some standard, but I'm not clear just what standard you are talking about. Is it, for example, some management standard, some technical standard, or is it some group standard about what the behavior of an employee should be? Take A, a high producer, for example. I gather he is conforming to management's standards; but in so doing he may not be conforming to the norms of his work group about what constitutes a fair day's work; whereas B, who is restricting his output, is conforming to the group norms about acceptable output, but in so doing he may be deviating from management's standards about working as hard as he should. Is the person in the case an A or B? Would it be worth knowing? What difference would it make in the action you take? Would you fire B and keep A; keep B and fire A; fire both of them; or keep both of them? If you did any of the first three, what do you think the consequences would be? If you decided to keep both, are there any other things you would do?

By selecting this rather wide assortment of different examples of what I meant by a nondirective response, I may be giving the reader a false impression of the classroom hour. Obviously if I kept up a steady barrage of such barbed questions, I would kill the discussion. In many instances, these questions are better examples of what was going through my mind than of what I actually said. My restatements were most often made in a lower key than my illustrations suggest. I have jazzed them up, so that the reader may see that by nondirection I did not mean no direction. Instead, I meant looking in a direction that was different from and sometimes at a 180-degree variance from the direction in which one looks in most discussions.

As a matter of fact, in the classroom I seldom was able to make any responses as clear, bright, or clever as the above illustrations suggest.

More often than not, I jittered in silence while the students tried to help me out of what was for them (as well as for me sometimes) an embarrassing situation. Not knowing what they could say to please me, they began to say what they really thought and felt, which I thought was in line with the independence of thought and judgment the case method was supposed to encourage.

MY LECTURETTES

In addition, because of the size of our classes, 80 to 100 students, it was often difficult to maintain the orientation of which I have been speaking. At the end of a class hour I would have liked to have been able to tie up neatly the different pieces of pointing fingers which were by then lying all over the place. I was seldom smart enough to do this. However, after I had had a night's sleep the pieces would begin to form a pattern. Certain common assumptions that had been under- lying the whole discussion began to emerge. Around these assump- tions I would sometimes give a short (10 or 15 minutes) lecture at the beginning of the next hour.

Many of these assumptions referred to distinctions which the stu- dents had failed to make in their diagnoses of the problem in the case and which I thought the skilled practitioner should make and use when assessing and dealing with the behavior of persons in organiza- tions. None of these distinctions is original with me. They have been made by many different investigators using many different terminol- ogies. I used them NOT for the purposes of theory construction but as aids for better diagnoses of and action in specific situations. I have already referred to a number of them in this as well as in preceding chapters. The following is a list of some of them.

Classes of Phenomena Which Needed to be Differentiated Before They Could Be Properly Assessed in the Concrete Situations Being Diagnosed

(1) Relations of ideas and matters of fact (Hume)
(2) Analytical and synthetic propositions (Kant)
(3) Logical validity and empirical truth (Russell) (Numbers 1, 2, and 3 are different ways of expressing the same distinction)
(4) Knowledge about and knowledge of acquaintance (William James)
(5) Knowledge and skill (Mayo)
(6) Maps and territories (Korzybski)
(7) Verbal and nonverbal behavior (Korzybski)

(8) Simple causation and mutual dependence (Henderson)

(9) Logical classes and concrete systems (Radcliffe-Brown)

(10) Descriptive and normative (the battle between "what is" and "what ought to be")

(11) Logical and nonlogical behavior (Pareto)

(12) Fact and sentiment (Henderson and Pareto)

(13) Individual needs and social roles (the two different reconstructions of behavior to which psychology and sociology address themselves)

(14) Intentions and consequences of behavior (Functionalism)

(15) Cultural values and social norms (Social Anthropology)

(16) Manifest and latent content (Freud)

(17) Preoccupation and attention (Janet)

(18) Proper evaluation and misevaluation (Lee)

(19) Gesellschaft and Gemeinschaft (Tonnies)

(20) Formal and informal organization (Mayo and *Management and the Worker*)

(21) Technical organization and social organization (*Management and the Worker*)

(22) External and internal relations, environments and systems (Whitehead, Claude Bernard, and Homans)

(23) Effective and efficient (Barnard)

(24) Meeting organizational requirements and satisfying individual needs (another way of saying number 23)

(25) Organizational goals and personal goals (Barnard)

(26) Organizational decisions and personal decisions (Barnard)

(27) Management standards and social norms (Mayo and Roethlisberger)

These distinctions can be the source of misunderstanding as well as of clarification. As can be seen, each one can readily be made into a false dichotomy. Although again and again I insisted that I was concerned with the relation of the two parts to each other, my statements to this effect were often heard by students as saying that I believed that one part was more important than the other.

During the early years of my teaching, these problems of communication were not my chief concern, though, as I will show, they later became so. At this time, I was interested in gross differentiations in the phenomena of organizational life, differentiations that I felt needed to be made before they could be thought about in an integrated fashion that would provide a framework for better observation and action. Each of the above distinctions at this time had for me this function. They became for me the important discriminations about human-social phenomena in organizations. I thought that practitioners who were dealing with these phenomena needed to keep them in mind. Underlying them was a simple and useful way of thinking about the phenomena of which they were a product.

As should be no great surprise to the reader, this useful way of thinking was for me Henderson's conceptual scheme of a social system. This conceptual scheme more than anything else was what I was attempting to communicate to my students. I wanted them to see the utility of this way of thinking as a tool for investigation, not as a theory of explanation. That is to say, I did not want students to explain the phenomena by the conceptual scheme; I wanted them to see how the conceptual scheme could be useful for understanding and investigating the phenomena.

As a result, I seldom lectured systematically about the conceptual scheme as such; I neither covered all the distinctions I mentioned in the preceding list nor always gave students the labels I gave in this exhibit. I used the labels to discriminate, both in the case and in the case discussion, one class of phenomena from another. Also, as can be seen from the list, I often expressed the same distinction in different terminologies. At that time this did not bother me, because the thrust was always the following: "Do you, dear students, see here and now in the phenomena the difference between this kind of ordering and that kind of ordering? Do you see the serious consequences for action if you confuse them?"

My reasons for keeping the conceptual scheme under-logicized had several sources. From my study of obsession I had become convinced that the chief error the normal obsessive makes is to treat the facts of his world as simple and to overcomplicate his thinking about them. This overcomplication in thought of an oversimplification in fact, it will be remembered, I called the false dichotomy. This tendency, it seemed to me, prevented learning and made realistic alternatives and decisions difficult.

From this observation I drew the conclusion that effective (skillful, competent) action was based on doing the opposite from what the obsessive does. Instead of treating the world of facts (the territory) as simple and making the map complex, one should treat the territory as complex and keep the map simple. A simple map applied to a complex territory could do wonders. It was the road to sanity. It was the road that my friend Occam suggested for the development of knowledge, that is "Do not multiply entities without necessity." It seemed to me like good advice for the practitioner and utilizer of knowledge.

Here was a dilemma. If one became enamored with the logicization of the map, so that this aspect became more important than its utilization for practice, the obsessive dilemma would persist. At this period of my life, for example, many of my friends were undergoing psychoanalysis. It seemed to me that among those for whom the analysis was unsuccessful, there were many who were more interested in understanding Freud and his theories than in understanding themselves. Obviously the psychiatrist employing psychoanalysis as his method of psychotherapy was utilizing the ideas of Freud in order to get his patient to understand himself. He was not trying to get his patient to be an expert on Freud's theory. But in many unsuccessful cases it seemed to me that this was just what happened.

Therefore, before presenting a conceptual scheme about human phenomena with which the students could become logically enamored, I felt I should first break down their old ways of thinking about them. Otherwise, the students would be trying to understand and to please me and my conceptual scheme instead of trying to understand and pay attention to the human phenomena occurring in their cases in the classroom, and in and among themselves. Hence, in the early part of the course, I spent the greatest portion of my time in what Kurt Lewin would have called an unfreezing process. This I did, as I explained before, by the method of nondirection.

While with one hand I was trying to unfreeze old ways of thinking about human phenomena, I was also trying with the other hand to present what I believed to be a more fruitful way of thinking about them. This was the purpose of my lecturettes. They were always addressed to something in the case or in our discussion of it. For example, I seldom lectured about the nature and function of formal or informal organization as such. Rather I tried to talk about how the distinction between formal and informal organization might help the students to see what was going on in the case or in their discussion of it. I hoped as a result that they might see some simple action step that they might be able to take if they ever faced the problem described in the case.

DIFFERENT VIEWS OF THE CASE METHOD

In my early teaching years I seldom tried to go further in the classroom than I have stated to develop either theory or personal insights among my students. That is, I limited the discussion to (1) an unfreezing process, as Kurt Lewin would have called it, or an extensionalizing process, as Korzybski would have called it, or a nondirective approach, as I called it, by which the students could get closer to the raw phenomena of human behavior; and (2) a refreezing process, as Lewin would have called it, or a conceptual scheme, as Henderson would have called it, by which the students could become more skillful observers and actors with regard to these phenomena. I was trying to make my students better observers and practitioners of human relations—not better theorists or explainers of human behavior—and I utilized the case method as a tool for achieving this objective. Therefore, I would not want the reader to believe that my version of teaching by the case method represents, in any shape, manner, or form, the official version (if such a thing exists) of the case method of teaching at the Harvard Business School. It was just my version.

Speaking generally, my version differed from other versions in several important respects. One of them was that for many of my colleagues the important "facts" existed in the written case and not in the discussion of it, whereas for me the important "facts" existed in the discussion of the case and not in the written case per se. It could be said that they were teaching the written case, whereas I was teaching the discussion of it.

Although this is obviously an oversimplification, these nuances tend to produce two different teaching styles, both of which are acceptable methods of teaching at the B-School. In the first style, the instructor spends hours in the preparation of the case. He knows the "facts," as stated in the case, cold and the "points" to be made in terms of them. In the second style, the instructor is less well prepared about the "facts" as stated in the case and the points to be made; he awaits—with pleasure and not anxiety—for the points to develop in the discussion and more often than not, an off-beat remark is grist for his mill.

To be honest, in my early days of teaching I tended to treat the case as an ink blot upon which the students could project whatever pattern they saw in it. I tried to correct this exaggeration later, when I taught cases I had collected myself rather than the cases my colleagues had collected. In the early days, when few facts about concrete human behavior were described in cases, I had to concentrate my attention upon where the concrete behavior existed, namely, in the behavior of my students.

There were other limitations in my style of teaching the case method. With my emphasis on observation and trying to understand what was going on, the question of action and what needed to be done came after the diagnosis of the problem had been made. Because in my classes this diagnosis often took more of the allotted classroom time, I seldom got to the action question until about 15 minutes before the class was to end. Sometimes, to be honest, I never got to this point at all.

On the other hand, many of my colleagues started the case discussion with the action question—that is, by asking the students what alternative actions could be taken in terms of the logical issues that the case presented and by asking them to decide in relation to the facts of the case which alternative would be the best. There is little question that for many of the cases written in the early days, this approach was the more logical, and it had the most adherents.

For me it had one drawback. By my approach I had difficulty in a class hour in getting to a discussion of what needed to be done. By their approach they had difficulty in getting to a discussion of how their logical solution of the problem in the case was going to be implemented. The human factor was obviously highlighted in the implementation of the solution, and this is why I was interested in the question.

I mention these differences now because in time they were to become the source of acrimonious debates about the case method among members of the Faculty. Most of these debates contributed more emotional heat than intellectual light, because the differences in our ways of teaching arose also in part from our different ways of thinking about our subject matter—that is, what we thought we were teaching as well as whom we thought we were teaching and what we expected the learner to learn. It seemed to me that if we could not relate what we were teaching with whom we were teaching and with how we were teaching, we were in bad shape.

The next two chapters will be concerned with my attempt to resolve these problems for myself. Chapter 10 will be concerned with what I thought I was teaching and Chapter 11 with who I thought the learner was and also with what I expected him to learn. This last question seemed important to me, because I did not think that what I should expect a student to learn—whatever his role as a practitioner in a business organization was to be—should coincide with what I needed to know as a teacher. In both chapters I will try to show how my answers to the questions were related to my method of teaching.

Chapter 10

Toward a Descriptive Theory of Behavior in Organizations

In this chapter I want to consider the first of the questions I raised at the end of Chapter 9. That is, what did I think I was teaching? What would constitute a better description of the behavior of persons in organizations—a description that would help students to investigate, diagnose, and understand better the concrete behavior that takes place in organizations?

I thought that such a description required in the first place an elementary classification of the kinds of relations which formed among persons in organizations. Among the kinds I distinguished were spatial, temporal, social, technical, status, superior-subordinate (hierarchical), purposive, rewarding, management-worker, and formal and informal relations. I will talk about each in turn.

SPATIAL, TEMPORAL, AND SOCIAL RELATIONS

It seems to me that among these relations, the greatest contrast occurs between spatial and temporal relations on the one hand and social relations on the other. Spatial and temporal relations occur among things as well as people, but social relations occur only among people. Although social relations exist in space and time, they cannot be reduced to these dimensions alone. A's job, for example, may be "to the left" or "right" of B's; or it may come "before" or "after" B's; but until A and B interact, these are spatial and temporal arrangements and nothing more. Once they interact, however, a social relationship is born. This relationship bears a contingent relation to their proximity to each other (i.e., the proximity provides them with an opportunity to interact) but cannot be reduced to it.

Social relations have—or lack—other properties that make them different from spatial and temporal relations. For example, if A is to the left of B, and B is to the left of C, then A is to the left of C, regardless of whether A, B, and C are peanuts, potatoes, monkey wrenches, or persons. Stated in the terms of logic, the relation "to the left of" is irreflexive (i.e., A cannot be to the left of itself); asymmetrical (i.e., if A is to the left of B, then B cannot be to the left of A); and transitive (i.e., if A is to the left of B, and B is to the left of C, then A is to the left of C), regardless of what entities are ordered in terms of the relation "to the left of." These properties of being irreflexive, asymmetrical, and transitive hold for the relation "greater than" in the set of finite integers. No integer is greater than itself. For any two integers u and v, if u is greater than v, then v is not greater than u; and for any three integers u, v, and w, if u is greater than v, and v is greater than w, it follows that u is greater than w. This order is also complete. For any two distinct integers, one has to be greater than the other.

But let us consider the relation "love." Here the entities that are being related and their properties make a difference. A may or may not love himself. If A loves B, B may or may not love A. If A loves B, and B loves C, A may either love or not love C. Such a relation in a particular situation may be symmetrical. When it is, this outcome is a matter of fact and not a matter of logic; that is, it cannot be derived from the logical properties of the relationship itself. Some persons may feel that "If A loves B, then B *should* love A," that is, they may feel that love should be symmetrical. Or to choose another example, some may feel that in football if Harvard beats Princeton and Princeton beats Yale, then Harvard should beat Yale; that is, the outcome should be transitive. Or some may feel that if under these conditions Yale beats Harvard, as has sometimes happened, then something incongruent is going on and hence something should be done about it, such as firing the Harvard coach. But no matter how strongly they may feel about the properties these relations should have, they cannot deduce what they are in fact from what they think they should be. Love may not be reciprocated and a tournament may end up in an intransitive outcome.

By social relations, therefore, I mean *matters of fact* and not *relations of ideas*. Social relations are not like the logical relations which exist among the conceptual entities of a conceptual system; they are not like the relations of similarity or difference from which a logical class or set of entities may be constructed, such as all the red-headed women in Boston. They are not the spatial and temporal relations in terms of which both things and persons can be ordered. They are relations of interconnectedness which exist among persons here and now at a particular time and place. They result from the interactions persons have with one another.

Although I do not think that these social relations often have the kinds of properties which allow the persons being related to be ordered in the way logicians or mathematicians would like, neither do I think they are random relations. They are ordered, but they are ordered *socially*.

One of the important ways in which they are ordered is in terms of how persons are expected to behave toward each other under particular circumstances. These expected ways of behavior may run the gamut from more implicit relations such as customs, routines, codes, norms, and roles to more explicitly stated relations such as rules, regulations, standards, policies, laws, and commandments. I do not equate these expected or required ways of behavior with the actual behavior of particular people in a particular organization; they are not phenomena. It is how these expected ways of behavior are in fact conformed to or deviated from by different concrete persons in concrete groups under concrete conditions here and now that bring them for me into the realm of fact and observation.

THE TECHNICAL ORGANIZATION

An industrial organization can be conceived as a coordinated system of activities or jobs. The activities or jobs come into being through the division of labor and specialization of function. They are ordered by what can be thought of as two sets of relationships: (1) the flow of work, that is, how the jobs are related to each other as materials and parts flow through the plant from their raw to their finished states (the horizontal or lateral system); and (2) the supervisory hierarchy, that is, how the jobs are arranged in terms of supervisor-supervisee relations (the vertical system). According to "good" organizational principles, every job should have a clear place in both systems.

For me the horizontal or lateral system is a part of technological space. Its dominant relations are spatial, temporal, and sequential. These relations enjoy the properties of transitivity, so that the activities of people can be ordered logically. For example, it seems obvious to me that parts have to be bought or manufactured before they can be assembled, that a part or product has to be produced before it can be inspected and shipped, and so on.

Relations of this sort are present in working groups all over the world. Even in the Trobriand Islands in New Guinea the natives have to cut down the trees before they can build their canoes. In respect to such sequential relations no power structure and no magician can decree otherwise, it seems to me. I was an engineer to begin with, remember.

These sequential relations by which the products and the activities of people are logically ordered, I called the technical organization or system. It is that part of the organization which can be committed most easily to mechanical rationality and order and productive efficiency. Much of what was called scientific management at the time of which I am writing was concerned with the improvement of these relations; that is, for example, in trying to shorten the time interval between T_1, when raw materials entered the plant, and T_2, when finished products left it.

This technical system can be conceived apart from the interactions of persons, but sometimes the interactions between persons cannot be conveniently disregarded. As will be remembered, sometimes efficiency engineers, in order to reduce the time interval between T_1 and T_2, would keep the toilets hot in summer and cold in winter so that employees would not congregate there. Obviously if a worker spent more time on the job working and less time in the toilets on a non-job-related activity, the interval between T_1 and T_2 in theory should decrease and costs should go down instead of up. I did not argue this point; I learned my lesson well at M. I. T.! This was to me as plain as the nose on my face. I did not feel it required explanation, but there was another question that did bother me.

I could not see why in terms of technology any one job was more important or essential than another. In terms of technological rationality, it seemed to me the janitor's job was as essential as the president's in realizing the organization's purpose. If the janitor did not empty the wastebaskets into which much of the company's paper work usually went, there finally would be no room left for handling the other products the company produced. In fact from the point of view of technological space and mechanical rationality, the essentiality of the janitor's job was clearer to me then than the president's. Reduced to these dimensions alone, it seemed to me the president would have difficulty in making a case for what he was up to. I could see how the Hairy Ape, the stoker of a ship in Eugene O'Neill's play of the same name, felt when he said, "Not the Captain, but I run the ship."

If, in short, an organization was like a machine, such as an automobile, then it seemed to me absurd to argue about which part—the wheels, the chassis, the tires, or the motor—was more important than another. If any of them was deficient, the automobile became a piece of junk. If machine-like order and rationality were characteristic of an organization, to me it followed that the janitor's job was as important as the president's. In these terms alone one part could not be differentiated from another as being more or less essential or important.

This inference from the concept of machine rationality clearly did not coincide with the facts of organizational life which I was observing. In terms of these, the president's job was considered more important than the janitor's and hence was more highly rewarded. My conclusion at the time was that this concept of machine rationality could not be a scientific theory from which inferences could be drawn that could be tested against the facts. If so, it would have been refuted long ago. But equally so, it was not an inference from everyday observation. So what was it, if it was neither a theory nor an inference from observation? I concluded that it was not what something was like but what something would be like if interactions between persons could be disregarded. To this abstraction I thought the logics of efficient operation were addressed.

In short, at the time of which I am writing, I came to treat the technical system and its logic of efficiency as an abstracted system—a set of entities among which a set of sequential relations could be specified. It was not a concrete natural system. The entities had not ordered themselves this way. They had been ordered this way in order to attain the purposes of the organization. Years later, as I shall describe in Chapter 24, Herbert Simon called the study of this system the sciences of the artificial. As I have said, I treated this system with a great deal of respect. It made a lot of sense to me then, as it does now. But I did not treat it as a complete description of any system I was observing.

It seemed to me at the time that if a descriptive theory of organizations was to be achieved, a conceptual scheme which viewed an organization as a social system was needed. If an organization was conceived as a social system—that is, as a set of entities called persons among whom a heterogeneous set of relations could be observed—the relationships of efficient operations could not be ignored. They would be an important element of the organization in relation to other equally important elements in a state of some kind of equilibrium. On the other hand, if an organization was conceived as a technical system, the facts of social interaction had to be either ignored or subordinated. In the first case when an organization was conceived as a social system, the technical relations were not subordinated to the social relations; the problem was to find how the two were related (or could be better related) to each other. In the second case, when an organization was conceived as a technical system, the social relations had to be subordinated to the mechanistic rationality of the technical system; this was all there was, there wasn't anything else.

However, it was not the horizontal flow of work relations in an organization that I had difficulty in conceptualizing at this time; it was the vertical relations in them which gave me trouble. These vertical relations pertained only to relations between persons and their activities and not to relations between things. In this respect they were unlike relations in technological space.

I put two subsets of relations in this class of vertical social relations: status relations and superior-subordinate relations. Both were heavily charged with sentiments in terms of which persons and their jobs were ordered. To some extent both these sets of relations had the properties of irreflexiveness, asymmetry, and transitivity from which quasi-orderings (i.e., not complete orderings) could be derived. Let me discuss these points.

STATUS RELATIONS

Status relations are the evaluations made by persons in an organization of their activities in terms of *better* or *worse*. They often result in a rank ordering such that if job A is better than job B and if job B is better than job C, then job A is better than job C. But unlike the relation of "greater than" in the set of finite integers, there may be two jobs with the same status. For of any two jobs, one is not always better (or worse) than the other; that is, the ordering is not complete. Moreover, the relation "better than" is sometimes ambiguous; there is not always a consensus about the criteria for the relation "better than." These evaluations depend upon certain, often unconscious, common assumptions of the American society which the members of a group share. They vary somewhat, depending upon the position (class) in the American society to which the person belongs.

Thus, status relations are for me evaluations which do not follow from the operational rules of technology or even from the social rules of what behavior should be under certain circumstances. They are not, for example, like a rule of behavior which says, "In our group we eat peas with a fork and not a knife, and if you want to belong to our group, you better do likewise." It says something more; it says in effect, "We who eat peas with our fork are better than you who eat peas with your knife."

These evaluations of persons in a particular group based upon certain common assumptions of the wider society about the superiority (or inferiority) of the activities of its members have another peculiar property that I thought made this class of relations worthy of separate attention. For example, the rankings which can be made of a person's activities or characteristics in terms of the values of the wider society do not often add up in the industrial setting to a nice clean, well-established ranking by which it may be said in a particular case that this person is high (or low) on all counts. For instance, he might work on a job which is *low* in pay but *high* in cleanliness or *low* in autonomy and *high* in variety. He might be a long-service old man who is getting the same pay as a short-service young woman; or his job status might be higher (or lower) than his social status; or he might have a higher (or lower) status in the community than in the company; or he might be a highly respected member of his work group and have high status in one sense, but be doing a dirty job and have low status in another.

Probably no set of social relations attracted my attention more than these status-incongruent relations in my early interviews of employees and executives at the Western Electric Company, General Motors, and Macy's. They seemed to exist at all levels in those organizations. I began to associate a certain kind of trouble whenever these status relations were out of line. In *Management and the Worker* I tried to conceptualize this problem in a chapter on "Complaints and Social Equilibrium." I returned to the problem later in a joint research with George C. Homans, who I felt had done a better job than I of conceptualizing it (see Chapter 14).

For me then and for many years thereafter, this kind of "ouch" was only a syndrome (and not anything more conceptually elegant) which went like this: Status-out-of line $\longrightarrow$ expect a certain kind of trouble, manifested by such sentiments as "It ain't fair, right, just," etc.

In the few labor cases I arbitrated during World War II, it seemed to me that this condition was at the root of the trouble. It also seemed to me to be an important factor in many of the labor troubles that resulted in work stoppages.

SUPERIOR-SUBORDINATE RELATIONS

Whereas status-out-of-line relations evoke the responses of "It ain't fair or just or right," disturbances in superior-subordinate relations more often take the form on the part of the subordinate of "He treats me like a child or a schoolboy"; "He keeps breathing down the back of my neck"; or "He treats me like a machine, and goddamn it, I'm not going to take it anymore; I'm a human being and a member of the human race." On the part of the supervisor, the complaint often takes the form of "How do I get these lazy, irresponsible, good-for-nothing bastards to do what they are supposed to do?"

The production of such "ouches" is not the purpose or function of these superior-subordinate relations; they have another rationale. In them exist not only conflict but also those mysterious things called authority, control, and responsibility. Information goes up and down these relations. Orders go down and grievances go up them. Through them people are influenced and persuaded to do what they are supposed to be doing and are rewarded or punished for doing or not doing so. Powerful sentiments are associated with them. Depending upon which aspect one is considering, these relations may be called the line organization, the chain of command, the supervisory hierarchy, the communication system, the control system, the authority structure, the power structure, the formal organization, the formal status system, the establishment, the s.o.b.'s, and so on and on.

As in the case of status relations, superior-subordinate relations have to a certain extent the properties of irreflexiveness, asymmetry, and transitivity. A cannot be the boss of himself (not in organizational space anyway). If A is the boss of B, B is not the boss of A; and if A is the boss of B, and B is the boss of C, then A is the boss of C (so long as A behaves himself properly and does not undermine B by giving orders to C directly). In such a hierarchical structure composed of just A, B, and C, A is supposed to be the transmitter, B the carrier, and C the receiver of orders. A, however, can give orders to both B and C; B can give orders to C; but C cannot give orders to either A or B. In short, A has no superiors, C has no subordinates, and B has one of each.

As in the case of status relations, this hierarchical order is not complete. Of any two persons, for example, one is not always the boss of the other: D and E may be at the same boss level, so that neither one may give orders to the other.

For most organizations, then, these hierarchical arrangements have imperfections in their ordering, at least when compared with the beautiful complete ordering in the set of finite integers, in which between any two integers one is always greater than the other. At the same time, these arrangements tend to end up in (1) someone at the very top who has no superiors from whom he receives orders and who is the origin of all interactions; and (2) someone at the very bottom who has no subordinates to whom he can give orders and who is the terminus of all interactions and just does what he is told.

This hierarchical set of relations establishes a clear and explicit line of communication through which orders flow from the top to the bottom of the organization. Authority and responsibility also are supposed to flow in this direction. According to "good" management theory, each supervisor is supposed to give a certain amount of his authority and responsibility to his subordinates; that is, just the proper amount they need in order to get things done at their level of operation. This process of divestment goes on until the bottom or worker level in the organization is reached. At this point the process comes to a grinding halt, because the workers do not need formal authority and responsibility to get things done; they only have to do what they are told. Whatever authority and responsibility they need to improve cooperative effort, they have to assume for themselves; they are not given any from the top for such purposes.

A rational organization requires not only clear lines of authority and responsibility but also standard operating routines and standards of performance. According to the authorities at the time, each subunit of an organization should have had a subgoal that was clearly related to the total over-all goals or purposes of the organization. For each subunit there should have been specified practices by which these subunit goals were to be achieved as well as standards of performance by which their achievement could be evaluated. This setting of standards was management's major system of control; it permitted the performance of people to be evaluated in terms of specified standards of performance. In a rational sense it was required if the purposes of the organization were to be attained. Underlying it was a logic which went something like this. The more each person in an organization knows what is expected of him, the more he will do what he is told. The more he does what he is told and what is expected of him, the more reliable his behavior will become, the more rational it will be, and the better will the goals of the organization be realized.

Many managers believed that the achievement of such rational cooperation was their primary job. When I talked to managers about their jobs in order to learn what they were doing, this logic often would pop up, and the managers would make inferences from it that sounded to me very much like "all other things being equal, a straight line is the shortest distance between two points." I did not refute this logic. It made a lot of sense to me. But just as in the case of the technological relations I talked about earlier, I did not treat this logic as a complete description of the social system I was observing, but only as one very important component of it. I called both the rational social relations that this logic prescribed and also the technological relations required to achieve an organization's purposes parts of its "formal organization."

ORGANIZATIONAL PURPOSE

For me the formal organization was the system of coordinated activities required for the achievement of the organization's purpose. It involved what had to be done—the activities and interactions that were required—if the organization was to survive in and cope with its environment. These requirements were to me impersonal in character and not to be confused with the individual needs and goals of persons. The two were very rarely, if ever, the same. The production, marketing, financial, and corporate goals of the Western Electric Company, for example, were not any more the personal goals of the individual executives than they were those of the workers, although the executives might be more identified with them or more willing to contribute their services to them or have more to do with their formulation or articulation than the workers. For me the making of telephones and telephone equipment was not the goal of any individual in the Western Electric Company; it was the goal of the organization to which each of them was willing to contribute his services in order to satisfy his individual needs for food, clothing, shelter, safety, membership, recognition, status, power, self-esteem, individual development, and so on.

Once a purposive system was organized, it seemed to me, certain essential tasks had to be performed, if the purpose of the cooperation was to be achieved. These tasks were for me in the realm of objective facts about which, as I said before, no magician could dictate otherwise. The magician might dictate the incantations that had to be performed in connection with these essential activities, and different incantations might be recommended by different magicians; but what remained to be done, if the purpose of the organization was to be achieved, I thought of as logical means-ends relations.

For example, after the Greeks had made their sacrifices to Poseidon in order to assure the safety of their sea voyage to some destination, out would come the oars for the boat and also some rowers in order to help get them there safely. Objectively, the boat with its oars and its rowers were needed to get to the destination. The sacrifices to Poseidon were helpful in a different way.

This was the manner in which I viewed the means-ends relations of formal organizations. Some of them I put very definitely in the realm of the logical. But some of them were more logical than others and some had overtones which partook of the nonlogical. Let me explain by continuing with my example about Poseidon.

Poseidon for me was an important guy in relation to the successful accomplishment of the voyage. His function was different from that of the oars and the boat and I thought the two should not be confused. After making their sacrifices to him, the Greek rowers were more confident. They gripped their oars more firmly; they rowed more steadily; and when a big wave, howling gale, or drenching rain appeared, they met it with confidence instead of with terror, because Poseidon was right there behind them saying, "All's well in this world." All these factors worked in the direction of a successful voyage, getting safely to a destination.

The function of giving the rowers confidence, I insisted, was different from the function of the oars. Although Pareto, Henderson, and I called the sacrifices to Poseidon nonlogical and the oars for the boat logical, we did not mean that the sacrifices to Poseidon were functionless. We just meant that in the case of the oars for the boat there were some observable means-ends relations between them and getting to the destination, regardless of the sentiments of the rowers, whereas in the case of the sacrifices to Poseidon and getting safely to where they were going, the sentiments and feelings of the rowers were of the essence.

For me a successful sea voyage required both oars and Poseidon. They each had an important but different function to perform. In this way I interpreted many of the logics of management. Some of them partook of the logical; but some of them were the magical incantations that had to be made to the great god Efficiency in order to ensure that the products reached their destination, not only safely, but also with the least amount of time and cost. This god, unlike tired old Poseidon, was never asleep at the switch. To ensure a safe voyage he not only asked for the sacrifice of a few rams; instead, after reaching a destination safely, he said:

It took you five hours to get there; what about trying to do it in four-and-a-half hours? If you did, we might be able to make more trips in a day. Are you using the best kind of oars, the best kind of rowing methods, and the best kind of rowers? Have you told the rowers what you expect of them, how many strokes per minute is standard operating procedure? Have you selected out the rowers with the best physiological endowments for this job? Have you told our customers that not only can you get them to their destinations safely but also more quickly? I (the owner) have a heavy capital investment in this boat. I want a better return on my investment, or I'll invest my money in a citrus grove instead of this dilapidated old boat. And what about those fuddy-duddy suppliers from whom we get our boats and oars? Perhaps we should manufacture our own oars instead of buying them. Have you figured out whether buying or making them would be cheaper? Have you given a bonus to the rowers for getting there more quickly? What price are you charging the passengers for the trip? How did you determine this price? Have you criers in the market place advertising our trip, telling the hoi polloi that we have cushions on our benches, that slave girls with bare bosoms sell citrus fruits during the voyage? Get going! Time is money. And by the way—have you ever thought of getting something better than these silly old oars to propel the boat? We need some R&D around here!

So it seemed to me the great god Efficiency incessantly flogged his subects. Unlike Poseidon, he could never be appeased. Each day he demanded more sacrifices. "What a jungle," he would cry, "but how productive!" This great god was also different from Poseidon in another respect. Whereas Poseidon gave courage and confidence to the owner, captain, and rowers of the boat, not because he was democratic but because he felt they were all needed for the success of the voyage, the great god Efficiency struck terror in the rowers' hearts. "Hey," they said, in Greek, of course, "What's going on here? The more we sacrifice, the less we get. This ain't fair. As we perceive it, it's going counter to the rule of distributive justice, which says the more you sacrifice, the higher your rewards should be. What kind of a god are you anyway? Tell us, O god, whose side are you on?"

No more devastating question can be asked of any god or magician. If he cannot give comfort to both the virtuous and the sinner, the efficient and the inefficient, the high born and the low born, the managers and the managed, he had better close up shop; he is not in the right business.

Thus by a curious backing-into process, I discovered not only what Max Weber called bureaucracy but also what social anthropologists called culture. I did this not by going to the South Pacific, but by staying right in my own backyard at the Business School, listening to my colleagues and students speak about matters that were important to them: the absolute logics of our society, as Lloyd Warner called them, or those things you cannot have enough of, as George Homans called them, such as progress, for example.

REWARDING RELATIONS (SATISFACTION)

So far I have looked at the vertical relations in organizations from the point of view of the logical and nonlogical means-ends relations which resided in them and through which an organization's purposes were realized. Now I want to look at them from the point of view of the rewarding relations that existed in them and which resulted in states of satisfaction (or dissatisfaction) with the activities or jobs which persons performed while in them.

These states of satisfaction were for me properties of persons and not of organizations. They were an order of things different from the operating rules of technology or the logical means-ends relations of purposive space, although they were related to them. In organizational life, satisfactions were for me at the opposite pole from organizational purpose. They involved those matters which man found rewarding.

What an organization *needed* in order to realize its purposes, I felt, was something entirely different from what a person *needed* in order to be satisfied. As the needs of organizations were different from the needs of persons, I thought that different words should be used to refer to them, so that the one would not be confused with the other. I called the first, organizational requirements and the latter, individual needs. The individual needs were the properties of persons, whereas what was required or expected of persons by an organization was a property of the organization. In the way I used these words, an organization was not satisfied and an individual had no purposes.

Anyway, all those things a person wanted, desired, preferred, hoped for, aspired to, and valued, I put in a bag of things I called individual needs, and I did not try to classify them. Up to 1948 and for some time thereafter, they remained for me man's "itches" and I tried not to make value judgments about them. I did not say that one itch was better than another. I treated them as givens, because I was not trying to explain why the itches of man differed from those of pigeons, or why one man's itches differed from those of another, except in terms of his personal history. I was more interested in the relation of man's "itches" here and now to his "ouches" here and now. His "ouches" (complaints and grievances) I could listen to, but his "itches" I could only infer by assuming that his ouches were the manifestation of unsatisfied itches. I assumed that given *these* itches and given *these* opportunities—or the lack of them—in the environment to satisfy them, there would or would not be an ouch.

I phrased this conception of satisfactions in different ways: (1) as the relation between those things a person wanted and the opportunities that the environment offered for their realization; and (2) as a fraction in which the numerator was the objects in the environment which a person found rewarding and the denominator was all the objects he desired, irrespective of whether they were available. Viewed in this way satisfactions could be increased in three ways: (a) by increasing the numerator, that is, by increasing the number of obects in the environment that satisfied his desires, such as by getting two automobiles in his garage or two chickens in his pot; (b) by decreasing the denominator, that is, by reducing his desires, so that he asked and demanded less of his environment, to the point, theoretically, where his desires approached zero and satisfactions became nearly but not quite infinite, and Nirvana—or the "ouchless" state—was achieved; or (c) by doing a little of both and achieving some practical, if not ideal, satisfactory state of equilibrium between his desires and their realization in this actual but perhaps not best of all possible worlds.

No matter which way I conceived it, there remained a distinction between (1) what man as man found rewarding (a value for him) and (2) the rewards which were available for him in his environment and which he actually received. The resultant outcome determined his satisfaction.

There was another distinction which bothered me still more. This was the distinction between what man wanted and what he ought to want. In my interviews, dating back to the days when I counseled students, it seemed that many of them could not make this distinction easily. They more often told me what they thought they ought to want instead of what they wanted; in fact, they treated the two as if they were the same. They could not distinguish between what was expected of them and what they wanted. How often in dealing with a person suffering from indecision I would ask the innocuous question "What do you want to do?" only to find that this was far from being a simple question for him to answer! Indeed it is a difficult question to answer! After all, should not one want to do what his father, mother, brothers, sisters, teachers, sweetheart, husband, wife, children expected him to do? What else is there?

From these sorts of observations I inferred that the search for what man wants was a difficult achievement; it was not something he could treat as given and known, let us say, by him at birth. It was only by working through the itch-ouch balance that he could find out. And this might take a bit of doing and time.

I could see how a satisfied itch no longer was an ouch and ceased to motivate more scratching of it. I could see how by being born in a particular family and society, man was conditioned to have the itches which society could satisfy, so that he came to want those things which he ought to want, because those itches could be more easily rewarded than itches for things he ought not to want. All this seemed to me extraordinarily functional. I assumed that this was one of the functions of education, namely, to condition the young for the itches which, as they grew older, the social environment was capable of satisfying.

Also I could see that there was a cost attached to the satisfactory scratching of an itch. Because there was a plurality of itches and often a conflict among them, man had to settle which itch he wanted to satisfy the most. This meant that the satisfactory scratching of one itch left others unsatisfied; this was a cost that had to be paid.

Although all these problems bothered me, I felt that if I pursued them further I would get back to metaphysics, from which it will be remembered, I was trying to escape. I finally decided to tuck these questions in the back of my mind and bring them out for renovation if and when I needed to. For the time being, I would just try to understand the satisfactions of man-in-organization by the following set of relationships:

Man-in-Organization

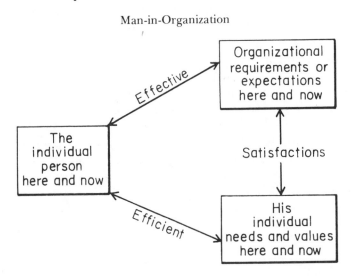

In this diagram I am using the words effective and efficient in Chester Barnard's sense. The reader needs to keep this clearly in mind. Particularly in the way Barnard defined efficient (1938, p. 92), he went against conventional usage and meant something different from what I meant, for example, when I used the word in speaking about Poseidon earlier in this chapter. When I use it in later chapters, I will specify the sense in which I mean it.

In Barnard's sense (1) if a person does well what is expected of him by the organization, he is effective; and (2) if what he does also satisfies his needs, he is efficient; so that (3) if he satisfies his needs by doing what is expected of him, he is in clover, i.e., satisfied. Obviously in these terms a person can be effective without being efficient; that is, he can do what is expected of him but not get any great boot from doing so—that is, not find it very rewarding, in which case he may either quit his job or keep it and do the minimum expected of him. Also, a person can be efficient without being effective; that is, he may get a great boot out of what he is doing, but still not meet the minimum standards of what is expected of him, in which case in the long run he may lose his job.

The social sciences are riddled with the problems that result from giving old words new meanings and from inventing new words in order to avoid the tricks that old words play on us when they are used in those ways. Barnard's use of effective and efficient is an example of the first of these practices, and Pareto's use of residues and derivations is an example of the second. I am not taking sides on these approaches; each has its advantages and disadvantages. But I am calling the reader's attention to the problem, because it is an important aspect of what makes the phenomena of behavior in organizations elusive. As I will be telling, I encountered the problem many times and in many ways; I will have to deal with it again, especially in my closing chapters.

In any case, effective and efficient are two quite different kinds of evaluations of a person's performance. Being effective is an evaluation from an external point of view, that is, from the point of view of the organization, whereas being efficient is an evaluation from an internal point of view, that is, from the point of view of the individual himself. And believe me, I think it is very important that these two different evaluations not be confused. As I looked at management-worker relations, it seemed to me that, more often than not, they were.

MANAGEMENT-WORKER RELATIONS

As will be remembered, most of my early researches were concerned with the productivity and satisfaction of workers, the people at the bottom of hierarchical relations. It was their ouches more than management's ouches that I had been trying to understand. As I pursued my researches further, I realized that I could not understand the workers' ouches apart from management's. They were inextricably intertwined. In fact it might be said that it was the same ouch as felt from two different frames of reference. Management's ouch was how could they make apathetic workers more willing to contribute their services to the organization's purpose—that is, to do more than the minimum of what was expected of them and became more effective. The workers' ouch was why should they become more effective, when this would not increase the intrinsic satisfaction they got from their jobs; they would still be paid for just doing what they were told. Moreover, if they increased their output, this might get them into trouble with their fellow workers.

The situation was complicated by many different notions about what the motivation of workers was or should be, about how and how much they should be paid for their labor, and about the rewards, other than pay, that were available in their work environment. In terms of my previous diagram and the concepts of effective and efficient, the situation in many of the plants I studied at the time looked peculiar.

Following Chester Barnard, I assumed that in the long run organizations had to be both effective and efficient. They had to realize their organizational purposes and also they had to have people willing to cooperate and contribute their efforts toward the realization of these purposes. At the workers' level this meant that the workers had to obtain satisfaction from the cooperative efforts. At the managers' level this meant that they wanted workers who were both effective and efficient. In terms of a Venn diagram, for example, management wanted the situation to look like this:

Effective Efficient

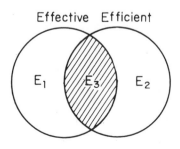

where ideally all workers should be E_3's and there would be no E_1's or E_2's.

This meant that the workers had to get satisfactions from doing what was expected of them, that is, from doing those things which constituted the conditions of effective operation. However, if the conditions for effective operation were not the same as the conditions for the workers' satisfaction, it could happen that what was effective from the point of view of management was not satisfying from the point of view of workers. Under such conditions, it could happen that the situation would deteriorate into something like this:

Effective Efficient

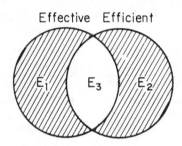

where the majority of workers did just what they were told, but got no satisfaction from doing it (E_1); where some slap-happy workers who were not effective were getting satisfaction, not from their jobs, but from throwing monkey wrenches into the machinery or enjoying the social conditions the work situation provided (E_2); and where few, if any, workers were both effective and efficient (E_3).

As this state of affairs could not continue in the long run in the majority of plants I studied, the situation was something like this:

Effective Efficient

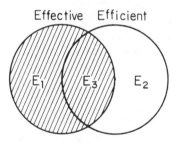

where most of the workers did the minimum that was expected of them, but with no great enthusiasm (E_1); where some workers felt rewarded by doing the minimum (E_3); and where hardly any slap-happy workers did not meet the required standards of performance before they got fired (E_2).

In some companies the workers did not find this state of affairs satisfying, so they joined a union in order to get more wages to compensate for the lack of intrinsic rewards they received from their jobs and also to improve their working conditions and have a little more to say about E_1. Under these conditions, in theory, the resulting outcome should have been an increase in the number of workers who were both effective and efficient, as shown in the first of my diagrams. But although in theory both management and the union now had the same objectives, in some companies it did not work out this way for a number of reasons.

Probably the most persistent reason was that E_1 was considered to be the exclusive prerogative of management. If the union interfered with it, the resulting state of affairs, according to management, would be disastrous. They argued that if you gave the workers an inch with respect to E_1, they would take a mile; and then, before you could say "Jack Robinson," you would have a situation like this:

Effective Efficient

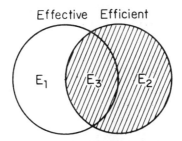

where there were only a few happy workers doing what was expected of them (E_3); a lot of slap-happy ones not doing what was expected of them but instead throwing monkey wrenches in the machinery (E_2); and no docile workers doing just the minimum of what was expected of them (E_1).

In short, at this time most managements could not envisage the more realistic possibility of this:

Effective Efficient

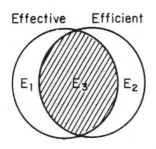

where most of the workers were getting a boot from doing their work (E_3); a few happy workers were doing less than the minimum expected of them (E_2); and only a few unhappy workers were doing what was expected of them (E_1).

In some companies the logics of the situation got still more balled up. Under the assumption that management was to be concerned only with E_1 and the union only with E_2, no one was responsible for E_3. Only the collective bargaining machinery (note the impersonal language of technology) could handle this integration. By the rules of this machinery it now became difficult for management to try to make the workers more satisfied without being accused of trying to break up the union. Likewise, the union in turn could not make the workers satisfied about their working conditions without interfering with the prerogatives of management. The bone of contention was often E_1, i.e., management's standards of work performance; this was often not talked about explicitly but in terms of wages.

Moreover, by now the union had found a way to deal with part of E_1 in a manner which was strictly in accord with its logics but to a degree that management in its most imaginative moments had never suspected was possible. In effect the union said to management, "We will do what you require us to do, but we do not think you have spelled out what we should do in sufficient detail. Tell us specifically what tools are required for our job, so that when a situation arises that requires a monkey wrench which you have not specified as required for the job, we can tell you, politely, of course, to go to hell and get the plumbers to do it." In this way in some companies, the union took over E_1 and had management making out job descriptions like crazy. Monkey wrenches were lying all over the place, but in some companies only plumbers could pick them up. Sometimes the situation got so bad that it looked like this:

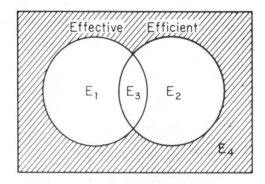

where no one was effective (E_1) or efficient (E_2) or both (E_3), and there was a strike (E_4).

INFORMAL RELATIONS

While I was trying to conceptualize the organization's vertical system in relation to attaining both the organization's purposes and the cooperation of workers, I realized I was ignoring a class of relations without which I could not make sense concerning what I was observing. In terms of those formal relations alone, the ones which Max Weber called bureaucratic and I call "formal," I could often hardly distinguish one business organization from another. From this point of view they all looked alike to me. In every company I studied I found some fairly explicit hierarchy of authority; some rules governing work activity; some standards of performance; some commitment to mechanical rationality, order, and productive efficiency; and some logics by means of which they were rationalized.

Yet in many smaller organizations I was impressed with how many of the rules remained implicit, not only the operating rules and standards of performance, but also the rules of communication, that is, to whom one was supposed to go for help. The managers of these companies seemed to get things done without having any very explicit operating rules, communication rules, decision rules, or strategy rules. Not that the rules were not there; but the rules were implicit in and intrinsic to the behavior of persons, instead of the behavior's being an explicit and extrinsic outcome of the rules. They resided in what I call *skill* and *judgment* and had not yet been operationalized, routinized, or, as we would say today, programmed.

For example, a carpenter strikes a nail with his hammer in a syncretistic fashion without having worked out the rule which settles when he should stop hitting it and without knowing explicitly such binary steps as the following which guide his action: (1) Strike the nail with the hammer. (2) Then ask the question, "Is the nail flush with the board?" (3) If the answer is "no," then lift the hammer and strike again. (4) Then ask the question again, "Is the nail flush with the board?" (5) If "no" then lift the hammer and strike again, and (6) continue doing this until the answer to the question, "Is the nail flush with the board?" is "yes." (7) Then stop hammering. (And by the way—you dumb jerk—put the hammer back in the place where it belongs. Do not leave it lying on the floor, because the electrician is not going to pick it up.)

But what interested me in these companies was not only that carpenters seemed able to stop hammering nails without having stated explicit rules which said when to stop, and executives seemed able to make decisions without clear decision rules by which to reach them. In addition, persons in these organizations were bound together by a set of relations that had nothing to do with what they were supposed to be doing. These relations seemed to me important indeed, not only for attaining the purposes of the organization but also for obtaining the cooperation of the people for these purposes. In fact, without these relations I felt that each organization would go to pieces. Yet at the time all the standard textbooks about what made management management never mentioned them. This seemed to me extraordinary and something worth looking into.

I began looking for these relationships in all organizations, large and small; although they were somewhat camouflaged in the larger organizations, I found them there also. The relations of interconnectedness which I am talking about had to do with matters such as *liking, trusting,* and *helping.* These relations seemed to me to emerge in outcomes that were more often cyclical rather than acyclical, symmetrical rather than asymmetrical, and closed rather than unilateral, so that they did not enjoy the property of transitivity. They were unlike structures such as this:

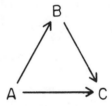

which, as in the case of status and superior-subordinate relations, had the properties of irreflexiveness, asymmetry, and transitivity from which quasi-orderings could be generated.

Instead these relations of liking, trusting, and helping resulted in social structures, such as for example, A ⇄ B, to which such empirical meanings as the following could be given: (1) A and B like, trust, and help each other; (2) if you scratch my back, I will scratch yours; (3) one good turn deserves another; or (4) even though you are a plumber and I am a carpenter and even though it is not part of my job, I will pick up the monkey wrench you left lying on the floor because you are my friend.

Or these structures might result in something like this:

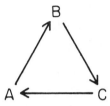

to which the following empirical meanings may be given: (1) We play cards with each other, but not necessarily all together; (2) we are all transmitters, receivers, and carriers of messages so that in our group everyone will get the message, no matter with whom it originates.

Or these structures might result in something like this:

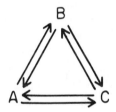

to which the following empirical meanings may be given: (1) We play games together; (2) eat lunch together; (3) take coffee breaks together; (4) like, trust, and help each other; and (5) share the same values, i.e., birds of a feather flock together.

These relations of interconnectedness among persons which resulted often (but not always) in structures that are nonhierarchical, I call the strong, close, and warm relationships. They make the cheese more binding. The hierarchical ones in contrast are weak, distant, and cold. I do not draw these conclusions from any logic, but from observing the behavior of the persons in the systems we studied.

It seemed to me that in most organizations the employees found these informal relationships rewarding. Whenever and wherever it was possible, they generated them like crazy. In many cases they found them so satisfying that they often did all sorts of nonlogical things (i.e., things that went counter to their economic interests) in order to belong to the small, warm, and cozy groups which these relations generated.

The two kinds of relations were in sharp contrast. Among members of hierarchical relations, there were few interactions, few close friendships, and seldom any small, warm, cozy groups. There was sometimes "respect," but quite often distrust, apprehension, and suspicion. Interaction was limited to what the task required. Helping was unilateral, not mutual. It flowed only in one direction, and sometimes the recipient found the help subordinating, not helpful.

It looked as if the logic of rational management generated weak, distant, and cold relations, whereas the employees as persons generated strong, close, and warm relations. The outcome, which was often conflict, was not because anyone was deliberately trying to throw a monkey wrench in the machinery. The logic of management could do only what it was supposed to do, its business, so to speak. It could only produce those relations in which rational order existed. To ask it to produce strong, close, warm, cozy, and comfortable relations would be like asking an icicle as an icicle to produce warmth for man. However, that man as man sought for these warm relations was also not being just ornery. He also was doing what his nature as man and the itch-ouch balance compelled him to do.

Thus, these two sets of forces could get locked into a struggle. But instead of a struggle for power, it seemed to me more like a struggle between cold relations in which some extrinsic rational order resided and warm relations in which some intrinsic nonlogical comfort resided. It was an unconscious battle between the logic of management and the sentiments of workers. I say unconscious because it was the unintended consequences of how the respective behaviors of managers and workers affected each other that caused the trouble in the first place. The imputation that these unintended consequences were intended followed and magnified the trouble in the second place. Each side *had* to impute bad intentions to the other. Each *had* to claim and show that its side was right and the other wrong.

The outcome was a jolly fight all right, but not quite like the kind of conflict that Karl Marx described. Although it reinforced the notion that management and workers had nothing in common, the conclusion followed because they were looking at each other's behavior in mutually exclusive ways and rationalizing their differences. Neither party was looking at the effect of his own behavior on the other. Each party was looking only at the effect of the other's behavior on him.

When I began conceiving of behavior in organizations in this way, I realized I could not make warm relations out of cold relations or vice versa, because I had created these classes of relations from differences in their properties. Hence, I could not have relations that were both warm and cold. But I could ask who were the persons in the system who were dealing with both cold and warm relations and trying to keep them in some state of equilibrium. This is how I came to look more closely at supervisors and managers and how I came to discover the man-in-the-middle syndrome.

This syndrome seemed to me *par excellence* the syndrome of management and paralleled closely the restriction-of-output syndrome that I had found at the workers' level. I wrote an article (1945) about this syndrome at the foreman level, which I called "The Foreman: Master and Victim of Double Talk," Chapter 3 in *Man-in-Organization*. At the time, I realized in an intuitive fashion that I had hold of something of much wider significance for the administrative process than just how this syndrome manifested itself at the foreman level. But I did not say so; I just felt so. I did not know then about the many different managerial and leadership styles that were to be discovered later to deal with this syndrome, nor about the battles that were going to be waged in respect to which one of them was best.

Chapter 11

The Administrator's Job

In the last chapter I tried to show how I walked into the subject matter of organization by what may seem a circuitous route. For me, though, the journey was perfectly straight. The route was dictated by a way of thinking that said, "Keep your eyes fixed on the phenomena and follow the ball wherever it bounces." I will continue this journey in this chapter, but with a slightly different question in mind.

In the last chapter I was concerned with the different kinds of relationships in which persons in purposive organizations found themselves and in terms of which their activities, interactions, and sentiments could be described. I found that from a systemic point of view both executives and workers were involved in the same kinds of mutually dependent relations and that the executives' problems as well as the workers' could be described by them. But was this point of view as useful to executives for taking action and getting things done as it was to students of organizations for the purposes of describing behavior? This question raised such others as who did I think my students were? Or better, for what role or roles in organizations did I think I was training them? And what did I think they should learn? These questions, which are the ones I shall consider in this chapter, were of special concern to me between the years 1938 and 1948, when my colleagues frequently told me that an executive could not just stand there and understand; he had to do something.

MANAGERS AND THE HUMAN FACTOR

Probably few topics are more riddled with oversimplifications and the fallacy of misplaced concreteness than so-called answers to the question of what a manager does or is supposed to do. According to the textbooks of the 1940s, the manager's job was to *plan, organize, staff, direct, coordinate, report,* and *budget* the activities of his subordinates. To me even then, this list did not get to the meat in the coconut; that is to say, these abstractions did not help me to observe an executive's behavior. I could not observe him directly doing any of these things. Moreover, when I would enter his office and say, for example, "Tell me, Mr. Manager, what amount of time do you spend each day in planning, organizing, supervising, coordinating, controlling, and so on, and how do you go about doing these things?" the conversation would dry up.

More often than not, he wanted to tell me about a persistently recurring problem he had which he could not completely eliminate. Stated in its most general form, this problem was that many people in his organization were not doing what they sould be doing, in spite of the policies and standards the manager and his colleagues had set up so that workers would do what they should. For example, the accounting people were not giving him the information that they were supposed to; the supervisors were not supervising in the way they should; the workers were not working as hard as they should (e.g., they were spending too much time in the toilets or on coffee breaks); the marketing people were not working well together with the production people; the R&D people did not understand costs and the wants of the consumer in the way that they should; and so on and on. I was fascinated by this; I could hardly believe my ears. It looked as if the organization was engaged in undoing all those things that the manager did, when he did what he was supposed to be doing, such as planning, organizing, staffing, directing, coordinating, reporting, and budgeting, or POSDCORB, for short.

Remembering my mathematics, I began to think in terms of reciprocal relations, i.e., those operations which undid what another operation had previously done, such as the operations of multiplication and division or of addition and subtraction. Could it be that the relation between the manager and the organization had this mathematical property of reciprocalness? Was the organization undoing what the manager had done in such a way that, as in the case of multiplication and division, the result was the identity number *one*; that is, the process of multiplying and dividing a number by another so that the first number was left unchanged? Or perhaps, as in addition and subtraction, was the identity number *zero*; that is, the number which when added to and subtracted from another number left the latter unchanged? In these terms could it be that the organization was constantly undoing what the manager had done, like this $n/1 \times 1/n \times n/1 \times 1/n \ldots$; or subtracting from what the manager had added, like this, $n - n + n - n \ldots$? The resulting "one-ness" in the first case and "zero-ness" in the second appalled me. I shuddered just at the thought that this might be an executive's contribution.

Yet I could not get this reciprocal notion out of my mind. It did seem at times as if there was some magic factor which was undoing what the manager was doing; that is, which was discombobulating his plans, programs, policies, control systems, incentive systems, communication systems, and so on and on. In the nonmathematical world in which executives lived, this factor which seemed to be undoing what they did or were supposed to be doing was not usually called a "reciprocal" but an "s.o.b."

From my point of view, the factor which seemed to bring an executive's contribution back to increased entropy (disorder) instead of toward negative entropy (or increased order), I called the "human factor." It was always present. This ubiquitous property caused me no end of trouble, for it made things look at times as if my subject matter became the whole wide world. I could not contain it within one of the traditional functions of business, such as finance, marketing, production, or personnel.

As I said in Chapter 8, when I started teaching about the human problems of administration, I viewed them from the point of view of the staff function of personnel. Persons in these positions were the ones who were supposed to be concerned with the "people" part of an organization. They were the ones, I was told, who selected people in terms of their aptitudes and attitudes, placed them in the jobs requiring such aptitudes and attitudes, and trained them to do what they were supposed to do. This seemed a good place to begin my teaching.

I did not stay long with these formal responsibilities of a personnel department, because the ubiquitous ball in which I was interested did not seem to bounce just there. Although personnel people were trying to fit square pegs into square holes or round pegs into round holes, they seemed to be suffering from the same troubles that the other functions of business were having. They also could not seem to get things done properly because, they said, their function did not report directly to the president of the company. Consequently they did not have the authority they needed to get things done as they should be. If only they did, the square pegs would stay in the square holes and the round pegs would stay in the round holes. This required, they explained to me, an authority they did not have.

During this period in the history of American business, the common diagnosis of why an executive could not get people to do what they were supposed to be doing was that his authority was not commensurate with his responsibilities. Many learned articles in the *Harvard Business Review* expressed this point of view, not only for personnel but also for other business functions such as purchasing, a function in which the executives seemed to be having the same troubles for the same reasons and for which the same remedies were proposed. The conventional wisdom of this period was that unless an executive's function reported directly to the president, he could not get people to do what they were supposed to.

Hence, I did not focus my attention exclusively on personnel people. If I had, though life might have been much easier for me, I felt I would have been once and sometimes even twice or more times removed from the phenomenological reality with which I was concerned. There would have been a clear organizational slot, both in business and at the School, such as personnel or labor or industrial relations, into which I could have been fitted. But the conceptual scheme I was following said live dangerously, even though my nervous system may still have been saying something rather different.

DIAGNOSIS AND ACTION: THE DASHMAN COMPANY CASE

Anyway, shortly after beginning to teach by the case method, I began to select cases in which not only personnel but also other departments were having difficulty in getting things done through people. I began to choose *any case involving any person in any business function in any position of responsibility and authority, no matter how low or high in the authority structure he stood, who was facing a problem of getting people to do what they were supposed to be doing.* At this period such cases were a dime a dozen; nobody was collecting them, because they did not fit uniquely into a course on production, finance, marketing, control, personnel, or labor relations.

Because I had no such restriction placed on me, I took any case that presented the problem I have described. Armed with the case, I entered the classroom. In discussions there, the students diagnosed first the total situation which might account for the behavior causing the problem, after which they discussed taking action to improve it. In this manner I hoped to penetrate the mysteries of getting things done through people.

At this time, as I have explained, taking action was an important ingredient of the case method of teaching at the Harvard Business School. It was what made the case method different from other methods of instruction. After the analysis or diagnosis of a case was made, the students, as budding executives, were supposed to take action; that is, to reach a decision about what to do and then, if they had time, say how they proposed to do it. This was the School's do-or-die version of the case method.

At one level of abstraction I agreed with it. We could not have students training to be executives just trying to understand problems without doing anything about them, could we now? Yet I thought that for practitioners, understanding preceded action, just as understanding preceded measurement for seekers of knowledge. Moreover, wasn't trying to understand something taking a certain kind of action? Indeed in most of the problems in which I became interested, it seemed to me understanding was an important first step. In the process, for example, a problem sometimes changed its character, although it did not usually disappear. It was not solved in a mathematical sense; it was resolved, even though its resolution might not be 100 percent complete. Understanding was just a first step along the way.

Hence, discussions in my classes in regard to proposals for what needed to be done often took a curious turn. Frequently they required the executive to assume a non-stereotypical posture. Instead of resulting in an executive's making a decision worthy of his stature, such as enunciating a new policy of how things should be done or firing someone for not doing so, the proposal for the next step to be taken often reduced itself simply to talking with someone who was not doing what he was supposed to be doing, trying to understand why he was not, and by this approach trying to gain his cooperation and understanding.

I can illustrate what happened with an introductory case which I frequently used in the course on Administrative Practices. It was a short case about a page and a half long, called The Dashman Company Case (the names are disguised; see Glover and Hower, 1949). The problem it presented went like this: A large industrial company during World War II was having difficulty in obtaining the essential raw materials for its twenty decentralized plants. A new person with considerable experience in purchasing, a Mr. Post, was brought in to coordinate the company's purchasing procedures. Mr. Post was made Vice President for Purchasing, a position which had not existed before. As Vice President he reported directly to the President, Mr. Manson. Mr. Manson gave him, so the case read, wide latitude in organizing his new job. Mr. Manson also gave Mr. Post an assistant, Mr. Larson, a man with long experience in the company.

One of the first steps Mr. Post took was to write a letter to each of the purchasing executives, saying that from now on any purchasing contracts they made over $10,000 should be cleared with the top office. He said that this would help him to coordinate their separate purchasing activities, and he asked them for their cooperation. Each of the twenty wrote back to say in effect that he would be pleased to cooperate.

But nothing happened; that is, no purchasing contracts above $10,000 appeared on Mr. Post's desk to be cleared. It looked as if the purchasing executives were not doing what Mr. Post had asked them to do; or as if they were no longer negotiating contracts over $10,000 because purchases of such amounts were no longer required—a most curious situation indeed; or as if they were in cahoots with their suppliers to buy amounts of less than $10,000, at a time, so that technically they would not need to clear their activities with Mr. Post. In this last instance it could be said that they were abiding by the letter but not the spirit of Mr. Post's instructions.

Each of these possibilities aroused uneasy feelings in the pit of Mr. Post's stomach. He asked Mr. Larson what he might do in order to obtain the more wholehearted cooperation of the purchasing executives. Here the case ended and the discussion began.

The discussion in my classes often started with an analysis of how Mr. Post had gotten himself into this fix. It was generally agreed that it happened because the letter had been sent by the wrong person to the wrong persons at the wrong time; that is, (1) the letter should have been signed by Mr. Manson, the President, not by Mr. Post, the Vice President for Purchasing; (2) it should have been sent to the general managers of the plants to whom the purchasing executives reported, not to the purchasing executives; (3) it should have been sent at a time when the purchasing executives were not especially busy, as they were at the time the letter was sent.

By ignoring these formal relations, it was said in class discussions, Mr. Post had inadvertently raised the issue of who was now or who in time would be the boss of the purchasing executives. Not only these relations but, in addition, the long-established and customary relations of the purchasing executives with their suppliers were being adversely affected. As a result of these uncertainties in their relations with Mr. Post, their general managers, and their suppliers, the purchasing executives were responding in a somewhat childish way. This was stage one in the usual analysis my students made and for which I gave them a Pass.

Stage two in the discussions arose when some students began to see that the solution implied in their diagnosis did not get to the heart of the matter. Granting that all these things that were wrong with the letter might have provoked this kind of response from the purchasing executives, could it be that no letter, no matter how well written, how properly routed, signed, and timed, could succeed in doing what Mr. Post was trying to accomplish? In short, had Mr. Post picked up the wrong ball? Although Mr. Post had consulted Mr. Manson and Mr. Larson about the letter and obtained Mr. Manson's approval, perhaps he should have sought the approval and under-standing of the purchasing executives (and perhaps of the general managers also) about the purpose of the letter. This could have been done by visiting each of them at his plant, or by inviting them to the central office for a meeting, where these matters about the alter-ations of customary relationships could have been discussed and clarified.

After my students had discussed the pros and cons of taking one or the other of these two approaches, and possibly even both, they usually reached the conclusion that any one of them would have been preferable to the bloody letter Mr. Post sent. For this I gave them a Pass Plus. Then some of them would remember that when Mr. Post had consulted Mr. Larson about the letter and when Mr. Larson had suggested that Mr. Post might want to visit the plants before sending it, Mr. Post had said, "I am too busy to do that." This brought stage three in the discussion, because this response, as-tounding in the light of the actions the students had suggested, raised the question of just what Mr. Post was busy doing instead of what the students had come to think he should have been doing. What was the nature of a purchasing executive's job at Mr. Post's high level? Was he supposed to do the purchasing himself or to be coordinating the activities of others? But what did the letter have to do with his own purchasing skill or competence? Could it be noth-ing? If so, what then were Mr. Post's qualifications for the job? Could they be zero? Was this Mr. Post's problem? Was he a purchas-ing expert but no executive? Did Mr. Manson know about this? Should he not be informed and do something about it? Some of my students went down this road—and back to Pass Minus in the grade I had in mind for them.

Other students thought that they had not yet gotten to the heart of Mr. Post's problem. Granted that his job had little, if anything, to do with purchasing, could it also be that his problem had little to do with trying to coordinate logically the purchasing procedures of the twenty purchasing executives (who in the students' minds now were not really executives but rather people who did purchasing)? Was this logical coordination the problem of the purchasing agents or of Mr. Post's definition of the problem? How was it related to the problem of securing the essential raw materials for the plants of the company? Did it have any or no relation? Who knew? Had Mr. Post tried to find out what the problems of the purchasing agents were, or had he been too busy to do so? Should he have done so? "Yes," the class shouted in unison, for which I now gave them a Low High Pass.

But would Mr. Post have difficulty in gaining this information? "Yes!" Why? Well, because (1) he was a new man, (2) his status was "out of line" (i.e., he was low on one dimension of it—length of service in the company—but high on others—purchasing experience and position of authority), (3) he had a new job that was ambiguous and not clearly defined, and (4) he was dealing with plant managers who had operated their plants in the past as separate and autonomous units. Under these conditions the class agreed that Mr. Post would have difficulty in gaining the cooperation and understanding of the purchasing agents and their general managers, for which I now gave them a Distinction Minus, because they had tied a few insights together.

But even at this high level of insight, the students were still disturbed. "No matter how you slice it," they would say, "Mr. Post did not know one part of his anatomy from another. He did not know what his job was; he did not know what his problem was. As a result he wrote a letter, which he should not have written in the first place, to the wrong people, at the wrong time under his (the wrong) signature, and so he had loused up the situation badly. This could not be allowed to go on. Something had to be done about it. Mr. Manson should be informed about it." But by whom? Mr. Larson? But wait a moment. If Mr. Larson did so, would it not possibly expose that Mr. Manson, as President, had not been doing what he was supposed to be doing? He had not helped to clarify the nature of Mr. Post's new job with the purchasing agents and their general managers. Why hadn't he? Had he not approved of the letter Mr. Post sent? How come? Moreover, might not Mr. Manson have said to Mr. Larson, "Why the hell do you think I made you Mr. Post's assistant? With your experience in this company you should have known that Mr. Post's letter would raise holy hell. Why didn't you prevent it? I can't think about everything."

By this time the class was deteriorating to a High Low Pass condition. Although stage three in the discussion had reached varying levels of higher insights, the conclusion now seemed to be that the purchasing agents were not doing what they should be doing because Mr. Post had not done what he should have done; and this in turn was so because Mr. Manson and Mr. Larson had not done what they should have done. The discussion now turned to the question of who was the biggest villain of them all. By the logics of organization, this had to be President Manson, and the class was in a quandary about how to fire him.

By this time the hour was drawing to a close, and from my point of view no one had suggested any action on the here-and-now situation presented in the case. Having been made action-conscious by my colleagues and the case method, I said to the class in my most nondirective fashion, "Dear students, so far we have been discussing what should have been done so that what did happen would not have happened. This is all water over the dam. As I remember it, the case ended with Mr. Post going to Mr. Larson to consult with him about what he should do now to get the purchasing agents to do what he wanted them to do. Isn't this a good first point of entry? The problem has been put right in your lap. Instead of saying you would go to Mr. Manson, why don't you tell me what you, as Mr. Larson, would say to Mr. Post here and now? With all your insights into this fouled-up situation, what would you say to Mr. Post, if you were Mr. Larson, that he might find helpful?"

Well, can you believe it? All the insights that the class had developed in the discussion completely evaporated. They harangued Mr. Post; told him what an incompetent nincompoop he was; gave him a complete rundown of his incompetence; and said that although he should visit the individual plants, they could not trust him to do so without lousing things up some more, and so his assistant, Mr. Larson, should visit them alone.

So about 30 seconds before the bell rang, I said feebly, "If you stop to think for a moment, none of us knows what the situation in the plants really is, because none of us has gone to the plants to find out. We have just been speculating about what the situations there might be. This applies to Mr. Larson in the case as well as to us in the class. Until these speculations are checked, we may be mistaken. Hence, whatever Mr. Larson can say that might help to move matters in this direction may be the first simple step needed. Perhaps Mr. Larson with one sentence can provide a simple logic for Mr. Post to take the first step. So, dear students, please reflect and ponder until we meet at the next hour about what such a simple one-sentence response to Mr. Post's query, 'What should I do now?' might be."

From my naive point of view, I thought that Mr. Larson's response to Mr. Post's query might be, "I don't *know*; but perhaps if you or I or both of us went to visit the plants, we might be able to find out." No matter how dim-witted Mr. Post was, I thought he might be able to accept the simple logic of this response, unless he thought that he could find out what was going on in the twenty different plants by sitting on his fanny in the central office, in which case I would be on the side of the students and feel that Mr. Manson might have to be brought into the picture. But let us be charitable and assume that one simple straightforward response might have put Mr. Post or Mr. Larson or both where they should have been in the first place in order to find out.

Let me make one more point: My suggested response (which I seldom got from students) began with the statement "I don't know." Without this admission, there was little need to visit the plants, except as a gimmick to secure the cooperation of the purchasing agents. Again and again it seemed to me that my students treated the course on Administrative Practices as a set of gimmicks by which supervisors or executives could get their subordinates to do what they should do. That they could not see that there was another rationale for the behavior I was recommending was a blind spot of theirs that baffled me but had me curious. Let me cite another example.

AN ANECDOTE WHICH DOES NOT PROVE BUT WHICH MAY ILLUSTRATE A POINT

In one of the early sessions of the Advanced Management Program, I had a student who presented for me in its most extreme form the problem I am trying to describe. When he came to the program, Hal, as I shall call him, an engineer by training, held a middle management position of some responsibility in a large company in the Midwest. From the beginning to the end of the program, Hal argued with me about what he as well as my colleagues felt was my soft-mindedness in the resolution of the human problems presented in the cases we discussed. "It just wouldn't work," he would say, "for reasons 1, 2, 3, 4, etc." Most of these reasons boiled down to such statements as "Goddamit, you got to tell people what to do and where they get off or they'll take advantage of you. Give 'em an inch and they'll take a mile," and so on and on.

Although Hal always provided excitement in the discussions, being somewhat more logical and considerably more articulate than most of his fellow students, his behavior toward the phenomena never changed; it was the same on the last day as it had been on the first. He almost had me convinced that "it" would not work—but not quite.

When Hal returned to his firm, he was promoted to the position of superintendent of the Maintenance Department. He had been on the new job only a few days when the telephone rang and an angry voice on the other end of the wire said, "What the hell is going on in your department?" Hal, who, as we have seen, was prone to making "signal responses" (i.e., to respond to words instead of what they referred to), was on the point of responding "Who the hell are you to be talking to me [the new boss] this way?" when, as he told me the story later, "I thought of you, Fritz, and I counted ten. Then I said 'I don't know. Why don't you come to my office and tell me?'"

Into Hal's office then came Bill, the shop steward, who was reputed to be one of the most difficult persons in the plant to get along with. Bill voiced his grievances and Hal listened to them. As a result of this conversation, a new relationship between them developed. Soon they seemed to be able to work through their differences better. In time Hal's colleagues began to ask him, "How the hell do you get along so well with that stinker, Bill? We can't get to first base with him. Tell us how you do it. GIVE!"

Hal was so astounded with this series of outcomes that he came all the way from Milwaukee, where his plant was located, to tell me about them. The gist of his comments was to the effect, "Goddam it, Fritz, 'it' works." He was almost inarticulate in his enthusiasm and excitement. From then on Hal became one of my most ardent disciples, although unfortunately "it" never worked again so well or so simply for him.

Although I have told this story many times in order to make a point which I feel does not need to be underscored, I have always been surprised at the many different points my hearers get. This time in order to make myself perfectly clear, I want to say what for me the interesting points of this story are.

(1) The point is *not* just that Hal counted ten, although this helped.

(2) The point is *not* just that Hal kept his mouth shut and did not shoot his mouth off. Although this is a physical prerequisite for listening, it does not constitute in itself hearing anything.

(3) An interesting point is that Hal said, "I don't know."

(4) It is interesting because it is a non-stereotypical response in the sense that an executive should know what is going on in his department.

(5) It becomes even more interesting when one sees that the response is truthful; being new on the job, Hal did not know what was going on in his department.

(6) It becomes still more interesting when one sees that Hal's response was not indirect, circuitous, gimmicky, manipulative, etc.; it was just stating what the situation was. He did not know! *That was a fact.*

(7) It becomes even more interesting when one sees that the statement "I don't know" had to precede the next step of how to find out. If Hal thought he knew what was going on in his department, there was no need for him to find out. Also if Hal's concept of himself as an executive was threatened by not knowing what was going on (see point 4), he would not try to find out. Check!

(8) The point is that Hal was not playing any tricks on Bill or performing any "ad prac" mystique. Bill was one source of information with regard to what was going on in the department. The most direct access that Hal had at that moment to this information was by listening to Bill. Bill might not have been the most accurate source of information, he might not have the whole story, and so on, but he was the most immediate point of entry that Hal had in order to find out. Hal did not need to go to any personnel records in order to obtain the information he needed. Bill was right there before him— no abstraction, but a living, breathing, though perhaps unwanted, here-and-now phenomenological reality.

(9) It is also interesting that Hal never told me what Bill told him about what the hell was going on in his department. That part of the problem seemed to disappear. Something new seemed to take its place, a new relationship between Hal and Bill that allowed them to begin and to continue to work well or well enough together.

(10) So this anecdote (soft data) has no points of departure or points of destination. It has no initial felicitous beginning or final happy ending. It may involve some points the reader did not get, such as, for example, that it illustrates a *point of entry* into an ongoing here-and-now situation that seems to make a difference in

respect to the development of the situation in a positive direction. I hope that is not a point which I have belabored too much.

PLANNED AND EMERGENT BEHAVIOR

As I have said, the kind of problems in which I became interested—problems in which people were not doing what they were supposed to be doing—were not difficult to find, even though they appeared in different guises and places and at different levels of organizations. For my students and even for some of my colleagues, each new guise or place or level in which the problem was found constituted a new and different problem. If it occurred at the worker level, it was a worker problem; if it appeared at the foreman level, it was a foreman problem. If the problem could not be solved at those levels because the people at them did not have the authority to do so—and alas, for my students this seemed to be most often the case—it became a top executive problem. Furthermore, depending upon the business function in which the problem appeared, it also became a production, marketing, cost, or personnel problem. If a single person was the chief offender, it became an individual or personality problem; if a group was involved, it was a group problem; if more than one group was involved, it was an intergroup problem. Of course it was also a lack-of-coordination or a lack-of-communication or a lack-of-authority or a lack-of-information problem. And furthermore, it was a problem of some particular person's not having the information or the authority he needed in order to solve it.

My eyes never left this ubiquitous ball, which it seemed to me nobody wanted to pick up. To employ another analogy which I frequently used in class, I asked, "How do we deal with this giraffe—the unexpected and unanticipated—which keeps poking its head in the window and distracting our attention and which we keep trying to legislate out of existence by some control device or other?" Somehow around this ubiquitous ball or giraffe, it seemed to me the job of the manager had to be conceptualized. If he (I mean the manager and not the giraffe) refused to pick up this ball, it seemed to me we would be in a sorry plight indeed. The manager would be dealing only with the best of all possible worlds in which the unexpected and the unanticipated had been outlawed. This could not be. No tough-minded manager could be concerned only with such a soft-minded Utopia. About such phenomena no rational manager could just shrug his shoulders in a Latin fashion and say, "C'est la vie," could he now?

So in all cases I collected and taught, I focused my attention and the attention of my students not only upon the intended or anticipated consequences of some control device but also upon the unanticipated and often undesired consequences; that is, upon the total behavior which resulted from some device designed to control the activities of the organization's members. It was this emergent behavior which interested me and about which I felt the practitioner had something to say or do. If not, it seemed to me the practitioner was residing in an ivory tower just as much as the theoretician.

In my endeavor to get the manager to pick up this ball, I landed myself in a most outlandish position. As the case discussions I have described above illustrate, the action to be taken tended often to reduce itself to small steps in the direction of talking with and listening to somebody who was not doing what he was supposed to be doing and trying to gain his cooperation by first trying to understand his situation. Although I thought that such an approach was as direct, practical, and down-to-earth as anyone could get, my colleagues and students often did not see it this way. For them I was being soft on action. It was said that I was indirect, nondirect, circuitous; "ad-prac-ing" someone; never firing anyone, just listening, being overly permissive, understanding, and passive; and, as a result, getting nothing accomplished.

How could this be? How could it be that I, who was dealing with what I thought were concrete and first-hand raw phenomena, was perceived by some of my students and colleagues as being abstract, theoretical, and soft-minded with regard to action, whereas some of my students and colleagues, who I thought were dealing with second-level abstractions, perceived themselves as being concrete, practical, and tough-minded? How could they perceive me as guilty of what I thought they were guilty; and how could I perceive them as guilty of what they thought I was guilty, namely, of being soft-headed or soft-minded, or for short just soft with regard to action? What a dilemma! This time I did not have to go to Spring Lake Ranch to resolve it.

Although I have already been around this difference of perception in both this and the previous chapter, let me consider it again by describing the different meanings that emergent behavior has under two ways of thinking of organizations—what I will call here the rational conception and the social system conception.

THE RATIONAL CONCEPTION OF ORGANIZATION

Under the rational conception it is difficult to deal with the unanticipated and unintended consequences of the devices designed to control the activities of the members of the organization in any manner except one which reinforces the continued use of the rational conception as a control device. I can illustrate what I mean by a diagram.

Rational Conception of Organization

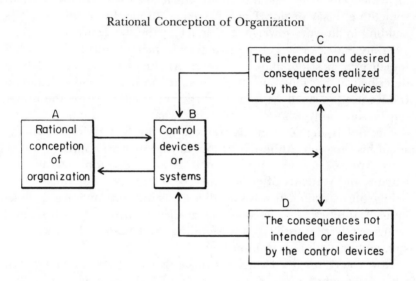

(1) Generated by the administrator's concept of rational behavior (box A), the control devices of box B are all of the same general character. They specify what something should be and are generally expressed in terms of standards. For example, they specify what the cost and quality of the product should be if the product is being produced by trained workers who use the prescribed methods, procedures, and tools and work at the required rates.

(2) As shown in box C, these control devices or systems have consequences that they are intended to realize, not only in terms of the cost, quality, and quantity of the product, but also in terms of the behavior of people. When this happens, the efficacy of the control device and its rationale is, of course, reinforced.

(3) Also, as shown in box D, these control devices have consequences not intended or desired by their designers. These undesired consequences take many different forms; let me mention three common ones, all of which have the peculiar property of reinforcing

instead of questioning the rational conception of control. This peculiar property was not just my personal discovery. It was also discovered by the so-called "bureaucratic sociologists," Merton (1957), Selznick (1953), Gouldner (1954), Blau (1955), and others, to whom I shall refer again in Chapter 18.

(a) When a control device does not achieve the desired improvement in the cost, quality, or quantity of the product that was expected, according to the logic of the rational conception, these unintended and undesired consequences have essentially only one meaning, namely, that someone did not do what he was supposed to do. Either the designer of the device did not set the proper standards, the supervisor did not properly implement the control device, or the worker did not do what he was told. Under the concept of rational behavior, there is no other way to explain these unintended consequences nor is there any way to deal with them, except by more and better—or better implemented—standards.

(b) However, many of the undesired consequences from standardized operations arise not only because people do not always do what they are supposed to do, but also because they do only the minimum of what is expected of them. It is most unfortunate but nevertheless often true that control devices encourage this type of behavior, because the standards often have to be stated in terms of minimum expectations. As we saw in the case of the wiremen in the Bank Wiring Observation Room and in the case of the purchasing agents in the Dashman Company, the members of the organization knew the minimum performance that was expected of them in order to keep their jobs, and they behaved accordingly.

To have people do only the minimum of what is expected of them, however, is not the intended consequence of a control device. Under the rational conception this unintended outcome arises because the people affected do not understand correctly the intended purposes. Thus, in many organizations, hours and hours of time are spent in the rather futile activity of explaining that the unintended consequences were not intended and that, if this was properly understood, the control device would work. Can you imagine the hours of time Mr. Post will spend in explaining to the purchasing agents what was not intended by his letter?

(c) Sometimes a control device has consequences for a line supervisor that were not intended by its designer. In theory the setting of explicit standards is supposed to help a supervisor to exercise a general instead of a close type of supervision. But the unanticipated consequences mentioned above, in which the worker does just the minimum expected of him, forces the supervisor into ever closer supervision. Hell or high water, he has to try to make the control system work in the way it is supposed to work.

If some readers feel that I have caricatured the rational conception of organizations, in a way they are right. This perception follows because I have been stating these generalizations at a fairly high level of abstraction and have not been describing the concrete behavior of people. Lord forbid that I think all managers or supervisors or designers of control systems are as constrained in their concrete behavior by the conception of a closed rational system, and act as rigidly in terms of it, as I have stated. But having said this, I do not believe for one minute that this way of thinking has vanished from the face of the earth. The assumptions and logics underlying this way of thinking are pervasive. They crop up again and again in one form or another and keep distorting the nature of the administrator's job. The chief defects of the rational conception are three.

(1) Being a logically closed system, the rational model cannot correct itself. It prevents an administrator from looking at the phenomena of human behavior and from becoming more adaptive with regard to them.

(2) The rational conception tends to see things from an external frame of reference. It puts the manager outside the system he is administering.

(3) It tends to confuse planned and emergent behavior. It treats the "control" of emergent behavior as being of the same character as "control" by technical standards. It equates control by standards with human motivation.

THE SOCIAL SYSTEM CONCEPTION OF ORGANIZATION

Let me now turn to the social system conception of organizations, which I thought corrected for these defects. Again I will draw a diagram to help shorten my exposition.

(1) In the diagram I place the administrator with his social systemic way of thinking (A) inside the social system he is administering. B, C, and D stand for exactly the same things they stood for in my diagram of the rational model: B stands for rational control devices or systems; C for their realized intended consequences, and D for their unintended consequences. D, however, is no longer something that should not be there. It is now a full-blown phenomenological reality on an equal basis with C. In this administrator's

Social System Conception of Organization

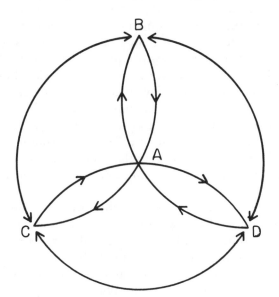

thinking D becomes the cost he has to pay for C, and D is ever present.

(2) I connect B, C, and D in exactly the same way as in the rational model except that now they look like a three-leaf clover figure in a circle, around which the administrator can still chase himself, if he wishes to. (I am a permissive guy, remember.) But I do not confine or constrain him to this cycle of futility. Though I free him from this fate worse than death by allowing him to move from B to C to D directly and in either direction, I do not release him from the pressures exerted by B, C, and D. He will have to learn to live with them and the realities they represent.

(3) The three-leaf clover routine can be thought of as the nonadaptive part of the system under conditions of uncertainty and change. It is the restricted way in which the administrator would behave if he suffered seriously from what is sometimes called goal displacement; that is, where the rule designed to achieve an organizational goal has a value in itself over and above the organizational goal to be achieved. In the extreme case, the observance of the rule becomes a ritual, when its observance becomes more important than what the rule is supposed to accomplish.

(4) As I have said, I release the administrator from this rigid behavior by allowing him to search for more alternative ways of

behaving than those prescribed by the three-leaf clover. These alternatives do not arise from any logic, but from his capacity to observe and learn from the concrete situation before him. In particular, he now has to learn to deal with D in a manner that is different from the way he tended to deal with it under the rational conception. Above all, he has to see how B, C, and D can be related in a way that is different from the way they are related by the three-leaf clover.

(5) In the social system conception, the administrator is an involved member of the system he is administering. He is both affecting and being affected by it; he cannot escape from it. Although he can think of himself as external to the system he is administering, as the rational conception allows him to do, the moment he acts he is constrained by it.

Trying to take action as though they were outside the system seemed to me to be what was getting my students into trouble. Often they proposed solutions which no one within a system could have implemented, because the solutions would have had consequences of such a magnitude that the system would have reeled with shock. The proposed action was directed to the solution of the problem as seen by someone outside the system. It was not the solution to the problem as internally felt or perceived. It was not capable of being implemented by someone from within the system. Viewed from the outside, the characters in the Dashman Company from the president down—except for Mr. Larson, and even he was not getting his message through—looked incompetent and were not doing their jobs as executives. The solution from this point of view would have been to fire the lot and hire some new executives who were more competent. This solution not only would have been difficult to carry out, but, if done, could have resulted in the end of the Dashman Company.

Obviously a social system can be studied and researched from the point of view of a disinterested observer outside the system, like this

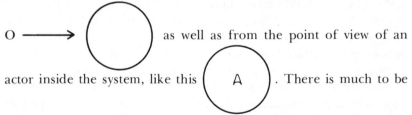

O ⟶ ( ) as well as from the point of view of an

actor inside the system, like this (A). There is much to be

said for both ways of looking at and understanding a system, but unless this difference is well understood, it can lead to wide differences when it comes to taking action. I shall have more to say about this later, especially in Chapters 25 and 26, when I contrast the scientific and administrative points of view. For now I will stay with my formulation of what I felt was the much misunderstood administrative point of view. I want to look once more at the headache from which Mr. Post suffered but which he could not seem to communicate, conceptualize, or understand.

Let me take Mr. Post outside of the system called the Dashman Company and place him wending his way home in his Cadillac to his wife and children, pondering the question of how he could tell them about the headache from which he was suffering. How could he tell them that he, the Vice President for Purchasing in the Dashman Company, could not get his purchasing agents to do what he wanted them to do and, by God, what they ought to want to do, if they understood that what was good for the Dashman Company was also good for the nation in its moment of peril at the beginning of World War II? Could they understand his problem? While he was coming to the pessimistic conclusion that the answer might well be "No," Mr. Post in his Cadillac went through a red light; so a traffic cop stopped him and said in effect, "Say, buster, that red light said 'No go' and you went 'Go.' That wasn't what you were supposed to do; so I'm going to have to give you a ticket. It's nothing personal. Please understand that I'm just doing my job. What's good for you is good for the country. We can't have people going through red lights, can we now?"

Well, how did Mr. Post respond? Did he say, "Yes, Mr. Officer, you're absolutely right. We can't have people going through red lights, and so I'm glad that you called my attention to this departure from a standard. I realize that you have to give me a ticket so I will not do this again"? Or did he say, "My dear Mr. Officer, I was wending my way home to my wife and children and suffering from a terrible headache which I felt that they—and I fear you also, Mr. Officer—wouldn't understand; so I went through the red light. Moreover, Mr. Officer, please remember that I am not 'buster,' but Mr. Post, Vice President for Purchasing in the Dashman Company, a position of high authority. People there salaam before me, even though sometimes they do not do what I tell them. Anyway, you can't talk to me this way."

To which the traffic officer might have responded, "You are not in the Dashman Company now, Mr. Post; you are in a different social system where you are just a citizen and I am the law enforcing officer. In this system I have the authority, people salaam to me, and I wield the big stick. Nevertheless, I try to treat all citizens, whatever the make of their cars, alike; I'm impartial. So you see you are just a 'buster' to me. No hard feelings, Mr. Post. You wouldn't want me to give you and your car preferential treatment, would you now?"

To which Mr. Post might have responded, "Say, Mr. Traffic Officer, I begin to see some parallels as well as some differences between my headache and yours. Some bells are beginning to ring for me. Can we go somewhere and have a cup of coffee or a bourbon on the rocks, perhaps, and chat about it?"

Well, let us not allow our imaginings to go too far afield. The chances are more than likely that to Mr. Post's statement, "You can't talk to me this way," the traffic officer would have responded, "Says who?" and this exchange would not have spiraled into an insight such as the one about which I just speculated. Instead it would have continued at a monotonic level for about, say, 15 minutes, at which point the traffic officer would have given buster the ticket; and Mr. Post would have continued his way homeward, feeling misunderstood now by both the purchasing agents and the traffic officer—but let us hope not also by his wife and children when he arrived.

Let us end this story on a more pleasant note and have her awaiting him eagerly at the door with anticipatory hugs and kisses. But when Mrs. Post saw her husband's glum look, she said, "Honey, why don't you lie down and relax awhile before dinner? From your face I see you are suffering from a frightful headache, and my favorite television program tells me that a few aspirins will do the trick." Now we have Mr. Post, lying on a chaise longue with only the aspirin tablets with which to communicate and from which to obtain an understanding of his incommunicable problem. I fear Mr. Post is on the verge of an ulcer.

Please do not think that I am becoming soft-hearted and trying to make you feel sorry for Mr. Post's plight. On the contrary, I just want to show how Mr. Post's plight, if understood a bit differently, is the source of the unique services that, as an executive, he might be able to provide. I want to get rid of Mr. Post's particular headache by universalizing it a bit, so that Mr. Post will not just be lying on his chaise longue, feeling that he is alone, misunderstood, and suffering from a headache that is unique to him. Such a nonexecutive posture, you must agree, is out of the question.

THE GENERALIZED FORMULATION OF THE ADMINISTRATIVE HEADACHE PROBLEM

Let me try to formulate the problem of administration by the headache from which Mr. Post suffered, which he felt no one understood and which he could not explain. In short, let me treat Mr. Post's particular headache as a concrete manifestation of a more general problem from which *any* administrator (let us call him or her A_i, just as Korzybski would have called any woman W_i) suffers. It is the headache of any person in a position of responsibility for the performance of others who is trying to effect a change in the system of which he is an involved member and who will be affected by the changes he is trying to introduce. Taking action from this position and in this context constitutes for me the administrative point of view, and it involves—not just sometimes but always—persons and their relations to one another. So for me this headache is not just the *human* problem of administration; it is *the problem of administration.* Period!

Although my A_i could be any supervisor, executive, manager, or administrator, in my early days I tended to use the label administrator more often than the labels of supervisor, executive, or manager, because when I changed these nouns into verbs, in order to give a slight cue about what my A_i might be up to when he became action-oriented, I thought the verb "to administer" expressed better in an etymological sense what I thought he should be up to than the verbs to supervise, to execute, or to manage. In time I ceased this verbal trickery and used these labels interchangeably. After all, I was not deriving my A_i from any of these labels, but from a phenomenological and contextual bind that followed from the nature of the system in which my A_i was involved.

For example, I did not make a class of all persons bearing the labels I mentioned above and then try to generalize, from all the different things they did, about what their essential contributions to their organizations were. As I have said, this would have constituted for me a hopeless mish-mash. Had I done so, for example, I would have had to put the purchasing executives in the Dashman Company in the same bag with Mr. Post and Mr. Manson. But although the former were called executives, they were not in the context or bind I described above. The purchasing agents were not performing in their jobs any executive or, to generalize, any A_i functions or contributing any A_i services. They were not in my terms A_is; they were doing the work of their organizations called purchasing.

Although Mr. Post was in the bind I described above when he was trying to elicit the cooperation of the plant purchasing agents, he could also have been doing some purchasing himself. I don't know whether he did; but if I had found him doing so, even though he had the label executive and the contextual position of an A_i, at that moment in that activity he would not have been performing an executive or managerial or supervisory or administrative or, to generalize again, A_i function. At that moment he was not my A_i, because he was not suffering from the A_i's headache from which I have generalized.

My A_i was derived from the nature of a system and the activities related to the maintenance and development of the system. It was not derived from all of the activities sometimes performed by persons bearing the label executive or other labels of a similar kind. It was not derived from some of the activities that they might perform on certain occasions, such as selling, purchasing, borrowing money, or giving a speech about the free enterprise system at a Rotary Club. Not that I underrated the importance of such activities for the business. Far from it. Mr. Post with his contacts in Washington might have obtained a contract with some supplier of great financial advantage to the Dashman Company. But no matter how financially rewarding to him and to the company such an activity was or might have been, he was there and then, as I am formulating it now, not performing an executive or A_i service. He was engaged in the business of the business, but not in the business of administration.

But what about "staff executives"—those people who designed the control systems that A_is administered? Were they A_is? In most cases, no. Not until they were in a position of having to implement the control system they had designed did they suffer from the headache from which I am abstracting my A_is. Although they were supposed to help the A_is to do a better job, they often became, as we have seen, more a source of interference than a source of help; that is, they were more often helping to give my A_is the headache from which they suffered than they were contracting this headache themselves.

But surely an A_i had to make decisions about what products were to be produced, at what cost and at what price they were to be produced and sold, whether to make or buy certain parts, and so forth. No, these were all technical decisions that required the information of experts about such matters. Obtaining the needed information from the different persons involved in order that a "good" decision could be reached was an A_i function. When a person was performing this function, he was facilitating the processes by means of which such decisions were made, but he was not then sitting in his office making them by himself alone. When he was doing that, no matter how important or good the decision he reached was, he was engaged in the business of the business and not the business of administration. He was not performing an A_i function.

What about "informal leaders," with whom business and industry abound, that is, those persons who might be performing what I am calling A_i functions and services but who do not bear the title "supervisors" or hold any formal position of authority which gives them the right to perform these functions and services? Are they A_is? Although these persons aroused my curiosity, because they often seemed to be performing the functions of an A_i better than those who had the formal authority to do so, yet I could not include them in the bind that gave my A_i the frightful headache he had. They were freed from that constraint called formal authority, which is why I called their contributions informal.

What was my A_i doing when he was *not* buying or selling or determining what the costs and prices of things should be or engaged in the business of the business or doing the work of the organization? In my terms, he was trying to get the cooperation and understanding of those who were doing the work of the organization for the purposes of the organization. He was trying to achieve a satisfactory condition of exchange between the essential services they contributed to the organization and the rewards they received in return; that is, a condition of exchange that was satisfactory both for them and for the organization.

For me the achievement of this balance required skills of communication that went way beyond the administration of a standardized system of rewards and punishments. That an administrator could not get things done through people by formal authority or formal organization alone seemed to me evidenced by the facts in most of the cases I collected and discussed in class. There were other skills he was using. These skills seemed to me to deserve attention, but they were seldom reported in the written cases that were available. I decided to turn my attention in the next period of my life to making these skills explicit.

Next to my meeting Mayo and my work with the Hawthorne studies, this decision was probably the most important event of my professional life. I never regretted it, for I do not think that science can progress without the commitment of its practitioners to a point of view. Nevertheless, my decision to pursue the social system conception of organization and its associated skills of investigation and action affected all of my work and what I did—and did not—accomplish from that time on. I shall have more to say about this when I revisit my subject matter in Chapters 23 and 24.

Part III

Human Relations as the Focus for
Development

1948–1957

INTRODUCTION

During the next period of my life, from 1948 to 1957, the cold war became hotter. The West Berlin air blockade took place in 1949, the North Atlantic Defense Treaty was signed by twelve nations in the same year, and the Korean War was fought from 1950 to 1953. Also in 1950 the Point 4 program of the United States government to assist economically developing nations was launched.

In this country fear of communism in high places and McCarthyism became rampant. Robert Oppenheimer became a security risk in 1954. The Supreme Court banned segregated public schools in 1954.

Gandhi was assassinated in 1948; India became an independent nation in 1950; King George VI died in 1952, and Elizabeth was crowned Queen of England; Stalin died in 1953. In this country Eisenhower was elected President in 1952 and Pusey succeeded Conant as President of Harvard University in 1953.

In 1950 the Ford Foundation reconstituted itself and undertook an enlarged—gigantic, it could be said—program of giving aid to the social sciences for the study of human behavior. For administrative purposes the Ford Foundation divided its undertaking into five programs, one of which was called Program Five. In one of the Foundation's position papers delineating the focus of Program Five, the term "behavioral sciences" was used. Up to this time this label had not been in current usage. Almost overnight it caught on and some of us, who were not quite sure what our discipline was, became behavioral scientists.

I was the grateful recipient of generous grants from Program Five, which lasted until 1957, when the Program was terminated and many social scientists returned to their individual disciplines. By this time I not only had no disciplinary home to return to, I also had no respectable label for my subject matter, because the words "human relations" had gone out of favor in both academic and foundation circles. I had to start a new cycle in my search for a subject matter.

Before this shift in academic and foundation climates occurred and while I was still in favor and where the money was, I spent my time cultivating my focus for the development of human relations. I no longer taught courses with my colleagues on matters of administration. I had courses of my own, in which I no longer needed to be concerned about the differences between my way and their way of conceiving the nature of organizations and administration.

This phase of my life continued until 1957, when my slumbers were disturbed, not so much by the termination of Program Five, but by the dissonant noises coming from the so-called knowledge explosion and the second industrial revolution and applied mathematicians and computers. Although all these forces were at work during this period I will be writing about, I will wait until the following period of my life to consider them. I want here to describe my search—or research—to make explicit the skills that administrators—the A_is I referred to at the end of Chapter 11—used to deal with the real and concrete phenomena of securing cooperation among persons in organizations.

Chapter 12

Human Relations Practice

In 1948 I organized in the second year of the MBA program an elective course I called Human Relations. I hoped the course would give me a framework within which I could address myself to the class of problems with which I had become concerned and in which I thought my students would also be interested. This class of problems had to do with trying to obtain the cooperation and understanding of persons in face-to-face situations; I wanted to understand better the skills involved in this process. These skills included ones which Mr. Post or Mr. Larson, or both for that matter, could have exercised in the plants, if and when they had ever gone to them. The data in the Dashman Company case, as it was written, only allowed me to get Mr. Post or Mr. Larson or both out in the field. Although I thought this was a very important first step, it left unclarified what they would say and do if and when they got into face-to-face interactions with the plant purchasing agents singly or in groups.

THE SECOND-YEAR ELECTIVE COURSE IN HUMAN RELATIONS

At first in this course I used mostly cases which reported verbatim conversations between two persons, in which (1) A was a counselor and B a client and where A was trying to help B about a personal problem B had. As the course developed, I also used cases in which (2) A was a superior and B a subordinate; (3) A was a staff person and B a line supervisor; (4) A was a field researcher and B a subject of the research; (5) A was a consultant and B a client; and (6) A was a trainer and B a learner. I also used cases in which (7) A was trying to obtain B's cooperation and understanding about a problem B or A or both had in these relationships.

Thus I used the counseling orientation as a model for a helping relationship; I explored these other relationships in terms of it. My course was never strictly a course on counseling. It was the extension of the orientation of counseling to the other relationships in an organization in which the component of listening was involved and might be of help to either A or B or both. It could have been called equally well a course in interpersonal communication, interpersonal behavior, skilled listening, or the helping relationship.

I gave the course each semester for four years. There were always more students who wanted to enroll than I was willing to teach, even though each section had over 100 students. I never published the materials I used; but a good many years later George Lombard, who taught the course for the next ten years, and Arthur Turner, who followed him, published theirs. In their book (Turner and Lombard, 1969) the topics and their sequence, also the cases and readings, included new materials but are representative of the course the last times I gave it.

As the extension of the psychotherapeutic model of counseling to role relationships other than those of a strictly counseling nature is what made this course not only unique, but also a source of confusion for some of my students and colleagues, I would like to be more specific about the first three kinds of relationships I mentioned. Most of the cases in the course were concerned with them.

(1) *The Counselor-Counselee Relationship.* I began the course with an examination of the counseling relationship. For this I chose cases in which B, the counselee, who in most cases was also a factory worker, had a personal problem such as the following: Should he quit or stay on the job and keep his nose clean? Should he punch his boss on the nose or suck up to him in order to keep his job? Should he be a rate buster or conform to the output norms of his work group? Should he go back to school or get more schooling while at work? Should he get engaged or married or stay single? If married, should he live with his parental family or with his in-laws or with neither? And so on and so on. Or B might be suffering from a sense of felt injustice about his work situation and he wanted to tell A how he felt about it.

I obtained many of the interviews that I used as cases from the counseling program at Western Electric. During the early years each counselor wrote up his interviews in verbatim fashion, stating not only what the employee said but also what he (the counselor) said in reply. Recording instruments were not used at this time; for details of the program at Western see Dickson and Roethlisberger, *Counseling in an Organization* (1966), the second book Bill and I wrote together. In my course I avoided cases involving physical symptoms or extreme forms of social deviation, since I was not training my students to be professional counselors or healers.

In the kind of situations I have described, A's job as counselor was to help B express what was important to him and thereby help him reach his own decisions about what he (B) wanted to do and not what A thought B should do. From records of interviews that had this character, we discussed in class such questions as the following: Did we think that what A had said in reply to B had facilitated or impeded the expression of B's feelings? What were B's feelings anyway? Had A, the counselor in the interview, heard them correctly? Had they, the students in the classroom, heard them? If so, what might have been a more helpful reply? And so on.

(2) *The Superior-Subordinate Relationship*. After I thought the students had obtained some feel for this kind of helping relationship, we looked at reports of interviews in which A was the superior and B his subordinate. The problems in these interviews were of the following character: (1) B was not meeting satisfactorily some standard of performance and A had to tell B this; (2) B's attitude was not what A thought it should be in some respect; for example, B seemed apathetic or hostile and A wanted to find out why before he acted; (3) B wanted a raise or promotion or transfer and A did not think B deserved it; or (4) B was so keyed up or teed off about something related to his job or the policies of the company that he went to A with the query "What the hell's going on here?" as I described earlier in the case of Hal and Bill.

In class we discussed such questions as: Did A understand what was bugging B? Did they (the students) understand what was bugging B or A or both? Had A helped B to understand how things felt for B? If the students had been A in the case, what appraisal would they have made of B's situation at the end of the interview? What next step, if any, would they have taken?

Obviously all interactions between a superior and a subordinate are not of this character. I did not choose cases, for example, in which A gave B an order and B happily complied with it. Nor did I choose ones in which B went to A for technical help or factual information about his job or the policies and rules of the company and A gave B what he asked for, so that B seemed satisfied. Instead, I chose cases in which A was trying to get B's cooperation and understanding about something related to B's job, the policies and rules of the company, or changes in them about which A or B or both felt there existed some misunderstanding on the part of the other.

Such cases constitute an important class of the situations that supervisors face with subordinates. Indeed, they are common. When they occur their characteristic is that A has the opportunity to try to understand B from B's point of view before taking action or telling B how things stand from his (A's) or the company's point of view. In short, I chose deliberately a kind of B with a kind of problem in which the skillful practice of listening on the part of A might be of help to B in the solution of his problem as well as of help to A in doing his job more competently.

These problems had not been pulled out of thin air or from any particular theory. They had been discovered by applying a way of thinking to the concrete relationships that existed between superiors (A's) and subordinates (B's) in many business organizations. During these studies I had found that the major form of influence or persuasion or communication used by the A's upon the B's was telling the B's how things should be or why things were the way they were from the point of view of the A's. The assumption seemed to be that the B's did not do what the A's wanted because they did not understand the organizational rationale or logic of the position of the A's. Once the B's saw the logic of a cost reduction or wage incentives program, for example, the A's assumed that the B's would do what they were supposed to do. As I saw little evidence for this assumption in the behavior of the B's in the plants I observed, I thought that a little listening to the B's by the A's from the point of view of the B's might be of help to the B's as well as to the A's.

Also at this time there was much concern about the lack of good two-way communication between the tops and bottoms of organizations. Orders coming from the top seemed to become attenuated by the time they reached the bottom, whereas information coming from the bottom got filtered in curious ways by the time it reached the top. The B's often seemed to tell the A's what they thought the A's wanted to hear and not "like it was, brother." As a result the further up the line the A was, the more he lived in a world as it was described in abstract economics and not as it was in a concrete social reality. The B's could not tell the A's "like it was, brother" and the A's kept telling the B's as it was logically and grammatically. This seemed to me a good place to start studying how to improve communications, that is, a place where a little listening might help.

(3) *Staff-Line Relationships*. There were staff people in organizations who were supposed to help first-line supervisors do a better job of supervision by providing them with standards for evaluating the performance of their subordinates. The curious thing about these helping relationships was that the supervisors often perceived these staff persons as a source of interference rather than as a source of

help. Lower-level supervisors could not tell staff people this, because the supervisors feared that this would activate the staff people to develop still more and better standards and controls, which in turn would require the supervisors to sit at their desks longer, with the result that increasingly they would have less time to get out on the floor to listen to the workers in order to find out what it was like for them there. So in the course I always had a few cases in which A, a staff person, was explaining to B, a first-line supervisor, how his (A's) control system would help B to do a better job of supervision. Here again I felt that a little listening by A to B's situation might help A as well as B do a better job.

THE PSYCHOTHERAPEUTIC COUNSELING RELATIONSHIP

As I said before, I started the course with an examination of the psychotherapeutic counseling relationship, because I thought that it provided the best framework that existed at the time for describing what constituted skillful listening in a helping relationship. Moreover, there was a body of clinical knowledge about this relationship. Furthermore, I thought the practice of the counseling orientation would help the student to see at a more microscopic level the phenomena of human relationships about which in the First-Year course, Administrative Practices, we had been able to talk at only a very general level. In the practice of the counseling orientation students would be able to observe, for example: (a) the dynamics of the influence process, that is, how a person affects the behavior of others as well as how he is affected by it; (b) the Alice-in-Wonderland character of the world of feelings and sentiments and the problems this character poses for persons who are engaged in dealing with it; and (c) how things look from the bottom up as well as from the top down. Not until he understood these matters could a student see correctly the relation of his interpersonal behavior to problems of administration.

It was these effects which I wanted my students of business administration to understand and to which my course was addressed, for I was not training them to be professional counselors. I will be concerned in this chapter primarily with what I expected them to learn about human relationships from the practice of the counseling orientation. Let me start with my own personal experiences as a counselor.

When I started counseling, I felt that the most important step was to get the counselee to tell me what was important to him. Although at first I thought that such a simple objective must have a simple means for achieving it, I soon realized that in order to achieve this objective, I could not just say, "Tell me like it is (for you), brother." In an intuitive way I realized that before a counselee was free to do this, I would have to stop saying and doing all the things that I thought would discourage him from telling me what was important to him, such as, for example, saying in effect "You should not feel this way," or "I approve of this feeling, but that feeling is a bad one to have," and so on.

Although I tried not to express approval and disapproval about the content of what was said, I did express my approval when B tried to express his feelings, both positive and negative, to me. For sweating things out like this for me, I felt I ought to give him something he wanted in exchange. I may not have rewarded him with love and affection for doing this very difficult thing, but I did try to reward him with understanding by saying something to the effect that "I think I understand a bit better the way things are *for you*. Let me test my understanding by summarizing for you what I have heard. You can tell me if I have it right."

Thus, in the counseling interview I did not start with the assumption that I was not influencing or being influenced by B and then discover later that I was. I started with the assumption that I was a member of a two-person relationship (a small social system). I was both affecting and being affected by B, as I tried to help B tell me what was important to him. I was in the bind I described at the end of the last chapter, but at a microscopic level where I could observe the bind closely. Although I was using the conceptual scheme of a social system, I was an involved member of the two-person system I was observing. In this system I was both an actor and an observer, and I could observe not only the effect upon me of what B said and did, and the effect upon B of what I said and did, but also what I hoped or intended to accomplish by what I said and did, and finally that awful discrepancy which so often existed between what was intended and what actually occurred.

In the counseling relationship I did not start by assuming that what was going on was primarily logical and then discover later that it was not. On the contrary, I assumed that what went on in most social exchanges between A's and B's could be roughly and approximately conceived as an interaction or exchange of sentiments. In such contexts A expressed sentiments to B, to which in turn B responded with similar or different sentiments, to which in turn A responded with similar or different sentiments, and so on. The resulting outcome of this exchange in time was sometimes a warm glow of shared sentiments between A and B and sometimes an argument between them, such as I described earlier, when A (the cop) called B (the citizen) "Buster," to which B replied "You can't talk to me this way," to which A replied in turn "Says who?" and so on and on.

As I did not wish these outcomes to occur, I tried to see that B's feelings did not act upon my feelings. Instead of reacting to B's feelings in terms of my feelings, I tried to reflect B's feelings back to B in as untwisted a way as possible. By so doing, I thought I would be putting B's feelings back in the place where they belonged, namely, in B himself. They were his feelings, not mine. Thus, I did not put myself in B's shoes, because then I would be saying what I with my sentiments and values would feel and do, if I were in them; and my feelings and his would easily get confused. Instead, I put B in his own shoes, that is, I tried to understand B's feelings from his point of view and not from mine. I realized that all of this was easier said than done. My performance fell far short of perfection; again and again I stubbed my toes, but I tried to maintain the posture I have described in this paragraph.

Thus in these exchanges I tried to "control" B's behavior by trying to "control" my own first, so that what was being circulated around this artificially contrived social system of two persons was B's feelings, not mine. B would bat his feelings to me and I would bat his feelings back to him as well as I could without twisting them and with the implied and often expressed query, "Is this the way you feel; that is, is this the way things are (for you)? Have I heard you correctly? If not, try me again." By this peculiar process of exchange, according to some theories, B's feelings would become ventilated and cooled off, so that in time he might gain some understanding about or insight into them and do something himself about them. Before accepting this explanation, let me continue to examine the kinds of exchanges that took place between A and B in this kind of relationship. That they were peculiar is not newsworthy; but why they had to be screwy in order to achieve certain results had me intrigued.

PROBLEMS OF CONCEPTUALIZING WHAT WAS HAPPENING

It would be impossible for me to state now in any chronological order either the increasing insights I had about the counseling relationship, or the different concepts I used to express what I thought

was happening in it, or the influence on me of the logical reconstructions that other investigators made about what was happening
in it. I do not think this matters now, because the interesting question for me resides in the fact that there exist so many different ways
in which this relationship can be conceptualized.

Starting with Freud, for example, one can say that in this kind of
A–B relationship the data for the new psychology of the individual
(B) began. Although this development started as a method of therapy called psychoanalysis, it developed over time into a theory of
individual behavior or personality also. Thus for those of us who
became involved in the development of the understanding of this
relationship, there tended to exist two foci for the logical reconstruc-
tion of what was going on. For some, it was the bees in B's bonnet
that needed better conceptualization, whereas for others it was the
kind of relationship between A and B which helped B to express to
A the bees in his bonnet that needed to be understood. In addition,
there was the underlying question of what good it did B, if any, to
express them. Would it not be better, or at least do as well and be
simpler, for A to tell B what bees B should have in his bonnet?
These questions were not unrelated, but some of us were interested
in one and not the other.

In my case it was the dynamics of the A–B helping relationship
that had me interested, because I thought the insights from it could
be extended into other relationships. This relationship was in some
respects very different from ordinary social relationships. It seemed
to violate the norms of elementary social behavior. To be interested
in and yet not to react to another person's feelings by expressing
sympathy for them was not acting like a normal social human being.
It looked as if I was structuring a kind of relationship that had no
counterpart in the social world of everyday life.

This relationship was also unusual in terms of institutionalized
forms of behavior. For example, I tried not to utilize any symbols of
status in order to influence B to talk to me openly and freely about
himself, even though on many occasions in terms of my academic or
professional rank or education I did have higher status than B. On
the contrary, by my behavior I tried not to do what persons in
positions of authority frequently do. For example, I would not have
done what a physician friend of mine did after he gave a student a
physical examination, namely, interview him while he was sitting
naked in a chair placed several inches lower than his in order to try
to get him to take his hair down. This would have smacked to me of
coercion and of playing tricks. If we were playing a game together, a

possibility I shall consider in a moment, it was to be an open and above-board game of mutual influence. Moreover, the game was a voluntary one on B's part, which he could terminate at any time, if he did not find it rewarding.

Although I tried not to utilize the symbols of authority, status, or power in order to influence B to tell me what was bothering him, I also tried not to establish a pretended relationship of equality with him. Whatever the differences might be in our status in terms of the values and norms of the wider society, they were what they were. These were facts I could not alter; I accepted them as facts by which B might be influenced but which I was not going to use overtly to influence him. And were he influenced by them too much, this would be something I would reflect back to him, by saying, "Are you telling me what you think I want to hear or the way things are for you?"

Let me now describe the exchanges between A and B in this relationship in terms of a game model, a now popular form in which to conceptualize exchanges between A's and B's. In terms of this model, what kind of a game was I playing with B and likewise what kind of game might B perceive he was playing with me?

Clearly from my point of view it was not a zero-sum game, that is, a game in which what I won B lost or vice versa. Nor was it the opposite, that is, a game in which no relationship existed between the preferred outcomes of the game on both our parts—that is, where the kind of help B wanted, expected, needed, or could accept bore no relation to the kind of help I could give him. In some sense B had to see me as a source of help and accept the kind of help I could give him, even though it was not the kind of help B thought originally he wanted, expected, or needed. Agreement about these outcomes could not be negotiated completely at the beginning of the game; it could be clarified and settled only by a series of interactions that occurred while the game was being played.

Hence, this kind of game was fraught with many dangers. For example, the kind of help B wanted or expected might not be the kind of help that A could give or the kind of help that in A's opinion B needed. For the outcome to be satisfactory for both parties, there had to exist finally a congruence of perception and expectation between the kinds of help A could provide and B could accept. If B kept asking for a kind of help that A could not give or if A kept giving a kind of help that B did not want, the relationship remained stymied. Then A could only get angry at B for not accepting the kind of help he could give, and B could only get angry at A for not giving him the kind of help he wanted. When such an outcome occurred, both A and B lost. From B's point of view he had not been helped; and although A had at first intended to be helpful, he had not succeeded in getting B to see him as a source of help. Hence, this was a kind of game in which one party could not win or lose without the other one winning or losing also. For the game to conclude successfully, both had to win or else both lost.

These outcomes, whether positive or negative, could not be predicted from the initial states of A and B; it was the interactions that occurred between them while the game was being played that determined the outcome. As this is often misunderstood, let me restate the kind of help involved in this kind of game and what the point of the game was. The point of the game was not just to have A understand B better; its aim was to help B understand himself better—that is, to get B to recognize and accept the feelings, sentiments, and values he had and with which he was trying to cope in the solution of whatever his personal problem was. It was a peculiar game in the sense that the successful outcome depended more upon B understanding himself than upon A understanding B. Although both outcomes were much to be desired, it was always possible that A could understand B without A being able to communicate this understanding to B. In this case too neither A nor B won.

In order to prevent this from happening, A set the rules of the game and rewarded B for playing the game according to these rules. As this gave A a big advantage, A had to see to it that he did not take an unfair advantage of this advantage, so to speak. For example, he could not set rules which would allow him to win the game at B's expense; this would have defeated the purpose of the game. Nor could he give B a complete set of instructions at the beginning of the game about how the game was supposed to be played; this would have defeated his purpose of allowing B to discover for himself the rules by which a cooperative game was played. This was the big point of this kind of game.

For example, when B batted his ball (feelings) into A's court, A could not pick up the ball and run with it. This was *verboten* by the rules which A had to set for the game to be played. If he did so, he ran the danger of claiming B's ball as his own, of saying, for example, "I (A) understand you (B) better than you (B) understand yourself." This was also *verboten*, because this would result in A batting B's ball back into B's court in a way that it would make it difficult for B to pick it up. Thus, this would defeat the purpose of what A was trying to accomplish, namely, to get B to pick his ball up and run with it, that is, to get B to recognize, accept, and take responsibility for his own feelings.

Thus, at the end of the game, if it was to be successful, B's ball had to be in B's court in B's hands. Although A set the rules of the game, B was the final authority about the outcome of the game. Only B could declare the game as being won. When he did, A won too. Once B picked up the ball and said, "By golly, it has taken me a long time to get the point of this game. I was refusing to pick up the ball by disowning it as mine, so I kept batting my ball back to you and trying to make you responsible for it. I see now what a silly game I was playing. You have helped me to discover it. Thank you, Mr. A, for helping me." At this point, there was perfect congruence of perception between A and B about what the game was all about. But this congruence, it should be noted, was not settled at the beginning of the game; it came in its final stage.

WHY SHOULD B CHOOSE TO PLAY THIS GAME?

This game was peculiar not only in terms of its final outcomes and payoffs. It was also peculiar in terms of the ongoing exchanges between A and B as they played. While the game was going on, what was it that A was giving to B and B was receiving from A, as well as A receiving from B and B giving to A? And how did these exchanges balance? For the moment let me disregard instances in which money was being paid for the services rendered.

Assuming a congruence of perceptions and expectations, it could be said that what A was giving B and B was receiving from A was understanding, while what A was receiving from B and B was giving to A was social approval, gratitude, and thanks, all of which built up A's self-esteem and feelings of competence. In shorthand terms, for the understanding B received, B gave A esteem. The understanding B received was of more value to him than the esteem he gave A, and likewise the esteem A received was of more value to A than the understanding he gave B, so that each received from the exchange what was of more value to him than that which he gave. Nevertheless, these exchanges were of a fragile nature in the ongoing situation.

If B had to give A too many thank you's (or too much money) in order to receive A's help, or if A had to give B too much "understanding" in order to get B's esteem (or money), either one could say "The cost I have to pay for the reward I am getting is too high; that is, the outcome from the exchange after I subtract the cost I have to pay for the reward I obtain has become negative. For me the game is not worth the candle." In short, under such conditions, the exchange would cease to be a rewarding experience for either A or B or both.

Moreover, as I have said before, if A gave no rewards at all to B for trying to play the game according to the rules A had set, that is, gave no rewards for the tears, sweat, and toil B underwent in order to tell A what it was like (for him), then why should B continue trying to do this? Of course A could hold out a big reward to B by saying to him, "After you have gone through this harrowing experience, Mr. B, you will feel better, be cured, better adjusted, able to make the decision, cope with life, be healed, and so on and on."

Although A could and often did try to develop such an attitude of expectant trust in the outcome, he could not guarantee it. If he did, he would be saying in effect, "Papa knows best; and if you do what papa tells you, you'll get better." This in effect might evoke on the part of B the feeling, "So I've got to become a dependent child in order to get your help. That does not sound like a cooperative game to me. It is the old-fashioned game I have been playing since I was a child."

Many learned articles and books have been written about the delicate balance of exchange that has to be maintained in these fateful encounters between A's and B's about which I am writing so cavalierly. But as I am not talking about psychotherapy *per se* but about what perfect cooperation, exchange, or communication between A and B in this kind of helping relationship looks like, if and when it exists, I shall continue cutting corners.

One of the solutions recommended by certain professional helpers or healers for this dilemma at this stage in the encounter is to take advantage of the fact that in most cases B wants A to be like a father to him and to tell him the answer. So although A never said to B he was papa and so knew best, he did allow B to make him into such a figure without calling it to B's attention. During the first phase of these fateful encounters, it was felt that there had to be what was called a "positive transference" on the part of B toward A.

During this phase, while B was sweating it out on the couch, A could wear a white coat, smoke a big cigar, look wise, make occasional cryptic remarks, sing a few bars from a Viennese waltz, or quote from *Alice in Wonderland.* But only in the manner of the wise old owl who lived in an oak tree, where the more he heard the less he spoke, did A allow B to believe that there were some profound thoughts going through his (A's) head which someday B would be able to latch on to and get help from.

After this first phase ran its course, sometimes lasting a year or more, and B was not feeling any better, but instead was feeling angry about the imbalance that existed between what he was paying and the services he was receiving, then and only then would A pull the rug from under B and change the rules of the game and say to B, "Don't you see what's the matter with you? Your present hostility toward me [now called a 'negative transference'] is because you expected me to be papa to you and I am not going to play this game with you any more. I fear it is going to take another year to get you out of the fix I allowed you to get into in the first place, but this is the way the ball had to bounce before you got better."

For some A's who were in the business of being professional helpers or healers, this two-game approach, even though the games were arranged sequentially and not played at the same time, was objectionable; they felt that only one game with one set of rules, such as I described earlier, should be played. In this game only the values of what for the moment I shall call the democratic, scientific, world view would prevail. This was the kind of game with which I became intrigued, and I read the books written by its professional players. Carl Rogers' two books (1942 and 1951) influenced me the most.

However, it is worth saying that during this period of my life, I did not think I was playing a game with the B's I encountered. As can be seen from my earlier writings, I never expressed myself this way or conceptualized what was going on in this way. For me the word "game" had a zero-sum flavor to it, and a game in which only both could win or both would lose did not sound like any game I had encountered. So why call it a game? Did not such a model distort the territory?

Moreover, had I thought of it as a game, I would have thought of it as a very different game from the games being played by religious healers, shamans, communist brainwashers, thought controllers, and so on, even though I recognized some similarities. For me the differences were more important than the similarities. Nevertheless, I want to continue with the analogy of a game, because it will help me to state what I thought I had in common with these other games as well as how I thought I differed from them.

CHARACTERISTICS OF THE GAME I WAS PLAYING

Obviously neither the B's nor the A's with whom I was dealing were mentally ill persons. Let me say again I was not in the business of professional healing. Nevertheless, I did have relations with many persons (students, employees, foremen, middle and top management persons) who wanted to tell it to me like it was for them. In order to facilitate this process, I developed, as I have tried to state, certain ideas about the uniformities that occurred in these relations. As a result, I found myself in practice structuring a kind of relationship in which the exchanges between A and B had the following characteristics:

(1) An exchange in which what A was giving to B was of more value to B than to A and what A was receiving from B was of more value to A than to B.

(2) An exchange in which, although A could influence B and B could influence A, A could not influence B to B's disadvantage; that is, A could not built up his own self-esteem at the expense of B.

(3) An exchange which both could find rewarding, although A could not obtain his rewards at the expense of B; that is, A could not make the costs that B would have to pay for the rewards he received from A so high that the relationship would cease to be a rewarding experience for B.

(4) An exchange of mutual trust; that is, A could not ask B to trust him without A also being willing to trust B.

(5) An exchange in which in time the perceptions of and expectations from the relationship could become increasingly the same for both A and B.

(6) A game in which A could not win without B also winning or lose without B also losing.

(7) A game in which although A set the rules of the game, B was the final authority about the outcome. When B, for example, said to A, "Yes, this is the way things are *for me*; you understand"; or when B picked up the ball and ran with it himself, the game was over.

(8) A game which was voluntary, which either A or B or both could terminate at any time.

(9) A game in which there were no guaranteed results and where the norm that A set for playing the game was stated in investigatory terms, "Let's try it and see."

(10) A game in which there were no arguments, so long as B told it as it was *for him* and not *like it was. Period.* The first—that is, like it was for B—was a fact with which A could cooperate completely. About it there could be no argument. Argument could appear only if A thought that the way it was for B should not be like that for B, or if A or B or both thought that the way it was for B was the way it should be for others.

As can be seen, I stated these characteristics in terms of A's behavior, not in terms of B's, because they implied rules for A to follow. If A behaved in accordance with these rules, it facilitated his achieving the purpose of the game—that is, giving help to B—from his (A's) point of view. B, on the other hand, was not compelled to live up to these rules, although A rewarded B in their exchanges if he did.

Although I have tried carefully to state these characteristics in terms of a specific limited objective in a given context in which they can be usefully applied, they can also be thought of as rules which can or should be applied to all human relationships in which cooperation is an aim. But when a person extends these rules to all such human relationships, he is in for trouble—and I don't mean little trouble but big—because both theorists and practitioners are on his back. This was the impasse which many of us in "human relations" reached, and it was one of the chief factors which resulted in the demise of that school of thought. I will return to it later.

Before I end this chapter, I want to state my conception of the nature of these rules for counseling and how I thought insights from their practice could be useful for practitioners such as the students in my course who were not likely to be involved in relationships of a strictly counseling-helping character. I will get at the issue I want to raise in this connection by asking a number of questions.

(1) Were these rules or norms of human behavior a set of higher moral principles which I had developed for myself and which I thought all practitioners of human relations should emulate?

(2) By means of these norms was I trying to induce the A's in business organizations to behave on a higher moral plane?

(3) Was I trying to eliminate conflict and show that cooperation was all?

(4) Was I still manipulating B, but now in in the name of science?

(5) Had I deserted my original intentions of describing the phenomena of human interactions and begun stating what they should be?

(6) Had I constructed an ideal type of behavior which could not be concretely realized?

(7) Did my rules state the conditions of perfect cooperation, communication, and exchange?

(8) Was I playing a zero-sum game with the devil (a shorthand term for the second law of thermodynamics) and trying to show how under certain conditions he could be outwitted?

(9) Or were my opponents still the brute and stubborn phenomena of human interactions from which I was trying to extract a uniformity, even though I had to stand, figuratively speaking, upside down in order to do so?

Although all these possibilities can be entertained (and surely no categorical denial on my part of any one of them is going to eliminate it), the last one had me intrigued. For me these uniformities were not higher moral principles of conduct which I was trying to get the A's in the business to emulate. Nor did I think I was manipulating the B's in terms of them. For me they were the conditions under which a B might begin to move under his own steam and in a more constructive fashion. Under the actual conditions by which a B was being influenced, he was often in a state of stable equilibrium with his social surroundings; under the new set of conditions I set up, B sometimes began to move in a direction of increased complexity toward them. This was the uniformity which had been observed in the Hawthorne Researches and to which the name "the positive Hawthorne effect" had been given. In the case of my counseling relations I could get this uniformity to emerge only by creating a kind of relation which had no counterpart in the actual (social) world, that is, by setting up what can be called conditions for perfect cooperation, exchange, or communication. Perhaps a diagram will help to illustrate how I conceived this.

In terms of the diagram I did not conceive myself as trying to change B. I could not alter G_1 and only for relatively short periods could I create conditions G_2. I conceived G_2 as a new relationship composed of norms which prescribed the activities and sentiments which would be exchanged between B and me. This new pattern of activities, interactions, and sentiments, together with its norms, I thought of as a new role model of behavior. I also saw it as approximating the conditions of perfect exchange, cooperation, and communication in the kind of helping relationship I have described.

Although G_2 was a set of prescriptive norms, the outcome O_2 I thought of as a descriptive uniformity in the phenomena. O_2 is what would be observed under the conditions G_2. I thought that this uniformity in the phenomena had been clinically observed by many investigators, perhaps not for all the different kinds of B's that existed in the whole wide world, but at least for many B's. This was good enough for me. In these terms O_2 was as phenomenologically real as O_1, even though the conditions G_2 under which it revealed itself I

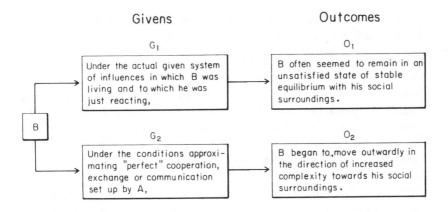

must confess looked to me at times as though they were out of this world. In spite of this, if it could be shown that under conditions G_2, O_2 could be observed, then I thought I had something.

This was as far as I could conceptualize the problem at the time. Later, in my final chapter, I will call O_1 a condition of reactivity and O_2 a condition of proactivity on the part of B with regard to his social surroundings. At the time I intuitively felt that O_2 (proactivity) was not a special case of O_1 (reactivity), but that the opposite was true; O_1 (reactivity) was a special case of O_2 (proactivity); that is, proactivity was the general stance of man's behavior toward his surroundings and reactivity was a special case of it.

At the time I was not capable of conceptualizing this insight. I did not have any idea of what the more general propositions about the phenomena of human interactions were that led them under conditions G_1 to reveal themselves in O_1 and under conditions G_2 to reveal themselves in O_2. I intuitively felt that there were some such propositions and that I would have to wait until a Newton, such as George Homans, came along, who would be able to state them. Until then I confess I felt that the area of "human relations" would oscillate back and forth. At times I felt as if it were getting off the ground and at other times as if it were grounded. The big stumbling block was G_2. Again and again G_2 was interpreted as the principles by which *all A's should behave toward all B's under all conditions.* Again and again but without much avail, I would say that G_2 were the conditions under which a certain kind of behavior on the part of some B's could be observed. There I remained hung up, except in certain respects which I will consider next.

LOOKING AT CERTAIN MATTERS FROM THE BOTTOM UP AS WELL AS FROM THE TOP DOWN

Even though I realized that I could not state the above clinical uniformities in a propositional form acceptable to science, I did not think that these grounds were enough to prevent them from being usefully applied by supervisors in matters relating to motivation, communication, authority, and control. These uniformities put matters from the right end up, in the sense that A was looking at and concerned about them from the point of view of B, not just from the point of view of A.

(1) In the case of motivation, for example, A was not concerned with motivating B; he was concerned with what was important and rewarding to B and thus in fact motivating him. Although A might have the authority to grant or withhold certain rewards, in the final analysis it was B who decided if these rewards were rewarding and the withholding of them punishing to him.

(2) In the case of communication, for example, A's goal was not how he could get B to understand his (A's) point of view. Instead, it was how he (A) could understand B's point of view without B fearing that he (A) would not accept it. Moreover, in the final analysis it was what B heard and not what A said that made the difference to B's response.

(3) In the case of authority, for example, A was not trying to influence B by his (A's) formal position of authority. Instead, A was trying to understand in what B said how he might be influenced by it. Although A might have the formal authority to issue orders, again it was B who in the final analysis settled whether or not he accepted what A said as authoritative. It was not the formal authority A had, but the authority B granted to what A did and said that made the difference.

(4) In the case of control, for example, it was how B controlled his own preoccupations and feelings, not how A could or should control them. Although A might set the standards for what B was supposed to do, it was B who settled if he would prefer to quit the job than abide by them.

Thus in the A–B helping relationship I have described, it was B and not A who did the motivating and the communicating, had the authority, and exercised the control about what he was going to do. This is what I meant when I said that in order to get at these matters from the right end, A had to look at them from the bottom up as well as from the top down. Although the counseling relationship offered an excellent opportunity to practice this way of thinking, I did not think that its methods had to be restricted to this relationship. I thought that the methods could also be extended to other A–B relationships, even ones in which A had a position of formal authority over B.

This did not mean that A had to stop talking, that he could no longer set up standards, tell B what was expected of him, exercise influence of persuasion, or give or withhold the rewards his formal authority granted him. It meant, though, that once and for all A recognized where the final locus of choice resided—namely, in B— about these matters in regard to what ought to be done. A could settle what needed or ought or should be done, but it was B who settled whether he was going to do it and whether he was willing to pay the costs of doing or not doing it.

Without a recognition of this fact, A could have all the power and authority any institution could grant him but no matter how great they were, they could evaporate into thin air when he started to exercise them, as we saw in the case of Mr. Post, unless he understood the limits of what power and authority could accomplish. Once A recognized these limits, there could be a change in the way he exercised his formal authority and power. I thought I could detect this difference in the behavior of any well-seasoned and successful practitioner in a position of authority. He knew only too well how real and also how ephemeral authority and power were, how carefully they had to be exercised and not extended beyond the point at which they disintegrated into dust. It seemed to me that with a way of listening such as I was advocating, there went a way of telling which, as would be said today, was less hot and more cool. This way of telling got motivation, communication, authority, and control from the right end up, that is, both from the bottom and from the point of view of B. Once this was understood, A could begin to exercise his authority and power more in accordance with phenomenological reality instead of in terms of what formalistic and legalistic stereotypes and abstractions had to say about them.

By 1951 I realized that I had reached the limits of what could be accomplished by the case method in the direction of training in the skills of human relations and interpersonal communications. Although the course in Human Relations had gone beyond Administrative Practices with respect to the skill aspects of the administrative process, it was necessarily classroom and intellectually oriented. Students were more likely to understand the fateful encounter between

A and B intellectually than they were to feel it emotionally. In the next chapter I will describe how I tried to find a way to deal with this problem.

Chapter 13
Human Relations Training

Although the human relations movement in industry started in the 1940s as a research activity, by 1951 it had become primarily a training activity confined to the lower ranks of supervision. Courses in human relations for first-line supervisors became very popular. Because I thought that many of these courses were superficial—in some cases even harmful—and also because I thought that my course at the Business School was touching only the tip of the iceberg in respect to training in human relations skill, I wrote a proposal for a Program for Advanced Training and Research in Human Relations and submitted it to the Division of Research at the Business School for funding.

At about that same time, the Ford Foundation decided to make available its first large grants for research in the behavioral sciences. In this program, the Foundation gave $300,000 to the president of each of three universities which were reputed to be research oriented and let the presidents decide how the monies should be allocated within their universities. This is how Mr. Conant, who was then President of Harvard, received $300,000 from the Ford Foundation; he gave $100,000 of the amount to the Dean at the Business School to support the program for which I had written such a timely proposal.

THE HUMAN RELATIONS CLINIC (1951–1954)

This program, which in time came to be called the Human Relations Clinic, was addressed to the training of what I then called second-level practitioners, persons who would someday be in positions of responsibility for improving the competence of human relations practitioners at the first level. First-level practitioners, as I conceived them, were persons who because of the nature of their jobs had some responsibility for obtaining the understanding and cooperation of others in order to get their own jobs done. Thus my first-level practitioner could be an administrator at any level in any kind of organization—those persons I called A's in Chapter 11. My second-level practitioner bore some resemblance to the persons who later came to be called change agents, but I thought of them as agents acting from within, not from outside the system or relationships which they were trying to improve.

As our program was designed to attract students who wanted to be where the action was and to utilize their knowledge there, the students or trainees were young men whose career objectives were somewhat different from those of most students in conventional doctoral programs. Although some of them happened to be doctoral candidates in business administration or one of the behavioral science disciplines, they were not sure that upon graduation they wished to go into academic teaching and research. Indeed, most of them felt no need for a doctoral degree. I purposely kept the program small. By its third year we still had only nine trainees.

The way their careers developed will help to show the kind of students we attracted. One, for example, set up a school in Mysore, India, for community workers in rural areas. Later he was engaged in a similar activity in Hyderabad, and afterward helped to develop a human-relations-type program at a southern university in this country. A second went into educational administration and became for a while vice-chancellor of a large midwestern university after having been first the dean of its business school; after a period of teaching, he returned to university administration. A third became a director of a non-university-affiliated research and training organization in the behavioral sciences in California and then became associated with the human potential activities at Esalen. A fourth, after becoming professor of human relations in a Canadian university, started working with management development programs sponsored by the Ford Foundation in developing countries, first in Egypt and later in Colombia. Later he became affiliated with the National Training Laboratories in Washington, D. C., and still later dean of a business school in the South. A fifth became first the director of alumni relations in a large eastern business school and afterward the head of a private executive development institute. Three others stayed in university teaching. Upon reflection, it seems strange that none of our trainees went into a business organization, that none of them strayed far from education in one form or another, and that a number of them returned to teaching; but I will not try to explain it. I will just treat it as a fact.

In the program I was concerned not just with the future careers of the trainees but also with exploring what the training for such persons should be; that is, what the training should be for those who wanted to act as multipliers of competence in matters of human relations. It seemed to me that the difficulty of this job was underestimated in many quarters and that this was why human relations training was coming to have a bad name. It tended to remain at either a superficial level or to degenerate into a cult. So the purpose of the "training design"—to use a highfalutin' term—of our program was to see if we could break through this barrier.

FIVE CONTEXTS IN WHICH TO LEARN HUMAN RELATIONS SKILLS

To accomplish this objective, we provided, as the program evolved, five contexts in which a trainee could learn to practice and improve his human relations skills in relation to the concrete phenomena of human behavior:

(1) *A diagnostic or research context,* in which the trainee would be trying to observe, diagnose, and describe the behavior that was going on in a small work group. In this context he would not take any action or intervene in any way to change or improve the situation. The product of his activity would be a written descriptive case.

(2) *A counseling context,* in which the trainee would be trying to help a person express his feelings and say how things were for him in relation to a problem he had. The aim of this activity was to help the person to understand his problem better and to make his own decision about what to do about it.

(3) *A membership context,* in which the trainee was a member of a small work group, in which he would try to be a helpful group member in achieving the group's task objectives, by which his behavior was in part being determined but also in respect to which he had a determining part.

(4) *A leadership context,* in which the trainee was the leader of a small group and in which he would be trying to practice the insights he had learned in the above three contexts but in this context from a position of formal responsibility and under the burden of responsibility for results.

(5) *A personal context,* in which he was not the counselor but the counselee and in which he had an opportunity to express his own

feelings, to say what things were like for him, and to understand why they were that way for him.

These five learning contexts developed in the direction of increasing complexity and involvement with the concrete phenomena of human behavior.

(1) In the diagnostic context, for example, the trainee was just observing and listening to these phenomena and *talking about* them in analytical terms.

(2) In the counseling context he was not only observing and listening; he was also *talking with* (and not just *talking about*) these phenomena and learning perhaps that talking with disturbed persons in a helpful way involved some other skills than just talking about them in a diagnostic way.

(3) In the membership context he was not only observing and listening to the phenomena and talking with them. He was also involved in the task to be achieved by the group, with the formal leader of the group, and with the problem of how to relate to this authority figure.

(4) In the leadership context the trainee was not only observing and listening and talking with the phenomena and involved in the task to be achieved. He was now also under the burden of responsibility for getting the task accomplished and getting the members of the group to cooperate toward this end.

(5) Finally, after learning how to observe and listen and talk about the phenomena of human behavior from an external frame of reference and to talk with them from an internal frame of reference as counselor, member, or leader of a group, he now had to learn to recognize, listen to, and talk to his own feelings and to learn the difficulties of coping with them.

These contexts allowed a trainee to move along a continuum from the extrinsic to the intrinsic aspects of learning and knowing. By the time he reached the fifth context his learning and knowing were completely intrinsic. This context was concerned solely with self-learning, self-knowledge, self-development, and inner growth. I mention this continuum because between these two different kinds of learning and knowing—the extrinsic and intrinsic—some of the most serious battles in the warfare among the social sciences have been fought. To one or the other of these juggernauts of knowledge many persons have blindly devoted themselves or been ruthlessly sacrificed.

Obviously I have been involved in this dichotomy since the beginning of my career. It is one of the themes of my life, what makes the achievement of a subject matter so difficult for me. For the time being, I want to describe how it manifested itself in the training program.

I called the problem then the problem of multi-dimensionality for the human relations practitioner. The problem arises because whichever of the five contexts a practitioner finds himself in, the territory to which he has to relate himself is composed of different dimensions, for example: (1) the needs of individuals; (2) the cohesiveness of a group; (3) the effective accomplishment of a task; (4) the values of science; and (5) the ideals of behavior. Each of these dimensions has its own prescriptions and injunctions about what behavior should be. In the order I have just listed, they are for example, (1) be true to yourself or else; (2) conform or else; (3) be effective or else; (4) be objective or else; (5) hold steadfast to the eternal verities or else.

These difficult injunctions often result for a practitioner in ambiguity, uncertainty, inconsistency, and imperfection as to how he should behave in a concrete situation. To the values of which dimension should he give priority? Yet unless he gives priority to one, how can he deal with the multi-dimensionality without becoming conflicted? At this time I thought that instead of trying to escape from this conflict or to seek for simple rules to deal with it, he might be able to learn to accept, live with, and deal with it at the level of skill and judgment—by what I called the clinical method. And by the clinical method I meant how the human relations practitioner dealt with, managed, and coped with his feelings of ambiguity, uncertainty, inconsistency, and inadequacy when dealing with the concrete. This was the direction in which I went full steam ahead in the training program.

Obviously this direction highlighted context 5 and the importance of knowing yourself before extrinsic knowledge about human behavior could be gained and usefully applied. At times it looked as if our program was leading our trainees slowly but surely (but not intentionally) to the analyst's couch. Let me stop describing the many bugs our training program contained and how we dealt with them; we described them in the monograph *Training for Human Relations* (1954) which I wrote with the help of George Lombard and Harriet

Ronken. Also I was beginning to suspect that these bugs were not going to be eliminated by any bigger and better training design.

MY EXPERIENCES AT BETHEL, MAINE

In the summer of 1953 I decided to visit Bethel, Maine, the summer training center of the Group Dynamics brand of Human Relations. Just as Elton Mayo was the father of the brand of human relations that I was practicing, it could be said that Kurt Lewin was the father of the brand of human relations called Group Dynamics that was practiced at Bethel. Born and educated in Germany and Professor of Psychology at the University of Berlin, Lewin came to this country in 1932. After short sojourns as visiting professor at Stanford University and Cornell University, he became Professor of Child Psychology at the State University of Iowa from 1935 to 1945 and Director of the Research Center for Group Dynamics at M.I.T. from 1945 to 1947, when he died at a tragically early age. Although Lewin helped in the design of the first training program at Bethel, given by the National Training Laboratories in Group Development in collaboration with the National Education Association in the summer of 1947, he died before he could participate in it. It was staffed that summer and for many summers thereafter by his close associates at the Research Center for Group Dynamics at M.I.T. and later at the University of Michigan. This program for trainers, educators, and administrators proved to be unusually successful and in time expanded into first a nationwide and eventually an international network of training centers and workshops.

When I participated in the program at Bethel in 1953, this expansion had not yet taken place, but the training design was fairly well developed. The concept of a cultural island was well established and the now famous T-group (T for training) was going strong. The label sensitivity training was not being used and the blood bath of the T-group was mild in comparison to the blood lettings which were to take place in the open encounter groups, confrontation groups, marathon groups, memory awakening groups, and voyaging-in-inner-space groups that appeared a decade or so later.

In 1953 the activities going on at the Harvard Business School in Human Relations training and the activities going on at Bethel in Group Dynamics were regarded as separate activities. However, it seemed to me and also to Lee Bradford, who was then the director of the National Training Laboratories, that in spite of differences in concepts and terminologies, we had some important characteristics in common. Generally speaking, each of us was looking at small-scale social phenomena in small groups and raising about the same sorts of questions about the cooperation, conflicts, and leadership going on in them. Each of us had a conceptual scheme (or theory). Although these were different, we were both interested in the relation of our scheme or theory to practice. We were both interested in the processes going on in concrete face-to-face relations. We were both zeroing in on the leadership process. Though both Lee and I were interdisciplinary and social-psychologically oriented, neither of us was strictly a sociologist or a psychologist.

There were also differences between us; some of them seemed to me more important than others. One of the less important, it seemed to me, was that from the point of view of practice, I had concentrated more on the two-person relationship than on the small group. Although I had researched the small work group—indeed from a research point of view, I was often regarded as a small group man—in practice I more often used or applied the insights I received from counseling. Yet I realized that in doing the work of the world, small groups were as important as two-person relationships and that the *here-and-now* processes going on in small groups were well worth the attention of the leader of the group, particularly in relation to getting tasks accomplished. I viewed these group processes as important, and I went to Bethel to learn more about them.

Of minor importance to me was the fact that I used "cases" and taught my version of the case method in small groups (if 100-student sections can be thought of as small groups), instead of using the *here-and-now* data generated in T-groups. I thought that I could take these differences in stride and that they did not constitute irreconcilable conflicts between us, because, as I have tried to show, I paid as much attention to the *discussion* of the case (here-and-now data) as to the case itself (there-and-then data).

Of more importance to me was the difference in our points of view that resided in the fact that I had been concerned with work groups in which the task dimension was more critical than it was in the training groups at Bethel. Also I had been concerned with the helping relationship in the administrative context in business organizations rather than in the context of professional helping services, such as social and group work. To put it another way, I had been concerned, not with a change agent who was *outside* the organization, but rather with the one who was acting from a responsible position *within* an organization in which he was trying to facilitate the processes of change, adjustment, and integration. I realized that these factors would make a difference between the backgrounds of the trainees attending Bethel and those of my students at the Business School. Still, I thought that these differences could be reconciled— or at least that I could reconcile them for myself—at a higher level of generalization, and that they would not interfere with my learning what could be learned at Bethel.

In short, I did not go to Bethel with the intention of persuading the authorities there about the superiority of my conceptual scheme, of the case method, of the clinical method, of the two-person relationship, of counseling, of task groups, or of my brand of change agentry in human relations training. Rather it seemed to me that in the small unstructured training groups at Bethel we had many objectives and values in common. I was interested in how they generated their own data for the purpose of having their members learn about themselves, about group processes, and about their relations with one another; for the purpose of practicing "good" human relations, "good" leadership, and "good" followership; for the purpose of implementing the helping relationship; for the purpose of helping their members become sensitive to or facilitate change; or for the purpose of dealing with conflict and encouraging cooperation (take your pick of the way you want to say this).

Although I had no intention of trying to convince the people at Bethel of the superiority of my conceptual scheme, nevertheless, I could not park it outside when I walked onto their cultural island. Honest to goodness, since it was an intrinsic part of me, I had to bring it along with me. Moreover, I could not stop myself from using it, because this was is its natural function. L. J. Henderson said it was an essential piece of equipment for the seeker of knowledge. Lewin said there was nothing more practical than a good theory. I felt that the utilization of theory in practice was cricket and consistent with my purposes. I came to Bethel to learn how they went about things but also to find out whether there were real differences between us or whether we were just hung up on words. In spite of what we had in common, were we without knowing it looking at and conceptualizing different phenomena? Were we raising different questions? Did we have different frames of reference, objectives, and values?

Thus, although I did not go to Bethel uncritically, neither did I go with my critical bifocals uppermost. Instead, as was my attitude in most field research, I tried to immerse myself as well and as much as I could in what was going on about me, to understand it, and only later after the whole experience was over to evaluate it critically.

I spent six—or was it eight?—weeks at Bethel. At that time the trainees were involved in a number of different kinds of groups—T (for training) group, S (for skill) group, C (for cozy) group, and so on. In one of the S-groups and one of the C-groups I was a trainer; in the other groups, I was a trainee.

The T-group experience was the one in which I was most interested. For my T-group leader I was fortunate to have Lee Bradford—a highly perceptive, insightful, and thoughtful person who exercised his talents in a most modest way. From his behavior as much as from any theory about the T-group that he or others expressed, I learned a great deal.

As I have indicated, at that time the "T" in T-group stood for training and not therapy. I was particularly interested in how Lee went about differentiating the group processes going on in the group from the intra-psychic (or personality or life style) processes of individuals and in how he addressed himself to these group processes. He helped to make the group processes explicit without ignoring the intra-psychic processes, but without making the latter so explicit that they became the object of attention or the subject of discussion.

From him I certainly got a better feel for group processes than I had had, but it was at a "syncretistic" rather than an "analytical" level. Heretofore I had studied groups which had a history because their members had worked together for a period and through time had generated certain norms of behavior in an organizational environment that was filled with standard methods and procedures. I had never looked at a group in the process of formation (except in my classes) or in an unstructured task environment. In my classes the task, because of the "case," was fairly well defined. Consequently, it was a new experience for me to see how 12 to 15 persons with different backgrounds, life styles, reference groups, and professional occupations, who had never known each other, could work together to accomplish a task that was never clearly stated by the leader. This approach highlighted the leader-follower relationship to a degree that I had not experienced. In comparison to my nondirective method it provoked more acutely and with more anguish the questions of "Tell me, dear teacher (or trainer), what should we do? What is the answer? Who is the villain? Who will our savior be, and what the hell is going on here?"

I also found that in these settings one could examine interpersonal relationships in more depth than I had been able to in my large case-method classes. In a syncretistic fashion, I was able to differentiate group from individual processes. I saw how this distinction could be applied, not by ignoring individual processes, but by calling the group's attention to what was going on in the group in relation to the needs of the group rather than in relation to the needs of individuals; that is, by clarifying how a particular activity of a particular group member at a particular time might be facilitating or impeding the cohesion of the group or the achievement of its purposes.

At this point I got hung up conceptually. What were the purposes of the T-group: trying to accomplish a common task as a group or examining and learning about the members' interpersonal relations? In a way, of course, it was both. But because of the training design, the task dimension was usually not clear and sometimes not even present, and the examination of the cohesion of the group always got priority. In a way it looked as if the more inefficiently the members of a group carried out the group's task, the better they were able to examine their interpersonal relations. But in relation to what? Again, not so much in relation to the accomplishment of a task, but rather in relation to whether they had become a good (cohesive?) group and were being good group members. Thus it seemed to me that the maintenance roles which the members of the group performed as good group members were more highly rewarded by the trainer than the task roles which they performed in order to get something done. In fact, attempts in the direction of task accomplishment were often interpreted as vying for leadership, that is, as attempting to get leadership in an undemocratic way. This emphasis on being a good group member rather than on getting a task accomplished seemed to me often to bring the life styles of group members sharply into focus—the factor which, according to its theory, the T-group hoped would be kept in the background.

As a result, it was sometimes difficult to keep the personality or life style dimension out of the picture. For example, although one could at times identify the role of a group member as a clown or blocker and raise a question about whether the role was or was not helping the group to satisfy what it needed in order to maintain its cohesion or achieve its purpose, it was difficult to avoid the question of why B (a particular group member) continued to play the same role at other times, when it was patently inappropriate for fulfilling one or both of these group needs.

With this question, of course, the dimension of life style raised its ugly head. Although attempts to explore the question were sometimes made—in fact, they could hardly be avoided—it seemed to me that Lee played down such explorations and hoped that the particular group member in time would see why the group needed different roles to be exercised by its members at different times and why playing one role on all occasions was bound at some times to be inappropriate. But Lee allowed the group member who played just one role to achieve this insight for himself. For example, I discovered that I was playing my customary mediating role in the group when there was nothing in particular to mediate and when the members were not ready for mediation. Lee could have said, "Stop being such a damn fool, Fritz," but he never did. He allowed me to get the point all by myself.

Other exciting insights also emerged. It followed that whoever by his behavior *here-and-now* most appropriately met the needs of the group became at that time its leader. Thus a particular group had no one leader, but different ones at different times; in a formal sense, it became a leaderless group.

As can be imagined, this idea had a great appeal for me. It was "of a piece" with many of the ideas I had been playing with for a long time, that is, that the leader did not get things done only by the exercise of power. Also, as my critics would wish me to point out, it was congruent with my non-power-oriented life style, or as they would prefer me to say, my fear of exercising power because I thought it was bad.

Even with these biases, I saw that the recognition of this insight was a difficult achievement, that its practice was filled with many perils; and that it was not something that could be learned in a few easy lessons. This was so in part because it set up difficult stresses and strains on any person in a position of formal authority who tried to practice and live by or with it. For example, in a T-group any group member who could satisfy the needs of the group more often than the formal trainer became *de facto* its leader. When this happened, what happened to the formal trainer? Was he satisfied with his accomplishments? Or were there queasy feelings in the pit of his stomach? And how did he handle these feelings? This seemed to me a taboo subject at Bethel, or at least one which at the time we were all too busy to consider.

In spite of these questions, my experiences in the T-group with Lee Bradford were rewarding; I learned a great deal. Certainly they were more rewarding than my experiences in other groups with my other fellow trainees and trainers. Here I found a number of things hard to take and cope with. I will mention a few:

(1) The generally hectic and unstructured climate. It seemed to be assumed that in order for people to learn about themselves and their relations to each other, everything had to be kept constantly in a state of flux. I felt that from eight in the morning until midnight I was kept circulating in groups with little opportunity for leisurely interaction or reflection.

(2) The Lewinian jargon, which was different from my own and often had me stuttering; e.g., I had difficulty in having to refer to the supervisory hierarchy in industry as the power structure.

(3) The many trainees who were trying to be grimly "democratic" or were awaiting with wide-eyed anticipation the moment when they would obtain the insight (peak experience or lesson) that they had come to Bethel to get.

(4) The assumption that everyone in business got things done only by power, whereas at Bethel things were different.

(5) The suspicion on the part of some of my fellow trainers that I was trying to introduce the case method and so adulterate the Bethel training design.

(6) The assumption of one best leadership style, which at times I thought was on the verge of becoming a cult.

(7) The norm of getting slapped down, if one vied for leadership in any other than a democratic way.

(8) The value of equality at all cost, even at the expense of the value of competence.

(9) The assumption that what needed to be learned or could be learned could be accomplished in a period of six weeks.

When I left Bethel, I must confess that I thought that the people there were in a bind that was rather similar to the one I was in. Although I had gained some insights, they were not capable of being made very explicit. Hence, it was not easy to communicate them without their being misunderstood or twisted into some questionable form. It did not occur to me that they could be practiced without considerable judgment and intuitive familiarity with the phenomena. What Bethel was up to could be as easily accused as what I was up to of manipulation, do-goodism, idealism, romanticism, being value-bound, normative, soft on power, and so on. At this level of semantic evaluation I could not see any difference. We were both in the same mushy pea soup.

BY 1954 I FELT THAT I HAD HAD IT

After my experiences at Bethel and my experiences during the last year of the Human Relations Clinic, when I tried to incorporate some of the insights I had gained at Bethel into the clinic's training design without satisfactory results, something came to an end for me. As the expression goes, I felt that I had had it; or perhaps that I had had enough of it. What was the "it" that I had had enough of?

Well, it was the experience of getting hung up by words in trying to communicate something of importance to me; the feeling that I could not get out of this box by juggling with words; the feeling that I had exhausted the clinical approach; and the feeling that although I might get new insights from its practice, I would not get any further clarifications or new knowledge at this level of investigation. Continued research at the clinical level would lead only to the continued rediscovery of the same results. Though these results could be interpreted by words, labels, and concepts in as many different ways as there were investigators, they would remain unexplained in a scientific sense.

Moreover for me, then, learning how to train human relations practitioners in the clinical approach had roughly been solved. Further refinements could be made, but they were likely to consist of different ways of packaging the same elements for different kinds of persons in different kinds of role responsibilities. The same old value questions would keep reappearing.

What disturbed me even more about this possible direction for development was that if we went in it under the assumption that we could communicate it in a few easy lessons, what we were doing would degenerate into a cult. Although the training of human relations practitioners in the clinical approach remained for me of the greatest importance and something in which I always remained interested, I felt that there was no magic about the approach, nor were there magical results that could be obtained from its practice. Whatever results could be obtained required a practitioner who was motivated by a desire to deal competently with the phenomena, who did not underestimate the difficulty, who did not think the approach could be learned in a few simple, easy lessons by taking short cuts, and who thus would give it his complete time and attention.

Let me conclude this chapter on a more optimistic note. I would not want the reader to believe that I was through with the conceptual scheme and clinical method I had been practicing, or that I thought either should be abandoned. Far from it—both had paid off handsomely for me. By thinking systemically and functionally and by practicing this way of thinking clinically in concrete situations, I had felt constantly rewarded. Armed with this way of thinking, I could go into situations and often see things that others missed; I could also, though not always, make a small intervention that sometimes made a big difference.

More than this, what had me excited and also pleased was that I was able to look at many different situations from the same point of view, without having to shift my frame of reference. I could look at both management and workers as interdependent parts of a social system. I could see how things looked different from different positions in a system of relations. I could understand situations from a B's as well as from an A's point of view and also in terms of their relation to each other.

Used as a tool of discovery, investigation, exploration, or diagnosis in concrete situations, this way of thinking seldom failed me. The possibility of translating this way of thinking into modes of action or intervention in concrete situations I found exciting and challenging. It opened up for me ways of doing things other than those generally considered by the textbooks in management. Particularly in dealing with a class of problems involving "itches" and "ouches," I found it useful. It revealed that there were sometimes more interesting and rewarding ways of scratching an "itch" or of dealing with an "ouch" than those recommended in the standard textbooks.

I also did not feel completely discouraged about being able to communicate this clinical way of thinking, looking, and acting to others. I thought it was possible to do this, so long as one did not reduce it to a gimmick that could be practiced without intuitive familiarity with the phenomena or without exercise of judgment under conditions of responsibility. The administrators-to-be whom I was teaching had to conceive of themselves as responsible practitioners, not as magicians. They had to see themselves as persons who were trying to become more competent, not just as whiz kids, in matters of human relations.

If everything at the time was as hunky-dory as I have just been saying it was, the question arises just what was bugging me? This is a good question, because in a way I could have spent the rest of my life at the clinical level I have been describing. I would have found it rewarding, and I find myself now wondering why I did not do it. Why did I allow myself to be sidetracked by other considerations? Had the charges of my critics gotten under my skin?

Although I can answer these questions more clearly now in retrospect than I could have answered them at the time, I will continue to stay as well as I can in the frame of mind I was in in 1954 for the discussion in the next chapter of one more aspect of what I was thinking about and doing during this period of my life.

Chapter 14
Human Relations Research

Although from 1942 to 1954 I was engaged primarily in trying to communicate a clinical orientation to administrators and practitioners of human relations, it would be incorrect for anyone to conclude that during this period I was doing no research. I say this because at times it seemed to me as if my critics thought that after we published the findings of the Hawthorne researches in *Management and the Worker* in 1939, I just sat on my podium at the Business School and pontificated about the Hawthorne effect and what human relations in industry should be. They seemed to assume that *all* the evidence I had for what I was saying came from those researches. There was a certain amount of justification for this belief, because it is a fact that during this period my publications were concerned more with ways of communicating and applying research findings than with developing new ones. Let me now make amends and describe what I was doing.

CASE RESEARCH

During the period from 1942 to 1954 I was engaged in case research, that is, in collecting or supervising the collection of cases for the courses I taught. These cases were not "armchair" cases; they were not anecdotes made up to illustrate or make a point. They were descriptions of actual concrete happenings that occurred in industry. In order to describe such happenings, someone at some time had to get up from his desk and chair, leave his podium, and go out in the field, even if only for an hour or two. This was the posture of all my colleagues at the Business School and one with which I was 100 percent in accord.

Where I differed was the way in which we went about collecting and reporting these cases. For my subject matter it seemed to me that we needed different procedures from the ones my colleagues used, so I instituted some changes. All these changes were in the direction of what I thought could legitimately be called descriptive research.

For most of my colleagues in production, finance, marketing, and control, cases were essentially teaching cases, that is, cases to be used primarily for instructional purposes. In order to collect them, a research assistant went into the field in search of an illustration of a particular problem which the professor needed to fill his teaching outline. For example, he might need a case about whether a manufacturer should make a particular part or buy it. With this in mind, the research assistant went to an organization where such a decision was in the process of being made or had recently been made, and he collected the data that he or the professor for whom he was working felt were needed in order to decide by good cost analysis procedures which alternative, to make or to buy, was better.

The cases which the students discussed in their classes were reports of these data. Let it be noted, however, that the data were not always those which the persons in a particular situation had used in reaching their actual decisions. The change occurred if the professor and his research assistant decided to put into the case data that they thought the decision makers in the actual situation *should* have used on the basis of "good" cost analysis procedures. After all, from a professor's point of view, it was sometimes important to show students that if decision makers would only collect the "right" cost data and analyze them in the "right" way, the decisions they would reach would be "better" than the ones which executives in real situations sometimes made.

From an instructional point of view, this kind of teaching case was useful for teaching about costs, and I had no quarrel with the practice. But if it was used as an accurate description of the total situation which determined the decision that had been reached, it bothered me. First, the cost data that had been used and analyzed in making the actual decision were not accurately reported. More important from my point of view, no data—I mean literally 100 percent none—about other influences which might have affected the actual decision were reported. Thus, if in fact some socio-human or other organizational matters had influenced the decision, the way in which the data in the case were reported left the impression that the decision had been made solely on the basis of cost data, when this had not been the situation. This bothered me no end.

These were not the only practices that concerned me. Often, for example, a research assistant would collect his data from just one person in an organization, the person, let us say, whose function in the formal organization resulted in his being the most involved and whose judgment should have been the most critical in making the decision. This was okay with me, so long as it was reported correctly. But was it?

More often than not, what appeared in the case was not what B, C, or D actually said or did or felt, but what A (from whom the case had been collected) said that B, C, or D said, did, or felt. What concerned me was that this fact was often disguised in the case. Most cases were written at the time in an impersonal, third-person, objective style, with the result that students in class often discussed what A said that B, C, or D said or did or felt as if what was reported was in fact what they did say or do or feel. And it was not; it was only what A—or worse, the case writer—reported they said. I thought this confusion could be and often was serious.

Still other things disturbed me. As the collecting and writing of cases became institutionalized at the Business School, the professors of large courses were given research assistants to help collect their teaching cases. These research assistants, in many instances, were not doctoral candidates, but MBA graduates who wished to stay at the School for a year or two after graduation in order to get this case-collecting experience before taking a job in business. As a result of this practice, professors themselves (particularly full and associate professors) went less frequently into the field and spent more of their time "editing" the data that their research assistants brought them. (I might add, as an aside, that it was often more financially rewarding for a professor to go into the field to consult than to collect a case.)

This division of labor, when done openly and honestly, did not bother me. What did bother me was the possibility that, in the editing of a case, it could unwittingly be slanted in the direction of what *should* have been happening out there in the field, where the full professor had not been. But because he was a full professor, he might feel that he knew better than his research assistant what was going on out there. If his views prevailed—and they sometimes did—in the written case, what we had going on was a self-fulfilling prophecy in full-blown operation. With my clinical orientation I shuddered at this possibility.

Still more was at issue for me in these practices. The philosophy of professors as interchangeable parts, which was at its peak during this period, also applied to research assistants. Just as it was held that all professors should be able to teach cases in production, marketing, finance, control, policy, and human relations, all research assistants should be able to collect cases in any of these areas. During this period, the case method had become such an inscrutable mystery at the Business School that one had to come there and spend at least a year in order to find out what it was all about. You taught by it; you did research by it. It had become an all-purpose tool. What made a case a good case could not be reduced to rational discourse; it had to be experienced to be understood. A la Gertrude Stein a case was a case was a case and so on. You had to sleep with a case or have a love affair with it before you could understand its potency.

Although I had some sympathy with this point of view, I felt that there was a difference between a research case and a teaching case. It was my belief that first we should do our research and get our facts straight; later—if necessary—we could arrange the facts in certain ways for the purposes of pedagogy.

Moreover, I did not believe that there were general rules for collecting all cases regardless of the situation to be described. The manual prepared by the Faculty for research assistants about how to write up a case seemed to me to give more attention to the rules of grammar and good English than to the rules of getting access to and reporting raw data accurately.

For these reasons, just as I had gone about cleaning up teaching by the case method in my subject matter, so I went about cleaning up doing research by the case method. What might be a good teaching case for my colleagues in production, marketing, finance, and control was not necessarily a good case for me. This was so not because I said so, but because the phenomena with which my subject matter were concerned said so. These phenomena might or might not be critical or important or relevant for *their* subject matters; they were for mine. No fooling!

Then too I wanted committed students to work with, preferably Doctoral candidates who had chosen the area of human relations (or organizational behavior, as it later came to be called) as their area of special interest. I wanted students who had committed themselves to a field of specialization, not because it was lucrative but because they were curious about it and felt it was important. Such men and women, it seemed to me, needed training in field work methods and in clinical observation and interviewing. In time, as our Doctoral program expanded, I organized a seminar to provide this training; I will tell about that in Chapter 18.

Before all that happened, during these years from 1942 to 1954; before my area became legitimate; before our Doctoral program became a new and real doctoral program; before I had any power as an area chairman (about all of which I will talk later); while I was still just more or less doing my thing (about which I have already talked a great deal); and while I had only a few lost souls in the old Doctoral program and the course on Administrative Practices to fool around with; I tried to institute some simple changes in the way we went about collecting and writing up cases. I feel somewhat sheepish about mentioning these changes, because they will seem trivial to my present-day sophisticated readers. But because at the time they had some revolutionary implications at the Business School and also because I think that, just as mighty oaks may grow from simple acorns, mighty institutions and subject matters may develop from simple choices about doing this instead of that, I will report them.

I instituted the following changes for myself and others in collecting and writing up cases for the Human Relations course. I said in effect:

(1) Collect and report the data that were actually used by the persons involved in making the decision, not only the data that they should have used.

(2) Collect and report the data about the problem or decision from the point of view of more than one person. In the case of a technological change, for example, interview not only the persons who instituted the change to get their reasons for it, but also the persons who were affected by the change to get their reactions to it.

(3) And no more sentences, please, of the character "It is reported that," or, "It was said that," or "B was reputed to say that." Goddam it, tell me who said what to whom, when, where, how, and under what circumstances; and tell me what he actually said in as a verbatim and uninterpreted a fashion as possible. Do not tell me that A reprimanded B; tell me what A actually said to B, and so forth.

As I instituted such (it seemed to me) simple, obvious, and minor changes in case research, I did not realize how revolutionary they would seem to my students and colleagues. For example, under my instructions, a research assistant could not collect a case in an hour or two; he had to stay in the field much longer. This reduced the number of cases he could collect. During this period the productivity of a research assistant was often judged quantitatively (as in industry) by the number of cases he collected. This criterion made a case collector who worked with me look bad.

My written cases also became longer. The short sentence "A repri-

manded B" had to be replaced by the dialogue, if it could be called
that, which A had with B. To what A said B said to him there had to
be added what B said he said to A, and so on. Some of my colleagues
thought that I introduced these transcriptions of conversations in
my cases to heighten their human interest. For them these were not
data; they were devices I used to make my subject matter of "human
relations" of human interest.

To make matters even worse, it began to look as though my cases
were filled with a lot of "subjective" data (i.e., things as someone
perceived them to be) and nothing objective (i.e., things as they
really were). To my colleagues this was disconcerting. How did you
deal with so many different perceptions and evaluations of the same
thing? "Let's not fool around with this dickey stuff," they seemed to
imply. "Let's get some hard data—the kind of data with which an
administrator should deal." So the issue of tell it like it is, baby, arose
in a new guise. From whose point of view was I describing the case?
Was my case illustrating the administrative point of view? Shouldn't
it? And so on.

The truth of the matter was that my cases were not illuminating
the administrative point of view; they were providing the data in
terms of which someone in the case or my students could exercise
the administrative point of view. If these data involved differences
of perception, I did not see how that could be ignored. Nor did I see
how I could make the administrator objective by denying these soft
data with which he often had to deal. Nor did I think that soft data
could be transformed into hard data by rules of grammar and good
English. I did not want my cases to be like candies that were hard on
the outside and soft and gooey on the inside, as I thought many of
my colleagues' cases were. Nor did I want to make these soft data
hard by disguising them in some ideology.

SOFT AND HARD DATA

Let's face it; my cases were filled with clinical or soft data, what is
sometimes referred to as anecdotal material. Yet I insist they were
not anecdotes. The deplorable status of my data was nothing new. It
had been true of the data of all my researches, including *Management
and the Worker*; in that instance my critics frequently commented
about it. They complained not only that the Hawthorne Researches
favored one group over another, but also that they had been full of
soft data, from which I had drawn too hard and erroneous con-

clusions. From the point of view of my critics, good research was drawing conclusions from hard data, that is, data which could be quantified and measured.

Also, the issue that my colleagues at the Business School raised about taking action primarily in terms of hard data (generally cost data) was nothing new. It existed from the first day I started teaching cases by the case method at the Business School.

Thus, this issue about soft and hard data or subjective and objective data or clinical and analytical data or anecdotal and nonanecdotal data (or various other ways of stating the same distinction) had been with me for a long, long time. In fact, it could be said that I had lived with soft data all my life—both in my private and professional life. I had become accustomed to and familiar with them. In my professional life I had become curious about them, nay, enamored of them; I took them to bed with me and even there they intrigued me. They spoke to me as no hard data ever could or did.

Early in my professional career, with Elton Mayo's help, I decided to accept these data for what they were—as soft and gooey—and I hoped that accepting this awful fact about them would set me free. And it did. This is what Mayo did for me; he set me free to chase these soft data like crazy. These were the phenomena for me, and I was in no hurry to wrap a hard covering around them. Not that I was just going to take a trip with them and enjoy them like a lotus eater. I felt very strongly that in these soft, gooey data there existed uniformities about human behavior that had to be coaxed out by a point of view and method that were perhaps different from those used by my more hard-nosed, realistic, objective, and scientific (choose your own nonevaluative way of saying this) colleagues. This was my method, the method of clinical observation and interviewing, which I was advocating for the administrator to use in relation to many of his problems. Although this method did not make soft data into hard data, it did make them more understandable.

Thus, step by step I became a clinician in almost every aspect of my professional life. I used the clinical method in both my teaching and research. I took it into the field; I took it into the classroom; I collected the material in the cases by it; I taught this material by it; I diagnosed this material by it; I took action by it; and above all I learned from it. It was what I was teaching about or trying to get my students to learn about. It was something which, when added to intuitive skill, made action, decisions, evaluations, behavior (again let my readers choose) correctable and so more skillful. It became for me a method of learning, of investigation, of discovery, and of taking action in relation to soft data. And to boot, I felt that it was the first step that had to be taken to obtain more systematic knowledge about the data.

There is little question that I was enamored of this steadfastness of focus. It motivated me and provided me with the "oomph" for what I was doing. It became for me almost a *weltanschaung*. I could not understand why my colleagues could not get equally excited about it. The clinical method had opened so many doors for me—its practice had been both so rewarding and rewarded—I could not see how it could be otherwise for others.

But still I had doubts. Was it not more art than science, more skill than knowledge, more intuitional than operational, more insightful than rigorous? (Again let the reader choose the way he prefers to state the distinction.) Was not the status of its evidence still shaky and soft? From one point of view, "yes"; but from another point of view, "no"—100 percent "no." At least this was so for me. Let me tell you why. I will in all probability be telling only a selected set of "you's"—my fellow clinicians—because for those of you who have not become curious about these soft data nor experienced their holy delights and terrors, there is little I can say that will be convincing.

For me the evidence I got about the phenomena of human behavior from my eyes and ears by the daily practice of the clinical method was more real than evidence provided by the more rigorous researches of my colleagues. Their researches could substantiate the evidence; they could not deny it. If there was a discrepancy between the clinical uniformities of field research and the correlations of more rigorous research, I trusted the former. The clinical uniformities I found daily from the practice of the clinical method, whether I was talking to a student, a worker, or an executive, and whether I was in the field, in the classroom, or at a Faculty meeting, were ever present. I did not have to wait until I went into the field to see and hear them. I did not have to design an elaborate research project or a questionnaire to see and hear them. I did not have to go to Timbuctoo to see and hear them. In fact, I did not have to go anywhere to see and hear them. Wherever I was, there they were to greet me and say "Howdy"; to which I would respond "Hello there, good old soft, gooey things; tell me your secrets." And if you can believe this now, they did—though not always, because on some occasions I was in a place or in a role in which I could not coax them out or check them such as at a Faculty meeting conducted under Robert's roles of order. It was important to check them, because there was a danger that while using the clinical method an observer could see or hear something in a situation that was neither there nor intended. (I will say more about these possibilities later.)

To come back to the question of evidence: What made evidence evidence seemed to me to have a soft side to it. The rules were not so clear and hard as we liked to believe. What was evidence for me might not be evidence for others and vice versa. There was a line between soft and hard data, but it could be drawn too tightly; one could go too far in chasing one or the other exclusively. Why some of us became more enamored of one or the other did not seem to me strictly a matter of logic. For instance, I felt that why some of my colleagues' correlations excited them but left me cold and why some of my clinical uniformities excited me but left them cold needed some explanation other than just that the colleagues were hard and I was soft.

To finish the point I started some pages back, I felt that during these teaching years from 1942 to 1954, I was not restricted to the findings of the Hawthorne Researches. Damn it, I was doing research! Granted that it was clinical research which resulted in descriptive cases and that much of it and many of the cases were not too hot, nevertheless, I felt that the research was in the right direction and that the data in the cases were of the right order. As time went on these cases became better. The case collectors spent more and more time at a particular company—sometimes as much as four months or longer; the result was not just one case but a series of cases written after the research was done, after the researcher had told me what he thought the data he had collected meant. It did not seem to me cricket to present data for students to interpret which had not already been interpreted by the researcher, even though his interpretation did not appear in the teaching case itself.

During these teaching years I felt that I had far more data of a research character than just the findings of the Hawthorne Researches. In fact, this case research substantiated many of the clinical findings of the Hawthorne Researches. Uniformities similar to those I found at Hawthorne appeared in many of the cases collected from other organizations. Hence, I did not think that the clinical uniformities found at Hawthorne were idiosyncratic to that one plant; they seemed to be present in many other factories.

Indeed, the good old rate buster or job killer or good Joe or deviant or man-in-the middle or autocratic leader appeared with great regularity in every factory I visited. Cases about them could be collected by the bushel. I could almost take a student into any old factory at any old time and pick up any old foreman and say to the student, "Listen to him. Do you hear that 'man-in-the middle' syndrome? Do you hear the plaintive melody; haven't you heard it sung before, perhaps in a slightly different key? Don't get 'balled up' with the particular words; listen to the underlying feelings and sentiments, listen for the melody. Doesn't it haunt you? Come on, let's go to another foreman in another factory and see if you can recognize it next time. Now go back to your desk and write your case and swing it, man!"

The regularity with which we encountered these findings had me scared. I thought that perhaps my clinical method had a self-fulfilling prophecy to it, because I kept finding the same things again and again. As George Homans said, I kept rediscovering America over and over. I was in a rut and the reason, according to George, was that I was staying at the level of clinical investigation. I was too enamoured of the uniformities in these soft data and too little concerned with the problem of explaining them. I should get interested, he said, in the problems of explaining them and not just the problems of investigating and "understanding" them. "Let's be men," he said, "and explain."

This pronouncement of George's came at a time in 1954 when, as I reported in the last chapter, I was having some qualms myself about the direction that human relations training was taking as well as about the limitations of the clinical method in the acquisition of knowledge. So George's highly normative injunction acted upon me in the manner of what in my youth would have been called a double dare, generally made after one had been called a scaredy cat. It was as if George had said to me personally, "I double dare you, Fritz, to leave your comfortable hideout and get a breath of good fresh objective air." At least this is the way I remember my conversations with George. To be fair to him, though, I should record that in his writings he emphasizes the importance of understanding, just as I do. Though George and I have our differences, I have always felt that our views about science were not far apart.

THE PREDICTION STUDY

Thus it came about that one day I happened to meet George Homans at the subway station in Harvard Square and said something like this:

George, old chap, let's do a research project together, something more systematic, definitive, substantive, analytical, and rigorous (you choose your own way of saying this, George) than my stick-in-the-mud clinical studies. Let us predict something for a change. We think we know something about small work groups. Let us find out if what we think we know clinically is really so, analytically. In *The Human Group* you reduced some of these clinical findings about small work groups into some simple *x varies with y propositions* relating to the motivation, productivity, and satisfaction of people.

Let's take some of these propositions and try to predict what we think we should find in a concrete work group, that is, under certain given conditions. I have two colleagues—Abe Zaleznik and Roland (Chris) Christensen—who would be interested in such an adventure and who are excellent field workers to boot. They could collect the data about the "givens" or "external system" (what you called later the "boundary conditions") of a group. From your propositions under these conditions, let us try to predict what should be found there. In the meantime, Abe and Chris can be finding out what is really there; then we can compare the two.

Because I am afraid that I might predict more from my clinical intuitions than from your propositions—you know me, George—I will hang around as a kind of "observer." I may try my hand at a few predictions, but I will not do this, George—honest to goodness and hope to die, if I tell a lie—unless I have a real proposition to predict from. Because I have only a conceptual scheme and a clinical method and some clinical uniformities and no general propositions, I am afraid I may not be too helpful. You be the chief predictor. Abe and Chris, of course, cannot make predictions because, in the process of collecting data about the external system, they may inadvertently find out something about the internal system. It would not be cricket for them to be the predictors.

And by the way, George, none of this correlation stuff. Let us make 100 percent on-the-nose predictions. Do not tell me that A is more likely to be a rate buster than B. You predict that A will be a rate buster. No fooling; O.K.?

Well, George was interested. Being an intrepid soul with a liking for calling a spade a spade and, unlike many of his colleagues in sociology, believing that research was done by the damndest methods, he said, "Let's go." This is how the prediction study got started.

In the beginning for all four of us—I think I am correct—it was an exhilarating experience. Our prediction sessions—which Abe and Chris attended because they had the data about the "givens"—were great fun. There was never a dull moment. Just from watching George make his predictions I learned a great deal, because there were many bugs in the simple and naive research design with which we started. But George ironed them out one by one, so that we could proceed with our monkey business—I mean research—in a somewhat less ideal fashion than we had at first envisaged; but at least we kept going.

I need to say a few words about George Homans in relation to me and my clinical outlook and about me in relation to George and his propositions. No two persons could have been more different in terms of social background and life style. George was a Yankee for many generations (for all I know, his ancestors may have come over on the Mayflower), whereas I was a first-generation American whose father had come over on a cheeseboat from Switzerland. George in his personal style was forthright and direct. No one had any question where he stood; he never seemed to care upon whose sensitive toes he trod. I, on the other hand, was timid in expressing my opinions, particularly if I thought they would offend the person I was talking to and prevent him from expressing his own.

But both George and I had been inspired in our youth by some of the same gifted then-alive persons: Elton Mayo, L.J. Henderson, and Alfred North Whitehead. Neither of us could wash them out of our hair. Perhaps in this respect George succeeded better than I, even though we both lost our hair in the process. Whether or not it was due to these common intellectual antecedents, I was always able to listen to George and read his books and feel I could understand what was "biting him" much better than I was able to with many of his colleagues in sociology. I always felt that we were in roughly the same ball park, even though each of us was interested in his subject matter from a different point of view. Although George had become a sociologist by being first a poet and then a historian and I had become a human relationist, or what have you, by being first an engineer and then a counselor, I always felt we were both concerned with essentially the same phenomena.

Although I felt that George had about as much intuitive skill in dealing concretely with these phenomena as Henderson had (which as I have said earlier was not much), I never felt that he sloughed them off as too trivial or unimportant to be reckoned with intellectually. I never heard George "pooh pooh" my clinical findings as such or the method by which they had been obtained. He was just as willing to seek his elementary and more general propositions in these clinical uniformities, which he did in *The Human Group* (1950), as in the experimental findings of his colleagues, which he did later in *Social Behavior: Its Elementary Forms* (1961). So we had one thing in common. George had become a sociologist without getting a Ph.D. in

Human Relations. It was the phenomena and not our degrees or our social backgrounds or life styles that kept us together.

When George would tell me—again I am quoting how I remember our conversations, not what he wrote in his books—"Let us not be sentimental softies and just understand these phenomena, let us be men and explain them"; or when he said "Let us not fool around anymore with conceptual schemes, let us get some propositions to test and explain"; or when he said, "Let us be curious about these phenomena for curiosity's sake and not for the sake of their immediate application"; and when he made other statements of a similar sort, I (or my super ego) did not feel attacked. When, more specifically, after I had written *Training for Human Relations*, George told me that I, who was supposed to be the resolver of the false dichotomy, was its chief perpetrator, I did not feel so much attacked as disturbed, in fact, disturbed enough that I will come back to this point later. For it is true, philosophically speaking, that I am more of a two-sy or dualist than a one-sy or monist.

In spite of these differences, I was able to take George's forthrightness (or directness or frankness or calling a spade a spade) as an expression of his life style and not as a personal attack against me. About the phenomena we shared a togetherness (forgive me for the awful word, George), even though he wished to explain them and not just to investigate them. In this there was no vital conflict. I was all for explaining them, even though I did not know how to go about it. From George I was willing to find out, because I respected him.

To be honest, there was more to it than that; many of George's propositions interested me a great deal. They were of this general character: if some aspect of a person's status was out of line with some other aspect, then an "ouch" could be expected. For example, if a person's job status was out of line with his social status or his group membership status; or if his job status or social status was not well established (i.e., if there was any out-of-lineness among the factors making up his job status or social status), then trouble could be expected. I was intrigued by these propositions because they coincided with many of the clinical findings I reported in *Management and the Worker* (especially in Chapter XVI, "Complaints and Social Equilibrium") as well as with those I found in my case researches.

Not by the wildest stretch of imagination would I have been able to reduce these different kinds of out-of-lineness to a simple formulation. This was George's skill, not mine. George said simply, "If a person's rewards are not proportional to his investments, then expect trouble. Why? Because if the investment of an individual member of a group is higher (or lower) than another, his rewards should be higher (or lower) too. Why? Because a balance between investments and rewards is a condition of equilibrium or 'felt justice.' Why? Because it is felt as 'just' by all the members of the group. When this condition of proportionality does not prevail, there exists a condition of disequilibrium or 'felt injustice.' One can expect as a consequence from a person in this condition a kind of behavior which will attempt to restore the disturbed reward-investment balance to a condition of in-lineness or 'felt justice.' And this kind of behavior often spells TROUBLE."

This was my crude understanding of George's theory of distributive justice. Note that it was made up of a more "general proposition" from which many of the clinical findings of small group research could be derived under given conditions. This had me fascinated, because such general propositions were a step up the abstraction ladder from my clinical findings and suggested to me a way by which my soft data could be made harder. This way was different from and more acceptable to me than the other ways that I had previously encountered and resisted.

For the prediction study we had three such sets of general propositions or theories from which we tried to predict the motivation, productivity, and satisfaction of the particular workers we studied under the conditions given by this environment. We called them the theory of distributive justice, the theory of social certitude, and the theory of external and internal rewards. Since these theories and the results of these predictions are reported in *The Motivation, Productivity, and Satisfaction of Workers* (1958), I shall not discuss them here. I do, however, want to talk more generally about the problems we had in verifying the predictions.

Abe Zaleznik probably bore the biggest brunt of this research in that in addition to being involved with Chris in clinical observations of the group, he became the person primarily involved in the verification of the predictions. Just as George was the chief predictor, Abe was the chief verifier. The verification process turned out to be a far more difficult job than we had anticipated. We found in our prediction meetings that we had to spend far more time making the independent variable (that is, our reward-investment index) in our propositions operational than we did discussing the operations by which we would measure the dependent variables (that is, productivity and satisfaction). In a way it could be said that Abe was left holding the bag.

The biggest difficulty he had was verifying George's theory of distributive justice. In the first way that Abe tested for the validity of this theory, he found no association between the condition of distributive justice and the satisfaction of the workers; that is to say, as many workers whose rewards were out of line with their investments were as satisfied as those whose reward-investment ratios were in line (as measured in terms of the reward-investment ratio we had constructed). This result threw a certain amount of consternation into our ranks—not so much for George as for the rest of us, because by this time he was on sabbatical leave at the University of Cambridge in England. In particular, it made trouble for Abe, because he could not throw out the theory on the basis of this simple test alone. To be sure, our measures for the dependent variable (worker satisfaction) were crude; but so too were our measures for rewards and investments (and hence for the reward-investment index, our independent variable). Neither provided a really adequate test of George's distributive justice theory.

It seemed obvious to me that there were many different ways in which a worker could behave to redress the balance of a reward-investment out-of-lineness and that diametrically opposite forms of behavior could even produce the same result. For example, to get back into line a worker could increase his rewards (by producing more) or decrease his investments (by producing less). But where did these different forms of compensatory behavior exist? Where could they be seen? The answer was in our clinical findings, in the soft data which we had collected from our interviews with the workers, but which in their full but soft richness we had ignored in order to make operational our test for the theory of distributive justice.

So we had to return to this soft gooey data in order to see what our findings meant. It interested me very much that in these data we could find in practically every case factors which we had overlooked and which were not present in the measures we used to make the theory of distributive justice operational and testable. If we had taken these factors into account, they would have made the theory more plausible. And what was the nature of these factors? In every case in which we had enough data about the personal history and social background of a worker to see what made a reward a reward and an investment an investment for him—that is, a value to him *from his point of view*—we could make the distributive justice syndrome sing its melodious tune. When we ignored these facts, the theory became as dead and mute as a doornail.

Here was our quandary: whereas in terms of our hard data, "No, the distributive justice syndrome was not there," in terms of our soft data, "Yes, it was there." Which were we to believe? And how were we to report this? Was or was not George's theory verified? Now, if the reader would like to believe that this quandary was a tempest in a teapot, he can do so, but it does not check with my experience. Around such an issue, particularly in academia, feelings and sentiments can get easily and deeply involved. Before one is aware of it, serious differences and disputes arise, in which no one it talking much sense. This happened somewhat to the three of us—Abe, Chris, and me—during the later stages of the prediction study. I was just as guilty as anyone else in contributing my share of the nonsense. Anyway, the research was no longer the enjoyable experience it had been in the beginning. We finally managed to write a book together, and I think it was a fairly good one. Abe's chapter on "The Theory of Distributive Justice and Worker Satisfaction" (Chapter VIII) was a fair and sensible one in spite of the silly, as I evaluate them now, disputes I had about it with him.

In reflecting upon this experience many years later, I think we never seriously considered at the time the larger question which the prediction study raised. This was the issue of prediction and explanation in the social sciences. I think George was aware of this when he returned from England and saw the quandary we were in. My evidence for saying this is that his future writings were pointed explicitly in this direction. This is another issue about which I want to talk later; at the time it was not a reality for me. As can be seen in the last chapter of *The Motivation, Productivity, and Satisfaction of Workers*, I ignored it completely and discussed the implications of our findings for administration.

I feel in retrospect that not only for George, but also for the rest of us, the prediction study had a personal influence far greater than the "objective" results we reported in our book. After the completion of the study, Abe went in the direction of psychoanalytical theories of investigation and explanation. Chris went back to the area of "policy," where the issue of what constitutes knowledge in the social sciences is not so acutely raised. I started teaching in the new Doctoral program, where the generalist–specialist issue was becoming a burning one. It was as if the prediction study helped each of us to settle the question of the level of abstraction at which he wished to work in the investigation, understanding, explanation, and control of the phenomena of human behavior.

ABOUT THE EQUITABLE DISTRIBUTION OF REWARDS IN
WRITING A BOOK JOINTLY

In joint research there exists a latent question about the relative ordering of the contributions each member makes to the research. This is sometimes indicated in the resulting book by the order in which the authors' names are listed. In the book about the prediction study Abe's name is first, Chris's second, mine third, and "with the assistance and collaboration of George C. Homans," George's is fourth.

This ordering, particularly with regard to the first two names, was reached by applying (perhaps unconsciously) the law of distributive justice: the person who invested and contributed most should have the highest reward. This unquestionably was Abe. We all felt this was just. Chris, by interrupting a brilliant teaching career in policy to join our research effort to learn how behavioral scientists talk, think, act, and do research (and who did this while he was still without tenure), invested a great deal in this joint venture. He also contributed a great deal by his excellent field work and invariable good humor at our meetings. Again, we all felt it was just that his name came second.

With regard to the ordering of the last two names, I am not sure what rule we applied. That our chief proposition maker and predictor should get fourth place seems now a bit strange. The only explanation I can offer is that the book was written when George was out of town, so he contributed nothing to the actual writing of the book.

But something else bothers me. For this research I was given the Ledlie Prize by Harvard in 1959. The Ledlie Prize is awarded every two years to a member of the Harvard University faculty who "has by research discovered or otherwise made the most valuable contribution to science or in any way for the benefit of mankind." When I received the prize, I thought it had been awarded for all my researches and not for the prediction study alone. This, I learned later, may not have been the case. Let me say now that if this prize was awarded for the prediction study alone, some law other than distributive justice was operating, except perhaps in some highly abstract sense that to whom that hath, shall it be given.

To sum up, this decade between 1947 and 1958 of work with human relations as the focus for the development of my subject matter did not take me very far. Though in one sense I learned a great deal that was new and interesting, in another sense the important lesson of the period re-directed me to what interested me from the beginning of my professional life: the phenomena of human behavior in organizations and the clinical methods of observation and interviewing for dealing with them. Previously I had seen how important these phenomena and methods were for the practice and training of first-level practitioners—persons who deal with them face-to-face in their daily life and in work in organizations. In this period I saw their importance for the practice and training of second-level practitioners, persons who endeavor to multiply these skills in others through programs of research and training.

To be sure, through the development of the second-year course in Human Relations at the Business School, I had come to see that the way of listening which I had learned through practice and study in the role of counselor was not enough for the complex role and multidimensional problems of administrators. We added a way of talking to take care of these new dimensions; but this way of talking, though going beyond the way of listening, was not essentially different. The two were of a piece, consistent with each other. More important, they were addressed to the same phenomena of human behavior.

At Bethel I learned to recognize and articulate patterns of group behavior in ways that seemed to me were nonthreatening and useful for the learning processes of individuals. Study of these patterns and of the interventions connected with them convinced me that they were based on the same kind of intuitive skillful observation of the same human-social phenomena that I had studied in work groups. Though absence or ambiguity of the task dimension in the Bethel T-groups highlighted aspects of work group behavior I had previously missed, it did not lead me to study different phenomena or different methods for dealing with them. Even the prediction study with all its excitements took me unexpectedly back to the same soft data that had me fascinated from the beginning of my professional life.

Exciting as many of the experiences of this period were, they also left me dissatisfied. I felt there was a kind of progress I could and should have been making which I was not. It seemed to me that my subject matter merited a development it was not getting and that there was a set of problems in business organizations that would not be touched without this development. This decade of my life ended with my drawing dissatisfactions as well as satisfactions from my work. Was I or was I not in a rut, still rediscovering America?

My readers know by now that finding myself in such a position was nothing new for me. This time I did not have a nervous breakdown to deal with the ambiguities of my situation. A new program at the Business School promised to give me a chance to walk around the whole ball of wax with which I had been so long connected and to view it from a slightly new perspective.

This opportunity was the decision of the School to start a new Doctoral program. I thought taking part in this program would allow me to build on the lessons I had learned about training second-level practitioners in the Human Relations Clinic. At the same time I thought it would allow me to go further, because the dimension of knowledge, which I played down without entirely ignoring in the Clinic, would be very much present. For the Doctoral degree certified that the recipient was competent to make a contribution to knowledge and to join the community of scholars. I thought that I would thus have the opportunity to rethink my work, not only in relation to the organization of the School, but also in relation to the academic disciplines. I felt that doing so might help me think through some of the tantalizing questions about hard and soft data that surfaced during the prediction study.

Before I can state my conclusions about these questions, which I shall do in Book Two of this account of my life and work, I need to tell about my experiences with the new Doctoral program. The place to begin is its organizational context at the Harvard Business School. This setting has been of the greatest importance in my life; I have already postponed discussion of it too long, while I sought in the single-minded way to which I am addicted to describe my intellectual development.

Part IV

ORGANIZATIONAL BEHAVIOR AS
THE FOCUS FOR DEVELOPMENT
1957–1967

INTRODUCTION

Up to now and in the role of researcher and teacher, I have stressed my intellectual curiosity about the phenomena of human behavior. At times, in order to keep the record straight, I have referred to my organizational involvement with these phenomena as a member of the Business School Faculty. Now I want to give this involvement the full attention it deserves. It can be viewed as my lover's quarrel with the School about what made administration administration, or to put it in the local language, what constituted the administrative point of view.

Later I will consider my involvement with the phenomena of human behavior from the point of view of the social science disciplines. This can be viewed as my lover's quarrel with the disciplines about what made science science. Obviously, these two involvements began before this period of my career. Nevertheless, I will write about them from the perspective of this period, because it was then that I became acutely aware of and concerned with them. Even when I will have to flash back to an earlier period to show how these involvements developed in my life, I will be writing about them from the point of view of the insights I had during the period from 1957 to 1967.

During this time more changes took place both inside and outside the University than during any other period of my life. Uncertainties, dissonances, ambiguities, paradoxes, and violence became the order of the day. Technology and knowledge exploded all over the place. Information was being processed by computers at a faster rate than at any previous time in history. In this explosive expansion of science and technology, gaps and vacuums appeared.

The Soviet Union lauched its first earth-orbiting satellites, Sputnik I and Sputnik II, in 1957. The United States sent up its first satellite, Explorer I, in 1958. Luniks I, II, and III went into orbit around the moon in 1959. Major Gargarin became the first human space traveler in 1961 and made one circuit of the globe. Commander Shepard of the United States rocketed some 116 miles above the earth and landed safely in the Atlantic Ocean some 300 miles away. A year later in 1962 Lieutenant Colonel Glenn became the first American to orbit the earth. He circled the earth three times. In 1963 the United States sent a man around the earth 32 times. Not to be outdone, the Soviet Union put both a man and a woman in orbit in 1963. Both landed safely, the man after 81 orbits and the woman after 48. In 1964 the Soviet Union launched the first spacecraft to carry three men. In 1965 for the first time a man stepped outside of a spaceship and walked in space. The race between the two great powers in the conquest of outer space was becoming closer. The gap between their technical accomplishments was diminishing. As time went on, it began to increase again—and in favor of the United States.

Exciting things were also happening on planet earth. To mention a few, General Charles de Gaulle became President of the Fifth French Republic in 1958. That year was also a year of triumph for Fidel Castro and of downfall for Batista. Castro entered Havana in January 1959; the United States severed relations with Cuba in 1961. The invasion of Cuba at the Bay of Pigs was crushed by Castro later in that year. John F. Kennedy was elected President of the United States in 1960 and was shot and killed in November 1963.

During this period many civil rights demonstrations took place in the South. James Meredith, a Black, registered at the University of Mississippi in 1962. Three civil rights workers were murdered in Fayetteville, Mississippi. Dr. Martin Luther King led the civil rights march, which had to be protected by United States troops, from Montgomery to Selma in 1965. Toward the end of the period a new philosophy about Black-White relations began to appear. Violence in the name of "integration" became passé and violence in the name of "power" began to appear. Malcolm X was shot to death in 1965. Race riots occurred in Watts in 1966 and in Newark and Detroit in 1967.

Ho Chi Minh—I nearly forgot him—how could I? In 1964, United States planes bombed North Vietnam bases and damaged 25 North Vietnamese patrol boats in retailiation against an attack on United States destroyers in the Gulf of Tonkin. In 1965 the undeclared war between the United States and North Vietnam and the Viet Cong escalated.

So many extraordinary things happened during this period that it is hard for me to select ones to mention. In 1960, 16 new African nations were admitted to membership in the United Nations. In 1965 Adlai Stevenson died; General Motors reported the highest profits of any company in history; Pope Paul VI visited New York City; a massive electric power failure blacked out most of the northeastern United States and affected a population of some 30 million people. In 1966 the Archbishop of Canterbury visited Pope Paul VI, three New York newspapers merged, General Motors announced a production cutback, the stock market trembled, and Medicare began.

By 1967 the established society was flat on its back, but the count of ten had not been officially declared. It is hard to date just when the final knockout blow was given but I want to close this period of my life—1957 to 1967—just before everyone was up tight, hung up, telling it like it is, alienated, and suffering from identity crises; just before nudity, the mini-skirt, and psychedelic drugs became a way of life; before Black became beautiful; before the youth culture, the militants, the hippies, the yippies, and the flower children took over; before the universities became embattled, the cities were in crises, women sought their liberation, the silent majority appeared, and air and water became so polluted that the earth people began to wonder what we were doing to our environment. I want to save my thoughts about all these wonderful happenings for the part of my autobiography that has to do with my retirement, when I had a final chance before I died to make clear where I stood in regard to these phenomena of human behavior. No joking any more.

Amidst this chaos or healthy diversity, I lived the rest of my life at the B-School until I retired in 1967. I cannot say that this was my happiest period. It was filled with some of my severest headaches. No longer was I able to cultivate my own garden in my own fashion. For my Doctoral students I had to relate it to other people's, both at the School and in the academic disciplines. This was not easy to do. All of us were so busy drawing such different lines around and about our gardens that it was difficult to integrate and consolidate mine. Often my attempts in this direction ended in justifying or defending the legitimacy of my own or in saying, "You can't do this to me and my garden," but this did not get me anywhere in particular. During all this period my negative feelings ran fairly high.

If these were not easy experiences, neither were they entirely new; I had had to relate my subject matter to other people's before this. But as I said in Chapter 8 when the matter first came up in connection with Administrative Practices in the first year of the MBA program, I had not really faced the question. I had turned my back and run away and "let George do it" when I started the second-year Human Relations course. to be free to do my own thing.

To describe the organizational context of the School and my relation to it when the new Doctoral program began, I need to go back to that time. I do not, however, need to describe step by step everything that happened in the interim, as I have with my intellectual development. I will describe only enough to show how things stood when the new program began in 1957. I shall take the next two chapters to do this. In the three following ones I shall describe my experiences in the program and in my seminar, particularly the problems I had in choosing the topics and relating them to the academic disciplines in the social sciences and also to mathematics, a subject which, for many reasons primarily related to the advent of Sputnik and the computer, received increasing attention during this period.

Once again, as I describe my involvement in the happenings of this period, I will try to restate and clarify the stubborn questions that still had me fascinated after a lifetime of work in my field, questions that I felt had not been answered. If the reader feels a certain sense of sameness, of repetitiveness, of a lack of progress in these chapters, well, let's face it: I too had those feelings. In a way I wished I could have dropped these problems, but they seemed too important, too central to unresolved disputes, conflicts, and confusions. Also, and increasingly as the years went by, I was looking forward to retirement, when I hoped to have time to think through these matters and the issues they raise and to write what my life and work had been about.

Chapter 15

The Social Organization of the Faculty

The issue of the relation of my courses to my colleagues' courses at the Business School had been present for a long time and had occasionally called forth sparks, but for the most part it remained dormant until about 1957. About then (perhaps somewhat earlier) a number of things happened in both the external and internal environments of the School which resulted in more attention to this issue. As I try now to clarify the factors underlying the issue, let me warn my readers that at no point in my autobiography are my perceptions and those of my colleagues more likely to be at greater variance. Obviously if we had perceived the issue in the same way, it would have been much easier to resolve. But this was not the case, and this was part of the problem.

THE DISTRIBUTION OF LOCALS AND COSMOPOLITANS AT THE SCHOOL

I will start by describing certain elements of the social organization of the Business School, some of which I have already mentioned in chronological order. Now I will tie these elements together, so that not just the individual beads, but also the necklace—should I say the neck yoke?—they fashioned can be more clearly seen.

In 1946, after World War II, the curriculum of the MBA program was changed, not fundamentally, but sufficiently to allow a few innovations to take place. At that time two new required courses in the first year were introduced: one was called Administrative Practices; the other was called Public Relations and Responsibilities. The remaining four required courses were in Production, Marketing, Finance, and Control. These latter courses had long been required first-year courses, although Control had previously been called Accounting. The subject matters of all six courses were conceived as a totality and referred to as the Elements of Administration. The six elements were supposed to be integrated in the only required course in the second year, Business Policy.

This combination of required core courses including Business Policy was supposed to be addressed to the problems of a line (not a staff) administrator. He was sometimes called the firing line executive, to emphasize that he was a responsible actor and not just a passive observer and student of business—a generalist as opposed to a specialist, a person who had the administrative point of view, that is, a point of view that was *not* specialized either in terms of one business function, such as production, or in terms of one academic discipline, such as economics.

The focus of this combination of required courses constituted the School's fundamental and unique contribution to the teaching of administration. It contained all of its most cherished norms and values with regard to matters of business education, action, and change. It was what made the Harvard Business School different not only from most other business schools, but also from most other graduate schools in the land. The cultivation of this big garden constituted the School's distinctive competence. Endless time and effort was given to this work. In terms of it the School became a great teaching institution.

The cultivation of this big garden, however, contained some implicit polarities. As can be seen, under this conception no individual professor could grow "his thing" unmindful of the other things being grown in the garden. He had to relate his corn to his colleagues' beans and show how in combination they produced the diet required for this person who was *not* a staff specialist, *not* a production specialist, *not* a marketing specialist, *not* a financial specialist, *not* an accounting specialist, *not* an economist (macro or micro), *not* a sociologist (concrete, general, or abstract), *not* a psychologist (clinical, social, or pure), *not* an anthropologist (physical, cultural, or social)—in short not any kind of specialist at all.

Although the negative part of this general focus was crystal clear, the affirmative part had some muddy elements. For example, it was sometimes not clear just what the general focus was which kept this set of alleged integrated courses from becoming a conglomeration of separate, specialized courses. Consequently it was sometimes not clear just how this integration was to be maintained. Was it to be maintained by fiat and power, by a common explicit conceptual scheme and method, or by a common set of shared values, concerns, and words implemented by a process of socialization? Was it to be maintained by all or some or a mixture of these things? Well, it seemed to me that it was maintained by a mixture of all these elements, but not by a common explicit conceptual scheme, and this concerned me plenty.

As I have said, the alleged purpose of these differentiated courses, although taught separately, was to keep production, marketing, finance, control, and people related. (Administrative Practices, it should be remembered, was a people course, or to be more accurate, a relations-among-people course.) Thus any professor teaching a first-year course in Production, for example, was supposed to be concerned not only with the production aspects of his case, but also with its financial, marketing, cost, and people implications. A student, in reaching his final action decision about a case, was supposed to take all these elements into account. In reaching a solution, he was not supposed to produce, for example, a conglomerate by financial means alone (no matter how profitable), because this would not have been practicing the administrative point of view. He also had to show that his solution consisted of an integrated and organized set of activities; that these activities could be socially as well as technically and financially integrated; and also that in some sense they could be made rewarding to all—and not just some—of the people involved in them.

Inasmuch as this focus was difficult to maintain in the first-year functional courses, it was the chief, main, sole, and single purpose of the required second-year course called Business Policy. In Policy, this focus was maintained by looking at the business from the point of view of a chief executive. Obviously he more than anyone else should look at his organization as a totality and not from the point of view of just production, marketing, finance, control, or individual and unrelated people. This solution bothered me, because by equating the practice of the administrative point of view with the position of the chief executive, the result seemed to me to avoid the difficult problem of conceptualizing the administrative point of view. The trick of the week was to get people *not* in this position to practice the administrative point of view.

Let it be noted that four of these required courses or Elements of Administration—Production, Marketing, Finance, and Control—had been explicitly carved from the formal organization of business enterprises. In most firms each one of these functions was a vice president's responsibility. This would also have been true of Administrative Practices, if the course had been conceived as a course in Personnel and Labor Relations. The same could be said of Public Relations and Responsibilities, if that course had been conceived as primarily concerned with the formal duties and responsibilities of a vice president in charge of public relations. But in neither course was this true. In both of them the cake was sliced differently; and, in both courses, disciplines other than economics were (or could be or should be) explicitly invoked.

The business functions of production, marketing, finance, and control were *not disciplines* in the sense that a discipline tries to state explicitly—sometimes with difficulty—the class of natural phenomena with which it is concerned. Their subject matters had been carved from the primary *activities* into which business organizations were traditionally differentiated. These activities were not natural phenomena; they were organizationally derived phenomena, that is, orderings of phenomena which, for organizational purposes, had been abstracted from total situations. Also, these activities of production, marketing, finance, and control could be developed as specializations apart from their organizational contexts and people implications.

Thus, from my point of view the subjects of Production, Marketing, Finance, and Control, particularly the first two, were conceptually inelegant, that is to say, they contained—so it seemed to me—"everything but the kitchen sink," and sometimes, believe it or not, they contained that too. I could not see how these courses in their state of unholy conceptual inelegance could be integrated. How could everything besides and sometimes including the kitchen sink be integrated? Nothing that I had been taught at Harvard or had learned from Henderson and Mayo or acquired from my readings about the "scientific method" said this was possible. But here were my colleagues doing it. How could this be? Something other than an explicit common conceptual scheme must be operating.

Applying my own conceptual scheme and clinical method, I sought for the missing element or elements. I observed, for example, that the word administration was the "hot" word. Any time that I suggested (in my most mild and innocent way) that any one of the business functions restrict itself to the technical problems of the function and leave the teaching of the "administrative point of view" to Administrative Practices in the first year and Policy in the second year, the function would rise in full wrath and become almost incoherent in its indignation. Such a suggestion would be enough to provoke a request at the next Faculty meeting for a change in the name of the course from Production to Production Administration, Marketing to Marketing Administration, Finance to Financial Administration, and Control to Control Administration. Even, as I remember it, Business Policy became for a while Administrative Policy; and I am sure that if I had pressed hard in this direction, I would have been able to change the name of Public Relations and Responsibilities to Administrative Relations and Responsibilities. But I didn't.

Therefore, whereas in my relation to George Homans we shared the phenomena but not the words, in my relation to my colleagues at the Business School we shared the word (administration) but not the phenomena. This was true not only with regard to the word administration; it was also true about the case method. Although all of us taught and did research by the case method, it was the connotative or intensional meaning and not the denotative or extensional meaning of these words that we shared. That is to say, the fact that (extensionally) I did research or taught by the case method differently from my colleagues was not so important to them as that I talked (intensionally) about the case method in terms of the same underlying values that we (i.e., those of us who were involved in these required courses) were supposed to have in common. They viewed with suspicion the use of words which suggested that we did not share these values.

It was these values more than anything strictly conceptual in terms of subject matter that kept these courses together and prevented them from becoming a conglomeration of separate, individual ones. These values were mostly maintained by emotionally laden words which pointed in the direction of activity instead of passivity (e.g., firing line executives instead of observers and students of business); "proactivity" instead of "reactivity" (e.g., being tough-minded and being capable of making tough decisions instead of being soft and sentimental and reacting to feelings and sentiments); and of doing instead of reflecting (e.g., being realistic or practical, not becoming immobilized by overthinking or getting hung up by words).

From the perspective of these values I began to see how the Faculty of the School had become socialized into an integrated whole. I began to see why a professor with a strong disciplinary allegiance had to spend time in different courses in the first year in the MBA program to get indoctrinated in these values, if he was to become an accepted member of the School and a full professor. I began to see how in terms of these values the professors had become interchangeable parts, how the institution had become ingrown, and how this was both its strength and its weakness.

This insight helped me to understand what happened at Faculty meetings, which for a long time remained a mystery to me. Let me illustrate by the squabbles we often had at those meetings between instructors who were teaching first-year and second-year courses in the MBA program. Again and again second-year instructors complained that the first-year ones were not doing an adequate job of teaching either the administrative point of view or the business functions of production, marketing, finance, and control. This struck me as peculiar, until I realized who were making the complaints.

In the second-year courses there were two classes of professors. The first kind was composed of professors who were more institutionally than disciplinary or subject-matter oriented. For them the institution, that is, the Business School with its values regarding the administrative point of view and the case method, was the chief reference. They were willing to forsake any allegiances they may have had to a discipline or specialization for the development of the nonspecialized administrator. Obviously the professors in Policy belonged to this group. A good many professors teaching advanced courses in Production, Marketing, Finance, and Control in the second year also had this orientation. The second class of professors—who taught primarily in the second year—was composed of those who could neither wholly accept the sacred cows of the institution nor wholly forsake their disciplinary or specialist leanings.

I will call the first class "locals" and the second class "cosmopolitans." Alvin W. Gouldner used these terms in an article which he published in 1957 to describe two latent roles which his research showed occurred widely in complex modern organizations. If I use these concepts in connection with what I observed at the Business School, I can make the following statements:

(A) The Faculty contained more locals than cosmopolitans up to about 1957. (B) The locals in the second year were on the whole the ones who complained that the first-year teachers were not doing an adequate job in teaching the administrative point of view. (C) The cosmopolitans in the second year were on the whole the ones who complained that their students were not getting adequate instruction in the first year about the technical problems of Production, Marketing, Finance, or Control. (D) A good but not outstanding local had a better chance than a good but not outstanding cosmopolitan of getting into the inner circle and of becoming a full professor. (E) A cosmopolitan could become a full professor only by being a cosmopolitan *extraordinaire*. (F) A good local did not rebel about being made an interchangeable part; he would teach Production, Marketing, Policy, or what not with equal relish. (G) When asked to do this, a good cosmopolitan would sit on his hindquarters and bay out loud (to the moon, perhaps), "You can't do this to me." (H) A good local was likely to be considered a better case method teacher than was a good cosmopolitan. (I) A good cosmopolitan was likely to be considered a better researcher than a good local. (J) The business function of marketing produced more locals than all the other functions, production, finance, and control, combined. And so on.

Thus, a high-status Marketing local was well on the road to becoming Mr. B-School himself. He not only espoused most fervently and eloquently the norms and values of the School; he also enforced and policed them and saw that young cosmopolitans did not get too far out-of-line. Such, for example, was Professor Malcolm P. McNair. When Mac, as he was affectionately called by the locals, gave his annual speech at Faculty meetings on being tough-minded, the locals would burst forth in applause: whereas the young cosmopolitans without tenure quaked in their boots, shivers ran up and down their spines, and perspiration dripped from their foreheads

Only a very high-status cosmopolitan indeed could talk back to a high-status local. Let us see why this was so. A prerequisite to becoming a high-status cosmopolitan (up to 1957) was having a Ph.D. in economics and a course to teach in a business function in which the discipline could be practiced without having to get balled up with the administrative point of view and the case method. Such persons (up to 1957) appeared primarily in three courses or areas: Finance, Public Relations and Responsibilities, and Labor Relations.

Probably no teaching group was composed of more individual prima donnas than the Finance group. Unlike the Marketing group, which was composed almost 100 percent of locals, the Finance group had both locals and cosmopolitans, and the cosmopolitans had higher status than the locals. That is to say, the Finance cosmopolitans had greater reputations outside the School than the Finance locals. The Finance cosmopolitans tolerated locals in their midst. They did not produce them, as the Marketing group did, but they allowed them to come in from other groups at the School. My impression was that Finance was not exactly a cozy group for a local to be a member of. It was more a collection of individuals than a social group; they did not go in for togetherness. I had less interaction with the members of this teaching group than with the members of any other of the teaching groups that were concerned with the elements of administration at the School. Probably this was because we were both willing to accept the fact that we were concerned with different phenomena, and we let it go at that.

The fact that Marketing over-produced red hot locals, whereas

Finance under-produced them, always interested me. I thought that it might be because Finance had a legitimate place in the field of economics, whereas Marketing had no place as a professional acitivty in classical economic theory. Not that classical theory ignored the marketplace. It did not, but it treated it as impersonal, subject to the inexorable laws of supply and demand; consequently it provided, at least conceptually, no more than a subordinated role for individual action and initiative. Thus, whereas members of the Finance group did not need the administrative point of view to achieve their identities, the Marketing group did. Hence, from the point of view not only of "Human Relations" but also of classical economic theory, the marketeers were bastards. Unlike the financiers, who had the sanction of economics for being tough-minded, the marketeers had to proclaim their tough-mindedness because of being somewhat soft on the consumer. Not only did they have to provide the consumer with everything his little heart might desire, but also in those instances in which he did not know what he wanted, they had to tell him what he ought to want. And for this kind of manipulation, classical economic theory did not prescribe.

Another home base for economists was the first-year required course in Public Relations and Responsibilities. When first introduced as one of the elements of administration, it had a difficult time fitting into the pattern, just as Administrative Practices did. No element of administration changed its title more often. During the years from 1947 to 1967, for example, it operated under four different ones: Public Relations and Responsibilities, or PR & R; Business Responsibilities in the American Society, or BRAS; The Manager in the American Economy, or MAE; and Planning in the Business Environment, or PBE.

Why it changed its name so frequently I never understood. Perhaps its instructors had difficulty in deciding upon a name for what they were teaching which would be fitting and yet whose initials would not spell out something so soft and feminine sounding as BRAS and MAE; or perhaps, because theirs was never a very popular element with students, they hoped that by MAE they could make their course sound more seductive (Why don't you come up and see me sometime?). But this is just wild speculation.

What I wish to point out is that the word administration did not appear in any of the course's four titles. I suspect that this was because it tended to be staffed with economic cosmopolitans. In fact, rumor had it that in this course, economics (that is, macro-economics) was being surreptitiously introduced as a required course in the first year, where, it will be remembered, it did not strictly belong. The course was not strictly an element of administration, because like *people*, in Administrative Practices, economics pervaded all of it. Hence, only by giving it a name different from its discipline could it be taught legitimately in the first-year program. Be this as it may, the course provided some economists with an opportunity to become identified with the primary educational purpose of the School and to satisfy the minimum requirements of locality without having to burn all their economics books or throw them in the Charles River.

The other place in which cosmopolitans could do their thing without becoming overly concerned or interfered with by the administrative point of view was the field of Labor Relations. In this field Labor Economics reigned almost supreme and, during the 1940s and 1950s, Sumner Slichter was its chief exponent. No more than I, Sumner never succumbed to the theory of interchangeable parts. But, unlike me, he never got involved in these God-awful (conceptually, I mean) courses addressed to the administrative point of view. He remained pure by teaching courses in Labor Relations—what I call Labor Economics—in the MBA program or the Advanced Management Program. By sticking to his knitting in this fashion he achieved high eminence in his special field and became a high-status cosmopolitan at the School. When Sumner spoke, both high-status locals and high-status cosmopolitans listened.

At this time there was another labor relations cosmopolitan at the School who did not see eye-to-eye with Sumner Slichter; this was Benjamin M. Selekman. They differed in something like the following way. Although Sumner had a real concern for workers and the importance of the union, through which the latters' grievances could be expressed and their lot thereby improved, the intellectual and economic aspects of the relationship interested him more than the nitty gritty aspects of the processes by which the relationship between a union and a management could be improved. To put it baldly, for Sumner the problem was essentially economic. For Ben this was not the case.

Brought up a poor boy in the coal fields of Pennsylvania, Ben had an intuitive familiarity with the phenomena of workers' behavior, with which Sumner, by social background and discipline, was not intimately acquainted. Moreover, Ben received his degree in sociology at Columbia before Robert Merton and Paul Lazarsfeld made sociology a science and when it was in a sense overly concerned with social problems and in another sense a branch of philosophy. Moreover, prior to coming to the Business School, Ben had been director of the Associated Jewish Philanthropies in Boston, and thus had been engaged in matters of social welfare, social work, and the New Deal, with all of which the high-status locals and the high-status cosmopolitans at the B-School had little to do.

To make a long story short, Ben Selekman brought to Labor Relations a set of attitudes and concerns which did not make him either an acceptable local or an acceptable cosmopolitan, but which nevertheless, together with a high sense of integrity, made him an acceptable member of the School. He developed a course in Labor Relations in the Advanced Management Program in which though the participants might have been hostile to him at the beginning, at the end they were eating out of his hands. Ben was a great teacher. He died with his boots on—in class lecturing to his students.

Although I could talk to Ben about my concerns much more easily than I could to Sumner, I never could reduce my concerns completely to the field of Labor Relations, of either the Sumner or the Ben variety. Although Ben and I taught together before World War II in the Human Problems of Administration and after the war in the Advanced Management Program, in which we each gave a separate course, we never saw eye-to-eye about the question of power. Ben always seemed to me to be trying to contain or civilize power by morality. Although this conception interested me, it did not do the trick for me in relation to my concern about knowledge.

As time went on—unfortunately, as I reflect upon it now—Ben with his interest in Labor Relations and I with my interest in Human Relations got further and further apart. By this time it was clear to most people that because I was interested in improving the worker's lot by changing the practices of management, I was on the side of management instead of the union. By such a route, so the argument went, the union would have fewer grievances to complain about and so ultimately in the long run it would lose its function. Obviously in this sense I was a union buster.

I mention this now, because it illustrates well one of those kaleidoscopic switches in which I more and more frequently became involved. Almost with one stroke of the pen I could be transformed from a "goodie" (an innocent seeker of the truth) to a "baddie" (a union buster).

Not only were there many locals and some acceptable cosmopolitans at the School; there were also a few deviants. Some of them achieved high status as isolates. Such, for example, was Georges F. Doriot. "Georges," as he was affectionately called by those who could say Georges in the way a Frenchman would say Georges, did not achieve his high-status isolation because of any disciplinary allegiances. Lord forbid! He got it because he could poke fun at not only the sacred cows of the professional manager and *le système du cas*, as he called the case method, but also at those of the social scientist. He was all for the pure and unadulterated free enterprise system with no holds barred. He lauded the creative and innovative—not the bureaucratic—aspects of this system. In terms of the latter Georges was a rule breaker and not a rule maker, and he had more than a bit of charisma about him. This charisma, as time went on, affected less and less the basic norms and values (or policies) of the School. He attended fewer and fewer Faculty meetings; he sat less and less on important policy-making committees; finally he came to the School only to give his course called Manufacturing, an optional course in the second year, which because of its title put him in the Production area. Actually it had about as much to do with Production or the administrative point of view, as conceived by the School, as the man in the moon. It was a course on entrepreneurship. Georges's course was always popular in the sense that he polarized the class quickly into those who were for or against him. No one could ever be neutral about Georges. He was either God or the devil incarnate.

WAS I A LOCAL OR A COSMOPOLITAN?

In the terms in which I have been writing, was I a local or a cosmopolitan or some screwed-up deviant or isolate? I have found that it is easier to put a colleague in a box than to put oneself in one (Don't fence me in that way), and I do not want to make myself an exception to this rule. So of course I was different; my situation was more complex. In terms of categories I was either a conflicted local or a conflicted cosmopolitan, depending on which way you wanted to look at it. In order to show how this came about, let me cite some things about the development of the subject of Human Relations. Although I have already mentioned them, now I will tie them together to highlight the beautiful pattern which they formed and with which I became intoxicated, though it left my colleagues cold sober and thus produced by juxtaposition the conflict in which I found myself.

Earlier I tried to show how Dean Wallace Donham, the actor and organizer, Elton Mayo, the clinican and visionary, and L. J. Henderson, the scientist and conservative, formed a constellation of roles which together produced the possibility of an intellectual underpinning (as well as a visionary one) for the development of the professional administrator at the School.

I think Donham was aware of this possibility. He realized that something more than clichés were needed to realize his dreams about the development of the role of the professional administrator. The development needed something that could appropriately be called knowledge and something that could appropriately be called vision; finally, it needed some emotionally dedicated persons to realize it.

In the ideas of Mayo and Henderson—two nonlocal boys, by the way—Donham saw the conceptual underpinning that was needed for this development and which he as Dean could organize so that something concrete would result at the School. Moreover, in Mayo he had a person who could make him think big about his job as Dean. Mayo provided a vision which made the development of the administrator something that was important, significant, worthwhile, and exciting.

You may remember that Mayo had little interest in any one of four notions about leadership: the dull rule-making bureaucratic administrator, the robber baron, the heroic charismatic leader, or the time-and-motion scientific management leader. When Mayo spoke about the administrator, he was not referring to the administrator of the established society or to making him a better rule maker, paper shuffler, bookkeeper or high-grade clerk; he was not referring to how to make a fast buck, how to become a Napoleon or a Hitler, or how to optimize time and motions. He was referring to the administrator of the newly emerging society which science and technology were slowly but surely creating and the knowledge and skills that this nonheroic person—still somewhat nonexistent—would need in order to do more competently the much-needed job of the twentieth century, a job which could *be* important, significant, worthwhile, exciting, and not just sound that way.

I think Mayo saw more clearly than Donham that before this development could take place, a great deal of the conventional wisdom of the nineteenth century about the motivation, productivity, and satisfaction of people would have to be liquidated. A great big unfreezing job would have to be done before this new administrator could emerge.

Mayo was then unaware of the modern methods (or mysteries) about how to intervene in an organization in order to make it more adaptive, and he made no attempt to change the Business School, its teaching curriculum, or its sacred cows. Donham could never have gotten him, for example, to teach a 100-student section of Administrative Practices. Nor could he have gotten Henderson to do it. Mayo exercised his influence in a two-person relationship or in a small group of a few highly selected students in whom he was personally interested. They might come from the Business School or not; this made little difference to him. Henderson exercised his influence on his colleagues and students across the River in the Society of Fellows, in his seminar on Pareto, or in his course on Concrete Sociology.

Thus I have shown how I was left holding the bag at the School, a bag filled with a most exciting assortment of concepts, methods, and visions, all of which I thought had tremendous implications for the training of this new professional administrator in whom Donham was interested but for whom I felt not many others at the School were doing very much, at least in an intellectual and conceptual sense. I thought I could help, but not at any price.

I have told how I helped to organize and teach the new course in Administrative Practices in 1947; how I got discouraged and introduced an optional second-year course called Human Relations, where I could do my thing without getting entangled with the sacred cows of the School; and still later, how I developed the Human Relations Clinic, where I could do my thing with research funds provided by the Ford Foundation. Along this road I was becoming, like Georges Doriot, a high-status isolate whose reputation and influence outside the School was much greater than inside.

But there was a difference, a big difference, I believed. Had I been satisfied to develop my thing as my private thing unrelated to the things going around me, I would not have become conflicted. This was not the case. Indeed, it could not be, because my thing came in time to be at the center of the big garden that the School was cultivating. It was related closely to the aims and goals of all those required courses in the first-year program and of Business Policy in the second-year program. In fact, from my point of view, I felt I could provide those courses with the conceptual scheme and method they needed to become really integrated and to grow and complicate beyond the level of clichés.

Let me further sharpen the underlying issue. In my opinion, if the Business School was to become something more than a trade school, if it was to become a part of a great university, and if the professional administrator it was developing was to become something other than a role bound by nineteenth-century culture, then the conceptual scheme and clinical method I could provide were essential. No kidding! Without them there could be no movement, no growth, no development; there could only be stagnation and obsessive ritualistic elaborations, such as changing the name of a course from Production to Production Administration.

Moreover, without practicing the conceptual scheme and for the time being, eschewing all other ways of thinking, there could be no development. For me the concepts of the social system and the clinical method were not just show pieces to be brought forth on special occasions in order to make a point, win an argument, or show how bright or sophisticated a person was. They were tools to be used.

About these matters I was in deadly earnest. As I showed in Part III, I cultivated this way of thinking to the exclusion of all others. I eschewed (an old-fashioned word which expresses exactly what I mean) all other ways of thinking. I was going to look at all organizations from the point of view of a social system, and I was going to look at the functions of this guy called an administrator from this point of view. I was not going to do this once or twice, but I was going to look at the world this way, wholly and steadily and all the time. If the going got a bit rough and I hit a snag, I was not going to abandon this way of thinking and choose another model. No siree! I was going to stick it out to some more bitter end, when even I would have to admit that something about my way of thinking had to be changed or modified. The conceptual scheme would have to fall of its own weight and not because I nudged it in one direction or another.

In this connection I often remembered what Whitehead said about Descartes. He said that Descartes' great contribution to knowledge had been to carry out a set of assumptions about the relation of mind and body to their final, bitter, inevitable, and totally unacceptable conclusions. Unlike Descartes, who did not find this bitter end before he died, I hoped that I might. I was neither completely fluid nor completely rigid. I was not exploring my universe in a rudderless ship, but in a ship with a rudder that I called my conceptual scheme.

Thus, what being tough-minded meant to McNair, the practice of my conceptual scheme meant to me. In both cases they had sacred and holy overtones. But there was also a big difference. With McNair's tough-mindedness you could *be* something without having to *become* something. With my conceptual scheme you could go places. Moreover, as I explained in Chapter 5, a conceptual scheme for me was an essential piece of equipment in the scientific enterprise. No conceptual scheme, no science. Period. And above all, I wanted to be scientific.

In these terms my reference group consisted of people who were associated with science, not business or administration. At no time in my life had I ever had any aspiration to be a businessman or to build or run an organization. I was willing to study executives, but I never wanted to be one. Never in class did I pretend to be a firing line executive who, from his vast experience, would be able to do better the dumb things that firing line executives in my cases often did. Perhaps this was why I was soft on action. From this point of view I was a cosmopolitan through and through. I was willing to act or intervene in a situation, but I wanted to know what the hell was going on before I acted upon or intervened in it. So here I was, a tender-minded cosmopolitan sitting among a group of tough-minded locals, whose every grunt and twitch disturbed me and yet to whom—can this be true?—I aspired to belong.

But not at any price. It was more that I thought I had the tools which could transform their mud heap into a beautiful flower garden. But my colleagues did not see it this way, for every time I opened my mouth in the direction of "Stop, look, and listen" (which I thought were necessary actions to gain knowledge), an image of a passive observer and student of business rather than of an active firing line executive would be provoked. We locals couldn't have this going on, could we now?

Moreover, here I was teaching a course called Administrative Practices, when I did not give a hoot about administrative practices as they were practiced in most business organizations at the time. I was not even interested in trying to improve them in any way that was comparable to adding epicycles to cycles. Every time a particular wage-incentive system broke down, for example, I was not going to bother tinkering with it by making some slight alteration in it. No, siree! I had been in that rat race during my days in scientific management at M.I.T. I was through with epicycles. I did not want to make a sharp break with them so much as to make a clean break through them.

To make my communication problem still more difficult, the kind of person I was training my students to become did not as yet exist. He had no identity here and now, though I hoped he might have one in the future. This was risky business. How could my students get a job for a role that did not yet exist? What kind of monkey business was I up to when I was training my students in skills for which no jobs existed? My students could not go into the job market and say "Dear Mr. Employer, I have an administrative point of view which does not coincide with your here-and-now bloody administrative practices. But in time I can improve them. Please give me a job." Could they now?

Thus, to conclude this sad story, I was conflicted. On the one hand, I could identify with the aims and objectives of the School about the need for the training of administrators; in this sense I was a local. On the other hand, I could not identify with the School's picture of what kind of person this administrator was and could and should be. I thought that this picture needed some renovation which a breath of fresh air from science could provide; in this sense I was a cosmopolitan.

This, then, was my organizational conflict in 1957. Now let us watch how a so-called expert in human behavior in organizations went about trying to resolve it.

Chapter 16

The Early Development of the Area of Organizational Behavior

In this chapter I want to begin the description of how the conflict I described in the last chapter was resolved organizationally at the Business School. The area of Organizational Behavior as a field of study gradually emerged during this resolution. In this chapter I will describe how the process began.

Let me be clear: In no course that I ever taught at the School—whether in the first or second year of the MBA program or in any other program—did anyone ever interfere with what I did or said in the classroom. About this I never was conflicted nor did I ever have any complaint. I was able to do my thing in any class I gave, even when I was teaching one or two of the seven sections of the required course Administrative Practices in the first year of the MBA program.

Yet it seemed to me that anyone teaching in this course had to be concerned, if only for the sake of his students and irrespective of his academic freedom, with what was going on in the other sections of it as well as in the other required courses which were addressed to the administrative point of view we were all supposed to have in common.

EARLY MEETINGS ABOUT THE CASE METHOD OF TEACHING
ADMINISTRATION

There was no disagreement about this among my colleagues. It was common practice for the teaching groups in the first-year program to hold staff meetings at which the instructors would discuss the case for the next day's classes. Because Administrative Practices was a new course and because it was a new venture for many of the teachers engaged in it, we probably held more meetings than any of the other groups.

When Administrative Practices was first introduced, as I have said, Edmund P. Learned (a full professor of about my age) was made course head; he chaired these staff meetings. Ed was a local *par excellence* in the best sense of the word. He had received his Doctoral degree from the School; his field was marketing; he had taught in other first-year courses; and he was identified completely with the aims of the School in respect to training administrators. Consequently, Ed was an excellent choice, because gaining the support of a high-status marketing local for a separate "people" course in the first year of the MBA program was an important step indeed for the course's future. The need for such a course had been hotly contested by the locals prior to its introduction, on the grounds that because people were involved in production, marketing, finance, and control and because matters about people and how to get things done through them were an essential part of these subjects, there was no need for a separate course.

In its early days the Administrative Practices teaching group contained more locals than cosmopolitans. From my point of view they were good locals in the sense that their nervous systems let them do well what my conceptual scheme said they should do: in fact, they sometimes did it better than I. They resisted making explicit what their nervous systems were telling them implicitly (a common phenomenon which has never ceased to astonish me). Just as in the early stages of many of my other ventures, we all had a good time, and we learned from each other. At our meetings I never felt that they were shoving their firing line executives down my throat, and I did not think I was shoving my conceptual scheme down theirs. As would be said today, our encounters were cool. I seldom used my "hot" (from their point of view) concepts and buzz words; they seldom expressed their hot (from my point of view) opinions about getting something done willy-nilly. Instead we practiced the art of extensionalization. Man, were we cool, as I look back upon it now.

Where we remained the most extensional and cool was in regard to the case method of teaching, as I described in Chapter 9. Indeed, it seemed easier for us to talk about *how* we taught our course than about *what* we were teaching in it. In respect to "how" questions, our discussions stayed cool; in respect to "what" questions, they got hot. This difference does not seem unusual, when I think about it now, because in our area the medium of communication contained the message the professor was trying to communicate to his students. It would have been strange indeed if his teaching style had not been congruent with the communication skills about which he was teaching. He could not do to his students in class what he was criticizing administrators for doing to their employees in the cases being discussed!

As a result, during the first years of Administrative Practices, from 1949 to about 1952, there was considerable excitement among the instructors about the case method of teaching. We held extra meetings with this as the sole topic of discussion, and we were joined by teachers from the Policy course and by Doctoral candidates. Some papers were written, and they were collected in a book, *The Case Method of Teaching Human Relations and Administration* (1953), edited by Kenneth R. Andrews.

I probably exercised my greatest influence on teaching at the School in these meetings. I first expressed in these discussions many of the ideas that I had about the case method. I was eager to extensionalize the method in relation to the learning process and not in relation to taking action, almost the only way in which it was being discussed elsewhere in the School. By means of the hot words used in these discussions, it seemed to me the case method of teaching was becoming an all-purpose tool, whose mystique belonged to the Harvard Business School, whereas I thought the method had much in common with other discussion and learning methods and that it could and should be developed in relation to the process of learning. In short I wanted to free the case method from its institutional bondage, give it wings, and let it soar into the wild blue yonder.

Well, live and learn. These meetings and the resulting book caused consternation in the ranks of the high-status locals. What seemed to bother them was the relative absence of their sacred words (the ones I have called hot) and the presence of words which I thought were cool, but which they thought were "buzz words" that contaminated all that for them was holy and sacred about the case method. Indeed to them it looked as though we were undermining the case method.

To correct this unhealthy state of affairs Professor McNair somewhat later edited a book of essays by members of the Faculty called *The Case Method at the Harvard Business School* (1954). Note this title carefully, because it communicated in effect: "Let's have no more nonsense about it. The case method is not a tool for learning about a subject matter; it belongs to the Harvard Business School, which owns the right to market it. The institution comes first, the subject matter second." Thus spoke a high-status Marketing local.

CHANGES IN THE TEACHING GROUP (1952–1956)

Administrative Practices enjoyed a honeymoon period of more than four years before stresses and strains around this issue—which I confess I am having a hard time clarifying, because it belongs more to the realm of feelings and sentiments than to the realm of fact and logic—began to appear within the ranks of its own teaching group. By this time, it will be remembered, I had left the group to teach Human Relations in the second year of the MBA program, where I felt I could do my own thing with less wear and tear on my nervous system. I say this to remind the reader again that I am still describing all this from my point of view.

The dissension, as I saw it, had its roots in the syndrome in the Faculty which I have been describing. The questions being raised included the following:

(1) Was the Administrative Practices teaching group introducing too many concepts and methods from the social sciences? After all, the course was not training social scientists but administrators.

(2) By its concern for the social realities was the course getting too far away from the economic realities of business—what was often referred to as the business of the business?

(3) Was not the course essentially concerned with matters of ethics and values? When all was said and done, was it just teaching the Golden Rule?

(4) Shouldn't the course fire more people as the solution to its cases? Wasn't the course creating the image that no one should ever be fired?

Lord forbid that I claim that by these four questions I have captured all the nuances of the matters that were conflicting the instructors in the teaching group. All I am saying is that their conflicts seemed to me to be roughly of this kind. They were not silly questions, but they were questions arising from a frame of reference entirely different from the conceptual scheme I advocated.

Anyhow, in time and in terms of these kinds of questions the Administrative Practices teaching group split more or less into two factions: (1) those who could emphatically answer "no" to the questions without getting conflicted and (2) those who had to say "yes" in order to remain unconflicted. This conflict was resolved over time, because, largely for other reasons, members of the second faction went into Policy or some other course where the questions did not arise so sharply. As I remember it, no one was fired; the process resembled more a game of musical chairs, in which the person who no longer found the chair comfortable in Administrative Practices was slowly eliminated but not fired. No, siree! He went into Policy where he could do his thing more comfortably. (Incidentally, I thought that allowing this to happen was good administrative practice.)

In the process, however, Administrative Practices lost three great case teachers—Ed Learned, Ken Andrews, and Jack Glover. Ed became course head of the Business Policy group; and Ken and Jack, along with Chris Christensen (who had never taught Administrative Practices, but who had been present at many of our meetings on the case method as well as involved with me in the prediction study), became his able lieutenants. Administrative Practices' loss became Business Policy's gain.

Curious as it may sound, these men could not wash Administrative Practices or Human Relations out of their hair. After all, "Policy" was an integrative course and people had always been one of the elements along with the business of the business that the course tried to integrate. These instructors wanted "people" in their course, but not too many and not just people alone; above all they did not want social science jargon about people. Ken was adamant about this last point, and I had a great deal of sympathy for it. Jack wanted to bring in ethics and values, for which I thought something could also be said, so long as it was one of the aspects with which we were concerned and not the only aspect to which everything was to be reduced.

THE THREE GROUP MEETINGS

Somehow none of us could leave well enough alone. We all felt that there was some more general conceptual framework under which Administrative Practices in the first year and Business Policy and Human Relations in the second year (George Lombard was teaching the Human Relations course now) could be integrated. We organized a set of meetings to discuss this question. It came to be called the "three group meetings" or the "AP-BP-HR combination." We held about a dozen meetings in 1956-1957 and somewhat fewer in 1957-1958. I do not remember who was the chief initiator of these meetings, but George chaired them in the first year and Ken in the second.

At these meetings we took turns stating the objectives of our respective courses, the concepts and methods we used, and how we thought our courses related to each other and to the School's over-all purposes of training administrators. But we could not agree about the development of an administrator's role and mission. Al-though I think these meetings served well the purposes of express-ing our differences and making them explicit, no general conceptual framework developed from them. It seemed to me we got hung up on words that we just could not extensionalize. Their intensional meanings were too holy and sacred for us.

The composition of the group had a good deal to do with these difficulties. By this time Ed, Ken, and Jack had left Administrative Practices and were associated with Policy; Paul Lawrence was now course head of Administrative Practices, having succeeded Joe Bai-ley, who had held the position for a few years. George Lombard, Abe Zaleznik, and I at the time represented Human Relations. Had these discussions been restricted to just these eight people, all of whom had worked together, we might have overcome our semantic difficulties. But this was not the case. Each of the two larger teaching groups—Administrative Practices and Business Policy—had added other instructors to staff the seven sections that were being taught. How had this been done?

As I have said, the School had no departments: There were only the teaching groups associated with the required courses. Each indi-vidual professor reported directly to the Dean. Although each of the teaching groups had a course head, he was not a department head; he had no budget, and nothing to say about salaries and promotions. In fact, at the time he had little to say about who would teach in the course of which he was "head." These decisions were the primary job of the Associate Dean for Educational Affairs. It was his respon-sibility to staff the required courses with a view to each individual Faculty member's interests and desires. In terms of the School's principle of interchangeable parts, any professor who expressed an interest in teaching Administrative Practices—perhaps simply be-cause he was interested in people—had a good chance of getting the assignment. Likewise, it was difficult to say "No" to a senior full professor who had a yen to teach Policy, because it was clearly just that when age, service, and rank were high, the rewards should also be high. And to teach Policy was the biggest reward the Associate Dean could give. You were now a high-status local for sure—for keeps perhaps, but let us wait and see about that.

The point I am getting around to is that the AP-BP-HR meetings drew about 15 people, 7 of whom had little or no experience in teaching the courses they had been assigned to because of their interest in people or because of the law of distributive justice. In my opinion they not only lacked experience but were also illiterate about the behavioral sciences and the nature of the scientific enterprise, and they were proud of their illiteracy.

In this conglomerate atmosphere, consensus about anything was impossible. After two years of the resulting confusion I became so frustrated and angry that early in 1958 I delivered my swan song in the form of a memorandum. The gist of this memo was that I had had it. I was through, finis, kaput with trying to reach any consensus about what we thought we were up to. I said that the values of science were my values; that I was committed to them and could not change. I wanted to go full steam ahead along this path. Should anyone with similar commitments care to join me, it would be fine and dandy. Let those who could not make such commitments do their thing, but please keep out of my way.

With this memo the meetings were disbanded, and we did not meet again to try to reconcile our differences. At the time I felt sheepish about my display of temper and felt I had "cooked my goose" for any possible future rapprochement among the three groups. In retrospect, though, I think it had some favorable consequences. It cleared the air in two important respects. It allowed each person to decide at what level he wished to investigate, understand, and deal with the human aspects of administration. And also it permitted a separate and explicit development of different areas at the School. For it was during these "three group meetings" that I first began to use the words Organizational Behavior instead of Human Relations as the label whose referent, if properly understood, might allow us to get together. Organizational Behavior was the study of the way people did behave—and not should behave—in organizations. The people could be workers, supervisors, middle or top management, staff or line, and so on. In this common ball park it seemed to me we could play our differentiated games and still remain related. But this was not to be.

AN INFORMAL LEADER OF AN INFORMAL SOUL GROUP

Although in the memo that was my swan song I implied that I was ready to go it alone, if I had to, this was not an accurate statement of my situation at the time these meetings took place. Through the years I had accumulated a number of followers—not blind followers, as my critics would have it, who said their prayers to Mayo and

Henderson and the conceptual scheme each night before they went to bed. Rather these followers were excited about the scientific and humanistic direction in which I was pointing and for which they felt there was much to be said.

This "soul group" as I shall call it, had no status in the formal organization of the School. In its very early days it had been called the Mayo group; later it was called the Human Relations group; now (circa 1957) it was coming to be called the Organizational Behavior group. After Mayo's retirement in 1947, I had become the senior member of the group and in a sense its intellectual, although informal, leader.

I want to mention some of the members of this informal group. I do so with trepidation, because I may leave out someone who thought he belonged and had contributed to it and who indeed may have done so, but about whom I have now forgotten.

First and foremost there was George Lombard, in age about ten years my junior, who worked with me over many years on so many projects that almost from the beginning I regarded him more as a colleague than a student. Although George was a product of the School and had received his Doctoral degree from it, he never succumbed to becoming an interchangeable part. He remained a committed member of this "soul group." His major contribution was in terms of judgment, perspective, balance, and characteristics of this order that are difficult to put one's finger on.

Again and again I would go to George to talk about problems about which I did not want any precipitous or immediate action or often even any action at all to be taken. He would listen, without agreeing or disagreeing, but allowing me to sort out the elements that made up my conflict, frustration, anger, and despair. This was something I never felt I could do with my trigger-happy, action-oriented colleagues. I always thought they would take some action that, however well intentioned, would mess up rather than clarify (for me) the show in which I was involved. George never did this to me, and for this I was ever grateful.

Again and again George could have said to me, "Well, Fritz, you have to cross the street to get on its other side, don't you now?" But he never did. He knew (in some intuitive sense) that I was terrified to cross the street, if by doing so I would remain deserted, alone, forsaken, and isolated there. I wanted autonomy (i.e., doing my thing), but also I wanted support for doing it. George never failed me in the latter respect, but he also did not comfort me by saying that this would be easy and without any headache. Probably more than any one else I have known, George could maintain a long pause in a conversation. Many times I would ask him a question, only to find myself answering it after a minute or more of unbearable silence.

There are no two students of mine of whom I am prouder than Paul R. Lawrence and Abraham Zaleznik. Both were young enough to have been my sons. Both were products of the School's MBA program, both received their Doctoral degrees from the School at the same time, and both were promoted to the ranks of Assistant Professor, Associate Professor, and full Professor at the same time. In their early careers both became members of this "soul group." Both had talents for teaching and research; in addition, Paul had talent for administration.

Paul, as I have said earlier, became course head of Administrative Practices in 1954 and spent many years developing the course. After the ranks of the teaching group for this course had become decimated by the departure of Ed, Ken, and Jack, the empty slots were filled with members of my "soul group." In time the course came to be staffed by those who had been exposed to me either in one of my courses or in the Human Relations Clinic. All were committed to the twin values to which the label Human Relations referred (human for humanistic and relations for science). Some perhaps were more committed in one direction than the other, but all were committed to the practice of the clinical method and to becoming competent field workers. They were also willing to expose themselves to the concepts and methods of the behavioral sciences. Yet there was no one who strictly represented any one of the behavioral science disciplines in the group. Most of them were products of the Business School who had acquired some knowledge of the behavioral sciences. In this latter respect they were inter- or multi-disciplinary. To use a label that was not current then but which I think could have been applied to them, they saw themselves as change agents of the second-level practitioner variety which I described in Chapter 13 when I talked about the Human Relations Clinic.

The group in Administrative Practices included Robert L. Katz, John A. Seiler, Charles D. Orth, James V. Clark, Louis B. Barnes, Arthur N. Turner, and James R. Surface. It was this group (plus Joseph C. Bailey and Ralph M. Hower) for whom Paul Lawrence became course head. Much of the future training of the group was under his direction. Under Paul's leadership most of them worked together to publish a book called *Organizational Behavior and Administration: Cases, Concepts, and Research Findings* (1961). The first case book published by the Administrative Practices group had been called *The Administrator: Cases on Human Relations in Business;* it was edited by John D. Glover and Ralph M. Hower (1949). Although some of the cases in both books were the same, the main titles and subtitles of the two books indicate the shift in orientation. The title of the original book had the overtones of the local. It was a collection of cases without a conceptual scheme provided for their analysis. The title of the second suggested the possibility of a subject matter based on research and a set of concepts for its development.

WHAT PRICE HUMAN RELATIONS?

Although I did not see it then as clearly as I do now, a number of factors were settling slowly but surely for me the direction in which I was going to make my future contributions to the purposes of the School in training administrators. One other incident probably clinched it for me.

On June 22, 1956, Malcolm P. McNair delivered a talk on "What Price Human Relations?" to alumni of the School who were attending a special program. The address was published in the *Harvard Business School Bulletin* (Winter 1957). The article was followed by an editorial in the *Harbus News*, the weekly student newspaper, on February 8, 1957. The editorial featured what it called McNair's "concrete and positive point of view," a platform which he stated as follows:

> Research in human behavior—yes
> Courses in human relations for mature executives—yes
> For MBA candidates,
>   courses in personnel management—yes
>   courses in business organization—yes
>   but courses in "ad prac" and human relations—no.

McNair based his proposals for action on five charges against human relations which I can summarize as follows:

(1) Though human relations should be taken into account as an integral part of other subjects, it should not be taught *as such* at the MBA level.

(2) Teaching human relations makes it easy for people to feel sorry for themselves, to find excuses for their failures, to slough off responsibility, and to act like children.

(3) The present vogue of human relations promotes conformity and teaches people to avoid conflict, to regard friction as an evil, and to become sloppy sentimentalists.

(4) Human relations encourages people who want to manage other people's lives to engage in amateur psychiatry.

(5) Human relations goes against the purpose of education in administration, which is to toughen and thicken a person's intellectual and moral veneer and not, as someone else has said, "to pick at the scabs of the wounds of his psyche."

As can be imagined, these charges and the resulting proposals for action resulted in considerable clucking of tongues inside and outside the School. It was the first time during my life there that the in-fighting among members of the Faculty about matters of the curriculum had taken place outside Faculty meetings and had been brought to the attention of the public, in this case, the alumni body. That Mac must have felt very strongly about something to have done this was obvious. It was clear to me that his proposals for action arose from these strong feelings, and as in my experience such feelings are generally accompanied by a need to do something, I felt I understood how Mac got to the point of taking the action he did. I also understood that according to the decision-making process advocated by the School, this was not the way tough decisions were supposed to be reached. They were supposed to be reached by a logical appraisal of the pros and cons of different alternatives based on the facts. Here was a proposal based on the strong opinions of an outraged local with few facts, with no idea (conceptual scheme) behind them, and with no consideration of alternatives. But because they were the opinions of a high-status Marketing local, they had a kind of pseudo-logical weight in the minds of the majority of locals at the School, and they could not be ignored.

How Stanley F. Teele, who was then Dean of the School, dealt with the situation I do not know, because I never had any discussion with him about it. (That he neither consulted me nor I him seems to me strange now, but I will not speculate about it.) At one point there was a rumor that there should be a Faculty investigation of McNair's charges to see if they were true. I shuddered at the thought of such a solution, because I thought the result would be stated by the locals in terms of tender- or tough-mindedness. I thought that in this way the issue would get polarized and that no new constructive synthesis could arise from it. I wished to avoid this outcome at all cost. A discussion by locals who did not differentiate opinions and feelings from facts and ideas would be more than my nervous system could stand. My personal solution was to let the members of the Faculty stew in their juice of rhetoric and semantics and to go ahead with my own way of clearing up the mess I felt we were in.

For as I saw it, we were in a mess. There was a half truth to some of Mac's charges, although not in the extreme form in which he put them. Mac had confused his reaction to the situation for a description of it. When done badly, human relations training did have at least some of the unfortunate, though unintended, consequences he cited. Ironically they arose in part because of the good, noble, and quite opposite intentions of the people in charge of the training. Surely Mac could not have believed that the consequences he cited were the intentions of the Administrative Practices teaching group: making people sorry for themselves, excusing their failures, sloughing off responsibility, avoiding conflict, becoming sloppy sentimentalists, managing other people's lives, engaging in amateur psychiatry, and pecking at their psychic wounds. Surely we could not have been advocating all these bad things, could we?

The problem for me was how teachers of Human Relations could produce consequences that were the opposite of what they intended. How could this happen? Were we involved in a pattern of circularity similar to the one I described in Chapter 11 when I talked about the bureaucratic model, but going now in a different direction? That is, did the unintended and undesired consequences of human relations training require more human relations training to correct them, and so on ad infinitum? In the absence of a conceptual scheme about a social system and of a clinical method of observation and listening, I thought this result was possible. Under such conditions the price being paid for human relations training was too high, and Mac was right. Accordingly, my solution to Mac's charges was similar to the one I suggested for the correction of the bureaucratic model (see the diagrams on pages 182 and 185). What was required was not more human relations practiced by more people with good intentions, but more human relations by people with more competence. It did not seem to me that Mac or the Dean or the Associate Dean or the locals could have both their policy of interchangeable parts and better human relations training. They could not staff their courses about people with people who did not know anything about people or themselves—and sometimes did not want to learn anything about people and their relations to each other and to themselves—and then complain about the results they got.

Taking one thing after another, here was the way the situation was for me in 1958. For the five years prior to Mac's blast I had been doing roughly what he recommended. From 1951 to 1954 I conducted the Human Relations Clinic—which was *not* addressed to MBA students. From 1954 to 1957 I had been engaged in research, the prediction study, an activity which Mac said was okay. Thus, since 1951 I had not taught Human Relations in the MBA program; even before that, since 1948, I had not taught Administrative Practices in the first year. In a way it could be said that all of Mac's charges had little to do with me, and I could have let the Administrative Practices group and George Lombard, who was teaching the second-year Human Relations course, bear the brunt of them.

Yet I was the informal leader of this informal soul group of young cosmopolitans, who were beginning to replace the locals in the Administrative Practices teaching group. Their ranks were solidified by Mac's charges. Moreover, as a result of the three group meetings, it was becoming clear to me who the members were who wished to improve their competence in matters of human relations and have careers in the field. Even though the Dean had not assigned me any formal responsibility for them and their careers, I could not avoid my feelings of responsibility for them. In a manner of speaking, if my chickens had come home to roost and if they were going to cluck in their nests, so help me God, I was going to see that they learned to cluck in a competent manner.

These were the events (i.e., the meaning they had for me) which led me into the Doctoral program, where I thought I could develop a legitimate area called Organizational Behavior in which students could specialize, become competent, and develop careers. In this program I spent the remainder of my life until I retired. With this choice, however, it could be said that I jumped from the frying pan into the fire. Up to now I had been primarily concerned with the School as an institution and with its norms and values about administrative action. Now I had also to be concerned with the most sacred norms and values of the University in relation to its highest degree, for which its holders became acceptable and respectable members of the academic community. I had to consider such questions as what made a scholar a scholar, a discipline a discipline, science science, and research research.

These headaches are the ones I will discuss in the next three chapters. I will start each chapter with enough history to fill in any gaps that remain in the account I have already given. I can be brief, because there are not many, and I want increasingly to focus on the questions that stayed with me throughout my professional life. Though I did not find that other people's books answered my questions, the study of these books for and with my Doctoral students helped me clarify these questions.

Chapter 17

The New Doctoral Program

I could not have joined the Doctoral program at a more exciting time than in 1957, when it was going through a period of renovation and rejuvenation as well as expansion. Up to that time the program had been a small show; the big show was the MBA program, of which the School was justifiably proud. The Doctoral program had been a side show, in which only a few of the cosmopolitan members of the Faculty were engaged. Its most important function for the high-status locals was to produce more locals for the Faculty of our own MBA program; there was no other place to get them.

Candidates for the degree—at the time called Doctor of Commercial Science (DCS)—spent most of their time collecting cases as research assistants for particular professors. After a few years of this training in case research (as it was understood by the professor for whom they worked), they often collected a half dozen or more cases of their own about some particular problem or topic. They added a final chapter about the administrative implications of the cases, and this constituted a thesis. Thus a graduate of the early program usually had training in only one method of research and one method of teaching. If he wanted to go into teaching as a career, he had to stay at the School or go to one which used the same methods.

Up to 1957 the limited nature of this training was not a big problem, because persons who wanted Doctoral degrees in business were few and far between. Not only was the teaching of business less rewarding than the practice of it; no one had established then—or for that matter, now—that the practice of business required an MBA or a DCS or a DBA. Thus there was no profession of business—if business can be called that—in which "he who can does and he who cannot teaches." Only a nut of a screwy kind like me could possibly think that some day a profession might come into existence!

By 1957, however, the so-called knowledge explosion hit the Business School. Lo and behold, the School and its celebrated case method (unless extensionalized with more sophistication than its tough-minded advocates recommended) were on the verge of going down the drain—or so some thought. In this exciting (for cosmopolitans) and anxiety-producing (for locals) atmosphere, I entered the fray in the Doctoral program. What fun! But I am rushing my hurdles.

THE ADMINISTRATIVE POINT OF VIEW

The first problem I encountered was in respect to my old friend the administrative point of view. The problem arose because around 1957 an increased number of MBA graduates from other business schools began to come to us for their Doctoral work. Most of them had not been taught by the case method. Thus they did not know what made a case a good case for either teaching or research. As for the administrative point of view, they were not only incapable of its practice, they were unaware of its existence. The problem was: How could we give a higher degree to a person who did not have the foundation upon which our MBA degree was based? We could not do that, could we?

In the old days when only a few students with MBA's from other business schools came to us, the solution to the problem was simple. Before they could become Doctoral candidates, they had to take courses in our MBA program, sometimes the whole two-year program. In those days student power was not what it became later. They cheerfully accepted their fate, perhaps with the hope that by this route they would some day find themselves teaching at "The" (and not any old) Business School or some replica thereof.

By 1957, however, some of the students, as well as the faculties at other institutions, began to believe (contrary to the belief of our high-status locals) that other MBA's were as good as ours. They resented the assumption of superiority on our part, a superiority which they did not believe was based entirely upon the facts. They even thought—if you can believe this now—that the administrative point of view could be learned and taught apart from the case method! All of this was hard to take, but change was in the air; and because we did not want to lose too many good Doctoral candidates to other schools, we were willing to compromise a bit. This is how we came to organize a semester of accelerated courses whose purpose was to communicate the administrative point of view.

These courses were patterned after the required courses in our MBA program: Production, Marketing, Finance, Control, Administrative Practices, and Policy. We set out to give these students with

MBA degrees from other business schools the point of view in four short months that it took us two years to accomplish in our own MBA program. Many of our high-status locals looked upon this task with great foreboding as a Herculean feat that could result only in disaster. But there were a few courageous locals (whose names I shall mention in a moment) and me (a conflicted local, you will remember) who were willing to give it a try.

The Faculty group which gave this set of accelerated courses was called the Doctoral Instructional Group, the "DIG group." In time, I suspect, two-thirds of the Faculty did not know what this set of letters stood for, except for what they spelled out and quickly came to mean; namely, that through this set of courses we were going to get the students from other business schools "to dig" the case method and the administrative point of view so that they could become full-fledged Doctoral candidates.

To be sure that this happened, we set up as the first hurdle a qualifying or general examination, as it came to be called. It consisted of six written examinations, one for each of the five elements of administration—Production, Marketing, Finance, Control, and Administrative Practices—and one on their integration—Policy—and an oral examination on the administrative point of view from the perspective of a chief executive.

In the oral examination the student received a Policy case to prepare in advance. He submitted his analysis of and action recommendations for it in writing. He was then quizzed on his statement by three examiners for an hour-and-a-half or more, after which the examiners had to decide whether he did or did not have "it," the administrative point of view, or APV, as the students called it. Well, if you can believe it, there were often serious disagreements among the examiners about the answer to the question. Some said, "Yes, he had it," and others said, "No, he did not."

I sat on many of these oral examinations, because by now I had reached the age and length of service that qualified me by the School's practices to know what policy was about and what the chief executive of a company was supposed to be doing. I had some ideas about this last question; but often what bothered me about the cases was why the chief executive was not doing what he was supposed to be doing, that is, getting his subordinates to do what they were supposed to be doing, and so on. (See the case of Mr. Post in Chapter 9.)

My problem in the examinations was that many Policy cases did not allow me to raise this question easily. Sometimes they were deficient with respect to the data which the students and I needed to consider it. Often the cases described no relations, apart from the formal and technical ones which existed in the company. Informal or social relations were just not there as far as the cases were concerned. Thus, in the examinations I often took the role of putting up hypothetically what these relations might be, so that students would have something besides formal and technical relations to administer.

My chief role in the examination, however, came in its third phase, after a candidate had discussed his analysis of the case and his proposals for action, when we asked him to consider how he was going to get his recommendations accepted and implemented. Until we reached this phase, I had little or no basis upon which to judge whether the candidate had APV. But when phase three came, "it" shone for me like a beacon light. For me, this phase separated the men from the boys, APV-wise.

I was usually very charitable (or soft) with my evaluations, because the context of the whole situation was almost ludicrous. To begin with, it was nearly impossible for a student to demonstrate the administrative point of view under the conditions of an examination. In this situation the student had little to administer except his own anxieties in relation to the hot question of his three examiners, among whom there were other relations and hidden agendas. Examining groups were not exactly cozy groups; often I found myself grading a student more in terms of how he administered the actual situation in which he found himself than in terms of how he talked about administering the situation in the case that he had been given on paper.

Making this evaluation was also tricky, because in time the examination became a kind of game at which the students became more skilled than their examiners. Even when the examiners did not agree on what APV was, the students came to know the rules of the game pretty well. For example, they knew how much to defend a position, so they would not be considered vacillating or indecisive (no executive could be that, could he now?); and when to shift a position, so that they would not be considered inflexible (no executive could be that either, could he now?). They knew how to make their proper bows and curtsies one at a time to the workers, the consumer, the investor, the wholesaler, the retailer, the supplier, and gee whiz, I nearly forgot—to the balance sheets, the profit and loss statements, the managements, and finally, the organizations and the relations of the people in them.

Frequently before his examination a candidate would be coached by older candidates (who had passed theirs) in regard to how he should conduct himself with particular examiners who had certain peculiar notions about APV. The students knew, even if the Faculty did not, that there was APV_1, APV_2, APV_3, APV_4, APV_5, and APV_6 (I will let the reader guess what 1, 2, 3, 4, 5, and 6 stand for), so that each of them had to be prepared for the ten possible combinations of the different points of view about APV which he might encounter among his three examiners. And if a student who had a yen for APV_5, for example, found himself with examiners who had APV_1, APV_2, and APV_3, it was unfortunate; but for some students that was the way the cookie crumbled.

THE DIG TEACHING GROUP

The situation was not as serious as I have made it sound, because during the first eight years of the new program, from 1957 to 1965, the Faculty members of the DIG group, especially those of us who regularly conducted the semiannual general examinations, remained fairly constant. Among the group were Franklin E. Folts, (Production), Harry R. Tosdal (Marketing), Gordon Donaldson (Finance), Ross G. Walker (Control), Richard S. Meriam (Policy), and I (Administrative Practices). Several of us had taught together in the early years of the Advanced Management Program.

With the exception of Gordon, all of us were full Professors, high-status members of our respective fields, and beginning to approach retirement. We knew the DIG candidates fairly well and had considerably more information about them than what the general examination itself provided. Moreover, the candidates knew us. We, that is, the Faculty group, met weekly for lunch; we got to know each other, our particular life styles, and our different understandings of APV pretty well. In short, we became a group, and this helped to make the general examination a less formidable obstacle for candidates. Moreover, we were evaluating our own products, the students we had had in our courses, so that it was not easy for us to flunk our own candidates. If the student had not learned, the teacher had not taught, had he?

My work with the DIG teaching group was by far the most pleasant experience I ever had with any group of locals at the School. I got to know them as persons, not just as representatives of their fields or as brands of APV; I came to regard all of them as my friends. Perhaps by then I had become more institutionalized, but I also thought we became a good working team with high morale. Yet some other things were going on in our group that had me concerned.

Here I was involved yet again in a Faculty group in which some common conceptual framework about administration could have been developed. In this case all of the so-called elements of administration were represented. Had I been younger, I am sure I would have tried to bring about a conceptual synthesis in the group; but by this time I had concluded from other experiences that you could not make a cosmopolitan out of a local. It was just not his line of country, and in the process you ran the risk of making him into a poor local. For me a good local was better than a half-baked cosmopolitan. Moreover, by this time, as I will be telling, I had other fish to fry than the DIG group's concern about APV. As a result, I just enjoyed this group, in spite of some of the difficulties we got into.

Thus, it was not a common explicit conceptual scheme that brought us together. Rather, it was a common concern for training students in administration. We came to feel we could do this better in a small group than it was being done in the large MBA program. In fact, we became pretty cocky about it. We came to think or ourselves as the last stronghold and guardian of the administrative point of view at the School. By means of the general examination we controlled for the Doctoral program who had or did not have APV. This brought us into trouble with some of our colleagues, particularly on those occasions when we flunked one of our own MBA graduates for not having the administrative point of view. Our own MBA's did not have to take the DIG course, but they did have to take the general examination. That some of our own MBA graduates could be deficient in APV was a proposition that could not be accepted. It just did not make sense. By this time some other unthinkable propositions were beginning to emerge in the Doctoral program, and to these I will now turn.

PRACTITIONERS, RESEARCHERS, AND TEACHERS

As I have said, the primary aim of the new Doctoral program, in which the degree of Doctor of Business Administration (DBA) was now given, was to train teachers and researchers in business—not practitioners. Training practitioners was the aim of the MBA program. This jump from a practitioner orientation to a teacher and researcher orientation was a difficult hurdle for us, for reasons that are not hard to understand. In most disciplines, going from a Master's degree to a Doctor's degree is of a piece; both degrees are addressed to the teacher and researcher, not the practitioner. Because of our emphasis on the training of practitioners in the MBA program, going from that to a DBA meant that after spending two years in graduate school, the candidate almost had to begin all over again.

In the early days, as I have said, this was not serious, because the recipient of a DCS degree was to be a bigger and better MBA graduate, that is, a bigger and better practitioner and not necessarily a bigger and better teacher and particularly not a bigger and better researcher. In the new Doctoral program with its emphasis on training for teaching and research, this issue came more and more into the foreground.

After we settled our first hurdle (the practitioner-oriented administrative point of view), it soon became apparent that one did not do research from this point of view. Research required specialization and a subject matter; it required more explicit questions, conceptual schemes, and methods of research than the implicit ones that underlay case research. But here we were, predominantly a Faculty of locals with little talent for or interest in going in this direction. Indeed for some of us doing so was anathema because of a feeling that the process would strip the big garden we were cultivating of what we believed was its major plant, the administrative point of view.

This apprehension manifested itself in a number of ways, one of which I thought was serious. After a candidate passed his general examination and demonstrated that he had the administrative point of view (from the point of view of the DIG Faculty group), the question was not necessarily taken as settled. He would sometimes be tested for it again and again, in his special field examination (the second hurdle we set up for the new DBA candidates), in his thesis proposal, and eventually in his thesis itself. This was likely to happen if his special field examiners and his thesis committee were predominantly locals. At each of these points, even though the candidate had demonstrated literacy in his special field and done a creditable job of research on his thesis, he could be failed for not having APV.

I thought this was too much of a good thing. Although I was all for APV (because it was the School's distinctive competence), one did not do research by APV; rather one did it by SPV, that is, the scientific point of view. It seemed to me that the APV tail was wagging the new DBA dog too much. I realized that this was not because our Faculty were meanies; they just could not get out of a bad habit. I was ready to import some persons with a scientific point of view from the social sciences into the Doctoral program and to allow them to do their thing to see if this would help to improve our research at the School, something for which, by the way, we had never received high marks. In so doing it was not my thought to dilute APV with SPV or vice versa. I wanted both better APV and better SPV. Although I realized that, like oil and water, they did not mix, I thought that at some higher level of abstraction or some lower level of processes of reality, they might become integrated.

I was not alone with these thoughts about the need for SPV in the field of administration. In 1959 the reports of two investigations about the state of affairs in business schools were published; one had been done under the auspices of the Ford Foundation and the other under the auspices of the Carnegie Foundation. The reports were heralded as doing for business education what the famous Flexner report had done much earlier for medical education. Although both reports concentrated more on undergraduate than graduate education, they had implications and recommendations about the latter, and their conclusions were astonishingly similar. The gist of them was that most business schools had too many courses, too narrowly oriented, and too superficially taught. (This applied more to the undergraduate than to the graduate schools.) But also, the reports said, too much attention was being given to the specialized skills and knowledge of the functional subjects (e.g., Production, Marketing, etc.) and too little to the basic skills that executives required (e.g., skills in problem-solving, communication, interpersonal relations, and organizational skills). They recommended a new set of required courses in which (1) courses in Administration, Organization, and Human Relations and (2) courses in Managerial Economics topped the list.

In short, the tenor of the findings was to the effect that in the new world that science had created, the days of intuitive business executives were numbered; business was becoming more of a science and less of an art. This new world needed executives with new tools (1) for analyzing the marketing environment; (2) for making rational decisions under conditions of uncertainty; (3) for dealing with interpersonal relationships; and (4) for dealing with changes in the firm's external and internal environment. The reports said that most business schools were not doing a very good job in providing students with these tools. As can be imagined, these findings resulted in consternation among all the business schools in the land.

According to these findings, executives, granted they were important and necessary persons in the modern world, were getting their results without usually knowing how they got them; they were working in a human-social medium they did not understand very well; and they were involved in this medium without understanding the nature of their involvement. Hence, they needed more knowledge about these matters. Where did this knowledge exist?

When the investigators sought for it in the business schools of the land, they could not find it. Like Old Mother Hubbard, they found that the cupboards were bare; or, as it was said in Washington at the time (circa Sputnik), there was a serious knowledge gap or vacuum between the knowledge that the executive needed and the knowledge that existed in the business schools. This was serious indeed. According to these findings, not only business executives but also business teachers were suffering from scientific obsolescence. Although many business exeuctives could accept this condition of ignorance gracefully, it was more difficult for business professors; for what air is to an automobile tire, knowledge is to a professor; that is to say, without knowledge the professor becomes flat.

Because human nature abhors vacuums and Washington abhors gaps, at all costs vacuums must be filled and gaps must be bridged. In my experience, the supply for these needs always exists in great abundance; that is, there is no dearth of people who want to fill vacuums and bridge gaps. Hence, there was no lack of solutions for the dilemma. As is likely to happen in such cases, most of the solutions produced more wind than knowledge. Consequently, for the few years immediately following the reports (1959–1961), the wind blowing through the business schools of the land began to reach the intensity and destructive power of tornados. Full professors of the local and APV variety had to seek shelter from the possible damage or do something to quell it. To use another analogy (at the time the confusion was so great I need more than one), there were just not enough locals to plug the holes in the dike and the water was spilling all over.

Consequently, to plug the holes, repair the flat tires, fill the vacuum, bridge the gap, or provide the victuals of which our cupboards were bare, we had to import some cosmopolitans. This was obvious, wasn't it? This in short was the gist of the two reports—about 600 pages each—which with the help of analogies I have tried to summarize briefly. To reduce all this to my own personal situation, it meant that, just when I had learned to live happily as a conflicted local, I had to learn to live all over again as a conflicted cosmopolitan. Before I tell this story, in order to tidy things up, I need to describe briefly one further aspect of my involvement with the Faculty organization at the Business School.

OTHER ORGANIZATIONAL MATTERS

In the academic year 1960-1961, Dean Stanley Teele appointed a Committee on Faculty Organization. George Baker was chairman and I was a member. By this time it had become clear that between the Dean and the now approximately 100 individual Faculty members, each of whom reported to him, the intermediate organizational structure needed clarification. Over a period of years, positions had developed for course heads, program directors, research directors, teaching groups, area coordinators, administrative directors, and assistant deans of all kinds and descriptions, whose duties and responsibilities and relations to each other were not always clear.

The one thing that was clear was the structure of our educational programs. If someone asked a Faculty member what he was doing at the B-School, for example, his answer would be to say in which program he taught—the MBA program; the Advanced Management Program (AMP); the Middle Management Program, interestingly enough later called the Program for Management Development (PMD); the now-defunct Harvard-Radcliffe Management Training Program (HR-MTP); the Trade Union Program (TUP); the International Teachers' Program (ITP); or the Doctoral program (DP)—which was sometimes called the displaced persons program! As we were all teaching the same thing, it was unnecessary to say what he was teaching; this was implicitly understood. He was teaching administration, or APV. Sometimes as an unnecessary and irrelevant addendum, one of us might say that he was in the area of Production, Marketing, Control, and so on.

In short, although we had a clear program structure, we had no clear area or subject structure, so that a program rather than an area was a Faculty member's home base. In 1957 Russell Hassler, the then Associate Dean for Educational Affairs, introduced the idea of area coordinators. It remained more of an idea than a reality, because many professors did not know which area they wanted or were supposed to belong to, and Russ was not willing to tell them. Nevertheless, he appointed area chairmen for some of the more obvious teaching groups in the School. For example, in 1957 he appointed Joe Bailey area coordinator for Human Relations, but Joe was never quite sure whom he was coordinating. Did the group include people from Labor and Personnel Relations and some from Policy? Joe stayed in this ambiguous position from 1957 to 1960. I was coordinator for the next two academic years, 1960–1962. I set up two informal committees, a steering committee and a committee of the whole, so that I knew—even if Russ did not—whom I was coordinating.

Anyway, in the Committee on Faculty Organization, which met for two years, I pushed hard for an explicit area or subject matter structure. I thought that having a home base in a subject as well as in a program was important, particularly for younger Faculty. I thought that two points of reference would help him establish better than one who he was and where he was going. It would help him to deal with the identiy crisis from which during this period both our Doctoral candidates and our younger Faculty members were suffering badly.

As I reflect on it now, I think I can say that this was the first time I ever tried to change the formal organization of the School, or as might be said today, buck the establishment, in any formal sense. I had previously succeeded in doing and getting what I wanted by working through its interstices, of which there always seemed to me to be plenty. I did not expect any great miracles to result from this formal change, but by this time, as Mac would have said, I was getting tough. I wanted an explicit area—no fooling—for my soul group, which would be recognized as important by the School officially and not just by me.

After two years of serious considerations, the Committee on Faculty Organization recommended that the Faculty provisionally set up an area structure with ten subject areas based on the special fields in the Doctoral program, namely, Production; Marketing; Finance; Managerial Economics; Control; Personnel and Labor Relations; Business and Government; International Business; Policy; and, whoopee, Organizational Behavior. After several hot Faculty meetings, the full Faculty voted in favor of the Committee's recommendations. An area was not conceived, however, as a department, and an area chairman was not a department head. What made a department head was having a budget and something to say about salaries and promotions. Our area chairmen were not given these formal responsibilities, powers, or prerogatives. They had to get their results by processes such as facilitation, encouragement, rewards, stimulation, help, and participation; this was OK with good old power-softie me.

I became area chairman for Organizational Behavior in 1962 for two academic years. In 1964, after Margaret died, Paul Lawrence became area chairman for the five years until 1969. So by 1962 my "soul group" had become an officially recognized area in the School as well as an officially recognized special field in the Doctoral program. As sociologists might say, my Gemeinschaft now became a Geselschaft. But it did not become strictly big business; some monkey business was still left in it.

As will be remembered, my old soul group had two seemingly opposing values represented in it, the ones I called humanistic and scientific. During the period before we achieved our organizational identity, while we were still seeking for it, these seemingly conflicting values were fairly well contained. We had the whole School to fight against, so to speak, instead of having to fight among ourselves. Now that we became more formalized, these opposing values began to heat up.

By this time the name of our area's first-year required course had been changed from Administrative Practices to Human Behavior in Organizations. Although this change in title indicated the changes in orientation which the Faculty members who were conducting the course intended, some of them thought there was left in it too much of the old Human Relations or APV or do-goodism or normative or optimistic elements about the nature of man. Even though we were bringing into the area accepted behavioral scientists representing some of the disciplines, some of us thought that they tended to be of a kind who represented these humanistic tendencies; that is, persons who were overly interested in T-groups or sensitivity training or Theory Y or Carl Rogers or Abe Maslow; that is, not the sloppy sentimentalists of whom Mac complained, but people who thought that there was some evidence that man was essentially good and that under certain conditions (perhaps difficult to specify) he might tend to go from bad to better instead of from bad to worse.

Probably no one felt more strongly about this humanistic and to him nonscientific trend than Abe Zaleznik, who by this time had become psychoanalytic in his interests. He felt that the area of Organizational Behavior was affected by this syndrome or disease, which he sometimes referred to as moral masochism. He felt so strongly about it that he finally chose to leave the area to develop a new special field in the Doctoral program called the Social Psychology of Organizations, a field which some of the social psychologists in the Organizational Behavior area thought could have been better named the Psychoanalysis of Organizations.

About these matters I do not wish to say more at this level. For me there are important problems here which go beyond the particular occasions on which they manifest themselves in particular personalities. I will begin to consider these problems in the next chapter, when I tell about my involvement with the academic disciplines, and I will be concerned with them at a different level of abstraction in Book Two.

By the time these problems became acute, I had reached retirement. Although President Pusey asked me to stay on half time for two more years until 1967, which I did, I was no longer actively engaged in the problems of the area of Organizational Behavior. I was pondering with renewed interest why it had been so difficult for me to build my subject matter and why the phenomena always seemed to elude any configuration into which for a while I thought I had them placed. It seemed to me that these experiences contained some uniformities that needed explanation.

Chapter 18

Theories about Organizational Behavior

Up to 1957 I had been able to cultivate my own garden at the School without much competition. Not many other academics were interested in digging into it. By 1957 things had changed enought so that I could not fail to notice. A profusion of academic gardeners had sprung up who wanted to grow gardens not of a similar, but of a better kind. They said my garden was suspect on two grounds; first, it was not "scientific," and, second, I favored one kind of plant over another.

Among these new gardeners there was little agreement about where the gardens should be planted, or what crops should be cultivated, or how the crops should be grown, or what should be done with the crops after they had been produced. All of us had in common one thing: No one wished to dig *in* anyone else's garden to help him grow what he was growing there. Some of us were willing to dig *up* someone else's garden in order to grow what we thought should be growing there. But in general each of us, including myself, had more or less his own favorite plant, hoe, fertilizer, soil, and name to designate what kind of garden he thought he was cultivating and what kind of crop he thought he was growing.

During this period I did not try to repress the negative feelings I had about these developments, but neither did I try to foster them. I just tried to "hold them," while I waited for some new and more pleasant, constructive feelings to emerge. Finally they did in the form of my becoming curious about why there were so many different ways in which we drew our lines around our gardens. I became interested in why we drew the particular lines which we were arguing about in respect to the investigation, understanding, explanation, and control of the phenomena of human behavior in organizations.

SCIENTIFIC KNOWLEDGE AND ADMINISTRATIVE ACTION

When I joined the new Doctoral program in 1957, the big line we were trying to draw was between scientific knowledge and administrative action; or as I expressed it in the last chapter, the line between the scientific and administrative points of view, as exemplified by the cosmopolitans and locals at the School. I was enamored of both points of view. I did not want to choose between them. Thus, my quarrel with my local colleagues at the B-School about the administrative point of view was not distinct and separate from my quarrel with my cosmopolitan colleagues at the School and at other universities about the scientific point of view. Even though I am reporting these quarrels separately and often engaged in them separately, they were intimately related in my own preoccupation about them.

From my internal frame of reference, having these quarrels about these two points of view was like living with two mistresses, each of whom was making different demands of me, yet both of whom I wanted to keep satisfied, so that we could live happily together in the new Doctoral program. This was often difficult to do, because they were jealous mistresses. Each of them nagged at me from a different direction. When one would say, "Get going and become engaged in the business of the business" and I was just about ready to do this, the other would say, "What is the business of the business?" and I would become immobilized. Under these frustrating conditions I had difficulty distributing my affection to them equitably. More often than not, I just got angry and conducted my spats with each of them separately.

So I sat in the new Doctoral program as a participant observer in the midst of different perceptions of precision and romance. What helped me to deal with these differences was an observation of Alfred North Whitehead, to the effect that the educational process went through a sort of Hegelian cycle from the stage of romance to its antithesis, the stage of precision, and finally to a synthesis, which he called the stage of generalization. This I thought might be a fruitful way of looking at my conflicts. It made me realize what I might have recognized sooner, that I had never really been in love with either of my two mistresses. My early love affair had been with the phenomena. Now this stage of my romance with them was over, and I was about to enter by way of the new Doctoral program into the stage of precision, in which I hoped that my two mistresses would know more precisely what our separate but interrelated quarrels were about. Although this stage took a bit of the edge off the stage of romance, being an antithesis to it, I felt it was perhaps a stage that one had to go through before a synthesis of broader and more fruitful generalizations could emerge.

It is neither Hegel's or Whitehead's fault that things did not work out for me in this simple fashion. I gradually found out that each stage had its peculiar hang ups, with the result that you could sometimes get stuck in one of them without *ipso facto* progressing to the next. I realized that you had to have a romance with the phenomena before you could become more precise about them and that you had to be more precise about them before you could generalize more adequately about them. I observed that these stages did not often go smoothly from one to the other of their own accord. A bit of tugging and hauling was sometimes required to get them to go in the right Hegelian direction.

Just as I had gotten stuck in stage one and, as George Homans said, "kept rediscovering America," so it was possible for some one to get stuck in stage two and to keep repolishing his analytical tools until he lost touch with the phenomena for which they had been fashioned. He could become so interested in being precise that he overlooked what he was being precise about. At each stage he could have a romance with the tools for investigating, understanding, explaining, and controlling the phenomena, to the extent that he did not keep his eye on the phenomena to which they could be fruitfully applied.

The reading seminar which I introduced in 1957 for Doctoral candidates in the area of Organizational Behavior helped me begin to think more extensionally and clearly about these problems. The purpose of the seminar was to help students prepare for their special field examination. This examination tested a candidate's knowledge of the literature of his special field, his understanding of its basic concepts, methods, findings, and theories as well as its different schools of thought. As time went on, this reading seminar came to be called (I think incorrectly now) "Organizational Behavior Theory."

My preparation for this seminar turned out to be a more formidable task than I had anticipated. During these years it became more and more difficult to select from the literature the researches, conceptual formulations, and findings which I thought were relevant to the developing field of Organizational Behavior. The literature was increasing at an exponential rate. By 1967 new books were appearing whose titles contained the word "organization" as a noun, in singular or plural, or as an adjective—e.g., formal organization, human organization, organizational behavior, organizational systems, organizational models, organizational theory, the social psychology of organizations, the sociology of organizations, and so on.

It looked as if each discipline of the behavioral sciences had discovered organizations and found in them a useful focus for studying its major topics, e.g., the distribution of power; conformity and deviance; rational and nonrational behavior; and individual, group, technological, and organizational development. My reading list became longer and longer and also increasingly difficult to arrange in a clear outline. The behavioral sciences, now singularized in some quarters to behavioral science, became almost synonymous with Organizational Behavior or with the now outmoded but still occasionally used label of Human Relations.

Obviously I had bitten off more than I could chew. The Doctoral candidates needed far more training than I could provide in a seminar on the concepts and methods of the behavioral sciences. I first dealt with the problem by encouraging them to take courses in Social Relations across the River or at other nearby universities. Although it made little sense to me to duplicate at the B-School courses that were being given in the vicinity, this solution was never entirely satisfactory.

In time and with the financial aid of the Ford Foundation, distinguished scholars came to the School from across the River and from other universities for a semester or a year to explain the findings of their research and to help us "tool up" our candidates for more sophisticated research. These visiting scholars could learn about APV and the case method, if they wished, but doing so was conceived as incidental to the main purpose of their visits. Some of those who came were Samuel A. Stouffer, George C. Homans, Edward T. Hall, Paul A. Lazarsfeld, and Murray Horowitz. In addition we added to our Faculty a few persons with backgrounds and degrees in the behavioral sciences disciplines.

Thus gradually I was able to place my seminar in perspective with other seminars in the Doctoral program. My main function was to act as a translator between (1) the pure social science disciplines; (2) the applied behavioral sciences; (3) the tradition of Human Relations as it had developed at the B-School from 1927 to 1957; (4) the distinctive competence of the School about matters of administration; and finally (5) the administrative practitioners, that is, those persons in positions of responsibility in organizations "out there" who were or were not practicing APV according to some particular theory. These five different frames of reference kept me busy—and shall I also say confused—for the next ten years of my life. I will not stress here their dysfunctional aspects, for I want to show how they helped me to clarify—just a wee bit—the burning questions of "Knowledge about what?" and "Knowledge for whom?" with which I thought we should be concerned in developing the area of Organizational Behavior.

This then was the background of the seminar and of the way I conceived its purposes. Thinking about the seminar in this way forced me to reexamine many of the assumptions I had been making about the investigation, understanding, explanation, and control of the phenomena of human behavior. Obviously I was drawing my lines about these matters very differently from my colleagues in the social sciences. In addition, each of them seemed to be drawing the lines around his work differently from all the others. My problem was to put this all together in a way that would be useful for my Doctoral students.

CRITICISMS OF MANAGEMENT AND THE WORKER

To explain what I did, let me go back once more to an earlier time, for my quarrel with the social sciences had a long history. It began in the early period of my life. In Chapters 3, 4, and 5 I told about the intellectual giants in the social sciences upon whose shoulders I stood in carving out the tools I used in my researches. Although they did not comprise by any means all the intellectual giants in the social sciences at the time, they included a good number of them—Freud, Piaget, Durkheim, Pareto, Malinowski, Radcliffe-Brown—as well as some of the persons—Mayo, Henderson, Warner, and Barnard—who made the theories come alive for me.

Let me repeat my principal debts to Henderson and Mayo. Those men abstracted from the work of the above-mentioned giants the two simple and useful walking sticks I took with me into the field. From Henderson I took the conceptual scheme of a social system, as he pared it down to the bone from his reading of Pareto. For him, be it remembered, it was not a philosophical theory, not a grand effort of the imagination, nor a quasi-religious dogma, but a modest pedestrian affair, to repeat, a useful walking stick to help on the way. From Mayo I took the tools of the clinical method of observation and interviewing, by which a concrete social system could be explored, as he had fashioned them from Freud and Malinowski. I thought both Henderson and Mayo had cleansed these simple walking sticks of their metaphysical trappings, so that I could now use them to help me on my way in fields other than those in which they had been originally used. But this was not the way my critics saw it.

Starting with the early days of *Management and the Worker*, the criticisms flew fast and furiously. Let me try to state them "objectively." I think I can do this now, because *Management and the Worker* is no longer "my" book. Its findings have been so often restated and misstated that it has a life of its own that has little to do with me. To put it another way, *Management and the Worker* has more or less achieved a permanent identity of its own, whereas, as Erik Erikson would have predicted, at each stage of my life I kept losing and searching over again for mine.

Over many years the major charges against Mayo, the Mayo group, *Management and the Worker*, and the human relations movement (these were for many of the critics the same kettle of fish) fell into three categories:

A. We were ideologically oriented or biased, because we
   1. favored management as against the union;
   2. de-emphasized the class struggle and accepted the status quo;
   3. excluded Karl Marx from our conceptual scheme;
   4. attacked bureaucracy;
   5. were being manipulative or soft on issues both of power and conflict.
B. We had neglected or overemphasized certain important aspects of the total situation because we
   1. ignored important external economic variables;
   2. overemphasized social needs;
   3. ignored formal structure or assumed that it was bad;
   4. ignored technology or the primary task the organization had to perform;
   5. favored conformity rather than individuality;
   6. favored equilibrium rather than change;
   7. emphasized convergent rather than divergent phenomena;
   8. were too psychiatric;
   9. ignored the logical and overemphasized the nonlogical;
   10. ignored Freud;
   11. were primarily concerned with face-to-face relations in small groups.

In addition,

    C. We had been methodologically naive and statistically unsophisticated because we generalized about all workers from a small sample of five workers (in the Relay Assembly Test Room).

Although I have placed these charges in three categories, they could be thought of as three forms of being unscientific or ideologically tainted or both. In time the charge became that we were unscientific because we were ideologically biased. Let me quote from Henry A. Landsberger's book *Hawthorne Revisited* (1958), in which he conveniently summarized and evaluated the charges made against the Mayo group and *Management and the Worker*. "Taken as a whole they (the charges) constitute as comprehensive an indictment of a theoretical system as could be imagined. Nothing more devastating could be said about such a system than that it is superficial and totally *misses the point* [my italics]; that it originates in the personal biases of its creators rather than in the facts it seeks to explain; and that it is deliberately formulated to favor one social group over another."

Without doubt this was strong stuff. Landsberger asked why we did not answer the charges. Why were we, particularly the authors of *Management and the Worker*, the school of thought's basic empirical study, so silent? His answer was that we were not guilty as charged if the books that expressed the school's ideology were distinguished from those, such as *Management and the Worker*, that reported its empirical studies. The authors "need not hang their heads in shame, for the book is indeed a classic."

I confess to being interested now in how I kept my equanimity in the face of these devastating charges before Landsberger exonerated the book. Was I a man or a mouse? What was the point which my critics thought I had missed and which in turn I thought they were missing? Why was my subject matter so elusive? As I have asked before, why did the controversies about it generate so much heat and so little light?

Lord forbid that I should convey the impression that I sat on Mount Olympus and viewed the charges with calm detachment. They had me disturbed, but I was by then fully committed to my "conceptual scheme" and by no means ready to throw it away. The method I used to "cool it," as we would say in the 1970s, was not to cool the charges made against me, but to cool my feelings about them. For this approach my conceptual scheme gave me plenty of reinforcement.

At a somewhat superficial level four injunctions comforted and sustained me. One was Pareto's and Henderson's injunction "Never dispute about words.' The second Mayo cribbed from the Old Testament, "Let the heathen rage," which he followed with "The cobbler sticks to his last." The fourth came from my mother when, during the First World War, I was disturbed about my first name. (A popular song at the time was "Keep your head down, Fritzie boy.") She would say, "Sticks and stones will break your bones, but names will never hurt you." About this last I confess I later had some doubts.

At a deeper level my silence was consistent with my understanding of a helping relationship. As will be remembered, in this relationship I tried to separate my feelings, my problems, my concerns, and what would now be called "my thing" from my client's feelings, his problems, his concerns, and his thing and never to confuse the two. In this way I hoped to avoid confusing what was bugging him with what was bugging me. I thought I was up against a similar problem in respect to my critics' charges; but I could not help my critics in the same way, because, not being in a counseling relationship with them, I could not say, "Tell it to me like it is for you, brother." The result was that when I wrote (which is the way we most frequently communicate in academia), all I could say was how it was for me, brother. This was the style in which I did my writing. I thought it constituted a refutation of the charges against me.

This kind of refutation was not heard as such, because for my statement to constitute a refutation, I would have had to say what I was not up to in terms of my critics' frame of reference, instead of what I was up to in terms of my own. This I thought would be not only difficult to do, but it would also involve me in that "You can't do this to me—Says who?" routine I described earlier in the cases of Hal and Bill and of Mr. Post and the traffic officer.

I would have had to keep saying, for example, "No, I am not trying to make people just happy or contented cows or conformists or organizational men. No, I am not trying to break up the union or humanize bureaucracy or eliminate conflict or equalize power or become willingly or unwillingly the tool of the established power structure and so on and on. These may be some of the unintended consequences of what I am doing, but they are not my intentions. Please do not confuse the two. If these unintended consequences should follow as night follows day, let me find that out in my own sweet phenomenological way; but until then please pipe down." To which, in turn, my critics could keep saying "Says who?" "Says who?"

"Says who?" on into the night in their monthly, bimonthly, quarterly, semiannual, and annual journals, and the process of my answering their answers could have become endlessly time-consuming and taken me away from possibly fruitful work. So why start the process?

There were still other factors, cognitive ones, that may have dictated my silence. At the time there was little question in my mind that the misunderstandings arose from the different assumptions my critics and I were making about all the distinctions I have been stating and using from the beginning of this book. The assumptions I made about the relations between knowledge of acquaintance and knowledge about; skill and knowledge; maps and territories; thought and action; skill and action; skill and learning; logical and nonlogical action; conceptual and concrete systems; manifest and latent content; action and interaction; intended and unintended consequences; planned and emergent behavior; cause and effect and mutual dependent analysis; functional and dysfunctional consequences; and so on—all this would be involved in any refutation of the kind I wanted to make. I did not then feel emotionally or intellectually ready to face these problems. Now for my Doctoral students I had to begin examining the factors underlying "my silence" and "my critics' complaints," and to say, as Portnoy's doctor said to Portnoy's complaint, "Now vee may perhaps to begin, yes?" Well, here is the way I began to classify the other main streams of development in the behavioral sciences from the perspective of what I thought would be useful for my Doctoral students.

HUMAN RELATIONS IN ITS EARLY PERIOD

During the 1940s and the early 1950s the phrase "human relations" was associated with three schools of thought that could be designated as:

(1) The school of Elton Mayo with its center at the Harvard Business School, with its emphases on the "social system," the clinical approach, the case method, a counseling orientation, APV, and the other "too much's" or "too little's" I have mentioned.

(2) The school of applied anthropology, associated with such names as Eliot Chapple, Conrad Arensberg, and William F. Whyte; and finally with the latter—Bill Whyte—at the New York State School of Industrial and Labor Relations at Cornell University with its emphases on sound field work and social observation.

(3) The Kurt Lewin school called "group dynamics" with its center at the University of Michigan and its affiliates at the Tavistock

Institute of Human Relations in England and the National Training Laboratories in Washington, D.C., and Bethel, Maine, with its emphases on group process, here-and-now data, and T-groups.

The human relations movement grew around these three centers of work. Two of them had journals: *The Journal of Applied Anthropology* (changed in 1949 to *Human Organization*) published by the Society for Applied Anthropology, beginning in 1941; and *Human Relations* (Studies Toward the Integration of the Social Sciences) published jointly by Tavistock and the Research Center for Group Dynamics in Ann Arbor, Michigan, beginning in 1947. The Mayo school never had a journal of its own.

Although there were differences among these three schools, there were also important similarities. They were all interested in the relation of theory to practice or action and in the utilization of knowledge. They were concerned with face-to-face relations in small groups. They shared both scientific and humanistic values, though perhaps in different proportions. They not only wanted to acquire knowledge about human relations, they also wanted to improve human relations in organizations. It could be said they were more interested in people or in people-in-organizations than in organizations per se.

As time went on and I think because of these similarities, some of the lines that had been drawn sharply between these schools of thought began to be less sharp. New names appeared in the 1950s and 1960s of people who were able to play in all three ball parks with a certain amount of ease without getting "up tight" about any one of them. Some of them were even able to establish little ball parks of their own which bore a family resemblance to the original human relations movements of the 1940s. If the differences were not stretched too far, it could be said that during the middle and late 1950s and the early 1960s such people as Douglas McGregor (M.I.T.), Rensis Likert (Michigan), Chris Argyris (Yale), Robert Blake (originally Texas), Robert Tannenbaum (UCLA), Warren Bennis (M.I.T. and Buffalo), Harold J. Leavitt (Stanford), Leonard Sayles (Columbia), and still others who became finally too numerous to mention, all achieved national prominence in the field of Human Relations.

HUMAN RELATIONS IN THE 1960S

Using the work of the persons I have mentioned as examples, it can be seen that the 1960 brand of human relations was in some respects different from, but in other respects astonishingly similar to, the 1940 versions. Let me state these similarities and differences in terms of the three categories I used to classify the criticisms of the Mayo school. I will do this in reverse order, starting with the category "C" charges that we were methodologically naive.

Certainly human relations 1960s style was methodologically more sophisticated. Survey techniques and rigorous statistical analyses had supplanted the 1940s emphasis upon clinical, participative-observation, and case studies. Along this dimension then there had been some scientific progress. Although many of the more sophisticated researches confirmed many of the early clinical studies about the determinants of worker satisfaction, they cast considerable doubt upon any simple relation between worker productivity and satisfaction. That is to say, a more satisfied worker was not necessarily a high producer. For some people this finding cast a big blight on the early human relations researches, which according to them had assumed the opposite. This statement was often made in spite of the fact that W_2—the rate buster and the highest producer in the Bank Wiring Observation Room as reported in *Management and the Worker*—was also described there as a very unhappy guy.

If we look at the category "B" charges (ignoring or overemphasizing something or other), we also find some changes and some things the same. In the 1960s there was more concern with management than with blue-collar workers. There was more emphasis on self-actualizing needs than on social (membership, affiliation) needs, more emphasis on leadership styles than on clinical diagnosis and action. There was a growing concern with formal structures, more emphasis on change than on equilibrium, and very much more on T-groups than on counseling and nondirective listening, the methods emphasized in the 1940s.

On the other hand, the 1960 brands were still concerned mostly with face-to-face relations in small group settings. They still emphasized feelings and sentiments in interactions between workers and supervisors and among workers themselves. They were still more concerned with employee and management attitudes and their effects upon each other than upon the decision-making process.

When we look at the category "A" charges (being ideologically biased and not value free), the similarities were astonishing. Although perhaps expressed less personally and more politely, human relations 1960 style was still being charged with being manipulative, normative, optimistic, and soft on conflict and power. Not only were the proponents of the 1960 version still trying to change organizations (being manipulative) and furthermore trying to change them in the direction of harmony and democratic values (being normative), but by God, if you can believe this now, they still thought they could do it. How optimistic can one get?

As I reflect upon it now, it seems to me the 1960 version was more normative than the 1940 version, assuming, of course, that one could be more or less normative instead of just being normative, period. Speaking for myself and also for Bill Whyte, I do not remember that in the early days we prescribed (1) what formal relations in organizations *should* be; (2) what itches individuals in them *should* have; (3) what emergent relations in them *should develop*; and (4) what ouches in them *should exist*. Nor, so far as I remember, did we try to eliminate all ouches or to design ouchless organizations. I do not remember that we advocated one kind of management or leadership style. We did not try to supplant or eliminate the bureaucratic model of organization or the labor relations or collective bargaining models of organization.

How was this? For us at the time human relations was first and foremost an *investigatory and diagnostic tool*. It was not a model of what an organization should be; it was a conceptual scheme for finding out what the relations in a *particular organization at a particular place and time* were, not what they should be. The questions we asked were "What were the itches and ouches and leadership styles that existed there? What were the needs, norms, and values of the people at the bottom of the organization as well as at the top?" Once this was ascertained—a diagnosis made—we thought we could consider the question of how the situation might be improved in this particular case. By whom? Well, in the first instance by those who were responsible for doing it. (Ho-ho, without consulting the employees? Ho-ho, did I say this?)

However, and speaking now just for myself, I was never completely non-normative or value free. How could I be? I was surrounded by a sea of *values*—the needs, norms, purposes, and cultural beliefs of people. For me taking action was *ipso facto* being normative. I did not think that I or anyone else could act non-normatively, that is, unrelated to some individual need, some social norm, some collective purpose, or some cultural belief. This to me would have been acting non-humanly. However, I thought there was a difference between (1) acting upon or intervening in a situation after the particular values in it had been assessed and diagnosed through clinical methods; and (2) acting upon or intervening in a situation in terms of so-called "science-based theories" about human behavior. Around this distinction I detected a difference between the 1940 and 1960 versions of human relations. The 1940 version talked the first way; the 1960 version talked the second way. I found these science-based facts and theories about human behavior riddled with ambiguities, to which I will return.

So far I have distinguished the old 1940 version of human relations, with which I was originally identified, from the 1960 version, with which I was also often identified and correctly so, because in spite of my reservations about the way some of its proponents talked, they were all involved in the same kinds of questions and ambiguities which also had me messed up. There were other similarities and differences which depended on the brands of psychology or models of man with which we identified. I will discuss them next.

CLINICAL, HUMANISTIC, AND EXISTENTIAL PSYCHOLOGISTS

Let me add the names of some persons in psychology with whom both the 1940 and the 1960 versions of human relations flirted, such as for example, Carl R. Rogers, Abraham H. Maslow, Erich Fromm, Robert W. White, Erik H. Erikson, Gordon W. Allport, James F. T. Bugental, Rollo May, and others too numerous to mention. This, I confess, is a varied array of psychologists of different persuasions, and differences existed among them, just as they did among the persons I cited above as belonging to the 1960 version of human relations. But for now, I want to emphasize the similarities in their intellectual interests with regard to the phenomena of human behavior.

Most of them were clinically oriented and interested in matters of therapy, mental health, and individual or ego or personality development. All of them admitted their indebtedness to Freud, but they differed from him in important respects. Their views about man and his capacity for growth and self-development were more optimistic. They were more interested in understanding mental health than mental disease. Most of them had explicit normative notions about what constituted individual mental health and also healthy and authentic relations between people. They were interested in therapeutic sessions of shorter duration than those that orthodox psychoanalysis prescribed. For them a couch was not a required piece of equipment. Most of them were not M.D.s. They were more interested in intrinsic growth than extrinsic knowledge.

These clinical psychologists or professional helpers or personality psychologists may be called humanistic—as opposed to behavioristic—psychologists. Both the 1940 and the 1960 versions of human relations tended to identify with studies done by these kinds of people. The 1940 version was associated mainly with Carl Rogers and his client-centered therapy and nondirective approach. When I discovered Carl Rogers and his nondirective approach after I had developed independently a similar approach in the Hawthorne researches, I thought he had stated the two-person therapeutic or helping encounter much better than I had, and I used his books in my classes in Human Relations from 1948 to 1951.

There is little question that during this period human relations almost became identified with the counseling approach. This bothered me, because, although the counseling approach was clinical and its data were collected under conditions of responsibility—two features I liked and thought important—it fell short in my view of being the only research tool for the investigation of organizational behavior. Nor was it in my opinion the only model for supervisory behavior. Remember that I sweated with the problems of making the clinical approach for research and action broader than "counseling." What the study of the "counseling relationship" did for me and what I hoped it did for my students was to highlight the differences between dealing with relationships in which one was intrinsically involved and observing relationships "out there" from an extrinsic point of view, a point of view which was much more common in "science." Unless one saw the differences, I did not think that research and practice in human relations could be usefully related.

As I mentioned, the 1960 version of human relations emphasized T-groups more than counseling, helping, or therapeutic relations. In one sense this shift in focus for the changing of attitudes represented an emphasis on group rather than individual performance. To oversimplify, it emphasized being a good group member rather than being an individual star performer. It could also be thought of as an emphasis on the human potential for change.

Though these two emphases were often at war with each other, the second is the one about which I wish to talk now, because that is the direction that some of the adherents of human relations in the 1960s took. The humanistic psychologists I cited above gave this direction plenty of support. They emphasized man's potential—too often unrealized—for becoming more sensitive, more open, and more authentic in relations with others, thereby becoming more interpersonally competent. They also stressed man's potential for becoming more congruent with himself and his feelings and thereby becoming more of a person. This shift in direction from counseling and psychotherapy to training for interpersonal competence and for becoming a person can be seen in Carl Rogers's work. The Carl Rogers of 1942 (*Counseling and Psychotherapy*) compared with the one of 1951 (*Client-Centered Therapy*) and the one of 1961 (*On Becoming a Person*) expresses this trend well.

The emphasis on man's potentials for self-actualization can also be seen in Douglas McGregor's Theories X and Y, for which his indebtedness to Abe Maslow's need hierarchy was clearly acknowledged. The writings of Warren Bennis (1966) and Chris Argyris (1960, 1964) also stressed man's potential for change, curiously enough in the direction that the members and leaders of bureaucratic organizations needed—and I mean needed badly, no kidding.

The 1960 version of human relations did not ignore man's social needs, that is, his needs for affiliation and belonging and for being an accepted member of a group. It did not address only his ego needs—his needs for achievement, competence, and self-actualization—any more than the 1940 version ignored man's ego needs in favor of his needs to belong. The difference between the two versions was a matter of emphasis. I became concerned about these emphases or nuances, because they seemed to be causing a lot of trouble.

In the trend toward the realization of man's potentials that was part of the 1960 version of human relations, the names I have mentioned—men like McGregor, Likert, Bennis, Argyris, and myself— were all moderates. The more extreme versions did not appear until the late 1960s, when the movement zoomed, and it was no longer clear what the T in T-group stood for. It might be said that the "T" came to stand no longer for either *training* in group development or *therapy* or *task* but something more intimate like *touching*. In fact, these "human potential" and "growth" groups differed so much from the original T-groups that other names had to be given to them, such as encounter groups, marathon groups, dialogue groups, creativity groups, nonverbal communication groups, relaxation groups, psychedelic groups, sensory awakening groups, and voyaging-in-inner-space groups.

In its early version the T in T-group stood clearly for *training* in group development. The school was interested in the processes whereby a group did or did not become cohesive or cozy and its members good followers or leaders. It was addressed to training both leaders and members of groups in interpersonal competence. This focus could be accused—and it was—of emphasizing "conformity" rather than "individuality." In fact toward the latter part of the 1960s, it became evident to some that the "principles"of T-group, sensitivity, or laboratory training could be utilized to train individuals in ideologies other than liberal democratic humanitarianism. Were not T-group methods similar to the brainwashing methods used by Chinese communists, for example? What was the difference between putting people in cells and preaching the gospel of Saint Mark or putting them on cultural islands and preaching the gospel of Saint Luke or even for that matter putting them on a couch and preaching the gospel of Saint Freud?

I shall not pursue those horrendous thoughts further. I want only to illustrate that these matters of emphasis and nuance were not to be treated lightly or casually. Without too much trouble, any social scientist interested in matters of action could find hidden ideological agendas in his fellow social scientists or in himself for that matter.

SMALL-GROUP RESEARCHERS AND THEORISTS

There were other foci for those interested in small groups besides training for interpersonal competence and personal growth or brainwashing. Other persons were interested in small groups for their own sake, not in order to improve them, but in order to discover what social processes were going on within them. These individuals tended to be more descriptive than normative, more knowledge-oriented than action-oriented, and more sociological or sociopsychological than purely psychological. Both the 1940 and 1960 versions of human relations utilized the contributions of these people.

In the 1940 version there was no better example than George C. Homans. Lord forbid that I suggest that George was in any way identified with the human relations movement. Nothing could be further from the truth. George was trying to create order out of chaos through general propositions and not by anything so inelegant as action. Nevertheless, I found George a healthy antidote to the human potentials movement; his book *The Human Group* (1950) was a "must" on my reading list for Doctoral candidates. The characters in the small groups George studied seemed to be affected more with snobbishness than with sentiments of equality. Nothing seemed to disturb them more than that they were rewarded less (along any dimension you can name) than someone else. Although these groups contained friendship subgroups, these friendships seemed to be based on factors more earthy and less ideal than those that made up a cozy democratic T-group.

Small groups could be studied experimentally as well as clinically.

Group processes could be observed and measured through one-way screens. Psychologists, sociologists, and social psychologists were all engaged in such activities. Many of these individuals were methodologically inclined. The 1960 version of human relations was indebted to these methodologically sophisticated persons. Again the names are too numerous to mention; among them, though, were Leon Festinger, Dorwin Cartwright, Alvin Zander, Daniel Katz, and Robert L. Kahn, all at the University of Michigan. These small-group experimenters and theorists also included such persons as Robert F. Bales, Robert T. Golembrewski, Theodore M. Newcomb, Paul A. Hare, and others.

BUREAUCRATIC SOCIOLOGISTS

The time has now come for me to stop using the label human relations. In fact I should probably have stopped before the last group I mentioned. The label would be not only misleading, but also unflattering, as applied to the group I want to talk about next. This school of thought was concerned with bureaucratic organizations. Thus it too had something to say about "organizations" and "organizational behavior." I included studies by its members on my reading list for Doctoral candidates, even though the studies were always a difficult kettle of fish for me to assimilate.

What Karl Marx meant to socialism, Sigmund Freud to psychoanalysis, Kurt Lewin to group dynamics, and Elton Mayo to human relations, Max Weber meant to sociology, particularly to that brand of sociology I call bureaucratic. He was its hero. With these individuals, and in particular Marx, Freud, and Weber, some of the greatest changes in the twentieth century about the nature of man and his relations to society were associated.

But here is to me an interesting fact: Among the intellectual giants on whose shoulders I stood in fashioning my simple walking sticks, two of those I have just mentioned, Karl Marx and Max Weber, were conspicuous by their absence—a fact which my critics did not fail to point out. By their exclusion was I not showing my ideological biases?

For example, my activist critics said, "Look at the persons you choose. For the most part they are soft on power, violence, and revolution as instruments of social change. There is no real revolutionary among the lot. They are all defenders of the status quo. Your social anthropologist friends turned Rousseau's noble savage into a big conformist and made him nature's first organizational man. Your psychiatric friends are trying to adjust people to the power structure. As for Durkheim with his preoccupation about 'Why does the individual, while becoming autonomous, depend more upon society?' the less said the better. Take another look at your good friend Pareto. Granted he believed in the use of force, wasn't he a Fascist? Didn't Mussolini use his ideas to seize power? It is all right for the elite to use power but not for the workers, isn't it now? No metaphysical trappings? Your walking-sticks are loaded. They are loaded against looking at the obvious facts. Karl told you where to look, man. The revolution of the masses is inevitable."

And then I could hear my more scientifically pure-minded critics saying, for example, "How do you account for the fact that you walked into the field of organizational behavior without having read the books of the man who has contributed more to the understanding of twentieth-century organizations than any other social scientist? How come you excluded Max Weber? Pareto was not interested in organizations; surely Freud was not, and as for Durkheim, well, only at a high level of abstraction. As for your social anthropologists, they looked at places where there was no modern technological or formal organization—no real honest-to-goodness power tools or even big power figures. Moreover, in the exotic places they studied, there were no Protestant ethics; there were only kinship relations, myths, and rituals. Your walking-sticks may not be ideolgically tainted, but they are lopsided, disciplinarily speaking. They have a small-group, *Gemeinschaft*, psychiatric and interpersonal flavor. You have not included a real honest-to-goodness sociologist interested in modern organization on your list. Look at the facts, boy; Max told you where to look. In the modern world, bureaucracy is inevitable. Stop being an incurable romanticist."

Well, perhaps unfairly, I have allowed my critics to state my case in part for me. Karl and Max could not both be right; both revolution and bureaucracy could not be inevitable developments of modern economic organization, or could they? I did not want to choose sides and say who was right. However, it could be that both might be right in the sense that too much bureaucracy led to revolution and too much revolution led to too much law and order of the bureaucratic kind. But I was not as yet prepared to make this statement. Moreover, my simple walking-sticks had not entirely ignored the cluster of variables which Karl and Max said I should be looking at. In fact, my walking-sticks had an almost compulsive urge to walk themselves in these directions but, as I have said, in a pedestrian, not grandiose, manner. In time I felt they would lead me to the "truth."

Also I was not denying some of the uniformities that Karl and Max had discovered; I was just not buying their explanations of them.

Enough of these claims for and defenses of my ideological leanings. My critics were detecting something important about me, but they gave it a twist that I felt was unwarranted and that I could not buy. That I personally brought sentiments and values to my work—yes; but that they were of a highly ideological kind—no. That I disliked conflict and violence—yes; but that I was a defender of the status quo—no. That I did not wish to make power, conflict, violence, and force principles for action—yes; but that I denied them as matters of fact—no; and so on and on. I will talk later about the values that I had as a human-social being and about their influence on me, my investigations, and their findings. Let me come back now to Max Weber.

Mayo and Henderson did not read much of Weber, I think, not because of any big ideological reason, but because of something more nonlogical, even nit-picking. Weber had a Germanic penchant for making nouns out of verbs, thereby making something sound "substantive." Weber was interested not only in identifying the characteristics of bureaucracies, but in explaining the process of bureaucratization. His followers, including Robert K. Merton, Alvin W. Gouldner, Peter M. Blau, Amitai Etzioni, and Reinhard Bendix as examples, were interested in the consequences of bureaucratization for bureaucracies. This is the way, following the style of their leader, the Weberians spoke!

According to Weber, the process of bureaucratization in its technical and nonpejorative sense involved the exclusion of any purely personal feelings, such as love and hate, especially of any irrational feelings, such as jealousy, or of incalculable feelings, such as uncertainty, from the execution of official tasks by the legitimated officials of a bureaucracy. It was never clear to me—and I think to many others—whether in such statements Weber was being normative or descriptive: whether he was saying this was the way bureaucracies should be or the way they actually were. But because Weber originated the famous phrase *wert frei* or "value free" that has plagued sociologists and some of the rest of us ever since, I assume he thought he was being non-normative.

Whether by *wert frei* Weber meant anything more than that the social researcher should not confuse his values with the values of the subjects he was studying (which was the kind of *wert frei* I and many others stood for) was also not clear to me. This is the way I finally interpreted his "non-normative" imperative for social science.

Clearly Weber's notions about organization and management were much closer to the views of scientific management and the classical school of management, which flourished in the 25 years between the two world wars, than to the views of the proponents of human relations, who began to express themselves after World War II. Weber was never as much interested in the motivations of people as he was in the rational characteristics of organizations. Thus, the bureaucratic sociologists and the human relations people did not often see eye to eye on many matters related to organization and administration.

Nevertheless, Max Weber had extraordinary and important sociological insights. One was the connection between Protestant values and capitalism, which he stated in *The Protestant Ethic and the Spirit of Capitalism, 1904–1905*. The other was his classification of three or four kinds of legitimated power or authority: (1) charismatic, (2) traditional, (3) legal–rational or bureaucratic, and possibly (4) professional or expertise. I state them in this way because the Weberian authorities cannot seem to settle whether Weber distinguished between 3 and 4. More than this, if you can believe it, after all the rationalistic shortcomings of which I have accused him, Weber sparked some first-rate empirical research. Two of his followers, Peter Blau and Alvin Gouldner, went into the field and talked to the natives of particular bureaucracies and came out with the interesting findings which I reported briefly in Chapter 11. They found that bureaucracies were not as functional as Weber thought them to be. That is, some of the unintended consequences of this form of rational organization were not as rational as they ought to be.

As I said, I thought these findings checked with some of mine and that a rapprochement between our schools of thought could be made. This did not happen, because we asked different questions of our data and tried to explain different things. As an aside, it always seemed to me that bureaucratic sociologists took great delight in knocking Max Weber down in the first parts of their books and then picking him up and putting him back together again in the latter parts. I think they felt that his conceptions could be refined, so that in time a systematic theory of organizations could be built from them. I shared their feelings, though not their hero.

SOCIO-TECHNICAL SYSTEMS

During the 1960s there was a difference of opinion between those who were emphasizing psychological factors and those who were emphasizing structural factors in relation to the question of how changes occurred in organizations. The issue centered on the question of whether behavioral changes preceded or followed attitudinal changes. According to one school of thought (the more psychologically oriented), attitudinal changes preceded behavioral changes; therefore, such training methods as counseling or T-groups, which resulted in attitudinal changes, could bring about behavioral changes. According to the second school of thought (the more sociologically and anthropologically oriented), behavioral changes preceded attitudinal changes. This school held that behavioral changes could best be accomplished by changing the patterns of interaction dictated by the formal and technological organization and that changes in attitudes would follow.

The difference between these two schools was in many ways subtle and difficult to state. For me, it related primarily to matters of strategy in particular situations; for others it was a more important difference. The difference was apparent in the ways in which we made interventions in organizations to bring about change. This difference appeared in both the 1940 and 1960 versions of human relations between those of us who were oriented to social anthropology (e.g., Eliot Chapple, William F. Whyte, and Leonard Sayles) and those who were oriented to counseling or T-groups (the group dynamics people, myself, and others).

In the 1960s this difference was accentuated by a school of thought which originated at the Tavistock Institute in England. For lack of a better name, I call this school "the socio-technical system point of view." I include in it such persons in England as Elliot Jacques, Eric Trist, A. Kenneth Rice, Cyril Sofer, Tom Burns, G. M. Stalker, and Joan Woodward and, in this country, such persons as Paul R. Lawrence, Jay W. Lorsch, Charles Perrow, and James Thompson.

This school emphasized those characteristics of organizations which, it was sometimes said, the early version of human relations deemphasized—technology, formal organization, and culture, for example. The representatives of this school accomplished this shift in emphasis not by calling human relations bad names, but by discovering interesting correlations between some of the characteristics of the formal and technological environments of organizations and some of the characteristics of their social environments.

Here again the difference was not that the 1940 version completely ignored the characteristics of the technological and formal organization. Rather, that version tended to treat these characteristics as "givens," whereas the advocates of the socio-technical system school of thought treated them as "variables." This approach became increasingly popular during the late 1960s. It became a direction in which many who were interested in research in organizations, as well as many who were interested in organizational development, thought their work should go. With this emphasis on matters of technology and complex formal organization went a relative de-emphasis of individuals and their feelings and interactions and group norms. These factors were not ignored, but in this school of thought they became less important as determinants of social organization.

In this school, for example, changing the attitudes of people by way of counseling and T-groups was small potatoes. The school's members were more interested in organizational design (O.D. as it was called) than in individual or group development. Here one has to watch out, for the advocates of T-groups were also interested in organizational development. For them, though, just as a doughnut needs a hole in the middle, so O.D. required individual and group development as prerequisites. In a manner of speaking, these people said the doughnut needs the hole, because without the hole there is no doughnut. For the advocates of organizational design, on the other hand, the making of a good doughnut with a nice hole in the middle was *contingent* upon external factors, such as the quality of the flour that was used and the technology by which it was made. Consequently they thought that one could make good doughnuts with different sized holes; organizationally speaking, one could design optimal organizations for different kinds of technological, cultural, group, and individual environments. As a result, in the 1960s two different kinds of organizational development were advocated— $O.D._1$ by way of T-groups and $O.D._2$ by way of organizational design.

To return to the doughnut analogy, the difference between the two groups raised the question whether the doughnut was the environment of the hole or the hole was the environment of the doughnut. It could be said, of course, that the doughnut ring was the hole's external environment and that the hole was its internal environment. But this left the ring without an external environment and the hole without an internal environment. These confusions about what were an organization's external and internal environments were rampant in the 1960s. Different schools of thought conceived of them differently. These differences resulted in endless arguments, about which I will write further, particularly in Chapter 24.

During the period from 1957, an additional school of thought about management emerged which I could not ignore, much as I might have wished to. As in the case of the behavioral sciences and human relations, this school of thought went by many names—decision theory, game theory, information theory, probability theory, operations research, applied mathematics, the quantitative management sciences, and so on. With its emphasis on logical decisions rather than nonlogical interpersonal relations, this school of thought presented a sharp contrast to human relations and the applied behavioral sciences. It dealt with totally new questions and made human relations theory sound old-fashioned and neo-classical.

Integrating the contributions of the different social sciences to management theory was difficult enough. Adding this truly modern and different theory made the task almost superhuman. Depending upon which way one wished to look at it, I was a Sir Galahad or a Don Quixote or a Simple (but not a Herbert) Simon. Anyway, I added this other weighty ball with all the power of logic and mathematics behind it to the ones I was already trying to juggle. Believe me, you could not toss this ball around lightly. It was a normative ball, to be sure, but normative in a more acceptable and respectable sense than the normative ball of human relations, as I shall explain. Before doing so, I will start a new chapter.

Chapter 19
Learning to Count Sophisticatedly

Decision theory seems to me different from any of the schools of thought I have already mentioned. In approaching the nature of organizations and administration it analyzes the decision-making process, the process with which executives or administrators are essentially involved. This school views the administrator's essential task as selecting a course of action from given alternatives. His problem is how to choose the best one.

DECISION THEORY

According to the school's chief proponents, James G. March and Herbert Simon (1958), man cannot be 100 percent rational about this problem. In order to choose the very best alternative, he would have to know not only (1) all the possible alternatives and (2) all the consequences of each alternative; he would also have to be capable of (3) assigning a relative utility to each set of consequences; that is, he would have to be able to say that he prefers consequence *a* to consequence *b*, consequence *b* to consequence *c*, and so on. Under such ideal conditions he could choose that alternative whose consequences would have the greatest utility, and his decision process could be 100 percent rational. In most cases this omniscience is not in the realm of the possible. So alas, man has to settle for what March and Simon call bounded rationality, which means he has to choose not the very best, but only the most satisficing alternative.

Let me point out that this bounded rationality is still rational. It is concerned with how man is able to act rationally (i.e., in a rational, goal-oriented fashion) in a complex environment about which he has limited information, for which he has limited tools (before the computer) for processing the information, and where, so to speak, he is not God. The computer helped with this tough problem, but it did not make man omniscient in exploring all possible worlds, which run into such astronomical figures as 10^{120}. It could help him search among a very broad range of satisficing alternatives. Three million consequences from certain given alternatives, for example, would not give a modern computer even a mild nervous breakdown. I shall say no more about these satisficing computational methods, because I want to return to utility theory and statistical decision theory in relation to decisions in regard to which it is still possible to search for optimal solutions. These theories are based upon some assumptions.

One assumption is that among the utilities or subjective values which I—or anyone—could assign to the outcomes of a particular course of action, an ordering could be made so that if I prefer a to b and b to c, I *should* prefer a to c; that is, the property of *transitivity* holds among my preferences. For example, if I prefer to punch my boss in the nose rather than to quit my job and if I prefer to quit my job rather than to state my grievance to the union, then I should prefer to punch my boss in the nose rather than go to the union.

However, before I decide upon such a course of action, it is often wise that I consider what the probability is that the particular outcome I desire will occur if I choose a particular course of action. Let us assume that I wish to keep my job as well as punch my boss in the nose. Then I would have to estimate the probability that I will keep my job (P_1) if I punch my boss in the nose. Let us say that under these conditions I assume that $P_1 = 0.1$. Then I have to conclude that the probability that I would lose my job (P_2) is 0.9, because much as I would like to believe otherwise—to believe, let us say, that $P_1 = 0.1$ and $P_2 = 0.3$—to do so would violate one of the conventions under which probability theory usually operates, namely, that the sum of the probabilities assigned to each of the possible consequences following a particular course of action should add to one.

I hope I have said enough about this school of thought's point of view to illustrate that it emphasizes heavily the rational component of man's behavior. In this respect it bears some resemblance to the older rationalities of scientific management and Weber's bureaucracy, but this resemblance is superficial. In other ways it is dramatically opposed to both. Both scientific management and Weber achieve a kind of machine rationality by treating members of organizations as passive instruments who are capable of doing only what they are told. On the contrary, this school of thought achieves its rationality by treating the members of organizations as *decision makers and problem solvers*.

When it does this, it seems to me that some interesting things happen. Social structure disappears from the scene and is replaced, so to speak, by psychological processes which are reduced in turn to a set of linear equations under a given set of constraints. Whereas traditional schools of management theory achieve their rationalities by emphasizing formal structures and ignoring motivation, this school of thought achieves its rationality by emphasizing rational motivation and ignoring social structures. In the process man's internal environment is no longer the passive machine of old, which can do only what it is told. It becomes rather a powerful thinking machine—curiously enough, just like the computer—capable of searching for satisficing alternatives of design for the problems of the modern world.

As can be imagined, the other schools of thought in that big mud heap called in the 1960s "behavioral science" or "organizational behavior" viewed this new model of man or organization or both with alarm and suspicion. The bureaucratic sociologists did not like to have their holy-of-holies, bureaucratic structures, reduced to psychological processes, no matter how beautifully rational. They said, "This ain't no theory of organization. It is a theory of human behavior in the context of an organization."

The neo-classical school of human relations—what I called earlier the 1960 version of human relations—did not like to have their socio-psychological processes involving interactions and sentiments reduced to mathematical equations. They said, "This ain't no descriptive theory of human behavior in organizations. It is a theory of how human behavior in organizations ought to be or someday in the distant future may be."

The social anthropologists did not like to have their cultural artifacts—and the psychiatrists did not like to have the unconscious—reduced to problems of rational design. They both said, "This school of thought ain't our bag."

Finally, practicing administrators—those people out there who were doing administrating, not theorizing about it—did not like to have their sound judgments, for which they were paid big fat salaries, reduced to rational processes that could be done as well, if not better, by machine. They said in their honest nonrational manner, "You can't do this to us," to which, as one might expect, this new school of thought in its rational manner replied, "Says who?" I shall not repeat the no-win consequences that this rejoinder set up. Instead I will tell you how I came to enroll in a course in mathematics and learned to count sophisticatedly.

MY INTEREST IN MATHEMATICS

In the early 1960s one of the conclusions that the authorities on matters of higher education in the land (i.e., the foundations) came to was that business education needed more sophisticated notions about mathematics, not only to improve their research, but also to improve the management skills they were teaching. Operations research was beginning to produce results and the computer was beginning to be used not only to process data but also to do many exciting things, such as to help make more rational decisions under conditions of uncertainty.

But at the B-School there was a fly—or should I say flies—in this exciting ointment that the new mathematics promised. These were the locals I described earlier, who were illiterate about the mathematics underlying these new tools for decision making. The data they collected for their teaching cases could not be put in the computer to be processed. The data were not in the proper form. They were not in the proper form because the locals did not know how to count. Strange as this may sound, they were still counting things (or accounting for them) in the most primitive way, that is, in terms of the 10 fingers on their hands. To remedy this shocking state of affairs the applied mathematicians at the School organized a course for their colleagues on the mathematics underlying computers.

I took this course during the summer of 1961 and the following academic year. The course was not concerned with the lower-level languages needed by computer programmers. It was about the higher-level languages of mathematics that underlay them. During the summer the seminar was concerned with calculus, probability theory, and so on. Not until the following academic year did I see how some of the pure mathematical structures that we played around with during the summer could be applied or given an empirical meaning. Even then, this remained somewhat vague to me. When the course was over, I had not seen a computer or learned any of what I am calling the lower-level languages of programmers. In this course I was at a much higher level of abstraction. Baby, was I up in the clouds!

This was okay with me. In fact, I would not have taken the course if it had been given at a more immediately practical and useful level. At the age of 63, I had no intention of becoming a computerologist. I was interested in how one got that way, not in getting that way myself.

Mathematics and logic had always fascinated me. I was not completely illiterate about them. At Columbia in preparation for becoming an engineer, I took courses in advanced algebra, analytical geometry, and the differential and integral calculus up to and through differential equations. After that, my formal training in mathematics stopped. I nearly flunked the course in differential equations, an experience I had not had in any course in mathematics; this disturbed me. Upon reflection now, I realize that up until then I had treated mathematics in a ritualistic way, solving equations by rules that had been well established but the logic for which I did not understand; this deficiency finally caught up with me.

At M.I.T. in my courses in engineering, I could stay (in the days before the computer) at a slap-happy and slipstick level. Although the mathematics underlying the slide rule fascinated me, I never saw the possibility of stating exponents on a base other than ten. In those days it was easy to remain a simple-minded slipstick or cookbook engineer and get by, and I did.

At Harvard, during my period in philosophy, my interest in mathematics revived, because of the then growing interest in mathematical logic as a tool for philosophical analysis, that is, as a tool for helping philosophers state more precisely what they were talking about when they were not talking about anything in particular. Although I could get somewhat excited about the "pure spaces" they created, I was then too upset with my own crumbling life space to become really concerned with them.

Thus my interest in mathematics gradually waned. This became increasingly true as my concerns turned in the direction of "life space" and "social space." The "preoccupations" and "dreams" of life space and the "interactions" and "sentiments" of social space did not seem to be tuned to or turned on by the seductive tunes of the pure spaces composed by the logical properties of numbers. Something nonlogical seemed to me to have composed the wild songs they sang. For a while it could be said, as I am sure it looked to some, that I was antilogical, antimathematical, antinumerical, antiquantitative and antimeasurement. I was having a ball, or so they could think, with matters that did not have any mathematical, quantitative, or measurable form whatsoever—administration, for example.

Nothing could be further from the truth. The seductive lure of pure spaces, as inculcated in me by the mathematical logicians at Harvard in my formative years, was still in my blood stream, so to speak. I confess it was lying there in a fallow state, for I did not talk about or use mathematics much. Occasionally, though, when the exposition of the "administrative point of view" got me down, I varied the diet and told my students how the non-Euclidean spaces had been discovered.

EMPIRICAL SAMPLE SPACES

Thus any antinumerical bias I had did not show up in relation to the pure spaces of mathematics. It showed up in relation to the empirical sample spaces produced by elementary statistics for describing social phenomena. The sets or classes these methods produced frequently set my teeth on edge. Let's face it; they annoyed the living daylights out of me. I was never at home with them. Often they seemed to me to prevent a researcher from observing what was going on right under his nose and to facilitate the asking of "wrong questions." I was not against the appropriate use of statistics. I was against their sole use and their misuse.

This attitude on my part has a long history. It goes back to the observations of those five women in the Relay Assembly Test Room, which I reported in *Management and the Worker*. Some of the generalizations I made had statisticians up in arms with such questions as: How can one generalize about all workers from five peewee workers who have not been selected by random numbers or by any method which by the wildest stretch of imagination can have made them a representative sample of workers?

Well, let's face the truth! You couldn't. The members of this "class" had been chosen because they were willing to cooperate with the experimental changes to which we were going to ask them to submit. We did this because we wanted to keep the factor of cooperation constant, so that we could study the effect of the experimental changes upon their productivity.

And what was the discovery of this great experiment? We discovered that these five women were not simply members of a *class* of workers but also a *social system* of five workers. That was the gist of this highly discussed and highly misunderstood experiment about which I wrote umpty-umth unnecessary (I would say now upon reflection) pages.

The generalizations I made were about *this system* of five workers and not about *some class* of which these five workers were a sample. What is the gist of the generalizations? It is to the effect that by looking at a concrete worker or a concrete work group or a concrete organization as concrete systems—and not, let me point out, by raising the question of whether they are representative of all workers, all groups or all organizations—one may observe something—and something very interesting—which the "class" abstraction of elementary statistics seems to ignore. This is the message of *Management and the Worker*, from which the human relations movement, the new posture for empirical research in industry, was born.

For many years I had strong feelings about psychometric tests of all sorts (intelligence tests, attitude and aptitude tests, and so on), survey methods, questionnaires, questionnaire design, sampling methods, correlations, and the 0.5 level of significance. My feelings about them can be expressed simply and briefly, if not objectively. They gave me one big, bloody headache. As Pierre Janet said to Elton Mayo and Mayo said to me, "Ce n'est pas la psychologie"; I might have added "Ce n'est pas aussi la sociologie." Why did I take this crazy attitude? Because it seemed to me that the *classes* that statisticians kept producing by the bushel and the correlations which in turn they made from them, also by the bushel, all excluded the element of social interaction—that element which for me was the holy of holies. Somehow it got squeezed out or reduced to insignificance by their bloody—I mean bloodless—classes.

In view of these strong feelings, it is astonishing to me that I would have considered taking a course in mathematics. But in the late 1950s many things were changing. Up until then I had no difficulty conceiving the area of organizational behavior as involving the behavioral sciences and not applied mathematics. But from about that time this assumption became more and more difficult to maintain. The literature on organizations was increasingly dominated by the applied mathematicians and their ways of thinking. I came to realize that their mathematical models introduced a way of thinking that was a far cry from my conceptual scheme and clinical methods of investigation. It seemed to me to be a radical departure from the other schools of thought in the behavioral sciences. The probability theory and statistics of this "newer" mathematics seemed to me to bear little resemblance to the elementary descriptive statistics about which I complained. I felt that these other men knew their mathematics much better than ordinary run-of-the mill social scientists. There was something here I could not ignore.

LEARNING TO COUNT

During the summer of 1961 I had John Bishop and Paul Vatter, both members of the Faculty at the School, as teachers. Their course on finite mathematics can be simply described as being concerned with getting students to count sophisticatedly. I also had Thomas

Lehrer, who was then better known for his satirical ditties than for his mathematical erudition, as an instructor in calculus. I did not have Howard Raiffa until the following academic year, when he showed us how we might apply what we had learned during the summer.

Only gradually did I realize that my instructors were facing a problem similar to ones that I had had. In teaching us about the pure spaces of mathematics, they were up against a blind spot. Just as interactions, norms, roles, feeling, sentiments, and culture were not there for many of my students, so the magical properties of numbers such as zero and one were not really there for many of us. How could you count something that was not really there? This was the teaching problem which I though they had and with which I could identify.

Let me illustrate with my favorite probability problem—what mathematicians call the birthday problem. It seems to me that the mathematicians have a way of pushing their thinking by trying to find a solution to all sorts of paradoxes, dilemmas, and wacky problems, of which the birthday problem is one. It goes something like this: What is the probability that at least two people among x people selected from a large group will have the same birthday; and how large will x have to be so that the probability of finding two people with the same birthday will be greater than 1/2? In terms of this problem, I will illustrate the problems that John Bishop had in teaching me to count by describing what I thought about at night, while John was trying to teach me during the day. Though I listened to him during the day, at night I tried to reconcile what he was teaching me with the kind of real events I had learned about from practicing the clinical method. I could not stop myself from doing this. The point of my telling about this is that I want to use my experience of learning how to count to communicate how difficult it is to relate the pure spaces of mathematics to the concrete systems which I studied with the clinical method. As you will see, whenever I tried to do this, even with the aid of mathematics—that most precise of all languages—they kept getting so entangled with each other that I could not keep clear just what, in terms of the elusive phenomena, was being counted. I will not tell all of my nightmare—indeed, not enough to show how much I learned about mathematics, which was a good deal—but only enough to make this other point.

Lest the reader get the wrong impression, let me also say that my night-time dialogues with my math teacher about the birthday problem present an imaginary John Bishop, not the real John and what he and I might have been thinking, feeling, and saying if I had seen fit to raise during the day the problems I lay awake thinking about at night. It is in no sense whatsoever—mais non, mille fois non—what John actually said or did. He was most kind and gentle in class whenever he had to expose my ignorance. These are my nightmares—not reports of John's teaching—even though I give the dialogue from his point of view.

MY NIGHTMARE ABOUT MY MATH TEACHER

"Start counting, boy! ... All thumbs, eh? ... Well, let me help you. Let's number the days of the year 1, 2, 3 ..., 365. We'll omit people born in leap years on February 29 and give each person's birthday a number. For example, give to the person born on January 1 the number 1; on April 28 the number 118; and on December 31 the number 365. Everyone in the whole wide world now has a birthday number. Check?

"You're worried about the people who don't record birthdays by the Gregorian calendar and the people possibly living on some other planet who may be recording their birthdays by some other time system? Let's forget them. Even without them, you have a large enough population to select from.

"We now have a set of birthday numbers and each birthday is an element of the set A = 1, 2, 3, ..., 365. Right?

"Now let's perform an experiment. To keep the experiment simple, let's make n = 5. Please select five persons from your large group and record their birthdays.... No, you don't have to ask five redheaded women at the B-School for their birthdays.... Yes, that's right. Each of those five redheads has a birthday number. Her number is in the set A, but she's not there; you got her number. That's a joke, son.

"Okay, if you are that up-tight about counting, think of those five redheaded women. Select RHW_1 and ask for her birthday number. Let's assume, hypothetically speaking, she says 6; do the same for RHW_2, RHW_3, RHW_4, and RHW_5. Be sure to take them in this order; let's assume each says in turn 18, 78, 119, and 210.

"You have now recorded a typical outcome of your mental experiment. It's (6, 18, 78, 119, 210). That is an ordered 5-tuple. Now start counting, son.... Counting what? Well, counting the number of ordered 5-tuples in set A.... What's an ordered 5-tuple? I'll give you a strict definition later in the course; for now (6, 18, 78, 119, 210), (17, 3, 100, 40, 5), and (6, 5, 4, 6, 365) are examples.

"What's this? You want to know which particular five persons you should select next to ask for their birthday numbers? For goodness sakes, boy; choose any damned five people you please, because in the end no matter what answers they give, the five ordered answers are going to be one of the outcomes of your mental experiment and a simple event in your simple space.... Yes, even the actual ordered birthdays of RHW_1, RHW_2, RHW_3, RHW_4, and RHW_5 will be one of the elements in your sample space. We're giving them no preferential treatment. What I want to know is how many other outcomes, in addition to this particular outcome of (6, 18, 78, 119, 210), will there be in your sample space?

"What's a sample space? Well, roughly speaking it's all the possible outcomes of the conceptual experiment you are in the process of performing. Let me tell you, although I don't like to do this. Your sample space $S = A \cdot A \cdot A \cdot A \cdot A$. It contains 365^5 elements. I'll give you the proof for this later. That's a lot of elements, son. Your sample space contains $365 \cdot 365 \cdot 365 \cdot 365 \cdot 365$ or something in the neighborhood of six trillion, 500 billion elements, or if you wish to say so, simple events or ordered five birthdays or ordered 5-tuples. How does it feel counting this way, son? ... No, I don't mean you actually counted 6,500,000,000,000 outcomes. How long do you think that would take? I've only got a summer to learn you how to count.

"You're worried that the actual ordered birthdays of your five redheads at the B-School are lost in this vast, fast-moving set of 6,500,000,000,000 elements? Don't worry, boy, they're there. They're one of the 6,500,000,000,000 possible outcomes of your mental experiment.... You want me to show you this particular ordering, so you can be sure it's there? For goodness sakes, son, I can't show it to you, because I don't know what it is.... Yes, even though I don't know what it is, I know it's there.... Where? In your sample space, son. Even though I can't find it for you there, it's not lost. It's there. I can prove it to you, boy.

"What I want to know is among the 365^5 elements in your sample space, how many of them will have at least two people with the same birthday. Start counting, boy! We want to find out n(E), where E is the event that at least two people have the same birthday and E is a subset of S.... Let me help you again. Perhaps it would be easier for you to count E', that is, the complement of E, where E' is the event that *no* two among the five people selected have the same birthday. Once we know n(E'), then we can find n(E) by subtracting n(E') from n(S), which by now I hope you know is 365^5.... That's right, (E) + n(E') = n(S) = 365^5. I'm going out for a smoke while you count E'.

"Having trouble? Well, let me help you. How many ways can the first person's birthday be chosen from the full set of 365 possible birthdays? ... Did you say 365 ways? That's a good boy! What about the second person ... 364 ways! Excellent! You're going to be quite a hot counter someday soon, I hope. But keep counting! The third person can be chosen in 363 ways, the fourth person in 362 ways, and the fifth person in 361 ways. So applying the fundamental principle of counting, we find that

$$N(E') = 365 \cdot 364 \cdot 363 \cdot 362 \cdot 361.$$

"That's a pretty big number, boy; but by inspection, we can see that it isn't as large as 365^5, that is to say, n(E) which is $(365 \cdot 365 \cdot 365 \cdot 365 \cdot 365) - (365 \cdot 364 \cdot 363 \cdot 362 \cdot 361)$ will not exceed, let's hope, the gross national product.... No, don't multiply it out, son; I know you can multiply. What I'm trying to find out is whether you can count—sophisticatedly, I mean.... OK, multiply it out, long hand, if you have to restore your ego. I'm going out for a smoke.

"Did you determine n(E)? It's about 175 billion, you say? Well, that sounds about right.... No, I didn't say there are 175 billion people who have the same birthday as Ho Chi Minh. I said that among the approximately 6,500,000,000,000 ordered 5-tuples in your sample space, approximately 175 billion ordered 5-tuples have at least two birthday numbers in common.

"What's that? You want to examine each of the 6,500,000,000,000 outcomes and state how you personally feel about the probabilities of each one of them? You think that personal feelings should count or be counted? Say, man, what are you, a nut or anti-establishment? I've been as permissive as I can get in allowing you to assign probabilities to your 6,500,000,000,000 outcomes—all the way from zero to one—but there comes a time, son, when enough is enough. Your demands of me have become non-negotiable. We're going to assume that the probability of each of the 6,500,000,000,000 outcomes in your sample space is 1/6,500,000,000,000. That's final, man. Let's start counting.

"What's the probability of the event E that at least two among the five people selected have the same birthday? ... What's P(E)? Well, it's clear, at least to most nonscrewballs, that

$$P(E) = n(E)\frac{1}{365^5} = \frac{175{,}000{,}000{,}000 \text{ (approximately)}}{6{,}500{,}000{,}000{,}000 \text{ (approximately)}}$$
$$= .03 \text{ approximately.}$$

That's to a rough approximation, but I know you can divide, although you better watch out for your decimal points! Yes, you can now say with some confidence that the odds are 97 to 3, against any two of the five redheaded women at the B-School having the same birthday.

"Anyway, it's time for lunch; so if you want to check, run along now and ask the five redheads what their birthdays are. I think you'll find them in the cafeteria.... Eating lunch together? Well, I wouldn't know about that! ... What did you say? You mean a possible real outcome of such an experiment would be a punch in the nose? Didn't I tell you to ask for their birthday numbers and not birth years? ... You like real experiments better than conceptual experiments? That's fine and dandy, son. I'm glad you like 'em. ... No bones are broken in a conceptual experiment, you say? There's no confrontation or observation or interaction in a conceptual experiment, you say? $1/365^5$ doesn't carry much weight, you say? Don't talk philosophy or sociology to me, boy!"

AFTERTHOUGHTS

In this manner—by the case method, shall we say?—did I learn to count in the summer of 1961. Not only did I play with the set of all possible ordered birthdays, I also played with fair coins, fair red and green dice, fair red and black balls, and fair cards without ever touching or seeing a fair or real coin, die, ball, or card. I just performed mental or conceptual experiments with all these unseen objects. I think John Bishop or Paul Vatter would have slapped my wrist if I had brought into class some real dice or coins or balls or packs of cards. If I had, I think they feared that I would still be counting 6,500,000,000,000 on the fingers of my hands. And I think they would have been right.

Let's face it, this way of thinking went against my clinical bones. I marveled at John Bishop's and Paul Vatter's patience with me. I kept raising all sorts of irrelevant questions. At times I could get excited about their pure mathematical structures, and occasionally I did. Howard Raiffa, in particular, often had me sitting on the edge of my chair with his creations and his expositions of them. Such beauty and grandeur! But I could not stay in this rarefied atmosphere for any length of time. After a day or two, I would revert to my clinical outlook. As I said, I turned my math class into a social system and described how it might look from this point of view. I just could not stop myself from doing it!

It was clear that I never was going to learn to think like a mathematician—not in 10 or even 10^n (where n was greater than 1) easy lessons. This was not my cup of tea, and this limitation I could accept for myself. The problem came up with regard to my Doctoral candidates. How much time should they devote to becoming proficient in this way of thinking? Did not a lifetime of sweat, tears, and toil have to be given to its development?

It seemed to me that Howard Raiffa ate, drank, and slept with mathematics; this was what made him a great teacher. He had devoted a lifetime to it; it was his career. But Howard knew the limitation of what he was up to. When he started to apply mathematics to the empirical world, he knew that the phenomena were more complex than his pure structures revealed. Never—not once—did he pretend otherwise. I wondered how long it took him to learn this. In Howard I saw no superficial, fly-by-night mathematician applying numbers to things just for the hell of it, an impression, frankly, I had about some of the new mathematical model-makers in the area of Organizational Behavior. I saw a dedicated man, dedicated to his subject matter and its possibilities for application to real-world problems of business.

Although I thought my Doctoral students should be exposed to all the research tools that were available, I wondered with how many they could play around and at the same time cultivate understanding of any one of them in any depth. In the Doctoral program, were we not in danger of training jacks-of-all-trades, superficial jackasses?

An attitude which became prevalent about this time particularly disturbed me. This was the attitude that now we could take for granted that students knew field work and clinical methods of research. The assumption seemed to be that the behavioral sciences had reached a stage of development in which the capacity to make insightful, first-hand observations could be assumed as part of a student's normal background. What he needed was rigorous and sophisticated tools for research and theory building.

I saw little evidence for this assumption in the literature I read. An unsophisticated field worker was to me just as superficial as an unsophisticated mathematician. A sociologist not capable of making first-hand observations was just as unsophisticated as a sociologist who could not count.

To me there was a difference between a clinical outlook and a mathematical one that could not be glossed over. Not that I wanted to make a false dichotomy between these two different ways of thinking, but neither did I want to make a superficial, sentimental, and verbal integration. There was a problem here that needed attention. The problem was not a way of thinking about numbers, but a way of thinking about relationships to which numbers could or could not be applied. The problem concerned the differences among the relations which composed what I call technological, purposive, social, and life spaces. Perhaps these different spaces required not only different modes of investigation, but also different modes of explanation, application, and control. The 1960s highlighted all these questions, to which I will turn, as soon as I describe the views I reached as a result of giving my seminar about the theories that were available in the field of organizational behavior.

SLEEPING DOGS THAT WOULD NOT LIE STILL

In this and the previous chapter I have described some of the similarities and differences among the schools of thought that existed in the 1960s about matters of organization and about what the behavior of people within organizations (employees, administrators, or technical specialists) is, or might be, or should be. By making only a few more distinctions I could easily increase the number of different schools, but this is unnecessary to show that a diversity of conceptual frameworks existed and that no single one was dominant. This state of affairs led to some bothersome consequences:

(1) Each school of thought could be accused of having overemphasized or underemphasized some dimension of organizational behavior—individual motivation, social interaction, formal structure, or the environment (technological or cultural) in which organizations have to survive.

(2) Since each dimension represented some human or social value, each school of thought could be accused of taking—either explicitly or implicitly—some value position.

(3) Since each dimension also represented the province of some discipline, each school of thought could be accused of trying to reduce someone else's discipline to its own.

(4) As a result, there were differences of opinion about what constituted the legitimate scope of organizational behavior, of the be-

havioral sciences, and of the individual disciplines that comprised them.

(5) Because there were no accepted principles of legitimacy about these matters—many persons held that there should not be any— there was no way of settling these arguments rationally. The arguments tended to degenerate into statements of the "You can't do this to me—says who?" variety.

(6) Some social scientists thought that because differences of conceptual outlook were merely matters of convenience for purposes of investigation, the findings and not the tools by which they have been discovered were what we should be concerned with, quarreling about, and trying to consolidate.

(7) This was easier said than done. Often it was difficult to specify whether the findings of one school contradicted or confirmed the findings of another. Was it a real contradiction or was the uniformity masked by differences in the conditions under which A had found this and B had found the opposite?

(8) Moreover, it was sometimes difficult to say whether the findings of one school were relevant to the findings of another. Was what one investigator meant by "power" the same as or different from what another investigator meant by "influence" and another by "status"?

(9) In terms of the explanation of findings, it was often difficult to see how the way one investigator explained "change" differed from the way another investigator explained "social structure" or how the way one explained "conformity" differed from the way another explained "deviance."

(10) In terms of the application of findings, it was often difficult to say whether what one investigator called "the management of conflict" was the same as or different from what another called "the management of cooperation." Could it be that the management of one involved the same processes as the management of the other?

(11) This state of affairs provided a field day for any investigator of organizational behavior. All one had to do was set up the conceptual scheme of a fellow investigator as a straw man, point out what it overlooked, and demolish it with one fell swoop. Then he could start *de novo*, with a new conceptual scheme or model and a new vocabulary (called "concepts") and claim a breakthrough.

(12) Unfortunately the new concepts did not explain any better than the old ones, because concepts in and by themselves do not explain anything. Thus we remained where we were in the beginning, arguing about our different concepts and conceptual schemes.

These were the conclusions to which my seminar in organizational theory led me. The more I read the literature on the sociology of organizations, the social psychology of organizations, the social anthropology of organizations, the clinical psychology of organizations, the scientific management of organizations, and the management sciences of organizations, the more I was driven back to questions about the nature of the scientific enterprise. What constitutes a scientific theory, a scientific explanation? With what class or classes of entities and relations is a science of organization or administration concerned? With what classes should it be concerned? Can there be a science of organization or of administration? Is there just one science of human behavior rather than separate sciences of individual behavior, social behavior, organizational behavior, and so on?

It seemed to me that the literature was bursting with these questions. Unlike sleeping dogs, they could not be made to lie still. Clearly, these questions could not be settled by observation, experiment, or logic. How then were they to be settled? By faith and conviction or by convenience and utility? If by utility, for whom were these different conceptual formulations useful? For the scientist in his search for truth for its own sake? For the administrator and leader in his search for effective behavior and control? For the employee in his search for justice? For the human being in his search for identity?

Were these different aims of knowledge unrelated? In matters of human behavior was there a bifurcation between descriptive knowledge about things as they are and the utilization of such knowledge for the improvement of things as they might be? Why did normative questions about how things should be always rear their ugly heads? Could there be a normative science? Was there a difference between the logics of scientific description and the logics of normative action? Does the scientist in the acquisition of knowledge use one logic and the administrator in the utilization of knowledge use a different one?

With these questions, which went around and around in my mind, it was obvious that I was back in the realm of philosophy, from which in my early career I had tried to escape. Mayo turned me off from many of these philosophical questions by saying "rubbish" to them, and turned me on to empirical questions which could be answered by clinical investigation. Even Henderson said that in the first instance scientific explanation did not require a philosophical theory but only a simple walking-stick that would allow me to carry on investigations. Thus these questions bought me back not only into the realm of philosophy but also to concerns that bothered me at the beginning of my professional career. I was back to considering the explicit and implicit assumptions I had been making about the acquisition and utilization of knowledge.

It seemed to me that the most serious obstacles in achieving a science of human behavior in organizations arose from:

(1) a failure to distinguish between a *conceptual scheme* for purposes of investigation (one kind of theory) and a *conceptual system* for purposes of systematic explanation (another kind of theory); and furthermore,

(2) a failure to distinguish this second kind of *conceptual system*— a system of logically related concepts—from a *system of logically related propositions or findings* which can be arranged deductively from the more general to the more specific (often called a "scientific theory of explanation"); and furthermore,

(3) a failure to distinguish between these three different kinds of theories and the *concrete systems* to which they can be applied; in particular,

(4) a failure to distinguish between the various *conceptual systems* by which a concrete system can be analyzed; hence, a difficulty in keeping them related to each other and to the concrete system; and in particular

(5) a failure to distinguish between the external and internal equilibria of concrete systems; and hence, an additional difficulty in keeping them related to each other and to the concrete system.

With these difficulties I shall now be concerned.

Book Two

RESTATEMENTS AND REFLECTIONS

Introduction:

The Turbulent Sixties

There are many interpretations about what happened to the social order in the United States during the 1960s. Particularly during the latter half of the decade there was little question that something was out of whack. Almost all the established ways of doing things came into question; change and revolution were in the air, though there was no consensus about what needed to be changed and how change was to be accomplished. Even the nature of the revolution was not clear. Two revolutions seemed to be occurring simultaneously, a scientific and technological revolution on the one hand and a counter-cultural revolution on the other. Most of the social science futurologists, curiously enough, had not predicted this state of affairs.

It was both a good and bad time to be planning the concluding parts of this account of my life and work. It was an excellent opportunity to review the assumptions I had made about the knowledge enterprise and the relation of knowledge to effective action. On the other hand, things were so topsy-turvy it was difficult to maintain a balanced point of view. The pressures to take sides, to declare unequivocally one's value position and where one stood, to tell it like it was, to go where the action was, to be authentic, to politicize, to cut out the bullshit, and to still be scientific, were terrific. To do otherwise was to be labeled "square."

I hesitate to say the number of times I had the urge to write something in which I would express unabashedly my feelings about the state of affairs and say who I thought the chief villains were. Sometimes I succumbed and wrote a piece, which I later tore up, when I found that my feelings were not clear-cut but ambivalent.

For I shared many of the values of the counter-culture. In fact the human relations movement in its early days, with its emphasis on the importance of the group and the need to belong, could be said to be a forerunner in the industrial arena of the counter-cultural movement. It was counter to the overemphasis on technology and formal organization as the sole and dominant values of society. Yet I realized that you could not build and fly airplanes on the basis of the values of the counter-culture alone.

The presence of opposing processes—those in the direction of scientific and technological progress and those in the direction of social stability—precipitated the human relations movement. In Mayo's essay on "The Seamy Side of Progress" in his *The Social Problems of an Industrial Civilization,* he pointed out the undesirable consequences—in terms of anomie, disorientation, and loss of identity and social solidarity—that followed from a lopsided development based solely on scientific and technological knowledge without an equivalent advance in human and social knowledge.

Thus, in the early days the human relations movement was not solely an attempt to humanize bureaucracy (to which in later years it was often reduced). Nor was it only an attempt to adopt a more empirical and "scientific" stance toward the human problems of industrial organization. It also provided a focus for the direction in which social scientists could look to create the social knowledge that was so badly needed to keep these opposing forces in balance. In the ensuing years both behavioral science specialists and human relations practitioners, it seemed to me, forgot this focus.

Let there be no question about it: this focus was for me what gave the human relations movement its vitality. For me human relations was not a sentimental imperative to be human nor a lofty imperative to be scientific; it provided a much-needed orientation for a very real problem for which there was a woeful lack of knowledge. In short, I became a man with a paradigm (I have called it a "conceptual scheme") around which it seemed to me the liberal humanitarian, the social scientist, and the human relations practitioner could rally. I have tried to record—I hope faithfully—how all this did not happen and how in time my conceptual scheme became stigmatized as a tool by which management could co-opt the worker to the establishment.

I was not the only victim of this kind of a reversal. By the mid-sixties the air was filled with such reversals. In many quarters psychiatrists and clinical psychologists and even—if you can believe this now—psychoanalysts and experimental psychologists were accused of being manipulators and advocates for the establishment. Psychoanalysts who tried to help women accept their femininity became male chauvinists, and functional sociologists became advocates of the status quo.

These reversals did not appear only in the social sciences; they were present almost everywhere. Black became beautiful; White became ugly; racial liberalism became racism; sexual emancipation became sexism; education became brainwashing or irrelevant; economic developers became environmental polluters; feelings became touchings; dialogue became confrontations; students became cop-outs, drop-outs, freak-outs, hippies, yippies, flower children, or political activists.

Every age has produced its reversals; but the 1960s were unique—it seems to me—by virtue of the number and rapidity of their oscillations and the confusions caused by them. It was no longer clear if women were or should be the same as or different from men; if Blacks were or should be the same as or different from Whites; if children knew or should know more than their parents or teachers. When in the morning a person had reached what he thought was a liberal conclusion that Negroes were like everybody else, by cocktail hour he was accused of being a racist and that nothing could be further from the truth, because they were as different from liberal Whites as anyone could get. When in the night a liberal father decided to rap with his children, by mid-morning the next day he was told how corny could he act. As can be imagined, in this atmosphere it became difficult for the liberal who wanted to be *au courant* and contemporaneous to say exactly where he stood. As he had no comfortable stool on which to sit, most of his time was spent on the floor sitting most inelegantly on his behind or lying flat on his face.

But the 1960s were characterized not only by the slapstick comedy of pratfalls taken by those who wished to be *au courant* about where they stood. They were also characterized by the fact that forces for and against progress, modernity, science, technology, and a growth economy were all flourishing at the same time. In the face of the counter-cultural revolution, the technological and scientific revolution did not come to a grinding halt. In some ways its pace increased, though the opposite could also be said, for in the face of the scientific and technological revolution, the counter-cultural advocates did not fold their tents and quietly disappear into the night. Rather their resistance to unbridled economic development increased.

As a result, in the 1960s conglomerates and multinational corporations flourished side by side with communes. Outer space was being explored by the computer at the same time that inner space was being explored with psychedelic drugs. Economic growth for backward areas abroad was advocated at the same time that a nongrowth economy was considered at home.

But were these phenomena entirely new? Had not their underlying forces been with us for a long time—ever since the first industrial revolution? Except for their exaggerated manifestations, what was so different in the 1960s from what Mayo diagnosed in 1940? What was so surprising about what was taking place? If Mayo's diagnosis was correct, could it not have been predicted? For me the interesting question was why had it not? Why had the behavioral sciences not focused more on these questions? Why had their knowledge been so difficult to apply? Where had my colleagues and I gone off the track, so that we had not seen what was coming?

These questions are very much in my mind as I begin the following chapters about the assumptions that I make about the knowledge enterprise and its utilization for the human problems of a technologically and scientifically oriented civilization. Although these questions provide a useful focus for reflecting about and reassessing my assumptions, they can also be used defensively to say how, not I, but my colleagues had been off the track.

Let's face it: I often have defensive feelings, but by being aware of them I think I can correct them. I also feel that the important question is not who is right and who is wrong, but what is it that makes the achievement of scientific knowledge about human behavior such a very difficult enterprise—an enterprise whose difficulty perhaps all of us underestimate? This latter problem is the one with which I shall be primarily concerned in the next chapters. I hope that this concern, not my ruffled feathers, will come through to the reader.

In these chapters I will consider some of the assumptions I make about the different levels, processes, and products of the knowledge enterprise. None of these assumptions is original with me; they have been made by many others, though in different words. I shall not dwell on the authorities I could cite for their sources. Instead I will state the assumptions as I have come to see them.

I will take three chapters to discuss the three levels of knowledge which I call skill, clinical knowledge, and analytical or scientific knowledge and the boundaries and relations between the three. I think that one of the confusions that afflict social scientists occurs because we fail to separate these levels of the knowledge enterprise. Thereby we tend to reduce all levels to whichever one interests us most. Having made these distinctions, I will try to use them to reconceptualize the phenomena in ways that I hope will help to clarify the subject matter of human behavior in organizations. Then, finally, I will write about the relation of knowledge to action in modern society.

Part V

LEVELS OF THE KNOWLEDGE ENTERPRISE

Chapter 20

Skill

In this chapter I will consider the assumptions I make about skill and its relation to the higher levels of knowledge. At the level of skill the practitioner is more concerned with improving his relation to the phenomena, that is, with action, than with the acquisition of knowledge. Hence, in a strict sense it can be said that skill lies outside the knowledge enterprise and knowledge begins with what I call clinical knowledge at the second level. I prefer the view that skill is a level of knowledge, the foundation on which the other levels rest. At the level of skill all the elements that lead to the acquisition of systematic knowledge can be found. Without this level the higher ones would have nothing to support them. The big gap between knowledge and action, if it develops, appears as I see it at the analytical level. There the emphasis is on the truth of a proposition and on explanation rather than on the utilization of knowledge for action.

THE NATURE OF SKILL

By skill, viewed externally, I mean *concrete behavior* in relation to *concrete entities and relations,* either physical or social. Skill involves *concrete operations:* it produces *concrete results and concrete outcomes.*

By skill I do not mean verbal skill—skill in manipulating words, symbols, and abstractions; neither do I mean that in the practice of skill, words, symbols, and abstractions are absent. Indeed they are very much there, a part of skill, but in a form such that if their meanings are challenged, the concrete entities, relations, operations, or results to which they refer can be pointed to. The way in which a woodcarver behaves in fashioning objects from wood is an example of what I mean by skill. To the original concrete material (wood) he adds certain concrete operations, called skill, by which he fashions certain concrete objects, let us say, a bowl.

Although this description of skill from an external point of view emphasizes clearly that skill deals with the concrete, it falls short of specifying the nature of skill from the point of view of a skilled person. In fact, in the sequence I have just mentioned of wood $\longrightarrow$ woodcarver $\longrightarrow$ bowl, I have already made certain distinctions by which, in time, skill may be programmed out of existence and may become as dead as the proverbial doornail. Let us look more closely at skill as it is first practiced by a practitioner, the woodcarver, for example.

Viewed from this perspective, skill becomes the way by which man begins to improve his relation to his surroundings. It becomes the response of the whole organism, acting as a unit, that is more or less adequate to a particular point in a given situation. This response of the total organism, acting as a totality or unit, implies something different from a technique. Instead of being a technique to be learned, skill becomes a way of learning, a way of assimilating and ordering experience by which one's relation to one's surroundings can be improved. It becomes something intrinsic and not something extrinsic to the learner-practitioner.

Looked at from this point of view, the woodcarver is not learning, in the first instance, techniques of wood carving. He is learning slowly and gradually about the properties of the woods from which he can fashion certain objects. He is learning about the tools he needs in order to assist him. He is learning about the utilities of the objects he fashions. None of these elements is highly differentiated.

At first the woodcarver is not asking, "Am I using the best wood or the best tools to make this object?" or "Does there exist a consumer or market for this object which I am carving?" He is responding as adequately as he can to a particular point in a given situation. By a sequence of such encounters with his surroundings he learns to improve his relations to them. Skill, conceived in this way from the point of view of a practitioner, has three characteristics from which in time systematic knowledge about the nature of the phenomena may develop.

The first characteristic is the organic character of the skilled response. There is a balanced development between the outward and inward aspects of what is being learned. On the outward side the skillful practitioner learns something about the natural phenomena to which his responses are addressed. On the inward side he learns how to improve his responses to what he encounters in the environment. These two processes go hand-in-hand. The practitioner does not develop the one apart from the other, nor does he develop one of them more than the other; he develops them rather in a balanced relation to each other. His thinking about them does not complicate or develop beyond the knowledge he has about them from his experience with them. Thus his encounters with the external world and his capacity for response develop together. As a result, he gains growing and developing awareness of the complexity of relationships in the phenomena as well as a growing and developing confidence in his capacity to deal with them.

The second characteristic of this organized system of a capacity for response in skillful behavior is that it improves slowly and gradually, step by step, through time. An individual learns to creep before he learns to walk; he learns to talk before he can make speeches and become a politician. As Mayo said, "In our culture he learns to handle a knife and fork before he makes a notable contribution to conversations at the dinner table. To put it at a much higher level of abstraction, one has to be a Newton before he can become an Einstein."

The third characteristic of skill is that it develops through attention to the phenomena at the point of interaction with them. Although this seems obvious, it is often overlooked by the knowledge-seekers and by those who try to develop skill by reading a book or in ten easy lessons. This capacity of the practitioner to attend to the phenomena at the point of interaction with them is a necessary prerequisite for making the first elementary, useful discriminations about the phenomena as well as about his relation to them. Without the capacity to attend, there is little capacity to observe and discriminate. Without the capacity to observe and discriminate, there is little capacity to develop an organized system of response to the phenomena. And without a capacity to develop an organized system of response, there is little capacity to attend, observe, and discriminate among phenomena. As a result of this ring-around-a-rosy, no skill develops. Individual behavior becomes a "signal response" to an external stimulus. For me this is not skill but its opposite.

In these three characteristics of a skillful response reside, in rudimentary form, all the elements from which the knowledge enterprise develops. This response contains the roots of more effective observation of the phenomena, more effective ways of learning about them, more effective ways of dealing with or "controlling" them and thus of improving one's relation to them. Through its exercise the practitioner gains a sense of competence, achievement, and mastery and begins to exercise some intuitive judgments about them.

To these products of skill the word knowledge may be given. This knowledge is of a limited kind. It is not knowledge about things in a sophisticated or scientific sense. It is the kind of knowledge which William James called knowledge of acquaintance; which Henderson called an intimate, intuitive familiarity with the phenomena; which Mayo referred to as first-hand observation; and which Piaget called syncretistic—an apprehension of wholes without sharp delineation of parts.

This kind of knowledge is limited in space and time. Because skill deals with the concrete, its practitioner can use it only somewhere and sometime in particular. What is learned is extremely local. One may learn, for example, something about the ways of the buffalo and become a skillful buffalo hunter without knowing anything about the ways of the elephant and without becoming a skillful elephant hunter; and this skillful buffalo or elephant hunter is far from being a "zoologist."

In this lowly stage of knowledge there are no sharp distinctions between the descriptive and the normative. The skillful practitioner is not interested in describing the phenomena *as they are* for their own sake. He is no disinterested seeker of the truth; rather he is action-oriented. Nevertheless, in his endeavor to improve his relations to his surroundings, he does not ignore the properties of things *as they are*. The woodcarver, whether he is carving a bowl or, for that matter, an ornament (the outcome of the practice of skill does not have to be something practical), is attending to the properties of the particular wood he is using. In a syncretistic fashion he knows that to do his carving he needs an instrument harder than the wood he is carving; he may not know precisely how much harder it needs to be, but he knows it must be harder.

He has no strong notions about how things *should be*. He is not trying to make wood have the properties of stone, nor bamboo have the properties of pine or maple, if by some unlikely chance these different woods exist in his locality. He accepts the fact of these differences; the recognition does not throw him into despondency or get him "hung up" or "uptight." He feels that he can improve his relations to things *as they are*. In fact, in a syncretistically optimistic fashion he feels he can fashion things *as they might be* from things *as they are*. He feels that by taking into account the properties of things *as they are*, he can fashion things that never existed before. He can fashion necklaces, earrings, bowls, and so on, objects that were not growing in a natural state in his own backyard. In this sense he is being descriptively prescriptive or normative but, as I have said, in a syncretistic way. He is so naive, or should I say so intellectually non-obsessive, that the distinction between things as they are or might be or should be is no issue for him—as we would say in the 1970s, "no problem."

For the intuitive practitioner of skill, the distinction between theory and practice is also no problem. He practices his skill with no explicit theory about the nature of the phenomena with which he is dealing. Neither is he seeking to explain them. He just makes use of the uniformities in the phenomena he is observing. He knows perhaps, for example, that water tends to run downhill, that wood floats on water, and that it takes longer to boil an egg on top of a mountain than at sea level; but he does not know why. Without as yet being or becoming a zoologist, he may become a more skillful hunter by observing that he can kill more animals of a particular kind for food by going to a place where the animals tend to congregate than by waiting for them to come to his place of abode. Without as yet being or becoming a physicist and knowing that air has weight, he can fashion a hand pump to draw water from a well. Even though he may know that no matter how hard he pumps, he cannot draw water from a well deeper than so many feet, he does not know why. In fact he does not know precisely by how many feet he can perform this trick of the week or why.

HOW SKILL DEVELOPS

Although I am arguing that higher forms of knowledge are derived from skill and that skill is derived from a certain kind of experiencing of, learning about, or responding to, phenomena in order to improve one's relation to them, a question can be raised about how skill develops in the first place. After all, many games different from the one I call skill can be played with the phenomena. Why should this one have been cultivated, or as would be said today, "reinforced"?

I assume that skillful behavior develops because it is a rewarding experience and that the phenomena themselves do the rewarding; in the sense that the phenomena allow themselves, so to speak, to be manipulated or controlled better by the skillful practitioner than by someone who plays other kinds of games with them. A woodcarver, for example, who knows that some woods are harder than others, even though he does not know how much harder, is able to fashion articles accordingly. He thus achieves a mastery over his physical environment and feels competent to deal with it.

I would not say that the phenomena are pleading to be understood, explained, or manipulated. It is more as though the phenomena are saying, "If you take our properties into account, we will cooperate with you, allow you to understand and control us, and, in terms of the 1970s, give you a positive feedback. But if you abuse us by ignoring our properties, then, speaking more colloquially, we're going to let you fall on your big fat fanny."

The practice of skill is a rewarding experience in more than this sense; it is also often rewarded by others. Because he is able to produce better concrete results, the skillful practitioner often receives rewards from members of his group. He gains recognition for his skill. Because of it he may be asked for help. Sometimes he even becomes the leader of the group. Someone might say, for example, "Johnny seems to have a green thumb. He knows his onions, so let us ask him to help us grow ours." Or they might say, "Johnny seems to know his buffaloes. Let us make him our leader the next time we hunt buffaloes."

Much of the work on our planet is done by the kind of knowledge I call skill. This was true not only in the distant past or in primitive groups or in economically underdeveloped countries; it is also true in our highly technological society; going to the moon requires skill.

Important as I think this point to be, the question remains how higher forms of knowledge emerge from this lowly one. I assume that my intuitive practitioner of skill is more action-oriented than knowledge-oriented and more interested in practicing his skill than in verbalizing about it and stating the grounds for it explicitly. Nevertheless, if and when he begins to do this, the whole knowledge enterprise begins to unfold. This is all there is to this further development. No problem. Well, let just say there is no big, fat inscrutable mystery about it!

Lord forbid, though, that by saying, "This is all there is to it," I imply that "this-all" is insignificant. On the contrary, it is highly significant. It means that if skill is ever going to get beyond its limits in time and space and go places, logic and an explicit theory have to be added it. Logic and theory do not come from some never-never land. They too come first from practice. No problem? Well, yes and no. Let me stop here for a moment and catch my breath. There are a few more assumptions which I make about skill and to which I had better confess before I pursue this next point.

THE NATURE OF SOCIAL SKILL

Just as I assume that man's first-hand knowledge of his physical surroundings derives from skill, I assume that he obtains his knowledge about his social surroundings in the same manner. Following

Mayo, I call the former "technical skill" and the latter "social skill." This parallel causes many troubles.

One is that for many people "social skill" implies the manipulation of others by the practitioner for his own ends, and they consider this to be bad. It is treating persons as means to an end rather than as ends in themselves. This raises ethical issues which the practice of a technical skill does not; it is considered all right to manipulate things for one's own ends, but not persons.

Although I concur with the sentiments expressed by these criticisms, they do not address my concerns. I assume that even though physical phenomena and social phenomena are different (about this point I have absolutely no question, and I shall say more about it later), both may be viewed as "natural phenomena" and studied in the same manner. If knowledge about our social surroundings is gained by processes entirely different from those by which we gain knowledge of our physical surroundings, then as empirical scientists we are in bad shape.

I assume that in both cases the processes through which we gain knowledge about the phenomena reside in the first instance in a skill which may be developed over time to a stage called scientific knowledge. Viewed in this way, it is of the first importance in respect to social skill to underscore its intrinsic character, as I did when I said (a technical) skill is an intrinsic way of learning about the phenomena, not an extrinsic technique by which they can be controlled. If skill is viewed as something to be applied externally to phenomena (a technique) instead of a way of learning about them, it becomes manipulative in a pejorative sense. On the other hand, if skill is a way of learning about the phenomena instead of something to be applied to them externally, the meaning of manipulation needs renovation.

By social skill I mean the way any Tom, Dick, and Harry learn about themselves and their relations to each other and by so doing improve their understanding of themselves and their relations to each other. Social skill involves a capacity for being able to modify or change one's perceptions of others as well as a capacity to respond to these altered perceptions. In this process of seeking to improve one's responses to others, I see nothing sinister, bad, or manipulative.

As I have said, I view skill as a unitary and organic phenomenon; that is why I use the word in the singular. To break it down into separate and discrete skills does extreme violence to the way I understand skillful behavior. In the case of social skill it violates its intrinsic character. It violates the organized system of capacity for response—a response that is adequate to a given point in a given situation. By a given point I mean a point of interaction with another person; by a given situation I mean the ideas and feelings of the other person as well as the kind of relationship the responder has to him; by "adequate response" I mean that the desired communication to the other person is achieved; that is, the other person hears the ideas and feelings which the respondent intends to convey.

In these statements I am being too analytical. These distinctions are not explicit at the beginning in the practice of social skill. They are things that a person gradually learns as he becomes involved in a greater complexity of relations with others; that is, as he develops through time from relating to his parents in the family; to his peers at play; to his teachers at school; to his boss, colleagues, and subordinates at work; to his wife in procreation; and to his children and grandchildren as they are born and grow up. In this development I assume that social skill resides in *an ever-improving capacity to communicate feelings and ideas to another as well as to respond to the feelings and ideas of another in such a manner as to promote better understanding between them.*

I assume that in respect to learning about social phenomena, about which there is a great deal of knowledge of acquaintance, some people are more skillful than others. Much has been said and written about these phenomena in literary, poetical, evangelical, and practical forms. Uniformities have been observed in them and have been stated in maxims and proverbs, such as: "You scratch my back and I'll scratch yours"; "You can't eat your cake and have it too"; "To each his own"; "Whosoever hath, to him it shall be given"; "A stitch in time saves nine"; *"Noblesse oblige"*; *"Plus ça change, plus c'est la même chose"*; "Absence makes the heart grow fonder"; "Out of sight, out of mind"; "When in Rome, do as the Romans do"; "To thine own self be true"; "If the student hasn't learned, the teacher hasn't taught"; "If you're not part of the solution, you are part of the problem"; and so on and on.

These proverbs and maxims are far from being scientific propositions. They do not add up to any organic unity or coherent conceptual system. More often than not, there are inconsistencies among them. They do not appear in the form of "under certain circumstances" or "other things being equal" or "in our culture absence makes the heart grow fonder," for example. But in spite of these serious deficiencies as knowledge, for the most part they remain unchallenged. Only occasionally does someone say "Says who?" about them. In spite of their limitations from a scientific point of view, we accept them as part of the social chaos in which we live and about which we have some intimate, intuitive familiarity.

A socially skillful person is intuitively aware of these limitations and discriminates roughly among the situations to which the maxim may or may not be usefully applied. He does not get uptight, or to state it more elegantly, suffer from cognitive dissonance, when on one occasion someone says, "When in Rome do as the Romans do, and on another, "To thine own self be true." Only a nut of a very peculiar kind would want to bring order out of this familiar chaos. But alas, this was the kind of nuttery in which I became involved, and I thought that the socially acceptable word for what I was up to was "science." What a nut I was! Be that as it may, I feel and feel strongly that if we do not produce order out of this familiar chaos, as empirical scientists we are licked, *finis, kaput.* How can this spectacular transformation be accomplished?

When I am as uptight about something as I am about this, I find that a distinction helps. Let me return to the distinction I make between technical and social skill. Obviously these skills are addressed to quite different phenomena—to quite different entities and relations. Probably the most important difference concerns the role of words and language. In the realm of technical skill, whether the practitioner is skillful or not, the phenomena do not hurl words back at him: they do not object to the words he uses. A maple tree does not say, "I do not like to be called a maple tree." Nor is the technically skillful person hard put to it to explain his concept of a maple tree. He points to it. He does not know what makes a maple leaf a maple leaf and can only stutter, "This is a maple leaf because it comes from a maple tree"—a very poor explanation indeed, scientifically speaking. Still he sits in clover as compared with the situation of the person who uses words and concepts in relating to social phenomena.

In the case of social skill, not only are the phenomena capable of talking back, but they sometimes do, and not in polite· terms. In addition, the practitioner often has difficulty in pointing to the phenomena to which he wishes his words to refer and in differentiating between the words and the phenomena. He has what may be called a "map-territory bind," in which he is sometimes not sure what is map and what is territory. For example, the feelings and sentiments he and his relevant others have—which to me are the phenomena or territory and not words—are often expressed in words. This makes for no end of trouble. So far as I know, no effective rules of procedure have been developed and tested for interpreting what people say that are comparable to the effective rules of procedure that have been developed and tested for dealing with the phenomena of the physical sciences.

The trouble is that words are used for purposes of influencing behavior as well as for describing it. One has only to look at the language being used today to see that this is so. By 1970, when engagement rather than analysis became the social style of the day, the emotional use of language was clear and loud and sometimes even uncouth: for example, "Tell it like it is, man." "Swing it, baby." "Your penis envy is showing, sister." "Don't get uptight and fucked up, brother." "Do your thing, man." "Black is beautiful." "Get involved." "Confront." "Be authentic." "Express your negative feelings." "Rather than conform to the 'power structure' or 'establishment' cop out, drop out, freak out, or go out and out for force and violence." "Don't be a racist or male chauvinist." "Take a gut trip, not a head trip, baby." "Cut out the bullshit, man!"

Behavioral scientists, as well as administrators, private, public, and educational, had difficulty interpreting what such provocative and imprecise language meant. Amazing! Truly! Many different theories were proposed to account for it, namely, for example, alienation, anomie, an identity crisis, a generation gap, a breakdown in communication, a breakdown in law and order, a radical minority, the silent majority, a radical change in social norms and values, too much permissiveness and participation, and so on. We were living, the authorities said, in an affluent society, a temporary society, an outworn established society, a yet-to-be achieved adaptive society, a revolutionary society, a technological society, a great society, a go, no-go computerized society, a go-go swinging society, an urban society, a suburban society, a professional society, an industrial society, a bureaucratic grey-flannel-suit society. Need I go further to show that the interpretation of what people say is a difficult business? But I fear I am rambling, and of all things to a macroscopic level; let me return to the microscopic level, where skill resides.

At that level the socially skillful person addresses himself at a point of interaction to the properties of persons which I call feelings and sentiments in the same sense as a technically skillful woodcarver addresses himself to the physical properties of wood. In the same sense I assume that the phenomena of these respective entities allow themselves to be or are controlled and manipulated and influenced by persons who attend to their properties rather than by persons who do not. I assume that there is a great deal of intuitive knowledge about how to make friends, influence people, gain power over them, and persuade them to do what they ought to do or what you want them to do. This knowledge has all the limitations I previously mentioned. It does not specify clearly the limits or conditions under which A can influence, manipulate, or control B or under which B can be influenced, manipulated, or controlled by A. As a result, this intuitive knowledge contains possibilities of resulting in misunderstandings as well as understandings. Statements that say only how A can manipulate, influence, and control B without also saying under what conditions B can be manipulated, influenced, and controlled by A seem to me simplistic and dangerous. In fact, without making such distinctions, social skill is on the road to becoming a technique. Thus I restrict the words social skill to mean a skill of communication which includes not only the capacity to communicate feelings and ideas to another, but also the "capacity to receive communication from others and to respond to the feelings and ideas of others in such a fashion as to promote congenial participation in a common task" (Mayo, 1945).

This capacity for two-way communication in the setting of an organized task is for me the highest manifestation of social skill. The skill is not addressed to what the phenomena ought to be. Rather it is addressed to the phenomena as they are, but also as they might be if one wishes to improve his relations to them. The skill is to be exercised in organized work settings, not merely at parties. Without this latter condition it might not be practiced responsibly. I feel responsibility makes the cheese—I mean the social skill—more binding. One uses words in a responsible manner, under the burden of responsibility.

Social skill, in the way I delineate it, is in one sense rare, but in another common. It is rare, because it is not as commonly recognized as technical skill and its outcomes are not as highly visible. It is common in the sense that without it much of the work of the world cannot and would not get done.

THE RELATION BETWEEN THEORY AND PRACTICE

Throughout my professional life, I have thought that the social sciences or the science of human behavior in organizations could develop from social skill in the way I have been describing. In my trip to higher knowledge concerning the phenomena of human behavior I feel I need a point of departure as well as a point of return. Social skill gives me both. I do not want to go to the moon, so to speak, and not be able to get back. I think whatever higher knowledge may be achieved about the phenomena of human behavior will be in the direction of illuminating skill, not destroying it. It will break through skill, not break with it.

I assume that a little theory has to be added to the behavior of my intuitive socially skillful person in order to get him out of the frozen condition he is in, to allow him to develop and go to the moon, metaphorically speaking, yet not so much theory that he will be left stranded, unable to communicate with his fellow men on planet earth.

Even back in 1927, when I joined Mayo—before the atomic bomb, the missile, and the computer—technical skill was zooming into technical knowledge at a rapid rate. Meanwhile, social skill, like Cinderella, sat at the kitchen stove waiting for her Prince Charming to come along to give her the little recognition and also the little love and support that she needed badly—and I do not mean maybe.

If you are confused by the different roles in which my adventures in the realm of human behavior place me—Sir Galahad, Don Quixote, Sancho Panza, Simple Simon, and Prince Charming—please forgive me. I can only say in my defense that I think the phenomena are complex and that more than one role is needed to get them to reveal themselves. However, if you wish to interpret these different roles as manifestations of my confusion, I will buy that. If you think by this new role I want to go to bed with Cindy, you are not far off the track. Let's not quarrel about words. I confess I love Cindy.

What I am saying is that even back in 1927 there was an imbalance between the development of technical and social skill. One was zooming at an increasingly rapid rate, while the other was hung up, fucked up, balled up, not going places. To put it in more respectable language, there was a close relation between theory and practice in the development of technical knowledge which did not exist in respect to the development of social knowledge.

According to L. J. Henderson, both theory and practice are necessary conditions for the acquisition of knowledge. Theory without practice is metaphysics; practice without theory cannot get off the ground. Only a method which judiciously combines them succeeds widely and generally and is the road to success. This statement, Henderson asserted in his lectures in Sociology 23, is an induction from experience, a phrase he often used when he asserted a statement the test of which depends on its accord with experience, i.e., depends on observation and experiment. It therefore, unlike a definition, is not a statement that within limits is arbitrary and the test of which is convenience. When experimental evidence is lacking for inductions from experience, Henderson sometime appealed to "authority." For this one he quoted passages from Aristotle's *Nicomachean Ethics,* the gist of which was that there are essentially two kinds of "professional" persons: (1) those who practice but do not teach what they practice and (2) those who teach but do not practice what they teach. Between these two—men of action and men of thought—there is little communication and neither one gets far alone.

According to Henderson, among the sciences relating to man, medicine has progressed the furthest because there has been a close relation between those who teach and those who practice; in the social sciences this has not often been the case. For example, those in the universities who teach government and economics do not ususally practice what they teach, whereas the politicians and businessmen who run public and private organizations do not usually teach what they practice. For Henderson this little difference that makes a big difference was why medicine progressed and the social sciences stood still—why what Aristotle said about politics two thousand years ago makes sense to us now, whereas what Aristotle said then about physics or medicine sounds to us now like rubbish. So when it came to practitioners the difference that interested Henderson was between those who practiced with a theory and those who practiced without one.

Henderson also saw a difference between the kind of theory used by those who practiced with one and the kind of theory discussed by persons who did not practice what they theorized about. What was this difference? Well, you guessed it; the former used a conceptual scheme, a simple walking-stick that helped them improve their practice. Before I consider further the nature of this walking-stick in the next chapter, I want to consider some of the bugs that my notion of skill, particularly social skill, has.

SOCIAL SKILL AND SOCIAL PHENOMENA

The word "skill" is used so often in an extrinsic sense that I find it almost impossible to communicate the intrinsic properties I think it has. In the case of technical skill, this does not make much difference; not so with social skill, in respect to which the intrinsic properties are of the essence. For a while I dropped the term "social skill," though I never stopped considering the kind of relation between a practitioner and phenomena in reference to which I use the term.

The examples I have used show that I restrict the meaning of skill to dealing with and learning about natural phenomena—not to dealing with artifacts, bits of second-hand information, and high-level abstractions. These latter are the skills, or more accurately speaking, the techniques, with which the modern world is mostly concerned. These techniques of dealing with second-hand information have so supplanted the skill of dealing with natural phenomena that the latter seems to be on the road to disappearing altogether. The technology of milking a cow, to cite an example, has so replaced the skill of milking a cow that only a few people are left who can milk a cow by hand. Nevertheless, the skill of milking a cow the hard way and the first-hand knowledge thus derived have to precede methods of milking a cow more easily. I think this fact should not be ignored and forgotten.

Even before the eighteenth century, when it is claimed the industrial revolution was born, there existed a great deal of technical knowledge in the form of tools and machines, such as water mills, windmills, plows, looms, and potters' wheels. Much was known about the domestication of animals, about mining, metallurgy, dyeing, and glass blowing. Building the Gothic cathedrals required great technical skill and the solution of difficult technical problems without the aid of modern scientific knowledge. It occurred before the disciplines of physics, chemistry, and mechanics existed as we know them today.

However, before the eighteenth century the distinction I make between technical and social skill would not have made much sense. Before then they developed hand in hand; they had not become divorced from such each other. Technical skill in medieval times was utilized not only for achieving utilitarian ends, but also for expressing man's deepest subjective feelings, emotions, and sentiments. A towering cathedral was not built as an urban renewal project, but for the glory of God; it was as close to Heaven as any earthbound structure could get.

So far, in this chapter I have not specified the social ends (good or bad) for which technical skill may be utilized. I have been conspicuously silent about whether technical skill was or could have been utilized in earlier times for the glory of God or of some king or for engaging in some crusade; or in the case of modern times, for the profits of some corporation, for the making of weapons of destruction, for making man like a machine, for making a machine like a man, or for going to the moon. I was not unaware of these possible uses and misuses of technical skill, nor was I unconcerned about the difference between the labor-loving aspects of technical skill in the Middle Ages and its labor-saving aspects in modern times. In fact, much of my concern about giving social skill more love and attention arises from having noted this difference. What has dictated my silence is that I did not want to jump the gun and soar to higher levels of abstraction before I have skill well grounded at a point of interaction in a concrete situation, in the here-and-now phenomena with which it deals. Let me elaborate on this.

First, I wish to get the intrinsic here-and-now ends and not the extrinsic there-and-then ends of skill from the right way up. By intrinsic here-and-now ends, I mean the sense of satisfaction, mastery, and achievement that a skillful practitioner gains from the practice of his skill. These are why I think the cobbler—the metaphor gets too mixed if I say cheese maker—sticks to his last and does not become engaged in the ideologies of shoemaking.

Second, skill cannot be practiced in the there-and-then. Although I can talk about skill as it is practiced at some particular place and period of time, there-and-then that place and time were a here-and-now. You can see I am a here-and-now baby and no historian, except in a special sense, which I will explain later.

Third, and perhaps most important, I think that the natural phenomena from which science and technology developed slowly and gradually over a long period of time reside in the here-and-now and not in the there-and-then. To be sure, the outburst of science and technology which occurred in the eighteenth century required a new twist or ingredient. Nevertheless, it is doubtful if it could have occurred at all, if the technological developments of the Middle Ages had not taken place. The one had to precede the other, just as milkmaids had to learn to milk cows before milking machines could be developed.

I have already noted that no comparable development has taken place in respect to social knowledge. I assume that this is so because it has not been well grounded in a here-and-now social skill. This, I gradually learned, is because the phenomena to which this skill is addressed are more elusive and difficult to specify than the phenomena to which technical skill is addressed. Although skill is not verbal and no verbal statement about it can act as a substitute for it, yet social skill, more than technical skill, involves the use of words. Moreover, although social skill is a skill of communication, it is not a verbal skill of dealing articulately and sophisticatedly with words. It is the judicious and responsible use of words that are relevant to particular situations. This means that a socially skillful person can be and often is not only verbally inarticulate, but also sometimes verbally dumb or even stupid, but this deficiency does not make him a dummy. Far from it, it often makes him wiser than his more verbally articulate fellow man, for it often results in the words he uses being more pertinent to the situations he addresses than the words his more verbally oriented colleague uses in his situations.

Chester Barnard said that some of the brainiest and most competent and capable men he knew had been almost inarticulate. "Not what they could say but what they did showed the power of their minds." Some of the most competent counselors and psychiatrists I know are almost verbally inarticulate in their clinical interviews; and vice versa, some of the least competent are the most articulate.

I think even Freud may have been a bit verbally inarticulate, when he was trying to get his patients to reveal their secrets. Though I have no tape recording to prove this, I am confident in what I say, not because I say so, but because the phenomena, with which I have some intimate intuitive familiarity, say so. Of course Freud could also be verbally articulate, as his books well demonstrate; this contributed to his being the great genius he unquestionably was. But I insist, the verbally articulate skill Freud used in writing his books was not the skill he practiced in his clinic.

I hope it is clear by now that by skill I mean something to be practiced and not just talked about. Skill is not so much applying knowledge as it is *practicing* a point of view toward the phenomena from which knowledge may be gained. For me skill and practice go hand-in-hand; I often use the words synonymously. My notion of practice does not always coincide with the notion of "business practices," as the term is used by businessmen and my colleagues at the B-School. They use the term to refer to the organizationally required ways (rules, regulations, procedures, policies, standards, control systems, programs, and so on) by which certain things are supposed to be done and certain problems are supposed to be dealt with. These are "practices" for them; for me they are abstracted operations which have no skill in them, until they are applied in the here-and-now by someone to somebody in a concrete situation.

Only when somebody or something in an organization deviates from some rule or standard; only when someone feels he has to do something about it; and then only when he says and does something to somebody about it; then and only then, as I see it, does skill come into play. Not the standard or rule by itself, but the way in which it is implemented, administered, and applied by, for example, a supervisor in a particular situation having to do with concrete persons, brings into being the phenomena and the practice with which I am concerned.

Before a rule or standard has been applied there are for me no concrete phenomena to observe, no skill to be practiced. There is only an abstraction—a rule or standard whose properties of truth, goodness, justice, utility, or beauty in the abstract one can contemplate and about which people can and often do argue. But this is not for me. I do not see how one can practice by itself a rule or regulation or standard or policy. Nor do I see how a rule can apply itself; someone has to apply it. So until the bloody rule is implemented, I do not have anything to do with it. Only when it is implemented can I observe what I am calling social phenomena, about which I think I can make first-hand empirical observations and judgments. If I have a hard time talking about skill by means of words, the difficulty becomes even greater when I use words to try to talk about social phenomena. The latter are not words—no siree! Instead, anything I say about them is what they are not! This bind is not my personal bind; it is a bind in which I think the modern world is badly balled up.

Phenomenon in Greek means "that which reveals itself." Being a phenomenologist means for me letting the thing speak for itself. For example, if without touching the ash tray which sits at the edge of my desk I quickly remove the support of the desk, the ash tray falls to the floor. I did not actually push it there. It went there, in a manner of speaking, of its own accord. In this sense my ash tray reveals itself to me by its action when I no longer provide it with the support of my desk. Thus for me, that which reveals itself when I remove some of its constraints without coercing it or putting it in some conceptual strait-jacket is a natural phenomenon; and believe me, baby, that phenomenon is not a word, although I need words to talk about it.

This way of thinking about phenomena is more easily illustrated with physical than with social phenomena, because society is more man-made than, for example, a tree. As has been said, only God can make a tree. Although it can be said in the same sense that only God can make a man, only a nut could believe that God made society. Therefore, I assume that when man fell in disgrace from the Garden of Eden, God left the job of creating a society or civilization for man to do. What a good or a crummy job man made of it was no longer His responsibility. This was the job with which I felt I could be legitimately and without arrogance concerned.

My first startling, Eureka-kind of experience with natural phenomena in the social realm was probably with what has come to be called the "Hawthorne effect." In the Relay Assembly Test Room when the supervisor was replaced by an observer—that is, when one of the customary constraints in the work situation was removed—by golly, the five employees began to speak for themselves. Output rose and continued to rise, even when the better physical conditions of work they had been given were taken away. This so baffled management, it will be remembered, that they brought in Mayo to explain what had happened. They were so accustomed to thinking they controlled the phenomena that it was unthinkable for them to believe that if they took their man-made and God-damned controls away, the phenomena might speak for themselves and even control themselves. It was even more surprising that the phenomena might move in the direction that management wanted them to move!

For me Freud's great genius was that he allowed the phenomena to speak for themselves before he theorized about them. He went to such ridiculous extremes to get the phenomena to speak for themselves that many people thought he was a nut. If you can believe this now, he put people flat on their backs and removed the constraints of their daytime activities to get the phenomena—their preoccupation and dreams—to speak for themselves. What a nut, and what a genius! What the phenomena revealed under these screwy conditions shook the foundations of psychology in a way from which it has not even now completely recovered.

What I mean by phenomena in the social realm are not the artifacts of society, but the processes which produce them. I eschew the artifacts; they are constrained by so many conceptual straitjackets that the phenomena cannot speak for themselves and reveal their intrinsic nature in the way my ash tray did when it fell to the floor after I removed the support of my desk.

I think natural social phenomena reside in man's interactions with his fellow man and in their associated sentiments and feelings. I think the phenomena may speak for themselves and reveal their hidden secrets, if I have ears to hear them, in what takes place in that fateful encounter between A and B. Even in this simple situation this revelation takes a bit of doing, as I explained in Chapter 12 when I talked about interpersonal communication. As I listen to another person in a counseling relationship for what he wants to tell me and what he does not want to tell me and what he cannot tell me without my help, I do not coax, wheedle, or threaten the person to come clean. My interventions are in the direction of trying to remove constraints imposed by my behavior which prevent him from telling me what is important to him. The latter are the phenomena I want to understand and hopefully in time explain. The socially skillful person as I think of him deals with exactly the same phenomena in an intuitive and perhaps unconscious way.

Still, as I found out, there is a big difference between intuitive social skill and what I am up to. The more I try to get social phenomena to speak for themselves in the manner I describe, the more I seem to become some kind of nut and the less I am an ordinary social human being who can freely interact with my fellow man in a human way. The practice of this new communication skill seems to be in some respects at variance with intuitive social skill.

It looks paradoxically as if social knowledge, instead of helping to improve social skill and learning, on the contrary impedes its development. In the social realm it seems as if the more knowledge we have, the less our learning and the more one becomes an educated fool and loses his horse sense or, should I say, social skill. The more sophisticated the social diagnoses grow, the less they can be implemented. The more I try to extensionalize or professionalize the helping relation, the less helpful I become. Something is screwy. How can these things be?

What I have come to think is that we are asking the kind of statements or propositions about human behavior that we make at the level of intuitive social skill to do things for us which inherently they cannot do. In our rush to find general propositions, we regard statements about experiences with specific situations as the general propositions which we seek; but *they are not*. To explain what I mean, I need to move a rung up the ladder of abstraction and talk about the nature of clinical knowledge, which I assume is a stage through which the social sciences have to go before they can achieve the status of being truly scientific fields of knowledge with subject matters and disciplines of their own.

Chapter 21

Clinical Knowledge

At the clinical stage of the knowledge enterprise, as I see it, first-hand observations reign supreme. Rigorous definitions, measurements, hypotheses, and propositions are not the first order of the day. They are present, to be sure, but in rudimentary form. Definitions are nonoperational, measurements are not objective, and hypotheses are in the form of questions to the effect of what is going on in a particular situation. Findings are not strict propositions about how x varies with y. Rather they are of the character that under certain conditions x and y seem to appear together.

At this level of knowledge the prescriptive propositions of common sense take on a somewhat more precise and descriptive form. "When in Rome do as the Romans do" is now stated in the form that people in general tend to conform to the norms of the group with which they are associated, to which they wish to belong, or with which they wish to do business. More general propositions explaining why people tend to conform to these norms as well as sometimes to deviate from them simply do not exist. From the point of view of the clinician only a nut would ask such questions. For the clinician the answer is so obvious that it does not need to be stated; but one does not get very far up the knowledge tree without stating the obvious precisely.

Viewed from the top of the scientific knowledge enterprise, after arrival there, this level of clinical knowledge sounds like prescientific baby talk—as indeed it is. But let us remember that the social sciences, by any criteria we care to mention, have not arrived at the top yet, so these derogatory noises may be premature. To correct for this error, I want to look at clinical knowledge from the bottom up, not from the top down; that is, I wish to look at clinical knowledge from the point of view of intuitive skill, from which I think it can be derived. Let us see from this point of view what a giant first step it is.

Regarded from this point of view, the implicit conceptual schemes of common sense used in intuitive skill become at the level of clinical knowledge explicitly and simply stated. Stating these formerly implicit conceptual schemes helps in turn to make explicit the limited class or aspects of the phenomena or problems that the person is going to observe and talk about. Obviously before anyone can say anything at all precise about the phenomena, he has to know exactly about what phenomena he is talking. This, we shall see in a moment, is not so simple to ascertain as we would like to believe.

CLASSIFYING PHENOMENA: NATURAL SOCIAL SYSTEMS

In the beginning stages of the development of many sciences the early conceptual schemes are in the form of taxonomies. Although the intuitively skillful person is a bit of a taxonomist, he does not go heavily into classifying things and living beings in terms of different shapes and structures. He can distinguish a cat from a mouse without knowing where each would be placed in the animal kingdom. But once he decides to find out, he begins by observing the multitude of animals and plants on the earth and by giving them names and arranging them in some kind of order. That is, he goes first into the field and observes (not into the library to read) in order to find out how plants and animals can be classified according to certain criteria. In this manner, he finds out and later, from books in school, others including myself can find out, that there are about 1,000,000 known species of animals and about 350,000 known species of plants, living together on this planet earth.

This information does not exactly "send me," because in the first place I am not interested in observing the flora and fauna about me. Secondly, I feel that these taxonomic systems, if elaborated obsessively, are neither useful nor conceptually elegant, even though I have a great deal of respect for the patient and careful observation that went into their construction. It seems to me that the skill exercised by the taxonomist for identifying species, for example, often degenerates into a skill of putting living things into categories according to certain criteria and stopping there. After a taxonomist has identified a new species of bedbug, for example, and exulted in his discovery, his curiosity often seems to me to cease. It is as though once he has the bedbug pinned down in its proper place in the animal kingdom, he does not want to say anything more about it.

Sometimes a taxonomist gets such a kick from his skill of identifying things that the question can be raised whether the criteria by which he classifies a species are more artificial than natural and whether he is indulging in some subjective whimsy. It can look as though what constitutes a species depends on how good a connoisseur of them the taxonomist is in the same sense that a good book depends on how good the author is. As one might suspect, "objective science" does not like such subjective tautological statements.

Thus, to make a long story short, after the taxonomists arrange the animals and vegetables according to certain criteria in their respective kingdoms and in some hierarchical order of classes, orders, families, genera, and species, and then glory in the multifarious forms in which Nature appears, it becomes clear—at least to some botanists, zoologists, and biologists—that they are not getting higher on the knowledge ladder that way. By seeking only this kind of knowing, the scientific enterprise grinds to a halt, and the practice of a skill by which one can cope with the hippopotamuses, mushrooms, woodpeckers, bees, bats, and butterflies in one's environment comes to a dead end.

I am overstating my case. After the taxonomists give all the flora and fauna a name and put them in their proper places in the vegetable and animal kingdoms, they can, if they wish, observe the species again to see what other properties they have besides those that put them in their proper class, order, family, and so forth. For example, they can begin to look at a particular species or family of ants and observe how they live and cope with their environment, what food they eat, what other bugs or animals they are eaten by, and so on. In short, by means of the concept of a species the taxonomists can isolate classes of a natural kind about each of which further observations can be made. This is no mean achievement, as we shall see when we look at how social scientists have gone about the same task with respect to the kind of phenomena they study.

I am far from pooh-poohing classifications. I assume that all knowledge starts there. But I also assume that some classifications are more fruitful than others for purposes of investigation and discovery. Depending upon one's interests and purposes, one can classify anything any way one damn pleases. One can make, for example, a class of all the redheaded women at the B-School. The only trouble with this kind of class, it seems to me, is that one cannot say much more about it than that it contains the entities that have the properties by which one made it a class in the first place. It has little oomph and is as limp as a wet dishrag.

The knowledge seeker seems to me to be searching for a class of things about which he can make further observations and truthful generalizations. If he is to climb the knowledge ladder, he cannot stay at the level of giving names to things: he cannot remain a dictionary maker. He has to begin to make statements about the things to which he has given names; he has to stick his neck out and write sentences and make propositions about phenomena with which his colleagues can disagree. Ouch!

So finally after the taxonomist has discovered some 1,000,000 species of animals and after he has ceased speculating about whether or how Noah was able to get them all in his Ark, he has to go back into the field again to try to make some new observations about a species from which he can make some empirically true statements. In my terminology he has to become a clinician and to gèt some clinical knowledge about the phenomena he studies. He has to beard the wolf in his den, so to speak, and find out if he is as "wolfish" as folklore holds him to be.

Thus I believe that a fruitful conceptual scheme in the early stages of the knowledge enterprise is something different from a full-blown classification scheme. It has to isolate first what I call, following Radcliffe-Brown (1957), a *class of a natural kind*. By this I mean a class which is created, not just by logical definition, but so as to allow further empirical observations to be made about it. Horses are such a class, but so also are such chemical substances as tin, gold, silver, and oxygen and such entities as persons, groups, and organizations.

Now I am jumping my hurdles too quickly again. Let me return to the nonhuman level, where fortunately matters are less sticky, conceptually speaking.

What makes a class of a natural kind important for science is not only that it consists of a set of entities with a set of common properties, but also that it can be conceived of as a natural system, something that exists in the intractable reality "out there." It is a natural system which can be conceptually isolated from the rest of the universe (the environment). It exists not only as a set of entities with a set of common properties but also as a set of entities with properties and relations of interconnectedness which make it a naturally cohering whole or unity. Being able to produce such natural systems I regard as a great leap forward in the knowledge enterprise. For this step means roughly, and to a first approximation, as Henderson would have said, that a natural system, for which the rest of the universe becomes the environment, can be produced in the here and now. Now the researchers or practitioner can say, "By God, I am going to look at the system's internal nature and observe the relations between its constituent elements. That is what I am going to observe and make intelligible statements about."

I will try not to wax too eloquent about this great step forward. It falls far short of being conceptually elegant, as can be seen by comparing a natural system with an abstract system of entities and relations. One can make a system of any specified set of entities and the relations that exist among them, but the empirical status of such a system is sometimes in question. In abstract systems composed of abstract entities and abstract relations, one does not need to worry about whether they have empirical reality, even though a useful empirical meaning can sometimes be given to them. Euclidean geometry is such a system. Composed of points, lines, and spatial relations, its conceptual beauty and grandeur is its self-consistency; that is, no propositions can be derived from Euclid's five postulates which contradict each other. Non-Euclidean geometries have the same property. In this respect they are equally conceptually elegant. The difference is that it is easier to assign useful empirical meanings to Euclidean space than to non-Euclidean spaces.

The natural systems I am talking about at this stage of the knowledge enterprise do not have this conceptual elegance. Although these systems are composed of entities and relations, the entities have empirical properties, and the relations among the entities are empirical relations. They cannot be stated in advance; they have to be observed before they can be stated.

In my early days I thought of social systems as being of this character. I thought of them as concerned with a class of phenomena that included all events and processes in which interactions between two or more persons occurred. This class of phenomena was for me a class of natural kind and worthy of scientific investigation. It could be conceived as a natural system composed of persons with properties and relations that formed a natural cohering whole. Once it was so conceived, the rest of the universe became its environment, and I could begin to observe more carefully the system's internal nature and the relations between its constituent elements.

This kind of conceptualization was not a full-blown scheme of classification. It merely stated what I would look at (the class of phenomena) and the kind of problems with which I would be concerned. Events that involved interactions between persons and problems in which such interactions could not be conveniently disregarded became, so to speak, my cup of tea (1920) or my bag (1970). This conceptualization also defined *how* I was going to look at this class of phenomena. I viewed them as natural systems. But it did not classify the properties of the persons or the components of the system, except to say that they had *sentiments and feelings*, as well as some logical properties. Although in one sense this said a lot, it said it very imprecisely. It did not state the kinds of relations that persons in the system had with one another, except to say they were "social." In time I found out that this too covered a lot of waterfront.

In spite of this looseness—nay, because of it—I thought this kind of conceptualization was a step in the right direction. It fenced in nobody and nothing definitively. It pointed to open natural concrete systems rather than to logically closed conceptual systems. The former were capable of further empirical investigation in a way that the second were not. The important property of conceptual systems was self-consistency; the important properties of natural systems were not matters of logic. I assumed that the properties were empirical in nature and had, at the widest level of generalization that could be made, the characteristics of a natural cohering whole, namely, the property of equilibrium. In short, I assumed that in the social system the persons in the system with their properties and relations were in some kind of equilibrium, such that when a change that was not too great was imposed upon the system, the system would remain in a steady state. Under such conditions the system would not fly apart and dissolve into its separate component parts.

THE CONCEPT OF EQUILIBRIUM

The assumption of equilibrium or homeostasis was not original with me. Many investigators had made it before, particularly those involved with living beings at the physiological level. It has a long history. When Hippocrates, for example, made the widest generalization about the acute diseases of his patients which he felt his observations allowed, he said, in effect, that as a rule sick people recover without treatment. This principle came to be known as the *vis medicatrix naturea*; that is, let nature take its course; nature is the doctor. This was a crude but nevertheless useful conceptualization, that the natural history of acute diseases and the state of health are in a condition of equilibrium.

The statement was far from being a clear and distinct analytical idea; it was not even an explicit conceptual scheme. Hippocrates did not state explicitly the constituent parts of the physiological system he had in mind nor the relations between them that held them in a state of equilibrium. In spite of these defects, his crude view of the physiological system worked well in improving the treatment of disease in his period. It endures today in the precept of "Do the least harm"—a precept that still has utility in the practice of medicine as well as in the practice of politics and administration. Please note that it is not the precept of a do-gooder or of a reformer, but a generalization that derives from wide intuitive knowledge based on the responsible practice of a skill in concrete situations.

Although the definition of equilibrium as used by modern science has undergone much refinement since the days of Hippocrates, it seems to me that it still comes to much the same thing—a notion that a state of equilibrium is a condition of forces such that a slight modification leaves the forces substantially intact, so that they tend to reestablish the state that would have existed if the modification had not occurred. After I have gone to bed at night, for example, the depression I made by my weight on the box springs is restored when I get up in the morning. Similarly, the habits, routines, and sentiments which govern my everyday life seem to remain intact and tend to reestablish themselves after a modification, such as a hurricane, has brought about a few days of inconvenience (no electricity, telephone, etc.). Then my silly old academic ivory tower self reestablishes itself as if this peak experience (the hurricane) had not occurred.

The definition of equilibrium is not strictly operational. One cannot specify clearly when the system is in equilibrium or what makes a modification not too great. However, it has helped me to see that in many cases, for example, after a management has introduced a cost-reduction program, an improvement in the desired direction will take place for a limited period but then gradually, as time goes on, things return to their former state. It is as if the cost-reduction program does not touch the mainsprings of action, so that forces tend to reestablish the state that would have existed if the program had not been introduced. I could also see that this return to the former state did not always happen.

Let's face it; the notion of equilibrium is not a very clear idea. It is an induction from experience, not a creation of logic. It therefore suffers from the nonlogical limitations from which all inductions from experience suffer. Nevertheless, if one is trying to lift himself up the ladder of abstraction by his bootstraps instead of deducing himself down from a given set of axioms, such an idea is of great help. This is the way I think about the concept of equilibrium as applied to organizational phenomena. It helps, but there are problems.

These problems arise because the intractable reality "out there" does not seem to be all of a piece. Something needs to be differentiated from something else, yet not so sharply that the differentiated parts cannot be conceived as integrated parts of a system. Wow, this is one big headache!

Whether I am thinking about a person, a small group, or an organization as a natural system, the processes by which the state of equilibrium is maintained are exceedingly complex and difficult to identify. Three different kinds of relations to which the word "equilibrium" may be applied seem to be involved: the relations of the system to its environment; the relations among the components of the internal system; and the relations between the external and internal systems. For me the processes by which the system maintains an *adjustment* with its external environment are not the same as the processes by which the *integration* of the internal system is maintained. Nor are they the same as the processes by which these two seemingly opposing forces are kept together in some state of *adaptation*.

The distinction among these three kinds of equilibria appears over and over in some way or another in the literature of the behavioral sciences. Anyone who is trying to think systematically about phenomena, whether the system he is addressing is a person, a two-person relationship, a small group, an organization, or a society, becomes involved in them and has problems in stating them clearly. The first two do not present any great difficulty. It is the third kind of equilibrium—the resolution of the dichotomy set up by the external and internal systems—that presents problems of conceptualization. It is riddled with paradoxes and dilemmas which are difficult to resolve systematically. They are often settled by kaleidoscopic shifts, flip-flop twists, and nuances of meaning that fascinate me. The literature is filled with these twisteroos. One school of thought uses them to claim it has gotten itself out of the box or dilemma that it believes a rival school is in. To me these attempts seem more like shifts in metaphor rather than basic shifts in conceptualization.

EXTERNAL AND INTERNAL SYSTEMS

Let me explain what I mean by looking at the dichotomy which the first two kinds of equilibria set up. George Homans has said that I am a past master at setting up this dichotomy. Let us look at some of the many forms it takes, some of the forms being ones stated by me, some by others.

The dichotomy appears in the distinction between formal and informal organization; that is, the system of the activities of people as they are differentiated and consciously coordinated to achieve the purpose of an organization (the external system), and the system of social norms and values by which the individuals or groups are informally differentiated and integrated (the internal system). It seems to me that this is a useful distinction to make, so long as one does not make a false dichotomy of it. Formal and informal organization are not two clearly separate and unrelated sets of phenomena. At the same time, one cannot be reduced to the other. Formal organization can emerge from informal organization; informal organization can also emerge from formal organization. Their relation to each other is not that of one being "better" or more "important" than the other. There is a distinction between the two that cannot be eliminated, but the differentiation can be made either too sharp or it can be blurred. In either case there seem to be unfortunate consequences for practice as well as for research.

The distinction which Chester Barnard makes between "effective" and "efficient," which I used in Chapter 10 and which he applies to both the individual and the organization, seems to be of a similar character. In the long run, Barnard says, an organization has to be *both* effective and efficient. It has to be effective, that is, achieve its purpose (the requirements of the external system), and also it has to be efficient, that is, satisfy the needs of people (the requirements of the internal system), so that they will willingly contribute their services to the organizational purpose. The two are not clearly separate and unrelated. One cannot be reduced to the other; neither is one more important than the other. In a curious way both the actual and desired relation between the two is that they be in some state of equilibrium.

The distinction which George Homans makes between (1) the required or planned activities and interactions of the group (what he calls the external system) and (2) the emergent activities, interactions, and sentiments of the group (for him the internal system) is of a similar character. Both these phenomena are present in a group, not as two separate and exhaustive subsets of the system, but as mutually dependent consequences of the other which exist together in some kind of practical working equilibrium.

The distinction appears also in T-groups, as I reported in Chapter 13. Here it manifests itself in the form of task roles versus maintenance roles; that is, those roles the group needs for the achievement of its task (the external system) and those roles it requires to maintain its cohesiveness (the internal system). Again the group needs both roles. As I stated, the member of the group who meets these needs best at a given time becomes its leader at that time.

Although these distinctions help a group member to fix his attention on group process, they blur another distinction that it is important to make, the distinction between individual needs and group needs. Surely the needs of an individual are not of the same order as the needs of a group. Using the same word, needs, for such different phenomena seems to me to blur a distinction that it is important to maintain without making it into a false dichotomy. An action that may be functional for the cohesiveness of the group may not be functional for the needs of the individual and vice versa, though the two can also work together. Here again, it seems to me, it is useful to distinguish between the requirements placed on the group externally and the internal needs of the people in the system. The two need to be differentiated, not as opposing forces, but as mutually dependent ones that maintain themselves over a period of time in some state of equilibrium.

However expressed, these distinctions between the external and internal systems seem important for purposes of investigating and understanding the behavior of people in organizations. In and by themselves they are not false dichotomies, but they can be made false by pseudo-logical elaboration. The gist of my communication to my students about them was often to this effect:

(1) Do not confuse or equate the needs of individuals with the needs of groups, individual goals with organizational goals, formal organizations with informal organizations, planned behavior with emergent behavior, or an external evaluation (effective) with an internal evaluation (efficient).

(2) The two parts of each of these distinctions need to be differentiated before they can be related. But please do not relate them in any of the following ways:

    (a) Do not bifurcate them into two separate and distinct domains.

    (b) Do not reduce one to the other.

    (c) Do not arrange them in some value hierarchy.

    (d) Do not look for logical relations between them.

(3) Instead, look for the processes that keep them or fail to keep them empirically related in some state of working equilibrium.

If in my lectures to my students I made statements of the above kind once, I must have made them thousands of times and without much avail. So let me dig deeper into why these two seemingly opposing forces appear again and again in the literature and why their resolution seems to acquire metaphorical rather than analytical language. Let us look at the different kinds of entities and relations with which the two systems are populated.

The difference is perhaps most conspicous at the level of what I will for the moment call "ouches." In the external system of an economic organization the ouches are frequently stated in terms of: "We have to make a profit, if we are going to survive, don't we? We've got to reduce costs, if we are going to meet our competitive situation, don't we? We've got to have a little law and order around here, don't we? We can't have everyone doing his own thing, can we? We have to have some rules and standards, so that people will know what is expected of them, don't we?"

In the internal system, on the other hand, the ouches are often expressed like this: "Don't you see, brother, whose toes you are treading on, whose neck you are breathing down, whose meaningful ways of doing things you are disrupting? Well, if you don't see this, brother, let me tell it to you like it is. It's *my* toes you are treading on, *my* neck you are breathing down, *my* values you are ignoring. Get it?"

In the external system the activities of people are differentiated and coordinated. In the internal system the people themselves are differentiated and integrated. As a result, what is functional in the external system is not commensurate with what is functional in the internal system. The word function does not mean the same thing in both cases.

Applied to the external system, "functional" means that the activity is necessary for achieving the purposes of the organization and thus for the survival of the system; applied to the internal system, it means that the activity is rewarding to the individuals in the system. Of course I could have said that the survival of the system is more rewarding to the owners, financial investors, and managers than it is to the workers. If I had, I would have been using functional in the same sense externally and internally. If and when this is true, however, it is a question of fact and judgment, not a characteristic implicit in the conceptual scheme of a social system.

In one sense what is functional or dysfunctional for an individual has a clearer and more concrete human referent than what is functional or dysfunctional for the survival of a system. In the first case the ouch is emotional and human; in the second case it is logical and impersonal. In another sense the measures for evaluating the effectiveness of the external system are clearer and less ambiguous than the measures for evaluating the efficiency of the internal system. Measures such as cost, profit, and return on investment, for example, are clearer and less ambiguous than the measures used for evaluating "satisfaction, morale, cohesiveness, loyalty, willingness to cooperate," and so on. At the same time and within some limits they are seldom experienced as vividly as, say, love and hate.

Although the components of a social system are persons, these components are also systems or may be so conceived. When I conceive of an individual worker, for example, in that way, then I treat the social system of the organization as an important part (but not all) of the worker's external system; that is, that with which he has to cope and to which he has to adjust. The processes by which he maintains his identity and integrity I treat as his internal system. I treat the processes by which he may or may not become both a good worker (i.e., do what the social system expects or requires of him) and a good person (i.e., become himself), as the way he deals with the pressures produced by the two.

Many of the difficulties, problems, and dilemmas that exist when I treat an organization as a system are present when I treat an individual as a system. In this case also, the relation between the external and internal systems is difficult to specify. Statements about it may be characterized as being more insightful or perceptive than precise, vigorous, or operational. The world of poetry, fiction, and religion, as well as the literature of psychotherapy, are filled with statements of the first kind. In one sense how real they are and yet how difficult to reduce to testable propositions! Also how easily they can be twisted, get lost, or become cliches! What for a while is a blinding flash of insight, a great *aperçu*, becomes in time a source of misunderstanding and controversy, for which a new insight is required if it is to be corrected.

When the insight of "man against himself" got lost or twisted or misunderstood, the insight of "man for himself" was needed to correct it. "Love thy neighbor" becomes corrected to "If you are not capable of loving yourself, you will not be able to love your neighbor very well."

In the early period of psychoanalysis, what was being repressed—the powerful id, kid—occupied the center of the stage. To correct for this overemphasis, the repressing agent, the superego, became the center of interest. Finally, when the poor passive ego had been reduced by these two forces to a trembling, quivering piece of pulp, someone had a flash of insight of this order: "Let us support the ego by giving it something to do besides fighting the id and the superego." So "ego psychology" was born. But the problem I am talking about remains. It is not appropriate to call this new psychology a radical departure in conceptualization; it is rather a change of emphasis for which a new metaphor is required.

I do not sneeze at, thumb my nose at, or look down at these insights and the metaphorical language in which they are expressed. Far from it; they have a great fascination for me. At a clinical level, in particular situations, I find them very helpful. But they fall short of being scientific propositions. They highlight the difficulty of how to conceive external and internal frames of references in some state of equilibrium.

For me the internal system is more pregnant in meaning and significance, more real, more natural, and closer to the actual territory than the external. The property of homeostasis can more easily be applied to the internal system than to the external. In this sense an internal system may more properly be called a natural system than an external system. The external system seems to me to be of a higher level of abstraction, less concrete, and more artificial than the internal system. I think this is because the external system may often be conceived apart from individuals and their relations to each other. Technology and the formal organization, that is, the organization's consciously coordinated set of activities, may be conceived apart from the interaction of persons and their sentiments; the internal system may not be. Here one may not conceive the activities of persons apart from the associated interactions and sentiments. In fact, apart from the interactions and sentiments, activities in the internal system have no meaning.

As a result of these difficulties and feelings, I often find myself conceptualizing the relation between the two systems in different ways. One conceptualization is to say that I am concerned only with the phenomena of human behavior that occur where the two systems interact. Suppose I call the internal system A and the external system B and diagram their relation to each other in this way:

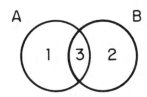

It may be said that I am concerned not with where A is apart from B (1 in the diagram) or with where B is apart from A (2), but only with where A and B interact (3). But this way of thinking is not very satisfactory, for what is A apart from B? Speaking metaphorically, it is a lot of monkey business; that is, it is the behavior of people that has no relation to the business of the business. It is difficult for me to conceive this as a system. B apart from A may be conceived as a system of the activities of people apart from the people who perform them; this is an abstracted system, not a concrete one. Hence, this way of thinking is not really helpful, and the problem of how to conceive (3) as a system remains.

Another conceptualization is to give up B, the external system, and say that it is not a system at all but the "givens" or boundary conditions under which the concrete behavior of the people being studied can be observed. A now becomes a full-blown concrete system which may be observed under different conditions, such as:

B = Givens

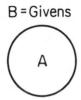

I probably use this way of thinking more than the other when I am researching a small group. From the point of view of taking action, though, this presents problems which I shall take up in Part VII, "Knowledge and Action in Modern Society."

Let's face it: A systemic way of thinking about behavior in organizations presents problems for knowledge makers in the social sciences. A system of persons with heterogeneous properties and heterogeneous relations is a crude concept that leaves much to be desired, both logically and aesthetically. From the point of view of logical clarity and elegance, a system made up of entities with homogeneous properties and homogeneous relations is highly preferable. But such a system can be created only by going to high levels of abstraction. In fact, the more abstract the entities and relations, the better the system from the point of view of a knowledge maker.

The kinds of systems that seem easiest to conceptualize are those in which the following three conditions hold: (1) the elements can be treated as unanalyzable entities or givens which have only external relations; (2) the system as a whole has only internal relations; and (3) the internal relations do not change over time. Such systems are generally called "closed" and "static" as opposed to "open" and "dynamic." Many machines are of this character or can be treated as such for purposes of understanding and explanation.

Although such systems can be abstracted by the bushel from concrete phenomena and under certain conditions are very useful, they fall far short of capturing in conceptual terms the nature of the concrete reality. To capture these realities we need to conceive of systems in which (1) the elements are themselves systems with both internal and external relations; in which (2) the systems themselves have both external and internal relations; and (3) in which both the systems themselves and their elements are changing over time.

Calling such systems "open" and "dynamic" does not alter the facts that they are difficult to conceptualize. The endeavors of the school of thought called "systems theory," whose purpose is to conceptualize the nature of open systems (that is, systems which have both external and internal relations), make this clear. Without question this school's logical analyses of different kinds of systems and its emphasis upon understanding the nature of dynamic systems, in which external and internal relations have to be related to one another, have contributed new understandings to the ways in which we conceptualize systems. But I am not certain that this school has surmounted the conceptual problems about which I am writing. There is no difficulty in relating external and internal environments, when the two can be reduced to commensurable terms. The problem arises when they are incommensurables. Before I take up that problems, though, I need to discuss the third level of the knowledge enterprise, the level of analytical or scientific knowledge.

Chapter 22

Analytical Knowledge

Nothing is more mystifying to me than the various means which people accept as legitimate ways to climb the knowledge ladder from its lowly level of personal knowledge to a level that may be called objective, analytical, and without reservation, scientific. Until 1954 I was primarily a clinician, what might be called an empirical scientist. Until then the conceptual scheme of a social system and the clinical or case method of investigation were sufficient for my purposes. But beginning at that time, I felt that for my own personal development as well as for the development of human relations as a legitimate area of substantive knowledge, I ought to attempt to climb up to the next rung of the abstraction ladder.

THE TRANSITION FROM CLINICAL TO ANALYTICAL KNOWLEDGE

I did not think the conceptual scheme and the clinical method I had been practicing were worthless and should be abandoned. Far from it—they had paid off handsomely for me. By thinking systemically and functionally and by practicing this way of thinking clinically in concrete situations, I had been constantly rewarded. Used as a tool of discovery, investigation, exploration, or diagnosis in concrete situations, this way of thinking seldom failed me.

More than this, I had found that the possibility of translating this way of thinking into modes of action or interventions in concrete situations was exciting and challenging. It opened up ways of doing things that seemed to me more productive than those usually considered in the standard textbooks about management. Particularly in dealing with the classes of problems that involved "itches" and "ouches," I found that there were more interesting and rewarding ways of scratching the itches and dealing with the ouches than those recommended in these books.

I could have continued to spend the rest of my life at this clinical level of operation. I would have found it highly rewarding. Alas, I did not do this—at least not 100 percent of my time. Ringing through my ears was what I remembered as George Homans' clarion call—""Let us not be mice and understand; let us be men and *explain!*"

Even more compelling was the fact that by this time I had qualms myself about the limitations of clinical knowledge. These qualms showed up in the following ways. Whenever I talked about or used human relations as a way of thinking for purposes of discovery, investigation, or diagnosis, I felt on sure ground; it made sense. However, whenever I talked about it as a body of knowledge, human relations as a way of thinking seemed to collapse. At this level I could not make clear what my subject matter was and what this knowledge was about. Although the clinical method was able to disclose certain uniformities in the phenomena under certain conditions, these uniformities—or clinical syndromes, as I called them— were so imbedded in the conditions under which they were obtained that it was difficult to generalize from them to other situations where the conditions and outcomes were different. So what kind of knowledge was Human Relations? In a strict scientific sense, it seemed to have no general propositions with which it could explain and by which it could apply its findings. Furthermore, since it was clear that these general propositions could not be obtained by the clinical method, Human Relations fell short of what I thought made knowledge scientific knowledge. This disturbed me.

Thus during the period that I conducted the reading seminar in the Doctoral program I was as interested in seeing the various methods by which my colleagues climbed the scientific knowledge ladder as I was in how they described their subject matter. To climb the ladder, according to the high priests of science, something more than orienting concepts and generalizations is needed. Operations, definitions, and concepts that refer to the properties of the phonomena and to the relations between them become of the essence. In addition, the syndromes of clinical knowledge have to be stated in rigorous forms in terms of which they can be tested and in time explained by more general propositions.

All this is much easier said than done. As I surveyed the literature, it was abundantly clear that there was no single accepted conceptual scheme for the sciences of human behavior. Instead the researcher has a wide range of conceptual frameworks and tools to choose from. So long as he stays at the level of discovery, this diversity of approach does not make too much difference. Not that everything is sweetness and light; there are differences of opinion about whose methods are more or less scientific. But on the whole these differences, it seems to me, are not serious. Discussion of them can even be fruitful and lead to exciting new insights.

The more serious problem arises when we try to explain our findings. Here the differences become sharp and bitter. In the absence of any generally accepted conceptual scheme or "shared paradigm," to use Thomas S. Kuhn's words (1962), it is impossible to build upon each other's findings. As a result, we keep opening new frontiers of inquiry without being able to consolidate what we have discovered and learned from earlier investigations. What one investigator treats as given, another treats as something to be explained. What one treats as an independent variable, another treats as a dependent one. A new line of inquiry can begin by shifting the age-old question of how a parent influences a child's behavior to the new question of how the child influences the parent's behavior. Such shifts are sometimes called "breakthroughs"!

By itself the difficulty might not be too serious, except for what it leads to. The development of each new frontier brings forth a new vocabulary of concepts, variables, and words. This proliferation of words makes it difficult to tell not only what has been discovered, but also what, if anything, has been explained. Thus, it is often difficult to determine whether what has been discovered is (1) wow! a new word for a new variable; or (2) just a new word for an old variable; or (3) even an old word for a new variable; or (4) ugh! just an old word for an old variable. Indeed it is often problematic whether the new or old word is pointing to any variable at all. Too often the words refer to clusters of variables, sometimes called dimensions, and then they are not real honest-to-goodness variables at all.

Just what does this verbal deluge explain? As George Homans kept saying, scientific explanation begins in propositions. Since a proposition expresses the relation between two variables, one variable alone cannot explain anything, no matter how "hot" the variable. Nor is it possible to explain one variable by another. Even a sentence expressing a relationship between two variables does not establish the statement in and by itself as a scientific proposition. It is not sufficient just to say that x is dependent upon y, or x is a function of y, or x correlates with y. To make a proposition a real honest-to-goodness scientific proposition, one has to explain—no more kidding now—*how* variable *x* varies with variable *y* under certain given conditions.

If the so-called variables in the statements being made are not variables in the first place, this makes matters even worse. Such sentences are not scientific propositions at all; but still further, one cannot explain anything scientifically by one proposition alone, no matter at what level of confidence it has been verified. To explain something scientifically takes three kinds of statements: a general proposition, a statement about certain given conditions, and an empirical proposition stated in the form of a deduction from the other two.

> If the general proposition is, for example, that the more established the social status of an individual, the more frequently he or she will interact with others;
> and if the given conditions are that: A is a concrete individual whose social status is well-established (e.g., he is an older, white male Anglo-Saxon who has been to college) and B is a person whose social status is not well established (e.g., she is a younger female whose parents came from southern Europe and who has not been to college);
> then the following empirical proposition can be deduced: A will interact more frequently than B.

The three statements together make up an explanatory, deductive system. Believe me, George was a hard taskmaster about matters of explanation:*

As I went through the literature in my special field of human behavior in organizations, I did not find anyone who took George's admonitions very seriously. Instead, I felt as though we had all been engaged in a tournament in which each conceptualizer, like a knight of yore, was trying to unseat his opponent–conceptualizer from his conceptual mount. We were fighting over each other's conceptual schemes, systems of classification, concepts, variables, or words, even though we were often not sure exactly what they referred to. Regardless of the difficulties, these were the entities we were championing when they were ours or trying to knock off their mounts when they were those of our colleagues! Each of us was trying to unseat his opponent in order to get his own favorite accredited.

---

* Editor's Note: Compare Homans (edition of 1974), pp. 8–11.

This jousting for accreditation results in what I have come to think of as a kind of kaleidoscopic twist or flip-flop effect, in which with one stroke (of the pen or the lance) heroes turn into villains, wise men into fools, advocates of change into defenders of the status quo, innovators into conformists, rational into irrational men, being "in" to being "out" of fashion, or vice versa in each case. These twists produce the in-words and the out-words. What has been said once in terms of anomie, for example, has now to be stated all over again in terms of identity crises. Words like bureaucracy, commonly used in a pejorative sense, are now used, or so it is claimed, in a nonpejorative sense. Words, such as trust, authentic, and open, that have been kicked out the front door because they have value connotations, are brought in again by the back door but, in some way that I do not understand, properly cleansed.

In this jousting for accreditation, acceptance, legitimacy, and being *au courant* (the reader may choose the term he prefers), I did not try to knock my colleagues off their horses; I just tried to keep from being knocked off mine. The astute reader should be able by now to predict that this would be my response, even though I have not provided him with a general proposition for making the prediction legitimately.

Anyway, this was my dilemma. Although I did not think my clinical horse was some super-duper Arabian steed, neither did I think she was some old grey mare I picked up in some farmer's backyard. Although she jumped the first hurdle (clinical investigation) with the greatest of ease, I confess that she was a bit balky about going over the second one (scientific explanation). Not that while she was grazing in the lush pasture between the first and the second hurdles, she ceased to be "l" and "h" (i.e., lean and hungry) and lost her "n-ach" (i.e., need for achievement) or "pe" (i.e., Protestant ethic) and became "f" and "c" (i.e., fat and complacent). It was more that my favorite horse could not see clearly what her rewards would be after she had taken the second jump because she had no way of estimating the probabilities that the new pasture would be any greener than the one she was in. In fact, let us face it: from the point of view of application, she might be worse off.

The social scientist could apply or practice the conceptual scheme of a social system—the simple walking-stick I have talked about all along—before the findings of the knowledge enterprise were in; but he could not apply the findings of real honest-to-goodness knowledge until such findings existed. To restate the obvious, in the absence of such general propositions there was no knowledge, in the strict sense, to apply. It seemed to me that this obvious limitation was not well understood by some of my colleagues.

THE DIFFERENT KINDS OF KNOWLEDGE MAKERS

Let me return to the different knowledge makers in the sciences of human behavior in and around 1957 to see at what level of the knowledge enterprise they were working. Rather than classify them from the point of view of their subject matter, as I did in Chapters 18 and 19, I will take them up from the point of view of their methodologies to see at what level they were trying to make contributions to knowledge, as well as to see what hang-ups they had at that level.

(1) Foremost are the conceptual logicians who are interested in defining their concepts and relating them to each other in some logically consistent conceptual system. They are the concept makers and concept systematizers, sometimes called (in spite of George Homans' cries of outrage) theory builders. Although the conceptual logicians have a useful contribution to make (after all, the phenomena have to be classified and their properties specified), the trouble arises when they try to logicize their conceptual schemes of investigation into conceptual systems of explanation. Because of this misapprehension these conceptual logicians or system makers tend to become dictionary makers, logic choppers, and word manipulators who create futile verbal arguments. Each contradiction of findings only produces more words, definitions, and terminologies. My impression is that contributions of the conceptual logicians dominate the literature. Although their contributions are valuable, my impression is that the behavioral sciences suffer from an overabundance of them.

(2) Entirely different from these conceptual logicians or magicians—in fact, almost at the opposite pole—are the clinicians, who are interested in matters of practice. They prefer staying close to particular concrete situations and tend to shy away from sweeping generalizations. Their contributions are insightful and perceptive. Their habitat is the field, not a laboratory or computer center. They are more comfortable inside a work group or sensitivity training group than inside the covers of a book. In debate with an expert conceptual logician, they may be reduced to putty, for their ideas are often not distinct or clear. But when matters of judgment are involved, they may make the conceptual logician look naive. They often call the conceptual scheme they bring to their fieldwork a

theory. This is all right, so long as they do not think it is a theory of explanation for the phenomena they are investigating and trying to understand. The clinicians are often good initial discoverers, practitioners, and understanders, but they are usually not so hot in verifying or explaining the clinical uniformities they discover or the insights they have.

(3) Indeed, the clinicians often leave verification and explanation to the correlation seekers and testers. The latter use questionnaires and survey methods to find out how some variable does or does not correlate with some other variable, such as productivity with satisfaction. They indulge little in theory, but sometimes they think that their correlations in and of themselves explain something. They are masters of transforming soft data into hard data by means of simple measuring scales and statistical devices. But no matter how hard they try, they cannot equate a correlation with an explanation. The literature, it seems to me, is littered with such unexplained correlations.

In the early days of my reading seminar the clinicians and the correlation seekers were having a running battle about the utility of field work versus questionnaire data. Ten years later they were having a love feast. They needed each other desperately to hold their own against the new knowledge makers that were coming into the field.

(4) The new knowledge makers include the hypothesis seekers and testers. They are concerned with the discovery and verification of causal hypotheses. They use rigorous methods of measurement, sophisticated statistical procedures for the analysis of data, and broad experimental designs. These are truly the methodologists, the hard-boiled and realistic men of science. They have little use for the insights of clinicians or for the nonoperational definitions of conceptual logicians. Their goal is to be operational; for them only what can be made operational is real. Their skills are technical and exacting. They live in a world of their own. When they talk about matters of application and practice—which is not often—they sound naive.

They are the high priests of independent and dependent variables. They often treat the independent variable as the cause of the dependent one and in this sense claim they have explained it. In a loose sense of explanation this is true.

(5) Strictly speaking, however, explanation is in the hands of the general-proposition makers. They search for general propositions from which the simple uniformities found at the empirical level can be derived under specified conditions. They are not analyzers, but synthesizers, and they synthesize propositions, not concepts. For

them a scientific proposition states the empirical and not the logical relation between two concepts. For them a concept describes a property of nature, not of logic. Once concepts are empirically related into propositions, however, then the propositions so stated (not the concepts) can be arranged in a deductive system, and this system constitutes a scientific explanation.

The skill of the general-proposition maker is to show how a variety of empirical generalizations follow logically from a small number of general propositions under certain conditions. In his search for general propositions, the general-proposition maker is willing to use the empirical findings of practical experience as well as those obtained by clinical investigation or by more rigorous and sophisticated methods of research. He is just as willing to take the findings of practical experience, such as "You scratch my back and I'll scratch yours," or "The wheel that squeaks the loudest is the one that gets the grease," or "Nothing succeeds like success," as he is to accept such unexplained uniformities as "The size of the nuclear family is an inverse function of position in the stratification system."

Because a general proposition is reached by intuition and invention, its discovery is a leap of creativity and imagination. When it has been achieved, the full-grown knowledge tree is in existence. There is always room at the top, of course, for a yet more general proposition to explain the ones that have already been stated. The knowledge tree looks very different when it is viewed from the bottom up than it does from the top down. Going from the bottom up involves sweat, tears, toil, a great deal of imagination, and little deductive logic. However, one goes from the top to the lower levels by pure logic. So the tree, when looked at from the bottom up, is indeed less elegant than when looked at from the top down.

(6) During the 1960s a new kind of knowledge maker and knowledge user appeared on the scene. These were the model makers or model builders. They built their mathematical models not only for attaining descriptive knowledge about phenomena, but also as normative knowledge to be applied to the phenomena. As they use their models (often not too clearly) in both senses and because I do not want to get hung up on this descriptive-normative issue now, I will confine what I say here to model builders who use their models for empirical discovery rather than for solving practical problems.

There is a similarity between the use of models for empirical discovery and what Henderson refers to as a conceptual scheme. Both are used for empirical investigation. There is also a big difference. Whereas a new conceptual scheme comes forth once in a generation or so, these new model makers, like the automobile manufacturers, put out a new model each year. Nay, I am doing them an injustice. About the time when I stopped teaching my seminar in 1967, the production of models rose sharply. It seemed that a new one appeared each day. Rumor had it that "a model a day keeps the doctor away." At this time I had difficulty in distinguishing model makers from the conceptual logicians and magicians I cited earlier.

The model maker also bears some resemblance to the general-proposition maker in the sense that the products of both the mathematical model and the general proposition are highly creative inductive leaps of the imagination to which empirical meanings can be given. But the general-proposition makers (at least the ones I know), once they have conceived their inventions, deliver their children slowly, one at a time, by simple deductive logic alone. The model makers turn out their progeny in much larger quantities and at a much faster rate by means of black boxes called computers.

PRODUCTS AND FINDINGS OF THE KNOWLEDGE ENTERPRISE

Thus far, I have represented the knowledge enterprise in terms of developmental levels or stages, of which I have distinguished three principal ones: skill, clinical, and analytical or scientific. I have argued that the passage from a lower to a higher stage requires some new ingredient. The first attempts to study a class of phenomena start with knowledge of acquaintance and skill in dealing with the phenomena. Going from skill to the clinical level requires a conceptual scheme and elementary methods of observation and interviewing. Going from the clinical to the analytical level requires concepts and definitions that refer more precisely to the properties of the phenomena and the relations among them. It also requires some elementary methods of measurement.

Within the analytical level I distinguish three sublevels: elementary concepts, empirical propositions, and general propositions. Going from elementary concepts to empirical-propositional statements requires operational definitions and rigorous methods of measurement. From empirical propositions to general-propositional statements requires a creative leap of an esthetic kind, by which it can be shown that statements about a great variety of different matters can be derived under certain conditions from a small number of simple, general statements. Once a general-propositional statement has been achieved as part of a deductive system, empirical propositions can be stated in a form that gives them the appearance of having been arrived at deductively. This appearance can be misleading, for empirical propositions often result from observation or other ways of building theories before a general proposition has been conceived. Indeed, many empirical propositions remain just such, without contributing to the leap of imagination that leads to the creation of the kind of explanatory system that is the goal of scientific statement.

Each level of knowledge has its own kinds of products and findings. Knowledge of acquaintance at the level of skill results in simple how-to-do-it statements of aphorisms about the phenomena. The products at the clinical level are descriptive cases about the phenomena or statements of clinical uniformities or syndromes in the phenomena. The products at the level of elementary concepts are statements such as x is the function of y; x is dependent on y; x has a consequence for y; or x correlates with y. The products at the level of empirical propositions are statements to the effect that x varies with y in such and such a fashion under certain given conditions (e.g., Boyle's law). At the level of general propositions, the products are sets of statements that include general propositions from which, under certain stated conditions, empirical propositions can be deduced (e.g., Newton's laws of motion). At this level, scientific theory and explanation have been achieved. I have summarized these views in the accompanying table.

If a knowledge seeker is satisfied with the stage of knowledge at which he is working, there is nothing which requires him to proceed to the next higher level of the knowledge enterprise. If he nevertheless proceeds to the next stage, he has to abide by the rules of the game at that level. Each knowledge seeker may become enamored with the tools and methods of his level, so long as he does not think these tools alone will get him over the hump to the next level. If he does not realize that by themselves they are not enough, he becomes "hung up" at the lower level. There is no more serious mistake than for a knowledge seeker who is at one level of the knowledge enterprise to think that he is at another; that is, he should not think he is applying a scientific theory before he has achieved one. If he does, he is not only kidding himself; he is also confusing others. It is equally serious when a knowledge maker becomes overcommitted to the tools of one level and takes a polemical stance with regard to their value in explaining the phenomena. The following are some examples of this mistake: the clinician who plasters descriptions of situations with diagnostic concepts and thinks that he is thereby explaining them; the conceptual logician who thinks that he is explaining phenomena by tying his concepts into neat logical bundles; the

The Knowledge Enterprise*

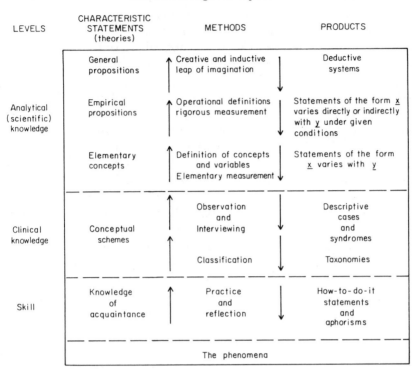

LEVELS	CHARACTERISTIC STATEMENTS (theories)	METHODS	PRODUCTS
Analytical (scientific) knowledge	General propositions	Creative and inductive leap of imagination	Deductive systems
	Empirical propositions	Operational definitions rigorous measurement	Statements of the form x varies directly or indirectly with y under given conditions
	Elementary concepts	Definition of concepts and variables Elementary measurement	Statements of the form x varies with y
Clinical knowledge	Conceptual schemes	Observation and Interviewing Classification	Descriptive cases and syndromes Taxonomies
Skill	Knowledge of acquaintance	Practice and reflection	How-to-do-it statements and aphorisms
		The phenomena	

*For the development of knowledge, read from the bottom up; for the practice of knowledge, read from the top down.

correlation seeker who thinks his significant correlations explain something; the causal hypothesis seeker who thinks he has the tools for getting hold of propositions that will explain themselves by stating what the causes of the phenomena really are; the general-proposition maker who is so enamored with scientific explanations that he ceases to understand the phenomena with which he deals.

PROBLEMS WE SHARE IN THE DEVELOPMENT OF KNOWLEDGE ABOUT HUMAN BEHAVIOR

In my conception of the development of knowledge, the general-proposition makers became the biggest troublemakers. They often argue that a set of general propositions about the phenomena is the only kind of statement that constitutes "scientific theory" and "scientific explanation." This reductionism—limitation of what constitutes science to only one kind of statement—raises questions about the different theories of human behavior that are embarrassing to answer. Are these other statements really theories in the sense of the general-proposition makers at all? If not, what are they? Does each of the behavioral science disciplines have its own set of general propositions? Or is there just one set of general propositions for the science of human behavior? If, as in the case of physical motion, there is not one set of general propositions for celestial motion and another set for terrestrial motion, but just one set applicable to both (Newton's laws of motion), then what is the nature of the general propositions for the science of human behavior? Are they psychological or sociological? In the 1970s these were hot questions. The masterpiece of understatement as an answer to them is "Wow!"

George Homans is more articulate. As I have said, George is not only a general-proposition maker; he is also forthright and believes in calling a spade a spade. Unlike some of the more timid general-proposition makers, he has a clear answer to these questions. He says, in essence, most of the so-called theories about human behavior in the different social science disciplines are not theories at all; they do not explain a goddamn thing. Most of their findings need general propositions to explain them.

Many social scientists found these Homansian declarations far out. Yet the worst was still to come, because when George, in his *Social Behavior: Its Elementary Forms* (1961), produced his general propositions from which empirical uniformities of elementary social behavior could be deduced, they turned out to be psychological in nature. This was the final straw which broke the sociologists' collective back. It meant that sociology had no general propositions of its own; and without propositions, it had no real honest-to-goodness theory. This was not just being far out; this was a declaration of war. Perhaps some psychologists, albeit more dimly, also saw the handwriting on the wall, because George's propositions also meant that there was no separate psychology of individual behavior. There was only one science of human behavior.

George's bombshell created havoc in the sciences of human behavior. The different disciplines were strewn about the field—out cold. Yet by a less spectacular route I reach the same conclusion about theories of organization and management: The fields of organization and management also may have no separate theories of their own. Thus, the empirical propositions of organizational behavior will in time be the umpty-umpth deductions from a set of more general propositions about behavior under certain given conditions.

And because I sometimes doubt that the general propositions that George produced can be fully realized, it is just possible that by this route no science of human behavior will develop. If perchance this happens, then there will be no descriptive science—in the sense that natural scientists use the term—of organization or management at all. Period.

Well, it has taken a lot of nerve, but now I have said it. What a load off my chest! Let me say one step at a time how I reach this conclusion. It all goes back to the conceptual scheme of a social system and the multidimensionality of the phenomena of human behavior (matters which I think George jumped over too easily, though I must say, most elegantly) and the problem of what constitutes science—a problem in which for too many years I have been involved.

Although I agree that only at the level of general propositions is explanation in the strict scientific sense achieved, I do not think that this stage can be reached without going through the earlier stages. I also think that at the general propositional level, once it is reached, one cannot discard as so much extra baggage the lower levels of the knowledge enterprise and their products. What I referred to earlier—in overly simplistic fashion—as the full-grown knowledge tree is the reconstructed logic by which what has been discovered can, after it has been discovered, be stated more elegantly. But these statements are built on and contain all the other levels of knowledge I have described. Without these earlier levels, general propositions are elegant but impotent. From the point of view of explanations, general propositions amount only to tautologies; without clinical skill and knowledge they are incapable of being understood or implemented in particular situations.

There is another problem in the social sciences today that bothers me. The question is: in the absence of any conceptual scheme generally accepted and shared by the practitioners of the social scientific community, what chance is there that agreement can be reached among the knowledge makers at the level of general propositions? As I see it, very little. If there is little agreement at the earlier stages of the knowledge enterprise, there can only be less at the later ones.

According to Thomas Kuhn (1962), the acceptance by the scientific community of a paradigm—the Newtonian paradigm, for example—allowed cumulative development to take place for a while in the physical sciences. Such a shared paradigm functions by delineating, on the one hand, what the important elements in the universe are, what the important questions for study are, what puzzles need solving, and what mop-up work needs to be done. On the other hand, it delineates what anomalies or $64 questions may at the time be disregarded. What makes science science (what Kuhn calls "normal science") and what makes it different from other forms of knowledge is just this: a shared paradigm in terms of which the soil can be tilled for a while by a group of practitioners, called "scientists," without at each turn raising a $64 metaphysical question.

In respect to this normal aspect of science, the metaphor of scientists as tillers of the soil is better than the one of knights jousting for conceptual legitimacy. Only in the pre-paradigm, post-paradigm, or revolutionary stages of science is the latter metaphor really applicable. Under the domination of a shared paradigm all is relatively quiet on a scientific front. During this stage the scientific practitioners busy themselves in tying up the loose ends that a good paradigm leaves open for solution.

A good paradigm, as I understand Kuhn to say, is open-ended. Although it is not completely articulate and true or false and does not provide all the answers, it is shared by the scientific community and provides a framework within which acceptable answers can be sought. It allows room for further observations, theories, methods, and instrumentation to be made. Although it cannot be overthrown by one negative observation, it may be unseated by a rival, which, when it has captured the imagination of the scientific community, may be cultivated in preference to the former paradigm. Why? Well, partly because it takes care of some of the anomalies the older paradigm failed to resolve; partly because it presents a more exciting picture of the universe.

Just as some members of the scientific community or "establishment" viewed Homans' concept of a "theory" with alarm, some viewed Kuhn's concept of a "paradigm" in the same way, although for different reasons. The concept of a paradigm seems to deny the objectivity and rationality of the scientific enterprise. To hop from one paradigm to another, because the new one offers a more exciting world view than the old one, does not sound, shall we say, objective, rational, and scientific. Also paradigms are more often than not incommensurable. Hence, to give up an old one for a new one seems to deny the traditional view according to which science progresses linearly by the accumulation of facts, rather than by paradigm hopping.

It seems clear to me that the practitioners of the social sciences do not yet share a paradigm in Kuhn's sense in the way that practitioners of the physical sciences did in the days of those sciences' early development. In those days there were rivaling paradigms—called "schools of thought"—under which what Kuhn called "normal science" was practiced. These different schools of thought represented in most instances incommensurable ways of viewing man and his universe, and there was little traffic between them.

In spite of claims of "breakthroughs" by the different schools of thought in the social sciences, there has been no scientific revolution in them comparable to the one that occurred when the discoveries of Einstein and, later, quantum mechanics broke through the Newtonian paradigm. To belabor the obvious, if in the social sciences the practitioners do not share a paradigm, then there is no shared paradigm to break through, is there now? There are still only candidates in rivalry for what the shared paradigm should be; that remains an open question.

After a scientific revolution occurred in the physical sciences, the defeated candidate for the dominant paradigm retired more or less gracefully from the field. After Einstein, for example, except for a few die-hards, the Newtonians folded their tents and disappeared quietly into the night. Not so in the social sciences, where the different schools of thought continue to flourish with equal vigor at the same time. No school disappears until its last exponent dies.

The notion of a shared conceptual scheme dominated a good bit of my behavior at the B-School. For me it almost became an obsession that the practitioners of human relations, administrative practices, or organizational development should share the same conceptual scheme or paradigm of a social system. I hoped that such a shared paradigm would enable the three course entities called in 1957 Administrative Practices, Human Relations, and Business Policy, to get together. That this did not happen is now a matter of history. Did this result follow from my maladroitness as a leader? In part, maybe; but some things in addition that were brute and stubborn seem to me to have also been at work. These matters are what I want to clarify in the concluding chapters. Before I go on, let me summarize where I think things stand in the early 1970s among practitioners in the social sciences. I do not think it is an exaggeration to say that the state of affairs is of the following order.

Among us there is still no shared skill, no shared conceptual scheme, no shared paradigm, no shared general propositions, and no shared truth or error. There is just confusion. According to Kuhn's conception, we have not yet achieved the level of normal science, and perhaps we never will. We are in some state of suspended animation, unable on the one hand to return to our lowly beginnings or on the other to proceed to the higher branches of the knowledge enterprise. It almost looks as though this state of affairs is endemic to the science of human behavior.

Before I conclude that this state of immobility is permanent, let me return to the phenomena of human behavior in organizations to see if keeping in mind the different levels, processes, and products of the knowledge enterprise, which I have gone to some lengths to describe in these last three chapters, helps to clarify the subject matter with which I have been and am concerned. Would the phenomena be clearer if they were not masked by the confusions that arise from our failure to distinguish between the different levels of the knowledge enterprise? How would the phenomena be conceptualized if we kept these distinctions clear?

I will write in the next two chapters from the point of view of knowledge makers. Then, in the last two chapters, I will turn to the problems of the relation of knowledge to action. Thus there is still much to discuss; but, as I am sure I have made clear, I find that seeking the elusive phenomena of human behavior in organizations is no simple task.

Part VI

REVISITING MY SUBJECT MATTER

Chapter 23

Classes, Concrete Systems, and Spaces

I now want to reconsider three different conceptual entities in which I often become entangled. These are classes, concrete systems, and spaces. I do not think I am the only person who has difficulty in discriminating among them, for knowledge makers use the terms in different ways. The confusions that result are considerable and, in my view, have impeded understanding of the phenomena of human behavior in organizations and the development of its subject matter. Let me try to disentangle the several meanings and the uniformities among the phenomena to which they refer.

CLASSES AND CONCRETE SYSTEMS

One common form of conceptualization is to establish a set of entities which can be clearly defined (extensionally) by enumerating its members or (intensionally) by stating the properties, attributes, or characteristics which the entities have in common, such as the set of all redheaded women at the B-School. Such a set is often called a class. To show how this form of conceptualization can easily become confused with the others. I will start with this class as an example and transform it hypothetically into the other forms.

In this class one redhead is as good as another. As members of the class, one cannot be discriminated from another. However, if one of them cuts off her hair, dyes it, or tints it, out she goes from this class. With this banishment, no tears are shed, for she receives no rewards or punishments to make her stay in or quit this class. So long as the women keep intact the properties of being redheaded and employed at the B-School, they belong to the class. Whether they share other similarities, speak to each other, or even know each other makes no difference—I mean 100 percent none. For the moment let me assume that they do not interact with one another.

Each of the women is also a member of the concrete system called the B-School and of some small concrete system or work group. Some of them may be more effective at, or satisfied with, their work than others. But they do not themselves form a concrete system, for there are no social interactions among them.

Speaking hypothetically, how might I make them into such a system? I could do this by removing all the physical and social barriers that interfere with their interacting with one another. I could put them all in the same department, the mail room, for example. I could choose them so that they would all be young, single, with similar social backgrounds, little service, and so on. I could arrange that their statuses in all these regards were so congruent that they would be well established at the bottom of the totem pole in the job structure at the School. In the process I might get such high "status congruence" among them that it would interfere with their doing their tasks efficiently. That is, they might have such a ball interacting with each other—talking about their boy friends, the food they like to eat, and what they would tell their boss if they had the nerve—that the productivity and quality of their work would suffer.

I would then have not only a class of redheaded women at the B-School, but also a concrete system of interacting redheaded women. I would have accomplished this by manipulating their activities and sentiments (elements of the system) in directions that allowed them to increase their interactions.

To create a concrete system, I need not have gone as far as I did in the example I have just given. I could have made the women's social backgrounds, length of service, and other interests very different and put them in the same department, let us say in Baker Library, where they would do more or less the same work. If I had done this, the members of the department would suffer seriously from "status incongruence." They might or might not do their jobs more efficiently than the young women in the first example, but their interactions would probably be low. Nevertheless, because they would interact, they would form a concrete system.

THE FOUR SPACES

The redheaded women at the Business School can also be conceptualized in terms of any of the different sets of relations used to reduce the phenomena of human behavior to a common scheme of analysis. In some abstracted, conceptual systems of this kind the units or elements may be the relations that I call technological, purposive, social, and personal or life. Thus, the women may be ordered in terms of the different kinds of relationships—technological, purposive, social, and personal—in which they are involved. Once abstracted, these relations may be treated as systems. Each such abstracted system is oriented toward one or more of these classes or sets of relations, not toward a particular concrete system in which these relations as well as others may be found. I call these four kinds of abstracted conceptual systems "spaces."

When I look at the behavior of persons in concrete systems, it seems to me that anything approximating a complete description of the phenomena I observe there involves all four of the systems I call spaces. I find this to be so, whether I am observing and talking about a concrete individual, a concrete group, or a concrete organization. For example, an adequate description of the behavior of any one of my redheaded women requires saying something about the following, each of which is part of a difference space:

> the physical location at which they work and how their tasks are related by space-time relations to the tasks that are being performed by the others who work around them (technological space);
>
> the formal channels of communication—what some sociologists call power relations—by which they are related to the purposes of the School (purposive space);
>
> the social relations they enjoy or do not enjoy in the social group of which they are regular, deviant, or isolated members (social space);
>
> and their anxieties and how they have learned to deal with them and express them here and now (life space).

Were I to make the living, breathing redheads at the Harvard Business School into a concrete work group or system—and believe me, baby, that would be no verbal class abstraction—and try to describe their behavior, all four spaces would be involved. In the same way, were I to describe the Harvard Business School as a concrete system, I would have to describe not only the purposive relations that exist there; I would also have to describe the spatial and temporal relations that exist among the objects and people there, the social relations that the people have there, the personally rewarding relations that they do or do not have there, and so on. Again, all four spaces would be involved.

Thus, I do not equate a concrete individual with life space, nor a concrete group with social space, nor a concrete organization with purposive space. To do so, in each case I would have to be interested in how all the other spaces related to it. Thus, I try not to confuse a concrete system with any one of the spaces.

The spaces are not four different classes of phenomena in a concrete system; they are four different ways of ordering the phenomena of human behavior that occur there. Although (a) no human event in a concrete system can be said to possess properties belonging exclusively to only one of these four spaces, and although (b) every event in the system has properties belonging to each of the four spaces, nevertheless (c) every event may be analyzed with respect to its position within the network of relations constituting one of these spaces. Thus, (d) each space conceptually has its own distinctive set of relationships. This is why I can make of each of my spaces an abstracted conceptual system; that is, I can treat each of them as having a specified set of elements among which a specified set of relations exists. Let me make these elements and these relations explicit. I will do this for each space in turn.

(1) In the case of technological space, the elements or units may be a specified set of physical objects, job activities, or individuals (e.g., redheaded women). The set of relations may be any one of a number of spatial or temporal relations, such as north, south, east, and west; to the left of, to the right of; up, down; before, after; and so on.

(2) By purposive space I mean the way that the activities of two or more persons may be ordered to achieve a collective purpose. The units of the system may be a specified set of activities, jobs, positions, or individuals. The set of relations may be those of inclusion, exclusion, means-ends, part-whole, formal channels of communication, and so on.

(3) By social space I mean the way that the activities of two or more persons may be ordered in terms of interactions and sentiments. The units may be a specified set of roles, social classes, activities, individuals, or groups. The set of relations may be those of liking, helping, better than, worse than, influence, power, conflict, cooperation, dependence, obligation, and so on. Associated with these social relations are the notions of exchange and reciprocity, often expressed in terms of norms, such as how someone is supposed or expected to behave in certain circumstances and in certain kinds of relationships, e.g., father-son, mother-daughter, foreman-worker, and the like.

(4) By personal or life space I mean the way in which an individual's activities may be ordered in terms of his own preoccupations, wants, needs, aspirations, feelings, sentiments, emotions, and cognitive structures, such as perception, skill, and so on. These are the entities that I found were so important when I discovered life space during the period when I was counseling students.

In short, if I extensionalize my spaces in this fashion (i.e., by stating as clearly as I can each time the entities and relations I am talking about), I can produce four different abstracted conceptual systems. The differences among these spaces or systems are as well recognized by common sense as by the academic disciplines. Each space seems to generate its own jargon, key words, and concepts. For example, it is difficult to conceive of social space apart from sentiments, interactions, norms, roles, expectations, belonging, deviance, conformity, exchanges, reciprocities, status, conflict, cooperation, and power. And it is difficult to conceive of life space apart from needs, skill, learning, preoccupations, perception, choice, becoming, life style, life cycle, self-concepts, superegos, and ego ideals.

To each of these spaces it is as easy to attach the words structure or organization as it is the word system. The work flows of technological space in the concrete system called a business enterprise, for example, become its technical organization or structure. The hierarchical and communication systems of purposive space become a firm's formal organization or structure. The relations of status, friendship, and influence become its informal organization or structure. The attitude, preference, and cognitive structures of life space become the personality organization or structure of persons.

It seems as though a researcher or observer can make a system out of any set of entities and relations he wishes. To an extent this is true; that is, a knowledge maker does not have to choose for his entities and relations only those that can be observed in a particular concrete system. He may create pure spaces, to which he can then give different empirical meanings.

By 1960 the word system was being attached to almost anything; and lo and behold, each time that this happened there emerged a new subject matter—and would you believe it?—a new theory. To mention a few, there were information systems (and theory); exchange systems (and theory); reward systems (and theory); hierarchical systems (and theory); personality systems (and theory); and cultural systems (and theory). In addition, there were open systems, closed systems, artificial systems, natural systems, rational systems,

and empirical systems, as well as the kinds of systems I am trying to differentiate: abstracted systems and concrete systems. And of course for each system there was at least one set of theories.

Lord forbid that by my jesting I convey the impression that I think the notion of a system is not basic and fundamental to the development of a science. But adding the word system to a set of entities does not make it a system. Unless the set of relations which exists among the set of entities can be specified, there is no system, but only a mish-mash of unrelated, over-related, or under-related entities. Furthermore, even if a set of entities and a set of relations are specified and a perfectly good conceptual system has been created, it may still fall short of being useful.

Despite this widespread use of the terms system, structure, and organization, the concepts are riddled with ambiguity and imprecision. For example, the structures of technological space are more visible than the structures of other spaces. For the specialists of life and social spaces, the term structure often refers to underlying processes, whereas for the specialists of technological and purposive spaces, structure usually refers to the visible and static aspects of the phenomena of human behavior.

These differences arise in part because the relations in the separate spaces differ greatly in the properties called logic and rationality. I have referred to these differences in bits and pieces throughout this book. Let me try now to state them abstractly and systematically in terms of the properties by which logicians would classify them; that is, in terms of the properties of reflexiveness, symmetry, and intransitivity and their opposites, irreflexiveness, asymmetry, and transitivity. Believe me, it is easy then to see the differences that exist among the spaces.

THE LOGICAL PROPERTIES OF THE SPACES

As I said in Chapter 10, relations that have the properties of irreflexiveness, asymmetry, and transitivity produce orderings about which certain statements may be made that are generally considered logical and rational. Logical inferences can be made from them. The relation of "greater than" in the set of finite integers, for example, enjoys these properties par excellence. This relation is clearly irreflexive, asymmetric, and transitive. Though such a distinct and complete ordering is hard to find among the entities and relations of concrete systems, it is more clearly approximated among the entities

and relations of technological space than among those of any of the other abstracted spaces.

For convenience and clarity of exposition I will construct a diagram of three points (A, B, and C) and three relations (r) in the form of three lines with arrows to indicate the direction of the relations among them, such as this:

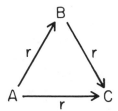

For the moment I will not assign any specific meanings either to the points or to the lines. Rather I will consider them as pure points and lines, as mathematicians would in pure logic. Then I can make the following statements—among others—about the diagram. For the points A, B, and C, I will say that the relations ArA, BrB, and CrC are no-go (i.e., the relation r is irreflexive). For the points A and B, B and C, and A and C, ArB precludes BrA; BrC precludes CrB; and ArC precludes CrA (i.e., the relation r is asymmetrical). And for the points A, B, and C, whenever we have ArB and BrC, then we also have ArC (i.e., the relation r is transitive).

Let me now assign different meanings to the three points A, B, and C (entities) and to the three directed lines (relations). Let us see what happens to the properties of irreflexiveness, asymmetry, and transitivity as we proceed from one space to another.

I will begin with pure logic and say that A, B, and C represent propositions and that the directed lines stand for the relation "to imply." I can then say that the diagram means that the propositions A, B, and C do not imply themselves (i.e., the relation "to imply" is irreflexive). I can also say that although A implies B and C, and B implies C, B does not imply A, and C does not imply either B or A (i.e., the relation "to imply" is asymmetrical). The diagram may also be interpreted in logic to mean that if A implies B, and B implies C, then A implies C (i.e., the relation "to imply" is transitive). Furthermore, in pure logic the properties of irreflexiveness, asymmetry, and transitivity hold not only for certain propositions, as illustrated by this particular diagram, but also for any old propositions A, B, and C, regardless of their content, that one cares to mention.

Let me take an example from geography and say that A, B, and C stand for San Francisco, Chicago, and Boston, respectively, and the directed lines for the relation "to the west of". Then I can say that the diagram means that San Francisco is west of both Chicago and Boston; that Chicago is west of Boston; and that San Francisco is not west of itself. If these statements are true, then Boston cannot be west of San Francisco and Chicago, and Chicago cannot be west of San Francisco. These statements are true even if A, B, and C stand for other places than the three cities or are "Of shoes—and ships—and sealing wax—Of cabbages—and kings," provided only that their locations in geographical space are the same in relation to each other as those of the cities I named.

Now let me move from pure logic into *technological space* and say that A, B, and C represent the activities of purchasing, fabrication, and inspection, respectively, and the directed lines the relation of "before." Then I can say that the diagram means, for example, that raw materials have to be purchased before they can be fabricated into final products and that the products have to be fabricated before they can be inspected. This is true whether the materials to be purchased are iron, wood, or cotton and the final products to be inspected are automobiles, battleships, or bubble gum.

Now let me move into *purposive space* and say that A, B, and C stand for persons and the directed lines for the relation "to give orders to." Then I can say that the diagram means, for example, that A may (shall, does) give orders to both B and C; that B may (shall, does) give orders to C; but that C may not (shall not, does not) give orders to A and B. Although this is true for this particular case—and there are many examples in concrete systems—nevertheless, this diagram may not be interpreted in purposive space to mean that if A may (shall, does) give orders to B and if B may (shall, does) give orders to C, then A gives orders to C, regardless of what persons A, B, and C stand for or what organizations they are members of.

Likewise, if the directed lines stand for the relation "carries messages to," it may be said that A is the transmitter, B the carrier, and C the receiver of messages. It is not always true in the empirical world, though, that if A gives messages to B, B may not (shall not, does not) give messages to A; or that if A gives messages to B and B gives messages to C, A may (shall, does) give messages to C. Least of all may it be said that C always receives the message that A gives B to carry to C.

What is happening? When we enter purposive space, where the entities are people and the relations are those which exist, might exist, or should exist among them, the properties of asymmetry and transitivity get shaken up and statements that follow logically in the case of the relations of "to imply," "to the west of," and "before" and "after" do not follow. It looks as if when the points A, B, and C represent persons and the directed lines represent their formal relations to each other, a wee bit of intransitivity comes in. That this is happening to the logical properties of the relations becomes increasingly clear as we move into social space.

Among the relations of *social space*, such as like, dislike, love, hate, trust, and distrust, the properties of asymmetry and transitivity are by no means guaranteed, and neither is the property of symmetry. To be sure, in social space there are many reciprocal relations which are symmetrical rather than asymmetrical. They can be symbolized by the diagram

to which the following meanings—among others—may be given: A likes B, and B likes A; A hates B, and B hates A; A trusts B, and B trusts A; and A confides in B, and B confides in A. It cannot be said of the empirical world, though, that if A trusts B, then B trusts A; or that if A trusts B and B trusts C, then A trusts C, regardless of who A, B, and C are.

Although there is a tendency to attribute symmetry to such relations as like, dislike, love, hate, trust, and confide in, and to attribute asymmetry and transitivity to such relations as dominate and fear, these logical properties are not always present. When they are absent, argument from a logical point of view that they should be present does not create them. Furthermore, the absence of these properties does not make these relations illogical; it means only that these relations have little to do with formal logic. This characteristic results from an empirical uniformity in the properties of either the entities or the relations being considered. It is explained by facts, not logic.

From the point of view of formal logic the worst is still to come. The relations of *life space* bring the property of reflexiveness into bold relief. This property, together with asymmetry and an unclear transitivity, sometimes makes for trouble.

Let us look at the feelings which emerge from interactions in hierarchical orderings such as those in which A is the boss of B and C, B is the boss of C, and C has nobody to boss, perhaps not even himself. In such orderings, C's feelings (not represented in the diagram on page 407) may cause a lot of trouble. This is because poor little old C—the receiver of orders and formal communications in purposive space and the recipient and terminus of interactions, influences, and communications in social space—has no one to whom he can communicate what it is like to be in his unique position at the bottom of the totem pole. He is not interested in the fact that the properties of irreflexiveness, asymmetry, and transitivity put him there; he is saying, "For Christ's sake, get me out of this bind." But alas and alack, C has no one besides himself to tell it to. For want of anyone else to hew or hack, C stews in his own juice.

Now stewing in one's own juice has the property of reflexiveness par excellence. Indeed, it is well recognized that one may stew in his own juice as well as in the juices of others. To correct for this kind of reflexive relation, I will modify my previous diagram, which was irreflexive, so that it refers to the feelings that characterize the relations of life space. To do this, I will reverse the arrows; omit the r's that referred to the relations of technological, purposive, and social spaces; and add an arrow to represent C's feelings about himself. The diagram then looks like this:

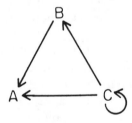

I can then say that this diagram means that A is stewing in the juices of both B and C, that B is stewing in C's juice, and that C is stewing in his own juice.

Life space is filled with these reflexive relations. Although they are bothersome from the point of view of formal logic, they do not always make for trouble. In fact, when they are combined with symmetrical relations so that A, B, or C is able to communicate with the others as well as with himself, as in the diagram

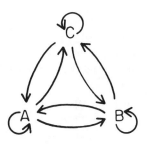

the possibility of making the relations of purpose and social space effective and satisfactory is vastly improved. But this possibility cannot be guaranteed by formal logic.

I could continue in this vein for a long time. However, I think I have already shown that although many of the entities in a concrete system may be ordered hierarchically in terms of some relation abstracted from the concrete system, nevertheless, as we proceed through the four spaces from technological space to life space, the properties of irreflexiveness, asymmetry, and transitivity become attenuated. They do not always produce complete, partial, or quasi-orderings which hold regardless of what the entities are that are being related. In many of the relations of purposive space, the property of transitivity, which makes for clear, distinct, and unambiguous orderings in technological space, becomes shaky. Many of the relations of social space suffer from intransitivity and have symmetrical rather than asymmetrical properties. In life space, the property of reflexiveness throws a monkey wrench into the logical machinery. For many of the important relations of life and social space, the properties of reflexiveness, symmetry, and transitivity and their opposites are ambiguous or entirely absent.

In these remarks I am not saying anything original. The points have been made, though perhaps in different terminologies, by philosophers for thousands of years and particularly by empirical scientists since the seventeenth century. I would not want to weary the reader with what is "old hat" and well understood. But I am no longer sure that all this is as clear as crystal or as clear as it may have been at one time. Sometimes I think that one argument after another, one debate after another, and even, God forbid, one research study after another about behavior in organizations proceeds as though these differences did not exist. So I will continue.

THE RATIONALITY AND IDEALS OF THE SPACES

In spite of the fact that many of the relations of social and life space have little to do with formal logic, it is incorrect to believe that rationality is absent from them. Indeed, each space has its own logic, rationality, and ideals; let me describe them.

Technological space has its optimal or "mini-maxing" rules and standards, by which the sequencing, allocation, and assignment of activities in concrete systems are evaluated and controlled to obtain maximum technical efficiency (to use the term in its ordinary rather than Barnardian sense). These rules and standards constitute "the logic of efficiency." This logic can be applied to people as well as to things. When it is, it concerns primarily their activities and movements in space and time that can be reduced to mathematical terms and equations; that is, to entities related to the activities of people which vary at a constant rate ("linear" equations) or at a varying rate ("differential" equations); or which achieve certain levels at specified times ("difference" equations); or whose outcomes can be arranged in a probability distribution.

According to the logic of efficiency (I am speaking now on a more low-brow level), a straight line is the shortest distance between two points; a chicken has to cross the street to get to the other side; and the least time and motion a worker spends on a unit of activity, the more units he will produce. The logic of efficiency has the rationality of a machine; its ideal is the condition of a perfect vacuum or frictionless state, where

$$\frac{\text{output}}{\text{input}} = 1.$$

The rationality of technological space, as I have defined it, lacks purpose. Like a clock it tells the time precisely up to, let us say, four decimal points; but it does not say where time is going. Purposive space supplies this ingredient in terms of procedural rules and production and methods standards by which the effectiveness of a concrete system can be evaluated and controlled and its goals achieved. Many of the means–ends relations by which the purposes of a concrete system are achieved also enjoy the properties of irreflexiveness, asymmetry, and transitivity, and they have logic and rationality akin to those of technological space. But whereas in technological space the entities being related are passive abstractions that may be manipulated apart from the people involved, the entities of purposive space are people who are actively engaged in doing the relating. As a result, in purposive space the machine-like efficiency of technological space loses some of its cold, objective, pristine beauty.

To distinguish the logic of the mechanical efficiency of technological space from the logic of purposive space, Bill Dickson and I in *Management and the Worker* called the latter the "logic of management" or the "logic of formal organization." This logic says what the formal relations and interactions between people are required to be and what they should be, if the collective purpose of the concrete system is to be achieved. The rationality of the logic of management consists not only in the fact that people have to cross the street to get to the other side but also in the fact that the activities of people have to be coordinated, if collectively they are going to get somewhere. Everyone cannot be crossing streets to get to the other side just for the hell of it. There has to be a little law and order (or structure, guidelines, and ground rules), if people are to accomplish something collectively. The rationality of the logic of management appeals to this fact of purposive collective living. However, because there is no complete agreement as to how much formal structure is needed to achieve the collective purpose, the logic of management does not enjoy the rational beauty of the logic of technical efficiency. It expresses a bounded rationality, in which the optimalities that characterize relations in technological space cannot be perfectly realized.

This unhappy state of affairs in purposive space can be seen in the ideals of that space. On the one hand, there is the ideal of perfect competition, in which, among other things, marginal revenues equal marginal costs:

$$\frac{\text{MR}}{\text{MC}} = 1.$$

On the other hand, there is the ideal of perfect cooperation, in which what the organization requires a person to do is the same as what he wants to do:

$$\frac{\text{Organizational requirements}}{\text{Individual need-satisfactions}} = 1.$$

There are still other factors which prevent the bounded rationality of purposive space from being achieved in a concrete system. These are the rules and standards of "fair exchange" of social space, by which the activities of concrete systems are also evaluated and controlled and by which so-called "justice" as well as technical efficiency and purpose are attained. The logic of fair exchange has a long history. It can be said historically that it preceded the logic of efficiency and the logic of management, which the modern world has in such abundance. Its rationality depends on a factor which does not appear—in fact, is conspicuously absent—in the logics of efficiency and management. This is the factor of sentiment. Following Pareto (1935) let me call the rationality of social space the logic of the sentiments.

The logic of the sentiments departs sharply from the properties of formal logic. From the point of view of formal logic, it is nonlogical, but this does not make it irrational. No, siree! The logic of the sentiments makes a rational music by its own sweet self which is sometimes dissonant but which often makes the logics of efficiency and management seem like aberrations of the human mind.

In most respects the logic of the sentiments is closer to the logic of everyday life than the other logics; in this sense it is closer to the concrete system than either the logic of efficiency or the logic of management. In social space to act in accordance with one's senti-ments and the sentiments of one's group is rational behavior. To act otherwise is not only nonlogical but is considered by many as irra-tional and nonhuman. In this ballpark a straight line is no longer the shortest distance between two social spaces; one crosses the street not just to get on the other side or to get somewhere but also in order to interact with another human being.

In this interaction the logic of the sentiments dictates what should occur and what the ideal outcome should be. The ideal of social space is the condition of perfect exchange or perfect justice, in which what one receives is equivalent to what one gives;

$$\frac{\text{what one receives}}{\text{what one gives}} = 1 \, .$$

This logic, like the logics of efficiency and of formal organization, is hard to realize. The relations in social space are not reflexive, symmetrical, and transitive. These relations do not enjoy the proper-ties of equivalence with which the logicians and mathematicians are concerned. Equality itself is the best example of a relation with these properties of logic; that is, where A is equal to itself; and where if A is equal to B, then B is equal to A; and where if A is equal to B, and B is equal to C, then A is equal to C.

In social space the rules of fair exchange are constantly being disrupted by deviant—shall we say—s.o.b.'s, who want to get more than they give or who want to be better than or superior to some-body else or have more power or influence than somebody else in some respect or other. The properties of equivalence, which are the basis of fair exchange in the ideal world of social space, are constantly being disrupted not only by the logics of efficiency and formal organization but also by the logic of life space.

In life space, though from a strictly logical point of view things are in a bit of a mess, nevertheless, they are very real. In life space it is rational that a person try to satisfy his needs. To do otherwise is to be a bit of a nut. This realization cannot be done in a vacuum; it has to be done within the constraints of technological space, purposive space, and social space. Therein lies the rub.

However, in spite of this difficulty, life space has its own rules and standards. They are the rules and standards by which the adaption of the individual to the concrete system is evaluated and controlled, so that his capacity to cope with it and to attain the states of satisfaction, peace, and happiness as well as those of growth, realization, and identity may be improved. Because of this multiplicity of foci, the ideals of life space speak in many tongues. I will mention a few.

For some the ideal of life space is the condition of perfect peace and happiness, where God's will—not man's—should be done; that is, where virtue is its own reward and where what God or society wants a person to be or to do (what Freudians call a person's superego) is the same as what a person himself wants to be or do (what Freudians call a person's ego): that is, in the language of psychoanalysis, where

$$\frac{\text{a person's ego}}{\text{a person's superego}} = 1.$$

For others it is the condition of "perfect self-realization," a state in which what a person wants to be (his ego ideal) is fully realized: that is, where

$$\frac{\text{a person's ego}}{\text{a person's ego ideal}} = 1.$$

For still others it is the condition of distributive—as distinct from perfect—justice, in which a person's rewards are proportional to his investments: that is, where

$$\frac{R}{I} = 1.$$

THE SPACES AND CONCRETE SYSTEMS

Of course, the ideals, equalities, and onenesses of the different spaces cannot be completely realized in the empirical world and its concrete systems. In concrete systems there are imperfect vacuums, imperfect competition, imperfect cooperation, imperfect exchange, and imperfect self-realization. This is so in part because the ideals of one abstracted space do not coincide with the ideals of another and in part because these abstracted spaces are not pure. They are always contaminated in concrete systems by the other spaces. As is obvious to the unsophisticated layman, the rules, standards, and values of the different spaces do not always mesh harmoniously. What is good for the technical performance or profits of General Motors, for example, is not always good for the life spaces of its workers or for the social spaces of the country.

Although the four spaces are man-made abstractions from concrete systems—useful abstractions, I feel, for the purposes of research by different space specialists—their status in relation to a concrete system is different from their status in relation to one another. This is the reason I keep distinguishing concrete individuals from the abstracted relations made by social space specialists, and concrete organizations from the abstracted relations made by technological and purposive space specialists.

Once the spaces have been identified, it is easy to stop seeing them for what they are; that is, as abstractions from the concrete. It is easy to confuse their status as abstractions and their status in concrete systems. As abstractions they are pure and manipulable. In a concrete system they are neither so elegantly pure nor so easily manipulable; they are once again parts of an interacting whole, a concrete system, as they were before they were abstracted by some space specialist for his purposes of making knowledge.

This is especially true of the relations of social space and of life space. Although the relations of these spaces may be treated as manipulable abstractions for the purposes of research, they cannot be pushed around so easily when they are brought back into a concrete system. They resume, so to speak, their phenomenological properties and become what they were before. This is also true, but not so easily apparent, of the abstracted relations of technological space and of purposive space. Under certain conditions the relations of these spaces can pass back and forth from the abstract to the concrete with the greatest of ease and seemingly without altering their status in reality. But when technological and purposive spaces are part of a concrete system in which their interactions with life and social spaces cannot be conveniently disregarded, the technological and purposive spaces—if treated by themselves—take on their true coloring and reveal the artificial properties that show they are abstractions.

In a concrete system the units are not abstractions, but concrete individuals. These concrete individuals have both nonlogical and logical properties (e.g., needs and sentiments as well as economic interests). The individuals are related to each other not only by purely social relations, but also by space-time relations and by the constraints of any larger systems of which they are subsystems. Both the units and the relations determine the nature of these concrete systems.

Henderson's conceptual scheme of a "social" system takes these complexities into account. It makes no value judgments as to which entities—the units or the relationships—are more important in determining the nature of the system. It makes no value judgments about which kind of relations among the members of the system is more important. It does say, to be sure, that the nonlogical sentiments (or residues, to use Pareto's term) of the components or units of the system—the concrete individuals—should not be ignored; but it does not say that these are the *only* properties of the concrete individuals or components of the system.

In short, according to Henderson's conceptual scheme, the state of affairs in respect to these questions in a particular situation is a matter of empirical determination; it is not a matter of verbal speculation; neither does it reside in the logic of the conceptual scheme. The conceptual scheme merely says "Look at the phenomena from this point of view and perhaps you may be able to settle how they are being determined in the particular situation you are observing."

Although a space in and by itself may be treated as a conceptual system, it cannot, by itself, become a concrete system. Life space, for example, may become a concrete system, a person, only when it is hitched to purposive relations, social relations, and technological space-time relations. Apart from these other spaces, life space is not a person but a zombie. This is true for the other spaces as well. Treated alone, apart from and unrelated to the other spaces, social space is a pastiche, purposive space a bureaucratic monstrosity, and technological space a technocratic nightmare.

The spaces are not abstractions which have only a set of characteristics or a class of properties in common, such as the class of red-headed women at the B-School. As I said earlier, in a class of that kind the members are not thought to be interacting units, as are the units of an abstracted system or space. Neither are my spaces pure conceptual spaces. That is, they are not systems of points (entities) and lines (relationships) to which different empirical meanings can be given, in the way I gave meanings to the points and lines in the diagrams I drew earlier in this chapter. The units and relations of my spaces have been selected by observation from the phenomena of behavior that occur in concrete systems.

Each of the spaces, as is true of the pure spaces of mathematicians, is man-made, so that its ontological status can be questioned. Each has been selected and abstracted from the behavior in concrete systems by some investigator for his own purposes (good or bad). Consequently, the biases of individual human beings may affect them. One kind of bias may be manifested according to whether the units (elements) or the relations among them are the more important in determining the nature of the space or system being considered.

If a researcher emphasizes the units and their properties, the possibility of confusion lies in obliterating the distinction between a class of elements and their properties, on the one hand, and an abstracted conceptual system on the other. Concepts such as personality and culture are examples of this kind of confusion. Each may be conceived of either as a *class* of elements and properties or as a conceptual *system* of interacting and related elements. Failure to specify which way the terms are being used then leads to considerable confusion.

If a researcher emphasizes the relations he has chosen rather than the units, he clarifies the abstracted system about which he is talking. An abstracted system is oriented toward these relations rather than toward the phenomena of behavior in a concrete system (which has these relations as well as others). The risk is that in the process of emphasizing the relations, the abstracted system and the concrete one will become confused.

Abstracted systems are common in the social sciences. In general they are associated with the different disciplines of the social sciences. So long as they are not confused with the concrete systems from which they have been abstracted, they can be useful. But when one group of scientists who are oriented toward concrete systems talks with another group who are oriented toward these abstracted systems as if they were both talking about the same thing, the confusion is terrible. This is particularly true when the talk is about the different kinds of systems that are called social. The problem arises in part because, while some investigators use the term "social" in reference to abstracted systems, others—including at times myself—have used it in reference to concrete systems.

SOCIAL SPACE, SOCIAL SYSTEMS, AND CONCRETE SYSTEMS

Because I find that this confusion is one of the greatest stumbling blocks to the unification of the sciences of human behavior, I want to illustrate the distinctions that I think exist between the concepts of what I call social space, the social systems of some sociologists, and the "concrete systems" for whose investigation Henderson provided a conceptual scheme.

By social space I mean a set of social relations by which the individuals in a specified concrete system may be given a position or place apart from the spatial or temporal relations by which they may also be ordered. Since there is more than one set of such social relations (e.g., power, influence, status, norms, social distance, social class,, etc.), an investigator may abstract and conceptualize a number of different social systems from a concrete system. In these social systems, the unit may be individuals or the properties of individuals and the relations are the variety of relations covered by the word social. Some investigators, for example, are more keen on conflict or power relations than on cooperative and helping relations, and so on.

By no stretch of the imagination can these systems be equated with concrete systems, even though I and others sometimes use the term concrete social systems, which, to make matters still more confusing, contain technological, purposive, and personal relations which are not strictly social in the sense I am now using.

Some social scientists, generally called sociologists, want to go still further in the process of abstracting social systems from concrete systems. Instead of having individuals as the units or elements of the systems which they study, these sociologists believe that the units should be the role relationships between individuals. Although this way of defining a social system helps to state the unit of analysis for the discipline of sociology, when a system so defined is confused with a concrete system—which as I have said is easy to do—the roles become, so to speak, more important than the individuals in the determination of human behavior. As one might suspect, other social scientists—psychologists, for example—do not like to be upstaged in this way, even though their abstracted personality systems in turn may as easily become confused with concrete systems and may thus lead them into making statements which upset sociologists.

Many times when I describe an organization in terms of social space—thereby intentionally neglecting matters associated with the other spaces—someone asks me, "Where the hell are the purposive relations? Where is the business of the business?" I retort, "Hell's bells, don't confuse the concrete organization with the particular space in terms of which for the moment I choose to describe it. The organization is a 'concrete system.'" Then to ball matters up still further, I add, "The concrete system, goddammit, has purposive relations." In this process of exposition, my swear words increase in number and vehemence, but communication does not improve. To my colleagues at the B-School, it looks as if I am trying to pull a rabbit out of a hat. In a way perhaps they are right, but not altogether, as I hope I have made clear.

I wish now to turn to the question of how the four spaces—the four different ways of thinking about the same phenomena—are related to one another. This is a problem that faces all of us who are concerned with investigating, understanding, explaining, and controlling human behavior in organizations. I, too, am now up against this question.

Chapter 24
The Battles of the Spaces

Up to now I have accentuated the value differences of the techno-logical, purposive, social, and life spaces. I have referred to these differences as logics—the logics of mechanical efficiency, of formal organization and management, of fair exchange and the sentiments, and of personal satisfaction and growth. I have tried to show that each logic expresses a dominant value position in terms of which each space is generated. Given what little we know about the human mind, it would be strange indeed if such widely disparate value systems had remained separate without attempts having been made to order them in terms of some criteria by which one space could be said to be "superior to," "more real than," "more rational than," or "more objective than" some other.

Well, the extraordinary has not happened. Arranging the spaces in some kind of order is a popular game indeed. It has been played not only by humanitarians who claim to know what this ordering should be, but also by space specialists enamored of the importance of their own spaces; by interdisciplinary space specialists who try to relate the spaces in some coherent whole; by generalists who try to administer them; and last, though by no means least, by laymen who try to live and cope with them. Among these separate groups the differences of opinion are terrific. Can some order be found in this chaos?

ORDERING THE SPACES ACCORDING TO
SOME CRITERION OF VALUE

One way that people frequently use to order the spaces is to arrange them according to some value criterion. There are at least three choices. The spaces can be ordered according to the fairly explicit values of different groups in society. They can also be ordered ac-cording to the more implicit absolute values of the wider society or culture. Or, third, they can be ordered according to the concepts, models, metaphors, and imagery of persons who are trying to bring order to the chaos "out there" in terms of some new subject matter or vision of the universe.

Whichever choice is made, there are 60 different ways in which any one of the spaces can lose standing in relation to the others. To put it another way, there are 15 permutations to the ways in which the four spaces, taken two, three, or four at a time, may be subordinated to technological space; 15 to purposive space; 15 to social space; and 15 to life space, a total of 60. This large a number adds to the confusion. Let me summarize the exercise by counting the orderings in tabular form. In the table, I refer to each space by its initial. TP, for example, means that purposive space is subordinated to technological space. Similarly TPS means that social space is subordinated to both purposive space and technological space and, in addition, purposive space is subordinated to technological space.

TAKEN		PERMUTATIONS
2 at a time	12	(TP, PT, TS, ST, TL, LT, PS, SP, PL, LP, SL, LS)
3 at time	24	(TPS, TSP, PTS, PST, STP, SPT, TPL, TLP, PTL, PLT, LTP, LPT, TSL, TLS, STL, SLT, LTS, LST, PSL, PLS, SPL, SLP, LPS, LSP)
4 at a time	24	(TPSL, TPLS, TSPL, TSLP, TLPS, TLSP, PTSL, PTLS, PSTL, PSLT, PLST, PLTS, SPTL, SPLT, STPL, STLP, SLPT, SLTP, LPTS, LPST, LTPS, LTSP, LSPT, LSTP)
Total	60	

I am not sure that all 60 of these ways were represented in the literature that I read during the period in which I was reading books for my seminar, but I found a sufficiently large number of them to become hopelessly confused. One of the main sources of my confusion was that the game of arranging the spaces in some kind of value ordering is not considered "scientific." Therefore, space and interdisciplinary space specialists play it covertly. As a result, they produce "infrastructures," a fancy word for "structures" as influenced by the sentiments of an observer. Hence, the results are of a kind to which the different "value-free" space specialists do not like to admit. If I take these infrastructures into account, it is my impression, though I have never researched the problem in an objective manner, that the 60 permutations are all represented in the flood of books published in the behavioral and management sciences during the 1960s.

Although this exercise in counting helps to show the number of ways in which the specialists of any space can reduce each of the other spaces to the specialists' conception of what is real, rational, and so forth, I am unhappy with these monistic solutions.

First, this approach seems to perpetuate the problem I am trying to get out of. In some sense each space represents some important value in the concrete system. To decide which one of the values is more important, significant, real, rational, etc., prevents looking at how the four spaces are empirically related in the concrete system.

Equally dead-end to me is the search for some super-map which conceptually puts together these four different ways of representing the concrete system. It seems to me futile to search for structures isomorphic to these four different analytical schemes. The four spaces are constructed for the purpose of differentiating the kinds of relations by which the activities of persons in the concrete system are being or can be ordered. The question is not how they may be related at some higher level of abstraction, but how they are related at the level of concrete phenomena.

Furthermore, I find it equally unsatisfactory to treat the different spaces as different phenomenological realities. Under this conception the four spaces become four separate subsets of phenomena that are exhaustive of the concrete system. Each space becomes regarded as an independent phenomenological unit with its own subject matter and theories. The trouble with this conception is that in the concrete system, as any practitioner or field worker knows, many problems exist which cannot be stated in terms of one space alone, because they involve two or more spaces. Neither the practitioner nor the interdisciplinary knowledge maker, who is trying to put these spaces together into some coherent whole, can ignore this state of affairs. In the concrete system the spaces are related; the question is how.

ORDERING THE SPACES EMPIRICALLY

Another method of ordering the spaces is to search for the way they are empirically related. I think that is the direction in which the behavioral sciences should go, so that these empirical relations can be pointed to in the form of recognizable syndromes or can be expressed in terms of explicit propositions. If there is no meaning to this way of ordering the spaces, then the science of human behavior, the science of administration, and the subject matter of "organizational behavior" are all in jeopardy. If the four spaces are not empirically related to each other in concrete systems, we are spinning our wheels in arid abstractions and lofty metaphors.

Let us look at the spaces once again. So far, except for my brief excursion with the 60 permutations, I have taken them up one at a time. Let me now take them up two at a time; perhaps this will help us to see simple uniformities in their relations.

When we take the spaces up two at a time, there are 12 possible permutations to consider: TP and PT; TS and ST; TL and LT; PS and SP; PL and LP; SL and LS. The question is what happens when we subordinate one space to another. In a simple-minded sense, let us ask if this step produces some well-known and recognizable tunes—not necessarily just sweet melodies, but perhaps also some ouches—with which, in an intuitive way, we may all be familiar. As can be seen in the chart, I express the results sometimes in terms of popular slogans, sometimes in terms of problems or issues, and sometimes in terms of false dichotomies. These expressions indicate the kind of responses that space specialists have, when the space with which they identify is subordinated to one of the other spaces.

Because this chart may be difficult to read, let me ask you not to wrap a wet towel around your head and wrinkle your forehead in trying to understand it. No great truth will be be revealed in this fashion. Instead I suggest that you put yourself in some reclined and not up-tight position in the hope that this will help you play with the obvious. While in this comfortable position and looking at the chart, I ask you to identify with some space and its value representatives when they are being subordinated to one of the other spaces. Let us say you choose technological space when it is being subordinated to purposive space and the logics or values it represents (box 1 in the top row of the chart). Then ask yourself how you would feel if you were a specialist identified with technological space. Don't be objective at this point; express freely both your feelings and the feelings you hear being expressed by the specialists of technological—the

Reactions Produced When One Space Is Subordinated To Another

Superior Spaces

Subordinated Spaces	Technological	Purposive	Social	Life
Technological	✕	**1** Positional authority overrides technical efficiency (bureaucracy)	**2** Social status and group cohesiveness override technical efficiency (economic underdevelopment)	**3** What is personally rewarding overrides technical efficiency (Theory Y vs. Theory X)
Purposive	**4** "Technocracy" "Computerology" "Scientism"	✕	**5** Informal organization overrides formal organization (getting along is more important than getting things done or getting ahead)	**6** Doing one's own thing overrides organizational loyalty (overpermissiveness)
Social	**7** Technical efficiency overrides cooperation (technical standards vs. social norms)	**8** Formal organization overrides informal organization (control vs. motivation)	✕	**9** Identity vs. anomie
Life	**10** Machine vs. man	**11** "Organization man"	**12** Conformity vs. individuality (society vs. the individual)	✕

subordinated—space. You will find that the feelings will be something like the ones conveyed by the phrases in box 1. Do this eleven more times, so that you have covered all twelve of the boxes. You will then have read the chart in the way I prepared it. No big deal; but when the interactions of logic with the variety and depth of human experience represented in the chart produce an orderly arrangement of empirically recognizable results such as this, my experience suggests that I am on the track of something that is relevant to the way things happen.

In no way do I think I have exhausted all the contexts in which these value nuances may be expressed. With a little effort I could write an essay and even a book about each box. In fact, in my opinion there is hardly one of the 60,000 or more cases collected by members of the Business School Faculty in the discussion of which the issues, problems, and dichotomies I have stated briefly in each box would not or could not be raised. In considering the problems of economic development in India, for example, the issues of boxes 2 and 5 can hardly be ignored. When industrialization, urban renewal, the ghetto, busing, management development, organization development, research and development, superior-subordinate relations, career development, or marriage—to mention just a few—are discussed, one or more of the boxes starts sputtering. Clinical reports and field reports are filled with one or more of the issues raised by these boxes. Hardly a day went by in my 40 years at the B-School in which I did not meet more than one of them in formal and informal interactions. Each chapter of this book cites examples that fit into one or another of them.

In a way I am being unfair, because the intractable reality with which interdisciplinary space specialists—including those who teach in business schools—deal is not all of a piece. This makes their subject matter more difficult to define than that of unidimensional space specialists.

Moreover, researchers have produced some statements resembling propositions that include variables chosen from two of the spaces in each of the twelve permutations TP and PT, TS and ST, TL and LT, PS and SP, PL and LP, SL and LS. In these statements the other two spaces are treated as givens, boundary conditions, or intervening variables. Some of the hypotheses that Abe Zaleznik, Roland Christensen, and I used in *The Motivation, Productivity, and Satisfaction of Workers*, especially in Parts III and IV, are examples. Some progress has been achieved by linking the variables from the different spaces in propositional form; so there is some progress in the direction that I think is fruitful. Still, by this approach it is very difficult to make propositions that state relationships between variables taken from three—and particularly from all four—of the spaces.

AFFINITIES AMONG THE SPACES

Up to now in both this chapter and the last, I have been writing as though the four spaces and their specialists were in serious opposition to each other. This is not entirely so; there are also affinities among them. The most marked are the affinities between the technological and purposive spaces and those between the social and life spaces.

As I have mentioned, the relations that are the basis of technological space and of purposive space are in a sense man-made, capable of being planned and designed. They are extrinsic rather than intrinsic in character and are concerned with required rather than emergent behavior and with aspects of behavior that can be easily and rapidly changed. An external frame of reference may easily be applied to them, and time may be treated externally.

The contrasts between the relations in these spaces and the relations that are the basis of social and life spaces are sharp. The relations in social and life spaces deal with the natural rather than with the man-made or the artificial. They are far less easily planned, designed, and changed, although not because people have failed to try. They are intrinsic rather than extrinsic in character and cannot be easily separated from the entities being related. An internal frame of reference is necessary for an understanding of them, and internal time and historicity are of their essence.

The differences between these two sets of spaces are often expressed in terms of two kinds of totalities or wholes. There are those wholes which may be broken down into their separate parts, either conceptually or concretely or both; the parts may then be recombined or reassembled to form the original or new and more exciting wholes. Such artificial wholes are the sum of their parts. Their behavior can be predicted from the behaviors of their separate parts. Their existence comes after their parts have been analyzed and conceived. For example, the computer could not have come into existence before the behavior of its parts was well understood.

On the other hand, there are also wholes which, though they may be analyzed into constituent parts, cannot be put back together again, like Humpty Dumpty. As the existentialists sometimes say, these wholes exist before they are analyzed and conceived. For example, a giraffe or even man exists before he is analyzed or conceived by a space specialist.

The differences I am now talking about resemble the distinction I made between the spaces and concrete systems. In the case of life and social spaces, for example, the concrete systems—the concrete individuals and groups and their relations—from which the spaces are abstractions may be said to exist before they have been conceptualized and analyzed by life and social space specialists. This may not be said of the technological or purposive spaces or of the relations that are part of them. For at least since the building of the pyramids, men have conceived and brought into existence new forms of organization in order to achieve their collective purposes.

If we equate life space with individual behavior, social space with social behavior, and technological and purposive space with organizational behavior, it looks as though individual and social behavior are concerned with the natural and as though organizational behavior is concerned with the artificial. This state of affairs has some curious results. For some interdisciplinary space specialists the differences make the intractable relations of the social and life spaces more concrete and real than the relations of the technological and purposive spaces. For others the same differences make the more manipulable relations of technological and purposive spaces the more concrete and real. But if human behavior cannot be so easily compartmentalized—and remember, individual, social, purposive, and technological behaviors all occur in concrete systems at the same time—we are left in the concrete situation with a mixed bag of the artificial and the natural.

These differences have a deeper significance, for they make up the mixed bag with which interdisciplinary space specialists have to deal and which these specialists have difficulty in putting together in some elegant fashion, either by concepts or by propositions. It seems an insurmountable task. Because the natural and the artificial cannot be treated as the same, the solution for integrating them that interdisciplinary space specialists seem compelled to take is that one has to be reduced to the other. In the 1940s and 1950s many specialists tried to reduce the artificial to the natural. When I tried this, as I said near the end of the last chapter, it produced the reaction, "You are ignoring the business of the business," meaning, in the language I am now using, that I ignored the artificial. In the 1960s, when it became popular to reduce the natural to the artificial, the shoe was on the other foot. The phenomenologists were up in arms and on the defensive, shouting "It can't be done."

To mix metaphors again, for social scientists this mixed bag is a hot potato indeed. No one, not even the interdisciplinarians, wants to pick it up. It seems as though the only way is to subdivide it into two cool parts and to choose between them. It seems as though it has to be one or the other and not both. Even among life space and social space specialists, whom, for purposes of exposition, I have so far treated over-simplistically as buddy-buddies with one another, it is not clear on which cool side of the hot potato they stand. There are bitter disputes among them about which side they should be on. Among sociologists the disputes produce "conservative sociologists" and "radical sociologists"; in psychology the battle is between "humanistic psychologists" and "behaviorists."

THE BATTLES IN THE BUSINESS SCHOOLS

Nowhere have these battles been fought more bitterly than among the experts on matters of organization in the business schools of the land. As far as I can tell from my hideout in retirement, the battle is still raging in the 1970s. And what a battle!

In most schools it has produced two camps. One is called management science, the other organizational behavior, interpersonal behavior, the behavioral sciences, and sometimes organizational development. The first camp is much clearer in regard to what it is up to than the second.

The first camp clearly champions the artificial. With the advent of the computer its adherents began making artificial wholes out of what had been considered the domain of the natural. According to them, decisions, intuition, and skill can be broken down into informational bits, out of which better and, they hope, more useful wholes for managers can be created. Their artificial posture may be clearly seen in statements made by their more enthusiastic disciples. They are not trying to make man into machines. Perish the thought! Rather they try to make computers human—to make the computer do in ways that are humanly rational what nonlogical man is trying to do by skill and intuition in ways that are nonrationally human.

The second camp believes that man's thought processes cannot be analyzed into bits and then built up into wholes. During the late 1940s and early 1950s, before computer models became the rage, the members of this camp were the champions of the phenomenological. They were "gestaltists" and "natural system" babies and believed in skill and judgment.

At first the two camps did not speak to each other very well or even very much; but during the late 1960s something strange (or perhaps not so strange) happened. In any science a new instrument for research—such as a computer—breeds a new language. During the 1960s a whole new language was born with such words as feedback loops, decision tress, trade-offs, spin-offs, interfaces, mathematical models, and information and artificial systems of all sorts—that is, systems that could be built from their differentiated parts. This was the language of the artificial.

During the 1960s this new language was in the ascendancy. Anyone who could not speak it felt he was prattling like a baby. This evaluation was hard for proponents of the second camp to take, particularly if they were junior faculty who wanted to become full professors. Gradually—so gradually that at first it was hardly noticeable—the proponents of the natural began to talk the language of the artificial, with the result that incommensurables began to be traded off. This produced a third group I call hybrids who, believe me, became the bane of my existence. I could talk with a good proponent of either the artificial or the natural, but I had difficulty understanding this new breed.

At first I thought this collaboration between the two camps would be a good thing; it would be good for each camp to understand the language of the other. But when the collaboration nearly became a one-way street, I changed my mind. What concerned me was not that the computer specialists failed to understand the language of social norms, codes, values, feelings, sentiments, perceptions, and internal frames of reference; in fact, at many meetings they acknowledged seriously the importance of these phenomena and of appropriate ways of looking at and talking about them. But they had little "knowledge of acquaintance" with them, with the result that the new instrumentation, about which they were ga-ga, transformed their talk about these phenomena as with a magic wand into the language of the artificial. Not that computer specialists were "meanies." Rather their cognitive style—or should I say the cognitive style of the computer—had to change the iconic and intuitive into the conceptual and systematic, or it would be going against its artificial nature. And we could not let that happen, could we now?

I think some of the more thoughtful computer specialists realized this problem. When they were temporarily off their guard—by means of alcohol or other tension-relieving procedures—they were able to express their feelings, and they acknowledged that their models were not really able to capture the richness and paradoxical nature of the territory. They pointed, sometimes sheepishly and sometimes bitterly, to the large number of unused and discarded models lying in the files of the great universities and corporations of the land. But did this dismay them? Not at all! In keeping with the best do or die, sink or swim tradition of Horatio Alger, they believed that the possibility still existed that somewhere and sometime a model would be produced that would say what is really going on in the intractable reality out there.

These computer specialists are not my main concern. They have technology on their side and they are riding high. My concern comes in relation to the field of organizational behavior in business schools and other institutions. What has this battle done there? Well, it has fragmented the field into two groups: (1) those who willy-nilly are going to study phenomena, even if in order to do so they have to change their field and (2) the hybrids who at one level are sincerely trying to achieve a rapprochement between the artificial and the natural, but who are doing this by talking the language of the artificial.

At least for a while these solutions produced what seemed to me a strange result. Those of us who remained in organizational behavior found ourselves talking the same language, but at the infrastructural and nonverbal level we meant different things. Besides producing new confusions, this shifted the battle to the infrastructural level, where it became less visible and audible but not any less bloody. At the verbal level things might appear peaceful and calm, but at the infrastructural level of feelings, there was much wailing and gnashing of teeth that could not be overtly expressed except in unhealthy ways. This state of affairs produced a lot of unresolved conflicts as well as unhappy hybrids.

The computer specialists were just as unhappy as the hybrids. As a matter of fact, there were both unhappy and conflicted computer specialists and unhappy and conflicted hybrids. Neither of them were pure knowledge makers. Even though they did not agree on what their subject matter was, they could not escape the fact that they were utilizers as well as makers of knowledge. Indeed, at business schools they were supposed to be training managers to utilize knowledge. As a result, the battle of "knowledge about what?" frequently turned into the battle of "knowledge for whom?" If we could not agree about the first, how could we agree about the second? Well, let's see.

Let me conclude my remarks about concrete and abstracted systems and the battles of their specialists. In this chapter and the previous one I have been concerned with the problems of conceptualizing the phenomena of human behavior in organizations from the point of view of explanation and the development of my subject matter. At this level of discussion, before I have taken up the problems of the relation of knowledge to action, I come to the conclusion that something like two contradictory but perhaps complementary principles—what I have called the natural and the artificial—are at work. For some purposes it is useful to look at behavior in organizations in one way; at other times and for other purposes it is useful to look at it in the other way. As long as this contradictory but complementary character of the phenomena is recognized, no harm is done. In fact, a step forward may have been taken, for there is no longer a need to argue about incommensurables. Discussion can move to more fruitful levels. But when space specialists and other advocates of concrete and abstracted systems do not recognize the differences, the battles and confusions develop rapidly.

The view that behavior in organizations needs to be looked at in complementary ways differs from the view that I held during most of my professional life. As I told in Chapter 11, I chose at that time to develop the social-system conception of human behavior in organizations and the skills of investigation and action associated with it—that is, observing, interviewing, and talking. I have no regrets that I did this. Indeed, I think it is only by some such process of committing oneself to a point of view and then pursuing it that science can progress. But I have already quoted Henderson as saying that a conceptual scheme, useful as a walking-stick to assist you here and now, is to be discarded when its work is done.

There remains for me a possibility that I have not yet discussed. Can that which interdisciplinary space specialists have difficulty putting together at high levels of abstraction be put together at the experiential level of skill? In their endeavor to be scientific, have space specialists thrown out the baby with the bath water?

These questions bring me back to the relation of knowledge to action. In the exploration of them in the two chapters which conclude this book, I will have more to say about the notion of complementarity as a suggestion for helping to understand the phenomena of human behavior in organizations.

Part VII

KNOWLEDGE AND ACTION IN
MODERN SOCIETY

Chapter 25

The Uneven Development of
Knowledge and Action

Action is for me related to the concrete and the particular in the here and now. Though one may act in relation to past experiences or to future expectations, action occurs in the present. It is taken by someone, somewhere, at some time. This property of action differentiates it sharply from the general properties of knowledge and provokes many of the intriguing questions about the relation between the two.

Although philosophers have debated these issues for many centuries, the questions have taken on a new meaning with the growth of the knowledge enterprise. This growth has brought an increasing division of labor between those who produce knowledge and those who utilize it or are supposed or assumed to do so. The result is an increasing gap between them. More strikingly than ever, the acquisition of knowledge has become one thing, its utilization in action another.

KNOWLEDGE VERSUS ACTION

This bifurcation of knowledge and action has produced some curious results. Clinical psychologists, for example, may acquire knowledge about human behavior through tests and research; but they are not supposed to apply it to concrete individuals in the form of psychotherapy. They may help in the diagnosis of a concrete situation; but they are not supposed to implement the diagnosis in the form of action because psychotherapy is the province of psychiatry. On the other hand, psychiatrists may practice psychotherapy with or without knowledge of clinical psychology.

The bifurcation of knowledge and action is also present in another field with which I am familiar. By the late 1960s the knowledge cupboards of the business schools were surfeited with knowledge which, despite its sophistication and respectability, administrators could not easily use. In addition, if you can believe this now, some students thought that this knowledge was irrelevant, perhaps even harmful, for the solution of the problems with which they believed administrators should be concerned. It was an elitist knowledge by means of which people could be manipulated and co-opted to the establishment. Thus, by the late sixties, the knowledge enterprise had lost some of its prestige. It was no longer the rock of Gibraltar, in which everyone could have an investment or, should I say, a piece of the action.

The bifurcation of knowledge and action has been one of my paramount concerns from the start of my intellectual career. It could be said that this book is a blow-by-blow account of my experiences with and reflections about the elusive relation between knowledge and action and the many guises which it takes. This relation has always been present, at least implicitly, in the action situations in which I became involved as a person, counselor, researcher, teacher, consultant, and administrator. Though the topic has not been far from the subjects about which I have written in the last chapters, I have not made it fully explicit. Indeed I have intentionally neglected it, while I concentrated on developing the knowledge aspects of my subject matter. I will now remedy this omission.

What I have to say will not be of a systematic character; that is not my forte. Neither will my statements go so far as to "resemble a primitive orgy after a harvest," as George Homans says the last chapters of a study may do. According to him, in the last chapters a researcher "is allowed a time of license, when he may say all sorts of things he would think twice before saying in more sober moments" (1961, page 378). Although I will not go as far as George's license permits, I will apply something of the spirit of it to my concluding remarks.

PROBLEMS OF TOO MUCH OR TOO LITTLE

In the world of practical human affairs there are some things of which we can have either too much or too little. This presents baffling problems to responsible actors in organizations—problems of maintaining equilibrium between the extremes of too much or too little. These problems of balance that confront administrators are different from the problems that the definition of equilibrium presents to knowledge makers, but they are no less important. Let me cite some examples. We can have too much or too little efficiency, progress, change, productivity, information, law and order, organi-

quandary. The x's, of which they cannot have enough today, become the y's, of which they cannot have too little tomorrow. Although this state of affairs keeps the learned journals going, it plays havoc with business administrators who want to deal responsibly with the phenomena in concrete organizations.

PROBLEMS OF DRAWING LINES

Closely allied to the problem of too much or too little and equally disturbing to responsible actors is the problem of drawing boundary lines between this and that: between, for example, a system and its environment, a society and an individual, a fact and a value, the subjective and the objective, the logical and the nonlogical, the descriptive and the prescriptive. Of course if there is a consensus between knowledge makers and knowledge utilizers about how the lines should be drawn, there is no problem, but in my experience this is seldom the case. According to modern scientific theory, knowledge makers may—indeed, for the purposes of research, should—draw their lines in arbitrary ways, so long as they state explicitly the purposes for which they are drawing them. If they do that, it is often said, they may draw them any damn way they please.

The responsible actor does not have this license. As a result, the way in which knowledge makers draw their lines for purposes of theory construction are often at variance with the ways knowledge utilizers draw theirs for purposes of action.

In the preceding chapters I have cited many examples of the confusions that result. Alas, in the process of trying to obliterate what I believe to be some false lines, I have made new distinctions and drawn new lines. Let me try to use them to deal with the relation of knowledge to action.

Although a systematic way of thinking is useful for knowledge makers, we have seen that it also presents problems for them. In Chapter 21 I used the concept of a social system as a system of persons with heterogeneous properties and heterogeneous relations to illustrate the problems. From the point of view of logical clarity and elegance, a system made up of entities with homogeneous properties and homogeneous relations is much to be preferred. These properties can be attained only by going to higher levels of abstraction. Doing so led me to consider the abstracted spaces I call technological, purposive, social, and personal (or life). In each case I endeavored to choose entities whose properties were of a piece with their relations. This was easier to do for the technological and pur-

zation, rules, standards, control, authority, cooperation, c
conformity, deviation, permissiveness, sensitivity, intuition, se
ferentiation, and integration.

Among this welter, there are, of course, values widely sha
the members of particular groups. The shared values of large
tivities are generally referred to as "cultures." In well-estal
cultures there is consensus about the values of which one
have too much (such as progress, health, education, truth, h
justice, happiness) and about the values of which one canno
too little (such as crime, hatred, bigotry, hunger, and po
These values are often dichotomized and stated in pairs of a
opposites. Thus, the value x, of which we cannot have eno
paired with the value y, of which we cannot have too littl
complete statement then takes the form, "We cannot have too
x and too little y." For example, we cannot have too much co
tion and too little conflict, too much law and order and to
violence, and too much love and too little hate.

Although this form of expression often helps to make a ca
value x, it also creates confusion. For example, in a dichoto
world such as I am speaking of, action-oriented persons usua
to maximize x, the value they want, and minimize y, the valu
do not want. If at the same time that they maximize x, they mi
y, then they are in clover. Thus, if by maximizing law and
they also minimize violence, everything is fine. Generally thi
pens only at the verbal level. At the nonverbal level things are
complex and do not work themselves out so neatly. Thus
happens sometimes throws action-oriented people back into
tradition. They find that sometimes they can have too muc
good thing and too little of a bad thing; that is, they can ha
much cooperation and too little conflict, too much conformi
too little deviation, or too much integration and too little
entiation.

This uncomfortable position is compounded by the fact t
modern societies there exist so many subcultures that there
general consensus about those things of which one can ha
much or too little. Each subculture has its own list. To com
things still further, the intellectuals and norm-setters of societ
changing their minds about these matters. One day they may s
society has too much conformity and too little deviation, or too
integration and too little differentiation, or too much coope
and too little conflict. The next day they may say the oppos
that mini-maxing, action-oriented persons find themselves

posive spaces than it was for the social and personal ones. Nevertheless, no matter how I sliced the cake, two different kinds of relations appeared again and again.

When something happens again and again, such as an apple falling to the ground—something in which the determining factors are so obvious that it staggers the imagination—I feel that a Newton should come along to tell us what it means. Surely such a pervasive uniformity should be expressed in some—let us say—three laws of human behavior. But alas, in the behavioral sciences, where we are all Einsteins trying to get meaning out of information in sophisticated ways, no Newton has appeared. We cannot seem to get back to a Newtonian level and state the simple and the obvious.

A-RELATIONS AND B-RELATIONS

Let me, therefore, list examples of the two kinds of relations that I kept finding. I will put them in separate columns, which I will call just A-relations and B-relations. I will curb my urge to declare these dichotomies false until I have considered them in their dichotomous state. Such pervasive and omnipresent dichotomies may be saying something important about reality, about ourselves, or about the relation between the two.

A-relations	*B-relations*
concrete relations	abstracted relations
nonlogical relations	logical relations
subjective relations	objective relations
internal relations	external relations
here-and-now relations	there-and-then relations
mutually dependent relations	simple cause and effect relations
exchange relations	unilateral relations
reflexive relations	irreflexive relations
intransitive relations	transitive relations
symmetrical relations	asymmetrical relations
cyclical relations	linear relations
intrinsic relations	extrinsic relations
satisfying, rewarding relations	optimal relations
process relations	structural relations
emergent relations	planned, designed relations
diffuse relations	specific relations
existential relations	probabilistic relations
etc.	etc.

A-relations and B-relations appear in both physical and social reality; I shall consider them only as they affect the problems of knowledge and action in social reality. I want to consider each of the columns as a whole, not the sets of terms in each row. In doing this I know that I am making one big dichotomy out of a lot of little ones. This is a dangerous thing to do. But because I am writing the last chapters of a book, not starting a new one; because the items in each column have a strong affinity for one another; and because as a totality each column expresses a common orientation, I am taking this route.

In A-relations the related entities are concrete persons, whereas in B-relations the entities being related can be abstractions from them—classes, aggregates, behavioral variables, and so on.

In A-relations the relations between the related persons are concrete relations and emerge from the concrete interactions, activities, and sentiments of people. The relations are intrinsic to the related persons and cannot be separated from them except by abstraction. In B-relations the abstracted relations are extrinsic to and can often be treated separately from the abstracted entities.

A-relations represent a concrete social reality, whereas B-relations represent an abstracted social reality. I treat A-relations sometimes as the phenomena themselves and sometimes as first-level abstractions from them. I do not think that this ambiguity is serious. From the point of view of action, A-relations have to do with concrete phenomena, while from the point of view of knowledge, they have to do with first-level abstractions from them.

B-relations always deal, from the point of view of either action or knowledge, with maps of phenomena and not with phenomena per se. Because there can be a map of a map of a map and so on, B-relations can produce maps that are two, three, or even more steps removed from phenomenological reality. Therefore, maps of them are always at least one step further removed from the territory of behavior than either concrete A-relations or first-level representations of them.

To state the point another way, although both A-relations and B-relations are the products of human beings, A-relations produce concretions arising from the interactions of human beings which can be regarded as phenomena, whereas B-relations can only produce or be the products of abstractions, which in and by themselves cannot be regarded as phenomena. Thus, A-relations represent naturalistic aspects and B-relations artificial aspects of society.

For these reasons, action from the point of view of A-relations is action at a point of interaction, here and now, whereas action from the point of view of B-relations is action from a distance, there and then. This is why for me the making of a decision or a policy is not concrete action and why concrete action does not take place until the decision or policy is implemented.

In A-relations apart from B-relations and at the level of elementary social behavior, distinctions between the knower and the known, the knower and the actor, and the knowledge maker and the knowledge utilizer do not arise as intellectual concerns. With the development of B-relations, this stage of innocence is gone forever, and all these distinctions occur.

B-relations tend to "objectify" the subjects of knowledge (the knowers), whereas A-relations tend to "subjectify" the objects of knowledge (the known). When the subjects and objects of knowledge are both active subjects—for example, when knowledge makers study knowledge users—these tendencies produce curious results. In the endeavor to obtain objective knowledge through B-relations (i.e., by objectified knowers), active subjects, as objects of this knowledge, become objectified and lose their quality of activity. As actors using A-relations, they resist being treated as objects by observers using B-relations. For them objective knowledge of their reality is for the birds. They tend, in turn, to show how subjective this knowledge is. This encourages the seekers of objective knowledge through B-relations to greater efforts to refine their methods in the direction of more sophistication and objectivity in terms of B-relations. All of the disciplines of the social sciences suffer from this problem.

This self-reinforcing, circular process describes the state of the social sciences today. The consequence is increasing sophistication of knowledge in terms of B-relations, coupled with decreasing relevance to A-relations and the phenomena of human behavior. Though many social scientists become pleased with their advances in knowledge, the application of this knowledge to real social problems does not progress.

For the purposes of both knowledge and action, neither A-relations nor B-relations can develop alone. The development of knowledge through A-relations apart from B-relations leads in the direction of self-knowledge and self-awareness on the part of the knower-actor. The development of knowledge through B-relations apart from A-relations leads in the direction of rationality. Apart from B-relations, A-relations cannot develop into a subject matter or discipline, what I prefer to call an "object matter." Apart from B-relations, the understanding of A-relations remains at the level of acquaintance with,

441

understanding of, skill in relation to, and clinical knowledge about separate events.

Thus, B-relations need the support of A-relations, if they are to remain in touch with concrete reality. In the process of objectifying A-relations for purposes of knowledge making, a knowledge maker has to select some of his variables and constraints from among them, and the question of whether he has chosen the relevant ones can only be settled by his knowledge or acquaintance with them.

From the point of view of action, A-relations apart from B-relations cannot develop or be developed into the large institutional structures required of modern society; the structures of A-relations remain subinstitutional. The cultivation of A-relations apart from B-relations leads to too much doing your own thing, doing what feels right, permissiveness, or *laissez-faire.*

On the other hand, there is much clinical evidence to suggest that the cultivation of B-relations apart from A-relations leads to excessive formalism, rigid controls, technical efficiency, procedural rules, and authority structures. B-relations need the support of A-relations, for without them complex organizations easily collapse, no matter how far they have developed.

Thus, neither A-relations nor B-relations can be cultivated apart from the other without producing anomalies in the development of either knowledge about or action in concrete reality.

THE EMPHASIS ON B-RELATIONS

In spite of this complementarity between A-relations and B-relations, the technologists of the social sciences today are addicted to B-relations. The reasons are clear. On the one hand, B-relations are considered more objective than A-relations, because they are more amenable to measurement. Their products may be stated in precise and operational terms and in propositional forms that may be tested by experimental and statistical procedures. In these respects they have the properties which are generally associated with "scientific knowledge." Yet first-hand observation is an important value of the scientific tradition; to be true to their phenomena, social scientists have also to be concerned with A-relations. These relations provide them with an elementary understanding of the phenomena with which they are concerned, even though they fall short of providing them with strict "scientific explanation" of them.

In fact, in order to get their fields of study started, the specialists of social and life spaces are compelled to distinguish between A-relations and B-relations. These distinctions are the basis of their orienting concepts—the concepts they need to point to what they are talking about (e.g., role, need, culture, self-concept, etc.). The literature of the social sciences abounds with these orienting concepts—so much so that some critics think that most social scientists, and sociologists in particular, are more often writing dictionaries than sentences or propositions.

But alas, these orienting concepts, because they are not capable of strict operational definition, do not provide a sound basis for writing scientific sentences. Thus, social scientists, if they are to remain scientific, need to seek concepts or variables that may be operationally defined. Hence, social scientists are in a bind. In order to get their disciplines started, they are compelled on the one hand to make distinctions between A-relations and B-relations; on the other hand, the distinctions become obliterated when to get their findings scientifically accredited they state them in terms of B-relations.

All this may be conceived as good clean fun among the knowledge makers, but it has serious consequences for action. It tends to reinforce the notion that until the study of human behavior has reached the kind of general propositions that characterize scientific knowledge, there is no valid knowledge to be applied. Obviously the search for general explanatory propositions is different from the search for effective action. The difference becomes increasingly true at the higher levels of the knowledge enterprise.

This two-step approach—knowledge first, action second—has been eminently successful in certain areas, for example, in electrical engineering, the atomic bomb, the missile, the computer, and going to the moon. In these areas the rapid development of successful applications followed the development of well-established theories in the form of general propositions.

I cannot find comparable examples in the human-social area. In this area where A-relations predominate, knowledge of or acquaintance with the phenomena involving those relations is being utilized and applied before it exists in the form of scientific propositions. The acquisition of this kind of knowledge—the kind I call "clinical" to differentiate it from the analytical kind that is associated with the ideals of science in the physical sciences—goes hand in hand with the practice of a point of view and a skill.

The emphasis on B-relations for the acquisition of valid knowledge about behavior in organizations has other consequences for action. It tends to reinforce an external frame of reference. If we regard B-relations as tending to produce more valid knowledge than

A-relations, it follows that valid action is more likely to be derived from an external than from an internal frame of reference. It also follows that an administrator should look at the system he is administering as though he were outside it and to act as though he were *not* an involved member of it. Because this prescriptive rule has little descriptive basis (that is, an administrator is in fact a highly involved member of the system and his behavior has important consequences for it), it tends to undervalue feelings and interactions (the administrator's as well as those of others) and to reduce the internal environment of the concrete system he is administering to the aspects which may be dealt with in terms of B-relations.

This misevaluation has still further consequences. In those cases where A-relations are recognized as being present and important, scientists and actors assume that they may be dealt with in the same manner as B-relations. This assumption manifests itself in thousands of ways. For example, if we define an action problem as a deviation from some specified standard and thus as a state of affairs about which something should be done, the assumption appears in the guise of treating a deviation from a personal standard or a social standard in the same way as a deviation from a technical or organizational standard. It appears in the form of correcting a breakdown in cooperation or communication by more logical coordination and formal rules. It appears in the search for optimal solutions where none obtain. Its most prevalent manifestation is in treating the implementation of a rule, standard, or policy as something any dummy can do, once the rule, standard, or policy has been stated.

If the reader has any question about the relative status of A-relations and B-relations in the application of knowledge to concrete situations, he or she should consider again the problem of implementation. It never ceases to astonish me that in modern organizations the implementation of rules, standards, policies, and programs is generally left to the lowest-status people. At the point of interaction, where A-relations prevail and where action most often is—at this most fateful encounter where the cookie is most likely to crumble—the knowledge enterprise folds up, and the knowledge makers say, "Let George do it." And who is George? Well, he is generally some unsophisticated, uneducated, economically unsuccessful person at the bottom of the totem pole. I do not understand how the task of setting rules, standards, and policies can be considered more difficult and more deserving of high reward than the task of implementing them.

The bifurcation of A-relations and B-relations that manifests itself in the knowledge enterprise in the ways I have just described permeates modern society. It appears when we contrast so-called primitive organizations with so-called modern ones. Primitive societies seem to be organized around A-relations, modern ones around B-relations. This is not strange, when we consider the kinds of "products" which are generated by and associated with A-relations, on one hand (e.g., tradition, custom, kinship, rituals, myths, social norms, codes, routines, friendships, etc.), and B-relations, on the other (e.g., technological innovation, machines, tools, technical products, procedural rules, technical standards, profit centers, etc.).

Modern organizations differ from primitive ones not only in the ever-increasing number of new products and tools but also in the number of new occupational roles that develop concurrently—for example, salesmen, investors, suppliers, retailers, wholesalers, advertisers, workers, managers, physicians, lawyers, teachers, counselors, consultants, and so on and on. These roles must number in the thousands when further subdivisions are included, such as airline stewardesses, programmers, astronauts, pilots, hematologists, cardiologists, urologists, radio and television announcers, disk jockeys, systems analysts, and so on. These new occupational roles and relations of modern societies are more abstract and specialized than the concrete and diffused roles and relations of primitive societies, for they refer primarily to roles in the occupational and economic sectors of society, as contrasted with roles in society as a whole. Thus, they are more readily capable of logical definition, and they can more easily be expressed in terms of B-relations.

In spite of this capacity for logical definition and specificity, these new roles and relations suffer more from ambiguities and conflicts than the less easily defined or definable and diffused relations of primitive societies. These confusions occur because in modern societies more people are involved in determining them. Take, for example, the role of an airline stewardess. Her role is determined in part by the airline management; in part by the union (if she is a member); in part by the pilot; in part by the passengers; and in part by the airline stewardess herself. They do not all necessarily agree upon what her role should be. Thus, her role as defined in organizational space is sometimes at variance with her role as defined in social space or by herself. As a result, she may not be sure about how far she should go in serving passengers' needs and wants; the airlines in their "Fly Me" advertising do not make it perfectly clear where and how the lines are or should be drawn.

These abstracted and specialized roles of modern society do not satisfy mankind's different needs equally well. They satisfy his needs for achievement, status, specialized technical competence, and economic success far better than his needs for friendship, belonging, and affiliation. These latter needs are better satisfied in small informal groups, in which he is not evaluated as an abstracted role in a system of abstracted relationships, but in which he can be himself, do his own thing, express his individual life style, and be accepted as a person.

Thus, in modern societies A-relations and B-relations are often manifest in a bifurcation of life into private and public spheres. In the public sphere, at work, and in his dealings with other abstracted roles an individual accepts up to a point being treated as a social security number, a consumer, a worker, an airline passenger, a client, a patient, a stewardess, etc.; but in the private sphere at home or in small groups and among friends he or she wants to be treated and is usually treated as a unique person.

Modern man does not find this bifurcation an easy or completely satisfactory resolution. Although he realizes that these abstract relations are essential for the running of modern complex organizations, he wants them to be human. He constantly seeks to humanize them, even though doing so may be like trying to get blood from a turnip. Let us see what happens in modern organizations to such time-honored and traditional characteristics of A-relations as sex, age, seniority, education, religion, ethnicity, and race. Do the status values attributed to these characteristics disappear? Does merit in terms of B-relations take over?

From my experience and reading, it is apparent that, far from disappearing, these values get lit up like firecrackers. Charges of discrimination against or in favor of every one of them increase. Today the form in which they are being most vociferously expressed is in charges of discrimination against Blacks and women. These characteristics of A-relations are in fact the values most out of line with the egalitarian ideals of a democratic society. However, in particular instances charges of discrimination may take either of two possible forms; that is, in favor of women and against men or vice versa; in favor of the young and against the old or vice versa; in favor of college graduates and against high school graduates or vice versa; in favor of Protestants and against Catholics or Jews or vice versa; in favor of Anglo-Saxons and against southern Europeans or vice versa; or in favor of Whites and against Blacks or vice versa.

Thus, in a modern society, in which B-relations are highly cultivated, there is likely to be (1) an increase in role ambiguity (e.g., it is no longer perfectly clear that man's work is from sun to sun and woman's work is never done); and also (2) an increase in status incongruence (e.g., younger and shorter-service women may get the same pay as older and longer-service men). As a result, there is (3) an increase in felt injustices, expressed in such forms as "Age, experience, loyalty, seniority, or education don't count around here any more," because the different status factors are no longer in line with pay. There is also (4) the increase in charges of discrimination in favor of or against age, seniority, men, women, Blacks, Whites, and so forth.

These felt injustices are not all expressed overtly in the same form or all the time. Some of them are manifest covertly in forms of behavior that are in opposition to the standards of performance required by B-relations (e.g., in forms such as restriction of output, featherbedding, moonlighting, etc.). Some of them go underground, where they fester until some incident sparks them off; then all hell may break loose. Some of them are expressed in the form of organized pressure groups and become highly vocal.

Some sociologists, speaking from a broad historical perspective, say that science and technology have liberated man from the narrow confines and traditional restraints of the tribe and the clan. This has allowed him to develop a system of relationships in which he has become a free individual with universalistic rights and obligations to other free individuals, but in which he is no longer a slave to the particularistic norms of custom. Although the forces of modernization have done a good job in this respect, the price paid for this liberation is alienation, which in time creates isolated and lonely individuals with no sense of community and no true identity. The pursuit of individual freedom—or at least too much of it—thus becomes transformed into the pursuit of loneliness.

These consequences are not recognized at once, because hope lingers on the part of the logical revolutionary that in time a new wholeness, a truly classless and nonalienating society, an all-embracing community, will emerge and replace the old society, dominated by tradition and custom, for which the old-fashioned romantic reactionary yearns. Alas, this has not happened. After a hundred years or so of pursuit—too long for the lifespan of a particular individual—this vision of an all-embracing community of free individuals grows dim, and a return to the particularistic rights of nations, Blacks, women, youth, etc., as against the universalistic rights of individual man, begins.

Although the mills of the gods have been grinding slowly but surely in this direction for some period of time—ever since the first industrial revolution, perhaps—in the late 1960s the consequences reached a really virulent form in the United States, where the greatest development of B-relations has been achieved. At that time the various forms of what is sometimes called the counter-cultural revolution arose: black power, the youth culture, the human potentials movement, student power, the women's liberation movement, the gay liberation movement, communes, and the attempt to modernize the Catholic Church by translating the mass from Latin into the vernacular.

Then the liberated but alienated members of our society no longer nursed their grievances underground. They now expressed them overtly and in forms that often seemed topsy-turvy. Many liberals who had spent their lives fighting for what they believed to be social justice (e.g., peace, brotherhood, liberty, equality, and integration) now found themselves accused of being old-fashioned white socialists, trade unionists, libertarians, or integrationists, and of belonging to neo-colonial, paternalistic, bourgeois, middle-class, white welfare organizations. "We don't want your love, help, and understanding; no more shuckin' and jivin'; we want self-determination and justice," said the militant Blacks. "Tell it to 'em like it is and not how the white man wants to hear it" was the slogan. "You can't do this to us," cried the liberal Whites. "You can't exclude us like this. We love you. You are our brothers. We are your brothers. We want to help you. What can we do? What should we do?" And the Blacks replied: "Look at your dirty white face in the mirror, white man. Leave us alone. Clean up your own dirty white power structure."

It looks as though the abstract universalistic rights of man are being supplanted by the concrete particularistic rights of groups and individuals. Who is the particular man in the universalistic "rights of man?" In the first place, he is a male; second, he is a white male; third, he is likely to be a white Anglo-Saxon Protestant male (how much more chauvinistic can you get?); and fourth, he is likely to be a member of the white power structure and the so-called establishment.

According to the disadvantaged, social reality is being defined by the people who are in power. They are the arbiters of what constitutes too much or too little; they draw the lines that put the disadvantaged in their state of powerlessness. Although the people in power uphold the universalistic rights of man in an abstract sense, in a concrete sense these people are loaded with racism, male chauvinism, Protestant work ethics, and prejudices of all sorts. When the chips are down, their hypocrisy shines through.

What does all this mean for social action? Well, in one big jump of the kind that the logic of the sentiments allows, it becomes obvious that power is what makes the world go around. Without power you get nowhere fast; only with power can anyone achieve social change. All the minority and disadvantaged groups seek for this kind of power, without which they are impotent. How do they do this? Well, they seek to demonstrate the illegitimacy of the establishment—even of the knowledge establishment; that is, they seek to expose its dirty white, racist, male-oriented, Protestant, work-oriented face. In this attempt, dialogue is out and confrontation is in; cooperation is out and conflict is in; law and order are out and violence is in. Almost everything—even experience—becomes politicized.

The counter-culture is also expressing another curious sentiment. It seems to be promising to liberate man from his isolation and to provide him with a sense of community and identity, the values he has lost when science and technology liberated him from the restraints of the tribe and the clan to become a free but lonely individual. Wow! How my ears flap! At times they stand at right angles to my face! It seems to me that Mayo predicted something like this when he wrote *The Human Problems of an Industrial Society* back in 1933.

THE PROBLEM FROM THE POINT OF VIEW OF ACTION

I could go on and say much more about these problems of modern society at the global level of analysis from which they are often discussed. This would open up so many diverse points of view that I fear there would be no end to them. Instead, let me restate the problem in terms of the concepts and points of view I have been developing and then raise, in terms of A-relations and B-relations, the issue of the relation of knowledge to action that is posed.

For me the following diagnosis of the times seems relatively clear: B-relations are essential to the running of modern society. The people responsible for running modern society are the upholders, defenders, and cultivators of B-relations. The technology of science supports them. Societies, whose dominant values they represent, reward them for cultivating B-relations. They find it personally rewarding to uphold these values. These two processes of reward reinforce each other, so that it is not surprising to find that the people who hold these values are at the top of the social structure; it would only be surprising if they were at the bottom.

Overcultivation of B-relations in society by leaders of organizations, however, has unfortunate consequences for those who are not in positions of power. It tends to result in their being considered objects rather than subjects; in their being treated as abstract categories rather than as concrete individuals; and in their being evaluated in terms of external rather than internal standards. As a result, they often resist the forces of modernization that B-values represent. But the managers of modern societies need their cooperation. Regardless of how managers feel about it, they have to deal with A-relations.

One of the characteristics of A-relations is that they tend to reveal themselves in polarities. Unlike the products of B-relations, which are linear, straightforward, clearcut, and logical, the products of A-relations keep flopping back and forth from one pole to another, for instance, from cooperation to conflict or from conformity to deviation. Moreover, like the little girl with the curl in the middle of her forehead, when they are good, they are very, very good; but when they are bad, they are horrid.

The conventional wisdom for dealing with these biformities is to reward them when they appear in their good forms and to punish them when they appear in their bad forms. When they appear in their good forms, they are often taken for granted by managers who are getting things done through people by B-relations. Thus, in their good forms they tend to remain ignored and unrewarded. As a result, a modern manager usually meets expressions of A-relations in their outraged state, that is, when A-relations are not doing what they are supposed to be doing. In order to get them to do what they should, the modern manager has one other piece of prescriptive equipment in his baggage, the principle of the carrot and the stick. However, when the people at the bottom of an organization are induced with a monetary carrot and prodded with a stick, they are being treated not only as objects, but also as jackasses. This adds fuel to the flames.

According to this analysis, it seems obvious that relations between the manager and the managed in modern society need to be improved. A simple and clear way to do this is to provide managers with more adequate skills and knowledge in dealing with A-relations. This is the road I have traveled throughout by professional life. I have not been the only one on it. It has been traveled by representatives of other schools of thought, including group dynamics, decision theory, and the other behavioral sciences. With so many prestigious groups on the same road, one might have thought we would have had little difficulty in reaching our destination in ten seconds flat.

Alas, this has not happened. Instead we have encountered every conceivable kind of roadblock and inconsistency. Some were thrown at us; others were of our own making. Lurking among them, I feel, and preventing clear understanding of the phenomena of human behavior are the confusions about A-relations and B-relations, about concrete and abstracted systems, about natural and artificial wholes, and about the relation of knowledge to action, concerning all of which I am writing.

Chapter 26

Complementarity as a Way of Correcting the Imbalance

When I first looked at the prescriptive rules of management, I found no descriptive theories about human behavior underlying them. As I have written, in the management logics of control through B-relations, there were no descriptive propositions about human behavior, other than conventional ones. I was about to declare my mission impossible—the mission of finding ways to improve administrative action through knowledge—when it occurred to me that executives could use the methods I was using to investigate A-relations. If they did, would they find what I had?

In trying to understand the polarized forms of too much or too little in which A-relations expressed themselves, I discovered the equilibrium-seeking properties of these relations. They seemed to be seeking states of practical equilibrium, which from the point of view of the participants in them—not that of an external observer—were rewarding and just. Furthermore, if someone paid attention to these relations instead of ignoring them, sometimes they also became efficient in an external sense.

With this insight I saw that I could conceive my method of investigation as a way of taking action. By listening to A-relations in their efforts to find states of equilibrium—rather than states of polarity composed of either too much or too little—I could both understand and take action in regard to them at the same time. And I would not be prescribing what I thought A-relations should do; I would be facilitating what they wanted to do. This for me was the lesson of "the Hawthorne effect"; with it, my scruples about taking action began to fade away.

Could this concept of action be accepted and practiced by executives? Obviously it was a far cry from the conventional one. Indeed, it looked as though it was 180° from it, as though it was nonaction rather than action.

The concept of behavior can be used in two senses which I now need to distinguish. There is first behavior in a *reactive* sense, when the behavior of an individual is a response to a stimulus in the familiar stimulus-response pattern. Then there is behavior in a *proactive* sense, the behavior of an individual when he is looking forward, initiating, innovating, acting from an urge or a long-range plan to change or add something to his situation. I am using the terms in Henry A. Murray's sense (1951, p. 439), when he wrote that psychology for the most part looked at behavior in terms of reactions to stimuli. He went on to say that this conception was inadequate to describe behavior that was guided by a plan or a goal, an intention to change or add something to a situation. Gordon Allport used the terms in the same way (1961, p. 550), when he pointed out that words beginning with "re" often connote "being pushed or maneuvered," whereas proactivity suggests "futurity, intention, forward thrust."

An individual can distinguish these two kinds of behavior in his own experience—for example, when he is in the mood to express his ouches without expecting any change in his situation to follow, or when he is in the mood to do something more active about them. Also, an external observer can look at another person's behavior from these points of view. He can perceive the other person as merely reacting to the forces impinging on him, or he can view him as a person who, with intention, is making choices and decisions about what to do to accomplish something new. In the first case, the observer is treating the person who is reacting to a situation as the object to his (the observer's) knowledge. In the second case, the observer is treating the object of his knowledge as a proactive subject. At a higher level of abstraction, this raises the issue of whether man's behavior is determined or whether he has free will. Let me stop short of this issue and use the distinctions between descriptive and prescriptive knowledge, the subjects and objects of knowledge, and reactive and proactive behavior to clarify some of the misunderstandings that arise in relations between scientists and actors.

MISUNDERSTANDINGS BETWEEN SCIENTISTS AND ACTORS

To begin with, a social scientist of the *pure* kind tries to explain a subject's behavior objectively; that is, he makes descriptive propositions in a reactive sense about actors. Since the object of his knowledge is a person whose behavior the scientist views as reactive, the scientist has no need to be concerned with subjects who want to use his knowledge proactively. In the scientist's view, descriptive knowledge is concerned with the truth (how things are), not with its utility for subjects who intend to use it proactively. For scientists, the utility of knowledge is not their problem, but their subjects'. (Some modern views of science question the objectivity of pure science. The implications tend to draw "pure" scientists into "impure" areas of which they had thought themselves free.)

Because a person who is being reactive does not care about a social scientist's descriptive knowledge (except, perhaps, to rationalize his own reactive behavior without doing anything about it), misunderstandings are not likely to arise between them. There is, however, another combination of scientists and actors between whom problems do arise. This combination is proactive subjects or actors who want to use descriptive knowledge to improve their own or someone else's behavior and descriptive social scientists of the impure kind who think they can help.

A descriptive social scientist of the *impure* kind studies and wants to help proactive subjects who want to cope more effectively with the situations in which they find themselves. This kind of scientist tries to make descriptive propositions about how well and how badly these subjects are carrying out their tasks in the hope that such propositions will help the subjects do a better job. These social scientists have a normative aim, even though they say that they are interested in descriptions. That is why I call them "impure"; man, have they got problems!

Prescriptive theorists have their problems too. A prescriptive theory is addressed to someone who wants to do something to improve his situation, that is, a proactive subject. Just as pure descriptive theorists (who are interested in truth) need not be concerned with proactive subjects (who are interested in utility), so pure prescriptive theorists (who assume they know how things should be done) need not be concerned with reactive persons (who have no interest in change). In this respect, however, there is a difference that gives descriptive theorists the edge over their prescriptive colleagues in terms of their standing in the values of the scientific enterprise. Being in their pure form reactive persons—that is, persons who are interested in things as they are—descriptive theorists are under no compulsions to make their theories useful to proactive subjects. They can claim proudly, "That is not our problem," whereas pure prescriptive theorists, being proactive persons who are interested in making things different, may have the compulsion to convince proactive subjects—managers, for instance—of the utility of their prescriptive theories.

The distinction between pure and impure prescriptive theorists arises out of these complexities. To state the distinction oversimply, pure prescriptive theorists *optimize;* that is, they are concerned only with the very best solutions to problems. Impure prescriptive theorists *satisfice;* they are willing to consider second or third best solutions in order to accommodate themselves to proactive clients.

It follows that just as there can be descriptive theories *about* but not *for* proactive subjects, there can be prescriptive theories *for* but not *about* proactive subjects. This possibility is a source of bitter controversy, for it means that there can be prescriptive theories with little or no empirical content. To descriptive theorists this is anathema. Descriptive theorists believe in the first place that there are no such things as prescriptive theories in a strict scientific sense. They also believe that prescriptive theories, if such exist, that do not include descriptive propositions about the phenomena for which the prescriptive theories prescribe, are just matters of logic. Worse still, from the point of view of descriptive theorists, these theories assume not only proactive but also rational actors. Of course prescriptive theorists can respond, "What's bugging you? Aren't you assuming irrational actors?"

Reactive persons have little or no concern with these debates. But misunderstandings do arise between proactive subjects who want to use prescriptive theories (in spite of the severe limitations that these theories have from the point of view of descriptive theorists) and prescriptive theorists who want to show proactive subjects how this can be done, either by optimizing (the pure kind) or by satisficing (the impure kind).

In summary, the people who have problems in relating knowledge to action for proactive subjects are descriptive theorists of the impure kind and prescriptive theorists. Thus, the questions that arise are how proactive subjects find descriptive and prescriptive theories useful. I will discuss these problems in the context of relations between managers and workers, and this will bring me back to A-relations and B-relations.

MANAGERS AND WORKERS AND A-RELATIONS AND B-RELATIONS

In our culture we tend to think of executives as being proactive and satisficing and of workers as being reactive and just plain satisfied or dissatisfied. These ways of thinking, of course, are oversimplifications. Workers are at times choosers and deciders; in addition to merely expressing their ouches, they sometimes exercise a skill in trying to improve their situations. And executives, as well as making choices and decisions, sometimes react to their situations without the intention of doing more than expressing their ouches. We consider workers' behavior as essentially reactive, because workers are not supposed to be involved in organizational decisions; hence, we view their decisions as restricted to personal decisions, the most important of which is whether to quit or stay on the job. We consider executives' behavior essentially proactive, because executives are supposed to make organizational decisions at work and to do their reacting and personal decision making at home.

These cultural factors have little to do with the relation of knowledge to action from the point of knowledge makers. From the point of descriptive knowledge, both workers and managers can be treated as either reactive or proactive subjects; from the point of view of prescriptive knowledge, they can both be treated as proactive. However, from the point of view of knowledge users, tbe cultural factors I have mentioned do make a difference, because of the difference between what workers and managers are proactive about.

At first glance, it would seem as though managers are proactive in terms of B-relations and reactive in terms of A-relations, whereas workers are proactive in terms of A-relations and reactive in terms of B-relations. There is a half-truth to this statement, but it is easily misunderstood because of a confusion about what is meant by being proactive in terms of A-relations.

Because A-relations are relations between people, they are most commonly expressed in terms of sentiments and feelings. The statement that most people most of the time react to their own feelings and sentiments and to the feelings and sentiments of others—and not to theories, descriptive or prescriptive—is so commonplace that I would not mention it, except that it has important consequences for the application of knowledge to A-relations. It means that a person under the burden of responsibility who intends to be proactive *cannot express his own feelings without regard to the consequences that his doing so has for others.* He cannot expect others to bear the entire burden of distinguishing his feelings from other matters of fact. Thus, he has to be aware that he is sometimes expressing his feelings and not making statements of fact about matters apart from himself. Consequently, in order to use knowledge in connection with A-relations, a proactive subject must have some skill in and knowledge about dealing with his own feelings as well as with those of others.

LIMITATIONS OF THE CLINICAL METHOD

This necessity raises big questions, perhaps the most stubborn that I met. It involves not only how one deals proactively with feelings—one's own and others'—but also how one deals proactively with the other forms in which A-relations manifest themselves, such as custom, informal organization, norms of behavior, etc. In our endeavors to find persons who have this skill and knowledge or to train them, we social scientists have fallen into one anomalous position after another.

Whereas getting things done through B-relations has been highly developed by science and technology since the year one, getting things done through A-relations has been accomplished largely by custom and the conventional wisdom of the times. It has remained at a fairly constant level of implicit social skill that develops only slowly over long periods of time.

Those of us who have been engaged in trying to improve managers' skills in dealing proactively with A-relations assume that there is some kind of knowledge lying around which will help managers and that there are some managers who are seeking to avail themselves of it. The transfer of this knowledge to these actors requires a relationship between a trainer or teacher or educator, who is in some sense a repository of it, and a trainee or student or client, who is seeking it. This relationship is not free of the misunderstandings that arise in the relation of knowledge to action that I have been describing. Let me add this trainer-client relation to the ones I am considering and then recall the many problems that I found in it.

I conceive of a client as a proactive person in a superordinate role, such as supervisor, manager, or executive. He (or she) is thus a person who is under the burden of responsibility, consciously seeking to gain and utilize knowledge about A-relations in order to improve his skill in coping with the concrete A-relations in which he is involved. I conceive of myself in the role of a trainer, teacher, or educator. We are both proactive learners.

To be sure, my conception of a client is idealized in that I cannot always assume that he is dissatisfied with the social skill he has and that he is eagerly seeking to improve it. I do not, however, accept that a trainer, including myself, is satisfied with his own skill. Instead, I assume that he is a dedicated and committed person who has some knowledge about A-relations. More than that, I assume that he has more experience in dealing with A-relations proactively than his client, and that he knows something about the problems of this endeavor.

I, as a trainer, do not wish to give my trainees theories that merely explain their behavior, but rather ones that they can utilize to improve it. Therefore, I choose from among the descriptive social scientists' bag of theories ones which they use to investigate behavior, not ones which purport to explain it. Indeed, I avoid the latter like the plague, because I want theories which my clients can practice, not just talk about glibly or apply without thinking, and also because I think that in the hands of proactive clients, theories that purport to be theories of explanation often become instruments that are more lethal than useful.

From the theories, methods, and skills which descriptive social scientists use to investigate behavior, I choose not the fanciest or the most sophisticated but the simplest I can find: The conceptual scheme or way of thinking about an organization as a concrete system and the skills of listening and social observation. My proactive client can practice this way of thinking and these skills in the situation he is in, and by these means he can seek to improve his relation to that situation. This point of view does not seek to substitute some different skill for his usual one. Rather it allows his existing skill to become explicit, so that he can learn to improve it.

I have already described the many problems and misunderstandings that I encountered in this approach: problems of communication, culture, linguistics, and semantics. I can summarize as follows the three most stubborn difficulties:

(1) The skills of listening and social observation are not as "simple" as I first conceived them. They cannot be learned in three easy lessons or packaged in a manual which any trainer without training can apply.

(2) The notion that an industrial situation can be changed by listening creatively to it is, I confess, idealistic. It requires a degree of self-awareness on the part of administrators that is out of this world. It leads to the Platonic conclusion that if kings were philosophers and philosophers were kings, then an ideal state of governance would be realized. I believe that this statement is a great insight, but it cannot be usefully practiced by proactive subjects.

(3) More seriously speaking, my approach tends to reach a paradoxical conclusion. It tends to treat B-relations as givens, as things which cannot be changed, when actually these relations are the factors over which managers have the best control and which they can most readily change. This was not an easy lesson for me to learn.

LIMITATIONS OF CHANGE AGENTRY

Let me now turn to some of my colleagues in the behavioral sciences to see how they dealt with the problems of misunderstanding that I encountered in the relation of knowledge to action. I shall speak first of the class of trainers who call themselves change agents and second the school of thought called decision theory.

Change agents assume, as I do, that a superior's behavior is an important determinant of a subordinate's performance and satisfaction. They also see the futility of giving executives concepts in psychology or sociology to apply in their work situations. From this common beginning, they move much more directly, quickly, and prescriptively toward "A-ing" executives with their theories than I move with my slow, patience-requiring clinical method.

I shall not go into detail about the different methods which change agents use to sensitize their trainees with regard to the feelings of others, to get them to see the effects of their own behavior on others, and to change their leadership styles to make them more democratic and participatory leaders. I thought that what change agents were up to and what I was up to were very similar; but as time went on, differences between us became apparent. What both intrigued and bothered me in their methods was that executives were being acted on more than they were acting. The trainers or change agents treated executives as reactive persons whose behavior needed to be changed. This role reversal flabbergasted me. Executives—for whom our cultural image is the last word in proactivity—were treated as reactive persons. And change agents—being scientists, for whom our cultural image is seekers of truth—became proactive subjects in getting things done! Wow!

One of the chief theories of change agentry, first stated by Douglas McGregor (1960), usually appears in a double-headed form known as Theory X and Theory Y. In this form neither is so much a theory as two different orientations toward motivation. If we put the two together, from the point of view of motivation, these theories say—in my terminology—that B-relations are as dead as doornails (Theory X) and that motivation resides in A-relations (Theory Y). The descriptive propositions that follow say that managers who administer in terms of A-relations achieve better results from their subordinates in terms of productivity and satisfactions than managers who administer in terms of B-relations. All the prescriptions to change the supervisory styles of executives from B-relations to A-relations are allegedly supported by this descriptive proposition.

How empirically valid is it? I hesitate to say how many researches have been directed to this question. At first the evidence seemed favorable; but as more and more findings came in, the descriptive proposition turned out to be a contingency statement of the "it all depends" variety. That is, its validity depended upon other factors in the total situation, such as the nature of the task. Hence, it could not be empirically verified, and there were no general propositions from which it could be deduced. It hung in the middle, unsupported at both the top and the bottom. I do not know how the proposition felt about it, but for persons in academic circles who held such a proposition, believe me, this was a most uncomfortable position to be in. Only a good clinician could take it.

Nevertheless, despite the proposition's lack of support by any strict scientific measures, the change agents forged ahead. They got support from top management, not for the proposition, but for the results they were able to achieve without it. They had a well-packaged and saleable product, which top managers could buy for their subordinate managers.

At first top managers were the clients who had to be sold but whose behavior did not have to be changed. They could still manage in terms of B-relations, while their subordinates were supposed to manage in terms of A-relations. This was a difficult position for any respectable change agent to maintain. Obviously, if a manager's behavior affects his subordinate's behavior, then the behavior of the manager's boss affects the manager's, and so on up to the top of the organization.

In terms of this analysis it was obvious that no enduring results could be obtained until the leadership styles of all managers were reduced to a common denominator. Not until all managers became democratic, open, trustful, authentic, and congruent could valid results be obtained. The contradictory findings that have been obtained come about because this condition has not been realized. So slowly step by step the change agents climbed the supervisory hierarchy, wooing each successive manager up the line in terms of marketing principles and B-relations, while they "A-ed" his subordinates in terms of A-relations.

From my point of view it was a sight to behold. Executives were expected to get results by having their behavior changed without having to utilize knowledge or exercise skill themselves. This was done for them by change agents who had the knowledge, skill, and mystique for changing the executives' behavior in ways that would improve the performance and satisfactions of their subordinates. I can think of no more reactive and B-oriented notions than these!

Let me now ask whether these attempts to change managers' behavior in terms of A-relations trickled down to the work level in terms of more productive and satisfied workers. This, after all, is where our concerns started and where in the last analysis the big payoff was supposed to be. But was it occurring? In a curious fashion, these questions seem to be becoming irrelevant. The work place has become a low-prestige place in which to do research. Even doctoral students in the 1970s do not do their theses there. Because nobody is looking at the work place, nobody sees that the work level is where organizations have changed the least in the last 30 years and more. Why? Because there B-relations are still dominant, and no hanky panky by "A-ers" will push them under the rug.

Although the itches and ouches at the work level have remained fairly constant for the past three decades, during the latter 1960s there was a change in the way the ouches were expressed. With the advent of the counter-culture and its underlying challenge to the legitimacy of the authority structure, a new note crept in and shook up the change agents more than a bit. Once the legitimacy of the so-called establishment came into question, the conventional rules of the game changed. How did change agents deal with this? T-groups became encounter groups, confrontation groups, and how-to-deal-with-conflict groups. Some change agents joined therapy groups and human potential groups, where the issue of authority was explicitly not present.

The most vocal attack on change agents came not from workers, but from liberals who allegedly represented the workers' interests. Questions arose about whose side the change agents were on. Who were their clients? For whom was their knowledge? Was their client the overdog, the establishment, the white power structure, the elite, or management? Or was their client the underdog, the alienated, the second-class citizen, the downtrodden, the poor, the uneducated, the lower classes, or minority groups? For change agents, many of whom were also liberals, this was a most uncomfortable position to be in. Thus the approach which the change agents used in developing the application of knowledge to action reached its limits in the itches and ouches, the twists and turns, of the responses of interacting persons, when they encountered the question "knowledge for whom?" Like my clinical method in its proactive applications, the change agent's approach came complete with its own inconsistencies, confusions, and limitations. As I have indicated, I accept the questions about the clinical method, but not the uncomfortable position they are supposed to put me in. As I see it, answers to the questions depend not on the resolution of ideological issues but on a clearer understanding of the nature of A-relations and B-relations.

Let me add that if I have been unduly harsh in my criticisms of change agents, it is not on the grounds of their motives. Rather it is because I feel that their endeavors have not assisted the search to clarify the relation of knowledge to action at the point of interaction. On the contrary, I feel let down, I think they have confused the issue. I regret this, because we had much in common. We started in the same direction and could have used each other's help along the way.

LIMITATIONS OF MATHEMATICAL MODELS

I now come to the school of thought called decision theory. Let me compare its approach to the relation of knowledge to action with that of the clinical method and change agentry. All three of our schools assume that executives' customary ways of doing things need renovating. But whereas I think that the customary social skills of executives can be improved, and whereas change agents think that their customary intuitive leadership styles can be changed, decision theorists think that the customary ways by which they make decisions can be improved. In fact, in many cases they think that decisions can be better made by machines!

All three of our schools draw on outside sources of knowledge. I borrow the conceptual scheme of a social system from descriptive sociologists of the pure kind (e.g., Pareto). Change agents apply concepts, methods, and findings from the behavioral sciences to change the leadership styles of executives. Decision theorists apply some of the theories and tools of mathematics to improving the decision-making processes which executives use.

Each of us has our ideal type of what an administrator should be. I have the picture of a self-aware administrator who makes differentiations among the kinds of relations in which he is involved and who has high tolerance for the amibiguities in which this multidimensionality places him. Change agents have for their ideal type a democratic, open, congruent, and authentic administrator. Decision theorists have for theirs a rational actor. Since a computer acts completely rationally, with respect to this ideal it is viewed as being more human than a human being. Therefore, the more an executive acts like a computer, the more he is acting in terms of man's noblest and most distinctive human characteristic!

We are also all doodlers. We all draw pictures to point out what we are talking about. We use straight lines, dotted lines, single arrowed lines, double arrowed lines, curves, loops, circles, triangles, squares, spheres, pyramids, boxes, and so on. Although I cannot differentiate which form of doodling each of us indulges in the most (the topic would make an interesting doctoral dissertation), my impression is that our doodling reaches its highest form when we try to copy the mathematician's way of representing concrete reality by variables and constraints in highly abstract models. Of course, a mathematician generally has linear equations for his variables and constraints, which can be quantified and expressed in terms of linear functions, which can be optimized. So, strictly speaking, he does not need to doodle. But when one has no equations at his disposal, yet wishes to appear quantitative, he has to represent the variables and constraints with which he is concerned with some kind of pseudo-mathematical doodling. By the mid-1960s this particular form of representation became an imperative. It was doodle or die. Researchers who could not state their proposals in terms of variables and constraints in highly abstract models feared that they could not get them funded by respectable foundations because the proposals would not be considered sophisticated research.

This restriction of doodling to only one respectable kind was hard on the clinical method. It was also hard on A-relations, which like to express themselves in terms of literary metaphors rather than in terms of variables and constraints. But the restriction was good for the computer, because this is the way that he (or it) thinks. Obviously under this way of thinking such words as skill, judgment, common sense, and intuition become obsolete, because we do not need what they refer to any more.

By the mid-1960s all the business schools in the land were "A-ing" executives by behavioral science on the one hand and "B-ing" them by mathematical models on the other. The clinical method had become a museum piece, and the case method was on the verge of becoming programmed. Had it not been for excesses committed on both sides, the case method and what it stood for would have gone down the drain. But when some "A-ers" started having executives take their clothes off, use four-letter words, and punch pillows to get them to express their real feelings and to become open and authentic, it was carrying things too far for the mores of the business community and the Harvard Business School. We were still uptight about sex, you see.

When one researcher's variables become another researcher's constraints, when doctoral students are madly trading off variables and constraints, and when a model a day becomes the order of the day, there is more than a bit of confusion. Business school professors could no longer effectively compare one doodle with another. This became a serious problem in our Doctoral program, for students could not find three professors for a thesis committee who could agree whether a thesis proposal was a doodle that had validity!

By 1973 the making of both authenitc administrators and authentic doodles reached a kind of impasse. It seemed as though the approaches that each of us were taking to the relationship of knowledge to action encountered problems and limitations. This result, of course, was not what any of us expected nor where we thought we would be, and our confusions became compounded. As a result, some professors entertained the idea of looking again at the clinical method and the case method to see if there was something there that they had previously missed. Thus do the wheels of progress turn and unsophisticated A-relations seek to restore the imbalance that too much attention to B-relations creates.

THE DILEMMAS WE FACE

The dilemmas we face in relating A-relations and B-relations are apparent if we look first at the relations of technological space and of purposive space as they would appear in concrete systems, and second at the relations of social space and of life space as they would appear in abstracted systems. In concrete systems the relations of technological space and of purposive space become phenomenalized; that is, they become the ways in which people relate to one another for purposes of achieving collective—as contrasted with personal—ends. In abstracted systems the relations of social space and of life space become impersonalized.

There are no objectified knowers—that is, scientists—in concrete systems, though there may be proactive actors. In abstracted systems there are objectified knowers—or at least the assumption of them— but no proactive actors. In concrete systems proactive actors produce natural wholes, which do not appear in abstracted systems. On the other hand, the objectified knowers of abstracted systems have problems relating the artificial wholes which they produce to the phenomenological reality of concrete systems.

As a result, from the point of view of objectified knowers, A-relations and B-relations in concrete systems have no clear subject matter—as my attempts to develop one demonstrate—even though these relations have a clear phenomenological object matter. In contrast, A-relations and B-relations in abstracted systems have clear subject matter, but no clear object matter. From the point of view of subjectified actors, just the opposite may be said; namely, A-relations and B-relations in concrete systems have clear subject matter but no clear object matter; in abstracted systems they have a clear object matter but no clear subject matter.

These confusions arise because, from the point of view of objectified knowers, such as scientists, the subjects and objects of knowledge are separate; thus, knowers and actors are bifurcated. On the other hand, from the point of view of subjectified actors, the subjects and objects of knowledge—and thus knowers and actors—are the same, that is, human beings. In the first instance the abstracted is treated as more real than the concrete; in the second, the concrete is treated as more real than the abstracted. Both are real enough; the difference is that the concrete are phenomena and the abstracted are not.

A PRINCIPLE OF COMPLEMENTARITY AS A WAY OUT

Thus, I come finally to the conclusion that the two ways of representing social reality as concrete systems and as abstracted systems are complementary ways of looking at it, neither of which can be reduced to the other. This conception of social reality offers the opportunity for the development of knowledge and action in ways that avoid the confusions and inconsistencies that we have fallen into. It makes it possible to keep *separate but related* the concrete and the abstracted, the A-relations and the B-relations, the natural (phenomenological) and the artificial, subjects and objects, the knower and the known, description and prescription, knowledge makers and knowledge users. Our failure to do these things during my lifetime has resulted in the issues and debates that we have been unable to settle and from which have emanated the inconsistencies and confusions that have limited the development of our understanding of the phenomena of human behavior in organizations.

In the physical sciences, I have been told, when a group of researchers comes to accept a principle such as the principle of complementarity, there is a gentlemen's agreement that certain questions are no longer matters of controversy. Applied physical scientists can then get on with the business of going to the moon without having to settle or have settled for them whether matter is a wave or a particle. Whether this belief of mine about the physical sciences is myth or reality I do not know. Certainly, there is nothing remotely like it in the social sciences.

For example, in the physical world it is usually said that rest is the general case and motion the special case. But it may also be said that rest, since it may be regarded as zero motion, is the special case of the general state of motion. In the same way in the social world it is usually said that reactivity is the general case and proactivity the special case of man's behavior. Instead, reactivity, since it may be regarded as zero proactivity, may be viewed as the special case of the more general condition of proactivity. Should I make such an assertion, though I might become the darling of the *Harvard Business Review,* I would have other, perhaps even more prestigious, groups on the back of my neck. Some descriptive social scientists, for example, might think I am saying that for all these many years they have been studying the special, rather than the general, case of human behavior.

The elusive point I am making is that the relation between knowledge and action in the social sciences is an intrinsic relation, such that the two cannot be easily separated, as they can be in the physical sciences. In the physical sciences when a question of a way of thinking about phenomena is raised, the question refers to its usefulness for the development of a body of knowledge, not to its usefulness for every Tom, Dick, and Harry. This is not so in the social sciences. These sciences are concerned with the actions of people. What people say and do constitute their phenomena and are what social scientists theorize about. Thus, their theories are useful not only to themselves for the development of their respective bodies of knowledge; they have an immediate and intimate utility for the subjects the scientists talk about.

This fact has a curious twist to it. The rapid developments in the different branches of engineering—civil, mechanical, and chemical—followed from and did not precede the basic sciences of physics and chemistry; the theories of the basic sciences were thus useful to developments in the different branches of engineering. Not by the wildest stretch of the imagination can it be said, however, that administration (the oldest of the arts and the newest of the professions) followed from the behavioral sciences. For this reason it cannot be taken for granted that theories of the behavioral sciences will be useful to administrators. It was not until the 1950s, as I remember it, that the Ford Foundation had this idea and asserted that it would be so.

I realize that when I assert a principle of complementarity and say that sometimes it is useful to think of organizations as concrete systems and sometimes as abstracted systems, I cannot restrict what I mean by "useful" to usefulness for knowledge makers in the social sciences. I have also to consider for knowledge utilizers such as administrators, even though knowledge makers may not have had them in mind when they created their theories. Therefore, a principle of complementarity as a way of conceptualizing social and organizational reality leaves open the issues of for whom and for what is one way of thinking more useful than the other. At the same time, I find too much evidence outside myself at the level of the phenomena of human behavior in organizations to believe that my resolution is solely within myself.

COMPLEMENTARITY AND THE SKILL AND TRAINING OF ADMINISTRATORS

A principle of complementarity as a way of conceptualizing social reality helps to clarify the role and skill of administrators at empirical levels. A-relations and B-relations are empirically as well as conceptually related. There is much clinical evidence that suggests that the overcultivation of one or the other in a society leads to problems of too much or too little. Just as it is difficult to conceptualize A-relations and B-relations as systems in ways that are useful to knowledge makers, so it is difficult to state scientific propositions about them in terms of too much or too little in ways that are useful to knowledge users, such as administrators. On all grounds such statements fail the test of having an objectified knower. No half-way respectable descriptive social scientist would assert them. Moreover, to ask scientists to say that B-relations can be overcultivated is to ask them to say that there can be too much of what they believe there cannot be enough of.

Propositions of the too much or too little kind, though, would be extremely useful for administrators. I have often speculated about what such propositions would look like, propositions which fail the canons of "objectified" science (the assumption of an objectified knower) but which would be useful to subjective, proactive actors.

Each time I do so, I come to the conclusion that if there are such propositions, they exist only at the level of personal or clinical knowledge. That is, they can only be stated in connection with a particular individual's personal commitments and beliefs.

As we have seen, there is no difficulty in integrating the internal and external environments of systems when both can be reduced to commensurable terms. The problems arise when they are incommensurables. If we express both environments of organizations in terms of B-relations, we are dealing with artificial systems, in which the relating of the internal to the external or vice versa can be done by a machine (e.g., a computer) as well as by a person. When the internal environment abounds with B-relations and their abstractions, the integrating of the two requires a human being.

A principle of complementarity as a way of conceiving social reality offers administrators a specific and unique role at empirical levels. Without it, there is no way to distinguish their contribution from that of other specialist or professional groups. They remain one more kind of specialist among many, specialists in leadership style or computer behavior, for example. But a specialists's way of thinking is not useful for dealing with the kinds of problems with which administrators have to deal, problems in which interactions between people cannot be conveniently disregarded, which have to be dealt with at phenomenological levels and not by abstractions, and which cannot be easily assigned to any of the specialist functions in business, such as marketing, finance, production, or control. With this conceptualization, the role and skill of administrators become unique, necessary in their organizations to maintain a balance between A-relations and B-relations and their abstractions. A balance must be maintained, else too much of the one or too little of the other leads to some form of social disruption and chaos.

It is not easy to grasp the nature of an administrator's role and skill, for they escape our traditional ways of thinking. The difficulty resides in the fact that both have to do with maintaining relationships between incommensurables. I have never ceased to marvel how A-relations and B-relations, which are so difficult to conceptualize in terms of an abstracted system and about which it is so difficult to make scientific propositions, are being related every day in the week by proactive subjects through such lower-order activities as skill, judgment, and personal knowledge. The persons who do this may not do it perfectly, but they do it after a fashion and without explicit knowledge about how they do it or how they should do it. I regard this as quite an accomplishment, one that many persons in organizations achieve under the burden of responsibility for action with no recognition, especially from knowledge makers, of the importance for their organizations and for society of what they are doing.

If a principle of complementarity and the unique role and skill of administrators which the principle implies were accepted by educators in the business schools of the land, it would cut down on much futile discussion. The arguments that remain would be at a higher level of discourse. A principle of complementarity would mean that knowledge makers, whether their interests are in concrete or abstracted systems, would state the usefulness and limitations of their respective views for the development of both knowledge and action. Neither side would appropriate the words "science" or "administration" for its own use. Each side would state in what sense it is or is not a science, subject matter, or discipline, as defined by whom, and to what kinds of administrative positions or problems it is applicable. Neither side would claim that its researches are more rigorous or sophisticated than the other. Each side would state the limitations of its position, not the limitations of the other.

If I apply this principle to the concrete-and-natural-system model that I use, I will say that it is more useful for line administrators than for staff specialists. The natural system model keeps the concrete and the abstracted related at an empirical level, just as it does the nonlogical and the logical, and the internal and the external. It provides the basis for the development of a generalist point of view. The generalist point of view cannot achieve the status of a science, a subject matter, or a discipline as presently defined by the proponents of the artificial system model. An understanding of this limitation is the source of the utility of the concrete system model for administrators as generalsits. Administrators do not need to seek for a kind of knowledge in the social sciences that many disciplines have not attained. They can practice their clinical outlook in concrete settings unabashedly but rigorously and sophisticatedly without having to seek higher levels of abstraction to sanction their actions.

From the point of view of administrators, the natural system model has limitations as well as uses. It focuses on the day-to-day, the here-and-now, the microscopic, the particular, what might seem to be the nitty-gritty, aspects of administrators' work. It tends to make human factors the major constraint in the development of organizations. Because of these limitations, the natural system model is not useful for the design and long-range planning aspects of ad-

469

ministrators' work. However, administrators can delegate these activities to staff specialists in ways that they cannot delegate their generalist functions.

From the point of view of research, the natural system model is also both useful and limited. It is useful for the study of concrete cases and the limited kinds of generalizations that can be drawn from them. It cannot be value-free; rather its users need to make its value assumptions explicit. Its body of knowledge is clinical and belongs in the domain of the clinical sciences. Its users cannot overcome this limitation through any method currently used by the social sciences, nor can they make it into a scientific subject matter as defined by the physical sciences. Once this limitation is accepted, users of the natural system model may develop their own methods rigorously and may define what makes science science in their terms. Although they may accept abstracted system models as useful for certain purposes, they do not accept the evaluation associated with those models by which the natural system model becomes a second-class citizen in the hierarchy of scientific knowledge.

The clinical knowledge that we need will be developed in the form of case descriptions of relatively stable patterns or syndromes of behavior. In a talk which I gave at the University of California at Los Angeles in November 1962 and which was published as Chapter 23 in *Man-in-Organization,* I summarized as follows the findings at the clinical level of knowledge that the researches of different investigators had brought out during my lifetime. Again and again the findings point to:

(1) the inadequacy of the motivational assumptions underlying the traditional principles of management;

(2) what little influence the employee was supposed to exercise, what few interpersonal transactions he was supposed to have, what little two-way communication there was supposed to be, and how doing what he was told and being obedient to authority seemed to be the sole integrative force under the traditional principles of management;

(3) the conflict between the principles of scientific management on the one hand and the determinants of cooperation on the other, i.e., how the application of these principles seemed to be at odds with the way members of an organization became identified and committed to its goals;

(4) how the more a supervisor managed in terms of what he was supposed to do in accordance with the principles of management, the less of an all-around, long-term job he seemed to be doing;

(5) how supervisors and managers who seemed to get the best over-all, long-term effect seemed to be displaying a leadership style quite different from those who did not;

(6) how supervisors and managers who were displaying a leadership style different from what they were supposed to be doing received little support from (a) their superiors, (b) the traditional theory, (c) any accepted new theory, or (d) any feedback of results, other than those of the traditional kind, that would reflect the good over-all long-term job that they were doing;

(7) how, under the traditional principles of management, informal leaders tended to appear in many work groups in order to take care of the maintenance functions that the task leaders failed to perform;

(8) "the restriction of output syndrome," i.e., how, under the principles of scientific management, employees tended to develop a concept of a day's work that was not too high or too low to get them into trouble;

(9) "the man-in-the-middle syndrome," i.e., the different ways supervisors resolved the conflict of trying to get the cooperation of their employees while at the same time trying to get them to do what they should be doing at the proper time and place and with the proper methods, and as a result, the different leadership styles which tended to emerge and to which many different names have been given, such as, for example, institutional, autocratic, laissez-faire, accommodative, personal, production-oriented, person-oriented, group-oriented, democratic, permissive, supportive, and transactional;

(10) "the staff-line syndrome," i.e., how staff people, who were supposed to be helping line people by setting standards for evaluating the results of employees, tended to be regarded by the line people more as a source of interference than as a source of help;

(11) "the distributive justice syndrome," i.e., the many complaints that took the form that it isn't fair or just that what I'm getting is not proportional to what I should be getting in terms of my age, seniority, education, sex, etc.;

(12) "the vicious cycle syndrome," i.e., how the unintended dysfunctional consequences of the traditional methods of control tended to encourage a continued use of them, e.g., the breakdown of rules begot more rules to take care of their breakdown or the breakdown of close supervision encouraged the use of still closer methods of supervision, and thus led to a continuous search for new control systems to correct for the limitations of previous ones;

(13) "the specialist-generalist syndrome," i.e., the sharp difference of outlook, skill, knowledge, and influence required and acquired by those who do the work of the organization (whether they be workers, salesmen, clerks, technicians, or scientists) and by those who are responsible for facilitating that the work gets done, well illustrated by the differences, for example, between the optimizing of this *or* that and the "satisficing" of this *and* that;

(14) "the frozen group syndrome," i.e., the kind of static accommodation which many work groups seemed to make to the organizational environments in which they had to survive; and

(15) "the underdeveloped individual development syndrome," i.e., the amount of apathy, uninvolvement, and uncommitment which existed among some members of an organization, particularly at the work level, and the needs for belonging, competence, self-development and identity which were not being tapped by management and which could not be tapped by the traditional principles of management.

We need more of the kind of knowledge represented by these findings to guide the decisions and actions of proactive managers. Even when we have it, their decisions, not being sanctioned by general propositions at high levels of abstraction, will be importantly characterized by skill and such personal qualities as judgment, commitment, awareness of their own and others' feelings, and authenticity. Clinical knowledge will help validate the conditions and directions within which such qualities operate usefully. If I am wrong and if valid general propositions do eventually emerge from study, my belief is that they will be at such high levels of abstraction that they will continue to be empty of content insofar as applications to specific situations are concerned. Thus, administrators will continue to have the important role of mediating between the concrete and the abstract; and they will continue to need the qualities of judgment, commitment, skill and the like that I have just mentioned.

We do not know a great deal about how to train people in the development of such qualities. I have few final conclusions about how this should be done. Nevertheless, I can say that from the point of view of instruction, a principle of complementarity means that an instructor should articulate the usefulness and limitations of the point of view he is using. My injunction to instructors is, "Do not mix or trade off incommensurables lightly or by verbal pyrotechnics."

As I see it, the representatives of each point of view should have equal time and an equal number of courses to cultivate their positions. It would be incumbent on each instructor to state clearly which model he uses and for what kinds of problems, theoretical or practical, he uses it.

I, as an exponent of the concrete natural system model, should not attempt to state the usefulness and limitations of abstracted and artificial systems. I leave that task to those who find that way of thinking a useful way of representing social reality. Many of the unnecessary problems I have encountered during my professional life and work arose because at times I tried to state the limitations of that way of thinking, As I see it now, that was not my business. For whom and for what that way of representing social reality is useful is up to its users to state—but they have to do so. For no longer is either the concrete system model or an abstracted system model the one true way of representing social reality; rather each becomes a useful way of representing it for certain purposes.

I have no illusion that I can make my principle of complementarity stick. The bifurcation of knowledge and action which has proved so highly successful for the development of the physical sciences remains the model for the social sciences. I want to say, though, that if behavioral scientists want to continue to be hung up by this bifurcation, that is their problem. It need no longer be a problem for those of us who want to develop a way of thinking and a body of knowledge that can be both *about* and *useful for* proactive men and women who desire to act on and change their environments.

References

EDITOR'S NOTE: I made up this list of authors, books, and articles. Most of them are mentioned in the text. I have added the titles of a few works which are not, when I knew that Professor Roethlisberger used them while he was writing this book.—G. F. F. L.

Adler, Alfred, *The Practice and Theory of Individual Psychology.* Translated by Paul Radin. New York: Harcourt, Brace & Co., 1924.

Allport, Gordon W., *Pattern and Growth in Personality.* New York: Holt, Rinehart & Winston, 1961.

Andrews, Kenneth, ed., *The Case Method of Teaching Human Relations and Administration.* Cambridge, Mass.: Harvard Unversity Press, 1953.

Arensberg, Conrad M., and Kimball, Solon T., *Family and Community in Ireland.* Cambridge, Mass.: Harvard University Press, 1940.

Argyris, Chris, *Understanding Organizational Behavior.* Homewood, Ill.: The Dorsey Press, 1960.

———, *Integrating the Individual and the Organization.* New York: John Wiley & Sons, 1964.

Bales, Robert F., *Interaction Process Analysis: A Method for the Study of Small Groups.* Cambridge, Mass.: Addison-Wesley Press, 1950.

Barnard, Chester I., *The Function of the Executive.* Cambridge, Mass.: Harvard University Press, 1938.

———, *Organization and Management: Selected Papers.* Cambridge, Mass.: Harvard University Press, 1948.

Bendix, Reinhard, *Work and Authority in Industry: Ideologies Of Management in the Course of Industrialization.* New York: John Wiley & Sons, 1956.

Bennis, Warren G., *Changing Organizations: Essays on the Development and Evolution of Human Organization.* New York: McGraw-Hill Book Co., 1966.

Bernard, Claude, *An Introduction to the Study of Experimental Medicine.* Translated by Henry Copley Greene. New York: The Macmillan Co., 1927.

Blake, Robert, and Mouton, Jane S., *The Managerial Grid: Key Orientations for Achieving Production through People.* Houston, Tex.: Gulf Publishing Co., 1964.

Blau, Peter, M., *The Dynamics of Bureaucracy.* Chicago: The University of Chicago Press, 1955.

————, and Scott, W. Richard, *Formal Organizations: A Comparative Approach.* San Francisco: Chandler Publishing Co., 1962.

Bradford, Leland P., *Explorations in Human Relations Training.* Washington, D.C.: National Training Laboratories, National Education Association, 1953.

————, ed., *Group Development.* Washington, D.C.: National Training Laboratories, National Education Association, 1961.

Braithwaite, Richard Bevan, *Scientific Explanation: A Study of the Function of Theory, Probability and Law in Science.* Cambridge, Eng.: Cambridge University Press, 1953.

Brinton, Crane, *The Anatomy of Revolution.* New York: W. W. Norton & Co., 1938.

Bugental, James F. T., *The Search for Authenticity: An Existential-Analytic Approach to Psychotheraphy.* New York: Holt, Rinehart & Winston, 1965.

Burns, Tom, and Stalker, G. M., *The Management of Innovation.* London: Tavistock Publications, 1961.

Cabot, Philip, *Addresses, 1935–1941.* Cambridge, Mass., 1942.

Cannon, Walter B., *The Wisdom of the Body.* New York: W. W. Norton & Co., 1932.

Carlyle, Thomas, *Sartor Resartus.* Edited by Frederick William Roe. New York: The Macmillan Co., 1927.

Cartwright, Dorwin, and Zander, Alvin, eds., *Group Dynamics: Research and Theory.* Evanston, Ill.: Row, Peterson & Co., 1953.

Chapple, Eliot D., *Measuring Human Relations: An Introduction to the Study of the Interaction of Individuals.* Provincetown, Mass.: The Journal Press, 1940.

———— and Sayles, Leonard R., *The Measure of Management: Designing Organizations for Human Effectiveness.* New York: The Macmillan Co., 1961.

Christenson, Charles J., "The Power of Negative Thinking." Boston: Harvard Business School Working Paper, HBS 72–41.

————, "The Structure of Science and the Science of Structure." Boston: Harvard Business School Working Paper, HBS 73–7.

Copeland, Melvin T., *And Mark an Era: The Story of the Harvard Business School.* Boston: Little, Brown & Co., 1958.

Cyert, Richard M., and March, James G., *A Behavioral Theory of the Firm.* Englewood Cliffs, N.J: Prentice-Hall, 1963.

Dickson, William J., and Roethlisberger, F. J., *Counseling in an Organization: A Sequel to the Hawthorne Researches.* Boston: Division of Research, Harvard Business School, 1966.

Durkheim, Emile, *Suicide: A Study in Sociology.* Translated by John A. Spaulding and George Simpson. Glencoe, Ill.: The Free Press, 1951.

Erikson, Erik H., *Childhood and Society.* New York: W. W. Norton & Co., 1950.

Etzioni, Amitai, *A Comparative Analysis of Complex Organizations: On Power, Involvement, and their Correlates.* New York: The Free Press of Glencoe, 1961.

Festinger, Leon, *A Theory of Cognitive Dissonance.* Evanston, Ill., and White Plains, N.Y.: Row, Peterson & Co., 1957.

_____; Schachter, Stanley; and Back, Kurt, *Social Pressures in Informal Groups: A Study of Human Factors in Housing.* New York: Harper & Brothers, 1950.

Freud, Sigmund, *The Interpretation of Dreams.* Translated by A. A. Brill. New York: The Macmillan Co., 1913.

_____, *Three Contributions to the Theory of Sex.* Translated by A. A. Brill. New York: Nervous and Mental Disease Publishing Co., 1916.

_____, *A General Introduction to Psychoanalysis.* Translated by Joan Riviere. New York: Boni & Liveright, 1920.

Fromm, Erich, *Escape form Freedom.* New York: Rinehart & Co., 1941.

_____, *Man for Himself: An Inquiry into the Psychology of Ethics.* New York: Holt, Rinehart & Winston, 1947.

Gardner, Burleigh B., *Human Relations in Industry.* Chicago: Richard D. Irwin, 1945.

Glover, John Desmond, and Hower, Ralph M., *The Administrator: Cases on Human Relations in Business.* Homewood, Ill.: Richard D. Irwin, 1949.

Golembiewski, Robert T., *Behavior and Organization: O and M and the Small Group.* Chicago: Rand McNally & Co., 1962.

Gordon, Robert Aaron, and Howell, James Edwin, *Higher Education for Business.* New York: Columbia University Press, 1959.

Gouldner, Alvin W., *Patterns of Industrial Bureaucracy.* Glencoe, Ill.: The Free Press, 1954.

———, "Cosmopolitans and Locals: Toward an Analysis of Latent Social Roles—I." *Administrative Science Quarterly*, II (December 1957), 281–306.

———, *The Coming Crisis of Western Sociology*. New York: Basic Books, 1970.

Hall, Edward T., *The Silent Language*. Garden City, N.Y.: Doubleday & Co., 1959.

Hare, A. Paul; Borgatta, Edgar F.; and Bales, Robert F., eds., *Small Groups: Studies in Social Interaction*. New York: Alfred A. Knopf, 1955.

Hayakawa, S. I., *Language in Action*. New York: Harcourt, Brace & Co., 1941.

Hegel, Georg Wilhelm Friedrich, *The Logic of Hegel*. Translated by W. Wallace. Oxford: The Clarendon Press, 1892.

———, *Lectures on the History of Philosophy*. Translated by Elizabeth S. Haldane and Frances H. Simson. 3 vols. London: K. Paul, Trench, Trübner & Co., 1892–1896.

Henderson, L. J., *On the Social System: Selected Writings*. Edited by Bernard Barber. Chicago: The University of Chicago Press, 1970.

Homans, George C., *The Human Group*. New York: Harcourt, Brace & Co., 1950.

———, *Social Behavior: Its Elementary Forms*. New York: Harcourt, Brace & World, 1961; rev. ed. Harcourt Brace Jovanovich, 1974.

Horvath, Steven M., and Horvath, Elizabeth C., *The Harvard Fatigue Laboratory: Its History and Contributions*. Englewood Cliffs, N.J.: Prentice-Hall, 1973.

Hume, David, *A Treatise of Human Nature: Being an Attempt to Introduce the Experimental Method of Reasoning into Moral Subjects; and Dialogues Concerning Natural Religion*. Edited by T. H. Green and T. H. Grose. New York: Longmans, Green & Co., 1898.

Inhelder, Bärbel, and Piaget, Jean, *The Growth of Logical Thinking from Childhood to Adolescence: An Essay on the Construction of Formal Operational Structures*. Translated by Anne Parsons and Stanley Milgram. New York: Basic Books, 1958.

James, William, *The Varieties of Religious Experience: A Study in Human Nature*. New York: Longmans, Green & Co., 1902.

———, *The Principles Of Psychology*. New York: H. Holt & Co., 1918.

Janet, Pierre, *Les Névroses*. Paris: Ernst Flammarion, 1909.

———, *Les Obsessions et la Psychasthénie*. Paris: Librairie Felix Alcan, 1919.

————, *L'Automatisme Psychologique: Essai de Psychologie Expérimentale sur les Formes Inférieures de L'Activité Humaine.* Paris: Librairie Felix Alcan, 1921.

————, *Psychological Healing: A Historical and Clinical Study.* Translated by Eden and Cedar Paul, New York: The Macmillan Co., 1925.

Jaques, Elliott, *The Changing Culture of a Factory.* London: Tavistock Publications, 1951.

Johnson, Wendell, *People in Quandaries: The Semantics of Personal Adjustment.* New York: Harper & Brothers, 1946.

Jung, C. G., *Psychological Types or the Psychology of Individuation.* Translated by H. Godwin Baynes. New York: Harcourt, Brace & Co., 1923.

————, *The Archetypes and the Collective Unconscious.* Translated by R. F. C. Hall. New York: Pantheon Books, 1959.

Kant, Immanuel, *Critique of Pure Reason.* Translated by F. Max Müller. New York: The Macmillan Co., 1896.

Kaplan, Abraham, *The Conduct of Inquiry: Methodology for Behavioral Science.* San Francisco: Chandler Publishing Co., 1964.

Katz, Daniel, and Kahn, Robert L., *The Social Psychology of Organizations.* New York: John Wiley & Sons, 1966.

Katz, Daniel; Maccoby, Nathan; and Morse, Nancy C., *Productivity, Supervision and Morale in an Office Situation, Part I.* Ann Arbor, Mich.: Survey Research Center, University of Michigan, 1950.

Kluckhohn, Clyde, *Mirror for Man: The Relation of Anthropology to Modern Life.* New York: McGraw-Hill Book Co., 1949.

Korzybski, Alfred, *Science and Sanity: An Introduction to Non-Aristotelian Systems and General Semantics.* New York: International Non-Aristotelian Publishing Co., 1941.

Kuhn, Thomas S., *The Structure of Scientific Revolutions.* Chicago: The University of Chicago Press, 1962.

Landsberger, Henry A., *Hawthorne Revisited: Management and the Worker, its Critics, and Developments in Human Relations in Industry.* Ithaca, N.Y.: Cornell University, 1958.

Lawrence, Paul R., and Lorsch, Jay W., *Organization and Environment: Managing Differentiation and Integration.* Boston: Division of Research, Harvard Business School, 1967.

————; Bailey, Joseph C.; Katz, Robert L.; Seiler, John A.; Orth, Charles D. III; Clark, James V.; Barnes, Louis B.; and Turner, Arthur N., *Organizational Behavior and Administration: Cases, Concepts, and Research Findings.* Homewood, Ill.: The Dorsey Press, and Richard D. Irwin, 1961.

Learned, Edmund P.; Christensen, C. Roland; Andrews, Kenneth R.; and Guth, William D., *Business Policy: Text and Cases.* Homewood, Ill.: Richard D. Irwin, 1965.

Leavitt, Harold J., *Management Psychology: An Introduction to Individuals, Pairs, and Groups in Organizations.* Chicago: The University of Chicago Press, 1958.

Lee, Irving J., *Language Habits in Human Affairs: An Introduction to General Semantics.* New York: Harper & Brothers, 1941.

————, *How to Talk with People: A Program for Preventing Troubles That Come When People Talk Together.* New York: Harper & Brothers, 1952.

————, *Customs and Crises in Communication: Cases for the Study of Some Barriers and Breakdowns.* New York: Harper & Brothers, 1954.

Lévy-Bruhl, Lucien, *How Natives Think.* Translated by Lilian A. Clare. London: George Allen & Unwin, 1926.

Lewin, Kurt, *Field Theory in Social Science: Selected Theoretical Papers.* Edited by Dorwin Cartwright. New York: Harper & Brothers, 1951.

Likert, Rensis, *New Patterns of Management.* New York: McGraw-Hill Book Co., 1961.

Lombard, George F. F., *Behavior in a Selling Group: A Case Study of Interpersonal Relations in a Department Store.* Boston: Division of Research, Harvard Business School, 1955.

————, *Interpersonal Behavior ....* See Turner.

Luce, R. Duncan, and Raiffa, Howard, *Games and Decisions: Introduction and Critical Survey.* New York: John Wiley & Sons, 1957.

McGregor, Douglas Murray, *The Human Side of Enterprise.* New York: McGraw-Hill Book Co., 1960.

McNair, Malcolm P., ed., *The Case Method at the Harvard Business School: Papers by Present and Past Members of the Faculty and Staff.* New York: McGraw-Hill Book Co., 1954.

Malinowski, Bronislaw, *Argonauts of the Western Pacific.* New York: E. P. Dutton & Co., 1922.

March, James G., and Simon, Herbert A., *Organizations.* New York: John Wiley & Sons, 1958.

Marx, Karl, *Capital: A Critique of Political Economy.* Translated by Eden and Cedar Paul. London: G. Allen & Unwin, 1928.

Maslow, A. H., *Motivation and Personality.* New York: Harper & Row, 1954.

May, Rollo, *Love and Will.* New York: W. W. Norton & Co., 1969.

Mayo, Elton, *The Human Problems of an Industrial Civilization.* New York: The Macmillan Co., 1933.

————, *The Social Problems of an Industrial Civilization*. Boston: Division of Research, Harvard Business School, 1945.

————, *The Political Problems of Industrial Civilization*. Boston: Division of Research, Harvard Business School, 1947.

————, *Some Notes on the Psychology of Pierre Janet*. Cambridge, Mass.: Harvard University Press, 1948.

Merton, Robert K., *Social Theory and Social Structure*. Glencoe, Ill.: The Free Press, 1949.

Morse, Nancy C., *Satisfactions in the White-Collar Job*. Ann Arbor, Mich.: Survey Research Center, Institute for Social Research, University of Michigan, 1953.

Murray, Henry A., "Toward a Classification of Interactions," in *Toward a General Theory of Action*. Edited by Talcott Parsons and Edward A. Shils. Cambridge, Mass.: Harvard University Press, 1951.

————; Barrett, William G.; Langer, Walter C., et al., *Explorations in Personality: A Clinical and Experimental Study of 50 Men of College Age*. New York: Oxford University Press, 1938.

Newcomb, Theodore M., *Personality and Social Change: Attitude Formation in a Student Community*. New York: The Dryden Press, 1943.

Ogden, Charles K., and Richards, I. A., *The Meaning of Meaning*. New York: Harcourt, Brace & Co., 1936.

Pareto, Vilfredo, *The Mind and Society*. Translated by Andrew Bongiorno and Arthur Livingston. 4 vols. New York: Harcourt, Brace & Co., 1935.

Parsons, Talcott, *The Structure of Social Action: A Study in Social Theory with Special Reference to a Group of Recent European Writers*. New York: McGraw-Hill Book Co., 1937.

Perrow, Charles, *Organizational Analysis: A Sociological View*. Belmont, Calif.: Wadsworth Publishing Co., 1970.

Piaget, Jean, *The Language and Thought of the Child*. Translated by Marjorie Gabain. New York: Harcourt, Brace & Co., 1926.

————, *Judgment and Reasoning in the Child*. Translated by Marjorie Gabain. New York: Harcourt, Brace & Co., 1928.

————, *The Child's Conception of the World*. Translated by Joan and Andrew Tomlinson. New York: Harcourt, Brace & Co., 1929.

————, *The Moral Judgment of the Child*. Translated by Marjorie Gabain. London: Kegan Paul, Trench, Trübner & Co., 1932.

Pierson, Frank C., et al., *The Education of American Businessmen: A Study of University-College Programs in Business Administration*. New York: McGraw-Hill Book Co., 1959.

Poincaré, Henri, *Science and Method*. Translated by Francis Maitland. New York: Thomas Nelson & Sons, 1914.

Polanyi, Michael, *Personal Knowledge: Towards a Post-critical Philosophy*. Chicago: The University of Chicago Press, 1958.

Radcliffe-Brown, A. R., *A Natural Science of Society*. Glencoe, Ill.: The Free Press, 1957.

Raiffa, Howard, and Schlaifer, Robert, *Applied Statistical Decision Theory*. Boston: Division of Research, Harvard Business School, 1961.

Rice, A. K., *Productivity and Social Organization: The Ahmedabad Experiment*. London: Tavistock Publications, 1958.

Roethlisberger, F. J., and Dickson, William J., with the assistance and collaboration of Wright, Harold A., *Management and the Worker: An Account of a Research Program Conducted by the Western Electric Company, Hawthorne Works, Chicago*. Cambridge, Mass.: Harvard University Press, 1939.

Roethlisberger, F. J., *Management and Morale*. Cambridge, Mass.: Harvard University Press, 1941.

————, *Man-in-Organization: Essays of F. J. Roethlisberger*. Cambridge, Mass.: The Belknap Press of Harvard University Press, 1968.

————, *Counseling....* See Dickson.

————, *The Motivation ....* See Zaleznik.

————, et al., *Training for Human Relations: An Interim Report*. Boston: Division of Research, Harvard Business School, 1954.

Rogers, Carl R., *Counseling and Psychotherapy: Newer Concepts in Practice*. Boston: Houghton Mifflin Co., 1942.

————, *Client-Centered Therapy: Its Current Practice, Implications, and Theory*. Boston: Houghton Mifflin Co., 1951.

————, *On Becoming A Person: A Therapist's View of Psychotherapy*. Boston: Houghton Mifflin Co., 1961.

Russett, Cynthia Eagle, *The Concept of Equilibrium in American Social Thought*. New Haven, Conn.: Yale University Press, 1966.

Sayles, Leonard R., *Behavior of Industrial Work Groups: Prediction and Control*. New York: John Wiley & Sons, 1958.

Selekman, Benjamin M., *Labor Relations and Human Relations*. New York: McGraw-Hill Book Co., 1947.

Selekman, Sylvia Kopald, and Selekman, Benjamin M., *Power and Morality in a Business Society*. New York: McGraw-Hill Book Co., 1956.

Selznick, Philip, *TVA and the Grass Roots: A Study in the Sociology of Formal Organization*. Berkeley: University of California Press, 1949.

_____, *Leadership in Administration: A Sociological Interpretation.* Evanston, Ill.: Row, Peterson & Co., 1957.

Simon, Herbert A., *The Sciences of the Artificial.* Cambridge, Mass.: The MIT Press, 1969.

Skinner, B. F., *Science and Human Behavior.* New York: The Macmillan Co., 1953.

Slichter, Sumner H., *Modern Economic Society.* New York: H. Holt & Co., 1931.

_____, *Union Policies and Industrial Management.* Washington, D.C.: The Brookings Institution, 1941.

Sofer, Cyril, *The Organization from Within: A Comparative Study of Social Institutions Based on a Sociotherapeutic Approach.* London: Tavistock Publications, 1961.

Tannenbaum, Robert; Weschler, Irving R.; and Massarik, Fred, *Leadership and Organization: A Behavioral Science Approach.* New York: McGraw-Hill Book Co., 1961.

Thompson, James D., ed., *Approaches to Organizational Design.* Pittsburgh: University of Pittsburgh, 1966.

Thompson, Victor A., *Modern Organization.* New York: Alfred A. Knopf, 1961.

Titchener, Edward Bradford, *A Beginner's Psychology.* New York: The Macmillan Co., 1915.

Tonnies, Ferdinand, *Vereins-und Versammlungsrecht wider die Koalitionsfreiheit.* Jena: G. Fischer, 1902.

Trist, E. L.; Higgins, G. W.; Murray, H.; and Pollock, A. B., *Organizational Choice: Capabilities of Groups at the Coal Face under Changing Technologies.* London: Tavistock Publications, 1963.

Turner, Arthur N., and Lombard, George F. F., *Interpersonal Behavior and Administration.* New York: The Free Press, 1969.

Warner, W. Lloyd, see Yankee City Series.

Weber, Max, *The Protestant Ethic and the Spirit of Capitalism.* Translated by Talcott Parsons. New York: C. Scribner's Sons, 1930.

White, Robert W., *Lives in Progress: A Study of the Natural Growth of Personality.* New York: The Dryden Press, 1952.

Whitehead, Alfred North, *Science and the Modern World.* New York: The Macmillan Co., 1925.

_____, *Process and Reality: An Essay in Cosmology.* New York: The Macmillan Co., 1929.

_____, *The Aims of Education and Other Essays.* London: Williams & Norgate, 1955.

_____, and Russell, Bertrand, *Principia Mathematica.* Cambridge, Eng.: Cambridge University Press, 1935.

Whitehead, T. N., *Leadership in a Free Society: A Study in Human Relations Based on an Analysis of Present-Day Industrial Civilization*. Cambridge, Mass.: Harvard University Press, 1936.

———, *The Industrial Worker: A Statistical Study of Human Relations in a Group of Manual Workers*. 2 vols. Cambridge, Mass.: Harvard University Press, 1938.

Whyte, William Foote, *Human Relations in the Restaurant Industry*. New York: McGraw-Hill Book Co., 1948.

———, *Street Corner Society: The Social Structure of an Italian Slum*. Chicago: The University of Chicago Press, 1955.

Woodward, Joan, *Industrial Organization: Theory and Practice*. London: Oxford University Press, 1965.

Wundt, Wilhelm, *An Introduction to Psychology*. Translated by Rudolf Pintner. London: G. Allen & Co., 1912.

The Yankee City Series. New Haven, Conn.: Yale University Press.

Warner, W. Lloyd, and Lunt, Paul S., *The Social Life of a Modern Community* (vol. 1, 1941).

——— and ———, *The Status System of a Modern Community* (vol. 2, 1942).

Warner, W. Lloyd, and Srole, Leo, *The Social Systems Of American Ethnic Groups* (vol. 3, 1945).

Warner, W. Lloyd, and Low, J. O., *The Social System of the Modern Factory. The Strike: A Social Analysis* (vol. 4, 1947).

Warner, W. Lloyd, *The Living and the Dead: A Study of the Symbolic Life of Americans* (vol. 5, 1959).

Zaleznik, A.; Christensen, C. R.; and Roethlisberger, F. J.; with the assistance and collaboration of Homans, George C., *The Motivation, Productivity, and Satisfaction of Workers: A Prediction Study*. Boston: Division of Research, Harvard Business School, 1958.

Index

EDITOR'S NOTE: In the Index, FJR stands for F. J. Roethlisberger, and HBS stands for Harvard Business School.—G.F.F.L.

Abstract(ed) systems, 402-411; technical systems as, 147; contrasted with concrete systems, 415-420, 431

Action: questions of in case discussions, 141-142; diagnosis and, 171-180; implementation of, in organizations, 444. *See also* Knowledge and action

Actors, problems of responsible, 435-439. *See also* Scientists and actors

Adams, Franklin P., 24

Adler, Alfred, 30

Administrative point of view (APV), 288-291, 292; and scientific point of view (SPV), 293-294, 301-304

Administrative Practices (course), 112, 115, 177, 236, 259-261; case books for, 112, 281-282; Edmund P. Learned made head of, 113, 273-274; introduction of, 113-114, 237, 269; FJR's teaching of, 114, 121, 271; changed to Human Behavior in Organizations, 114, 298; and psychotherapeutic counseling relationship, 201; as Element of Administration, 257, 264; and case method of teaching, 274-275; changes in teaching group of, 276-277; three group meetings on, 277-279; Paul R. Lawrence made head of, 278, 281; and administrative point of view, 288-289; failure of, to unite with Human Relations and Business Policy, 397

Administrator(s): and rational conception of organization, 182-184; and social conception of organization, 184-186; used interchangeably with executives and managers, 189; generalized formulation of their problems 189-192; training of, in contrast for observers and students, 258; and decision theory, 462-463; their role and skill, 468-473; and natural systems model, 469-470. *See also* Managers

Advanced Management Program (AMP), 110, 112, 115, 121, 177, 266, 296

Aesthetics, 36

Alger, Horatio, FJR's identification with, 17, 21, 23, 24, 52-53, 89, 430

Algonquin Group, 24

Allport, Gordon W., 116, 312, 453

American Book Company (New York, New York), FJR's employment as sales correspondent at, 23

American Smelting and Refining Company (El Paso, Texas), 84; FJR's employment as chemist at, 22-23

American Telephone & Telegraph Company, 46, 57

Anderson, Sherwood, 24

Andrews, Kenneth R., 113, 281; ed., *The Case Method of Teaching Human Relations and Administration,* 275; and Business Policy course, 277, 278

A-relations, 449-451, 452, 457, 463-464; description of, 439-442; and emphasis on B-relations, 442-449; equilibrium seeking properties of, 452-453; managers and workers and, 455-456; and limitations of change agentry, 459-462; in abstracted and concrete systems, 464-465; and principle of complementarity, 465, 467-468

Arensberg, Conrad, 55, 56, 308

Argyris, Chris, 309, 314

Aristotle, 73, 74, 130; *Nicomachean Ethics,* 360-361

Artificial and natural: characteristics of, compared 426-428; battle over in business schools, 429-431; usefulness and limitations compared, 469-473. *See also* Natural system models; Business schools

Athos, Anthony G., ix

Authority, in counseling relationship, 214-215

Bailey, Joseph C., 113, 278, 281, 296

Baker, George, 296

Baker, John C., 75-76, 77, 117

Bales, Robert F., 316

Barnard, Chester I., 66-67, 138, 364; *The Functions of the Executive,* 67; *Organization and Management,* 67; his definitions of effective and efficient, 158, 159, 376

Barnes, Louis B., ix, 281

Batista, Fulgencio, 254

Behavior, planned and emergent, 180-181, 377

Behavioral sciences, 116, 195; grants from Ford Foundation for research in, 217

Bendix, Reinhard, 318

Bennis, Warren G., 309, 314

Bernard, Claude, 138

Bethel, Maine, Group Dynamics program at, 222-229, 249. *See also* National Training Laboratories

Birthday problem, mathematicians', 330, 331-334

Bishop, John, 329-331, 334

Blake, Robert, 309

Blau, Peter M., 183, 318, 319

Bock, Arlie, 32, 90-91

Bodell, Prudence Celestine, 11

Boyle's law, 392

Bradford, Leland P. (Lee), and Group Dynamics, 222-223, 225, 227

B-relations, 449-451, 452, 457, 463-464; description of, 439-442; emphasis on, 442-449; managers and workers and, 455-456; and limitations of change agentry, 459-462; in abstracted and concrete systems, 464-465; and principle of complementarity, 465, 467-468

Brinton, Crane, 66

Broun, Heywood, 24

Bugental, James F. T., 312

Burling, Temple, 83

Burns, Tom, 320

Business Policy (course) 258, 259, 260-261, 262; teachers of, 277, 278; three group meetings with Administrative Practices and Human Relations, 277-279; and administrative point of view, 288-289; failure of, to unite with Administrative Practices and Human Relations, 397

Business schools: Carnegie and Ford Foundations' reports on conditions in, 294-295; battle over artificial versus natural in, 429-431; and principle of complementarity, 469

Cabell, James Branch, 24

Cabot, Hugh, 112

Cabot, Philip, 101; and FJR's study at General Motors, 76-77, 82; executive discussion groups of, 86-87; death of, 90

Cabot, Richard, 77

Carlyle, Thomas, *Sartor Resartus,* 31

Carnegie Foundation, 294

Cartwright, Dorwin, 316

Case, Everett, 117

Case method of teaching, 117, 119, 261; definition of, 123-124; objectives of, 124-125; FJR's qualms about, 125-126, 127; "perfect" solutions used in, 127-129; blind spots in, 129-132; FJR's observations about, 132-137; distinctions students failed to make in discussions, 137-140; different views of, 140-142; and diagnosis and action, 171-172; administration, early meetings about, 273-275; and administrative point of view, 288-289

Case research, 232-237

Castro, Fidel, 254

Change agentry, limitations of, 459-462

Chapple, Eliot D., 78, 84; and Yankee City studies, 55, 56; interaction chronograph of, 56-57, 62; and school of applied anthropology, 308, 320

Charles River, *see* Harvard University

Christensen, Roland (Chris), 426; and prediction study, 242, 245, 247, 248; and Business Policy course, 277

Clark, James V., 281

Classes and systems, 328-329; of a natural kind, 371-373; and concrete systems, 401-402. *See also* Social classes

Clinical findings (syndromes), listed, 470-472

Clinical method, problems in communication of, 229-230; practice of, in relation to soft and hard data, 239; Faculty views of, at HBS, 269; in relation to aims of HBS, 267-268; and clinical knowledge, 384; limitations of, 457-458. *See also* Conceptual scheme

Clinical psychologists, *see* Psychologists

Clinicians, 388-389, 392

Colgate University, 117

Columbia College, FJR's attendance at, 18-20, 132, 327

Committee on Faculty Organization, FJR's involvement with, 296, 297

Committee on Industrial Physiology, 32

Communication, in counseling relationships, 214-215

Complementarity, principle of, 431-432, 465-467; and skill and training of administrators, 467-473

Conant, James B., 195, 217

Concepts, elementary, 391, 392

Conceptual logicians, 388, 392

Conceptual scheme, 339, 373, 387; Henderson's, 65, 67-71, 139-140, 141, 224, 304, 390, 417, 419, 432; Faculty view of at HBS, 269-271; absence of a shared, among social science practitioners, 397-398. *See also* Social system(s)

Concrete systems, 328, 339, 373; classes and, 401-402; spaces and, 415-418; social space, social systems, and, 419-420

Consistency, notion of, 37

Control (control): course in, 257-260,

262, 288-289; in counseling relationship, 214-215

Convenience and utility, notion of, 37

Cornell University, 308

Correlation seekers and testers, 389, 393

"Cosmopolitans," at HBS, 257; defined, 262; 263-272 *passim*, 288. *See also* "Locals"

Cotter, Miss (Harvard University), 63

Counseling: with students, 33-35; 38; at Western Electric Co., 57-59; in psychology, 313-314

Counseling in an Organization (FJR and Bill Dickson), 59, 198

Counseling relationship, psychotherapeutic, 197-199, 201-203; problems of conceptualizing the, 203-207; viewed as a game, 205-212; communication between participants in, 207-209; characteristics of exchanges between participants in, 209-213; motivation, communication, authority, and control in, 214-215

Counselor-counselee relationship, 198-199

Counter-cultural movement, 343-345, 449

Curtis, George William, 12

Dashman Company Case, 171-177, 183, 186-190, 197

Data, soft and hard, 237-241, 246-247; in relation to (scientific) rules of evidence, 240

David, Donald K., 106, 114, 115, 119

Day, William, 76, 77

DBA (Doctor of Business Administration), 287, 292-293

DCS (Doctor of Commercial Science), 287

de Gaulle, Charles, 254

De Voto, Bernard, 66

Decision theory, 323-325; limitations of, 462-463

Derivation, 131-132, 158; defined, 131

Descartes, René, 26, 53, 270

Dichotomies, false, 39-41, 138, 139, 439

Dickson, William J. (Bill), 49; *Management and the Worker* (with FJR), 52, 53, 413; and counseling program at Western Electric, 57; *Counseling in an Organization* (with FJR), 59, 198

Dietz, Walter, 88-89

DIG, *see* Doctoral Instructional Group

Dill, Bruce, 32

Distributive justice, theory (law) of, 245-247, 248

Doctoral Instructional Group (DIG), 289, 293; members of, 291-292

Doctoral program (Harvard Business School), 296, 298; expansion of, 235-236, 250, 287-291; and DIG, 289, 291-292; aim of, 292-293; practitioners, researchers, and teachers in, 292-295; and Committee on Faculty Organization, 296, 297; line between scientific knowledge and administrative action in, 301-304

Donaldson, Gordon, 291

Donham, Wallace B., 30, 44, 82, 101, 105, 109; and Committee on Industrial Physiology, 32; and FJR's counseling of students, 34; and Henderson and Mayo, 61-62, 117, 267-269; retirement of, 90, 116, 118; his policy of interchangeable parts, 114; on Social Relations at Harvard University, 116; and human relations, 116-117, 118-119; and Visiting Firemen Program, 117, 119-120; influence on faculty of, 117-118; death of, 120; and case method, 123

Dooley, Channing, 88-89

Doriot, Georges F., 266-67, 269

Dos Passos, John, 24

Dreiser, Theodore, 24

Durkheim, Émile, 30, 31, 54, 304, 317

Edsall, David L., 32

Education, General, 115, 116, 119

Effective and efficient, 377; Chester Barnard's definitions of, 158, 159-163, 376

Efficiency, logic of, 412-415, 421. *See also* Logic

Einstein, Albert, 397, 439

Eisenhower, Dwight D., 195

Elements of Administration, 257-259, 264

Eliot, Charles W., 25

Elizabeth, Queen, 195

Employment, FJR's early, 22-23

Epistemology, 36, 71

Equilibrium: concept of, 373-375; problems of maintaining, 436-438

Erikson, Erik H., 305, 312

Ethics, 36

Etzioni, Amitai, 318

Euclid, 372

Evaluation: proper, and misevaluation, 134; external and internal, 377

Executive(s), *see* Administrator(s)

Existential psychologists, *see* Psychologists

Explanation (scientific): Homan's views of, 244-245, 385; and deductive systems, 386, 395-397

Fair exchange, logic of, 413-414, 421

Ferrand, Monsieur, 13

Festinger, Leon, 316

Finance, course in, 257-260, 262, 263-264; and administrative point of view, 288-289

Fitzgerald, F. Scott, 24

Flexner report, 294

Folts, Franklin E., 109, 291

Ford, Henry, 81-82

Ford Foundation, 116, 121, 269, 303, 467; Program Five of, 195, 196; grants by, for research in behavioral sciences, 217; management development programs sponsored by, 218; report of, on business schools, 294-295

Formal relations, 163

Fox, John, 88; and study at General Motors, 76, 77, 81; and study at Macy's, 83, 84

Francois (FJR's uncle), 14, 18, 19

Freud, Sigmund, 20, 54, 132, 138, 305, 317; impact of, on social science, 29, 304; FJR's reading of, 30, 31; influence of, on Mayo, 38-39; and obsessive thinking, 41; and neurotic thinking, 71; on experts in child psychology, 113; and psychoanalysis, 140, 204, 316; indebtedness of psychologists to, 312; articulateness of, 364; his handling of phenomena, 366

Fromm, Erich, 312

Fuller, Frances (Mulhearn), 120

Fuller, Stephen, 120

Galsworthy, John, 24

Games, models of, applied to counseling, 205-216

Gandhi, Mohandas, 195

Index

Gardner, Burleigh B., 55

Gargarin, Major, 254

General Motors, 85, 416; FJR's study at, 75-82, 83; employee cooperation and plant efficiency at, 98-99; strike at (1945-1946), 105; status relations at, 149; profits reported by (1965), 255

General-proposition makers, 389-390, 391, 393

George VI, King, 195

Gibbs, Willard, 68

Gibson, Hilden, 120

Gifford, Walter, 86

Gilson, Etienne, 26

Glenn, John, 254

Glover, John D. (Jack), 113, 172, 281; ed., *The Administrator: Cases on Human Relations in Business* (with Ralph Hower, ed.), 112, 282; and Business Policy course, 277, 278

Goals, organizational, *see* Purpose

Golembiewski, Robert T., 316

Gouldner, Alvin W., 183, 262, 318, 319

Gragg, Chuck, 113

Group Dynamics, 308-309; program at Bethel, Maine, 222-229, 249

Groups: small, 315-316; distinction between individual needs and needs of, 377

Hale, Merle, 77, 81

Hall, Edward T., 303

Hall, Max R., ix

Harbus News, 282

Hare, A. Paul, 316

Harvard Business Review, 87, 171, 466

Harvard Business School, 27; FJR's joining of, 29; increase in salary of FJR from, 35; and Hawthorne researches, 51; FJR's return to, 102, 105-106; grading system at, 110-111; policy of interchangeable parts at, 114-115; influence of Wallace Donham on, 117-118; case method at, 123-124, 141, 171-172, 232-237; Human Relations training at, compared with Group Dynamics, 222-224; social organization of, 257-272 *passim;* conceptual underpinning for, 267-272

Harvard Business School Bulletin, 282

Harvard Law School, 123

Harvard-Radcliffe Program in Business Administration (Management Training Program), 107-109, 110, 120, 296

Harvard University: FJR's attendance at, 24-27, 132, 327; Charles River, as a boundary in, 33-34; 65; 115-116; 119-120; Social Relations and General Education at, 115-121

Harvard University Press, 53, 87

Hassler, Russell, 296

"Hawthorne effect," 47, 50, 102, 109, 232, 365; defined, 46; "double-whammy," 51; requests for FJR and, 106; and counseling relationship, 212

Hawthorne researches, 35, 69, 212; described, 45-48; Elton Mayo's relation to, 48-51; publications resulting from, 51-54, 232; criticism of, 237; case research substantiating findings of, 240

Hayakawa, S. I., 72

Hegel, Georg Wilhelm Friedrich, 301-302

Hemingway, Ernest, 24

Henderson, Lawrence J., 38, 72, 101, 106, 138, 307, 338; on final task in science, vii; on acquisition of knowledge, 30, 352, 360; on two kinds of logic, 30-31, 153; and Committee on Industrial Physiology, 32; and Mayo and

Donham, 60-62, 117, 267-269; and Pareto, 61, 62-65, 66; his course on concrete sociology, 65-67; his conceptual scheme of a social system, 67-71, 139-140, 141, 224, 304, 390, 417, 419, 432; death of, 90; *Concrete Sociology,* 131; influence on FJR and Homans of, 243; and Max Weber, 318; on relation between theory and practice, 360; on natural systems, 371

Hierarchical relations, 165-166. *See also* Informal relations; Superior-subordinate relations

Hippocrates, 67, 373-374

Hiss, Alger, 105

Ho Chi Minh, 254

Homans, George C., 66, 138, 149, 155, 213, 261, 302, 384; and Mayo and Hawthorne researches, 49; and prediction study, 241-247, 248; *The Human Group,* 242, 243, 315; *Social Behavior: Its Elementary Forms,* 243, 394; visit of, to Business School, 303; on small-group researchers and theorists, 315; on FJR's setting up of dichotomy, 375; on external and internal systems, 376; on scientific explanation, 385, 386; and conceptual logicians, 388; general propositions of, 394-395; his concept of a theory, 396; on license allowed researchers in last chapters, 436

Horowitz, Murray, 303

Hostess House (later Lyman House), 33

Hower, Ralph, 113, 172; ed., *The Administrator: Cases on Human Relations in Business* (with Jack Glover, ed.), 112, 282; and Administrative Practices course, 281

Human Behavior in Organizations (course), 114, 298

Human Organization (formerly *The Journal of Applied Anthropology),* 309

Human Problems of Administration (course), 107-109, 113

Human Relations (human relations), 121, 195-196; Dean Donham's course in, 116-117, 119; practice, 197; second-year elective course in, 197-201, 215, 249, 269, 276; training, 217, 229; skills, contexts for learning, 219-220; practitioner, problem of multidimensionality for, 221; Group Dynamics brand of, 222-228; case research in, 232-237; three group meetings on, 277-279; use of words Organizational Behavior in place of, 279, 316; McNair's talk on ("What Price Human Relations?"), 282-285; area coordinators for, 296; in 1940s and early 1950s, 308-309; in 1960s, 309-312; humanistic psychologists and, 312-315; and small-group researchers and theorists, 315-316; and bureaucratic sociologists, 316-319; and sociotechnical systems, 319-321; failure of, to unite with Administrative Practices and Business Policy, 397

Human Relations (Studies Toward the Integration of the Social Sciences), 309

Human Relations Clinic, 217-219, 229, 250, 269, 281, 285; contexts in which to learn human relations skills at, 219-222

Humanistic psychologists, *see* psychologists

Hume, David, 36-37, 137

Hypothesis seekers and testers, 389, 393

Informal relations, 163-167

Intellectual life, divisions of FJR's, 2-6

Interactions, 56, 65-67, 146; as unit for study, 45; machine to measure, 56-57; at Spring Lake Ranch, 96. *See also* Social space

International Teachers' Program (ITP), 296

Jacques, Elliot, 320

James, William, 24, 137, 352

Janet, Pierre, 30, 31, 138, 329; *Psychologi-*

Index

cal Healing, 38; influence of, on Mayo, 38-39; and obsessive thinking, 41

Job Instruction Training (JIT), 88

Job Methods Training (JMT), 88

Job Relations Training (JRT), 88

Johnson, Wendell, 72

Journal of Applied Anthropology, The (later *Human Organization*), 309

Jung, C. G., 30, 39

Kahn, Robert L., 316

Kant, Immanuel, 37, 62, 69

Kaplan, Abraham, 56

Katz, Daniel, 316

Katz, Robert L., 281

Kennedy, John F., 254

Kennedy, Sargent, 76, 77

King, Martin Luther, 254

Kluckhohn, Clyde, 116

Knowledge: first element in acquisition of, 30; Hume on two kinds of, 36-37; extrinsic and intrinsic aspects of, 220-221; relation of skill to, 349, 351-352; of acquaintance, 352, 391; makers, different kinds of, 388-391; enterprise, products and findings of, 391-393; about human behavior, problems shared in development of, 393-398; prescriptive and descriptive, 452-456; subjects and objects of, 441; 453-455; 464-465

Knowledge, analytical: transition from clinical to, 383-388; three sublevels of, 391-392. *See also* Knowledge

Knowledge, clinical, 368-369, 391, 392; and classification of phenomena, 369-373; and concept of equilibrium, 373-375; and external and internal systems, 375-382; transition from, to analytical knowledge, 383-388; and case descriptions needed today, 470-472. *See also* Knowledge

Knowledge and action, 301-302; 435-436, 449-451; and problems of maintaining equilibrium, 436-438; and problems of drawing boundary lines, 438-439; A-relations and B-relations affecting, 439-442, 449-451; emphasis on B-relations affecting, 442-449; and principle of complementarity, 465-467; intrinsic character of relation between, 466-467

Knudsen, William, 80, 81-82, 86

Korean War, 195

Korzybski, Count Alfred, 129, 133, 137, 140, 189; *Science and Sanity,* 71; and general semantics, 71-74

Kuhn, Thomas S., 385; his concept of a paradigm, 395-397

Labor Relations, courses in, 263, 265-266

Landsberger, Henry A., *Hawthorne Revisited,* 306

Lawrence, Paul R., 278, 320; and Organizational Behavior group, 281, 297; ed. (et al.), *Organizational Behavior and Administration: Cases, Concepts, and Research Findings,* 281, 282

Lazarsfeld, Paul A., 265, 303

Learned, Edmund P., 109; and Administrative Practices course, 113, 273-274, 277, 281; and Business Policy course, 277, 278

Leavitt, Harold J., 309

Ledlie Prize, awarded to FJR, 248

Lee, Irving J., 72, 133, 134

Lehrer, Thomas, 329-330

Lévy-Bruhl, Lucien, 71

Lewin, Kurt, 69, 140-141, 224; and Group Dynamics program, 222, 308, 316

Lewis, Sinclair, 24

Life (or personal) space, 24, 79, 327, 336, 438-439; FJR's discovery of, 2, 36-39; preoccupations as a way of exploring, 39-44; definition of, 402-406; logical properties of, 409-411; rationality and ideals of, 415; relation of, to concrete systems, 416-418; ordering of, according to some criterion of value, 421-423; ordering of, empirically, 424-426; affinities between social space and, 426-428; relation of, in abstracted systems, 464

Likert, Rensis, 309, 314

"Locals," at HBS, 257, defined, 262; 263-272 passim, 288, 326. See also "Cosmopolitans"

Locke, John, 69

Logic: two kinds of, 31; of efficiency, 147, 412-415, 421; of management (or formal organization), 413-415, 421; of sentiments, 414, 421, 449

Logical and nonlogical, distinction between: as applied to behavior, 63-65, 153; as applied to merchandise, 84-85

Logical Properties, see Properties

Lombard, George F. F., 112, 116; role as editor, x; and study at General Motors, 76, 77; and study at Macy's, 83; Behavior in a Selling Group, 83; and Frances Mulhearn and Harriet Ronken, 120; course taught by, in Human Relations, 198, 277, 278, 285; Training for Human Relations (with FJR and Harriet Ronken), 221-222; and Organizational Behavior group, 280-281

Lorsch, Jay W., 320

Lowell, A. Lawrence, 60, 66, 67, 76

Lynton, Harriet (Ronken), 112, 120, 221-222

Lynton, Rolf, 120

McCarthyism, 195

McGregor, Douglas, 309; Theories X and Y of, 298, 314, 459

McNair, Malcolm P., 263, 270, 297, 298; ed., The Case Method at the Harvard Business School, 275; "What Price Human Relations?" (talk), 282-285

Macy's, 75; FJR's study at, 83-86; status relations at, 149

Malcolm X, 254

Malinowski, Bronislaw, 29, 31, 54, 304

Malott, Deane, 117

Man-in-the-middle syndrome, 167, 471

Man-in-Organization (FJR), 3, 48, 134, 470; "The Nature of Obsessive Thinking" in, 40; "The Secret of Success" in, 42; "The Foreman: Master and Victim of Double Talk" in, 167

Management, scientific, 84; logic of, see Logic

Management Controls (course), 109, 113

Management and Morale (FJR), 3, 87, 106

Management and the Worker (FJR and William J. Dickson), 42, 87, 106, 310, 329; Mayo's preface to, 49; writing of, 51-54; account of Relay Assembly Test Room experiment in, 109, 328; "Complaints and Social Equilibrium" in, 149, 244; criticisms of, 232, 237-238, 304-308; and "logic of management," 413

Management science, 429

Management-worker relations, 159-163

Managers: professional identity for, 3; and rational cooperation, 157-158; and human factor, 168-171; and reciprocal relations, 169; and workers, and A-relations and B-relations, 455-456; and change agents, 459-462; proactive, and knowledge for, 472-473. See also Administrator(s)

Mann, Thomas, 24

Index

Manufacturing (course), 267

March, James G., 323

Marketing, course in, 257-260, 262, 263-264; and administrative point of view, 288-289

Marshall, Alfred, 21

Marshall Plan, 105

Marx, Karl, 21, 166, 305, 316-318

Maslow, Abraham H., 298, 312, 314

Massachusetts Institute of Technology (M.I.T.): FJR's attendance at, 20-22, 23, 132; Research Center for Group Dynamics at, 222

Mathematical models, limitations of, 462-464

Mathematics: FJR's interest in, 326-328; and FJR's learning to count, 330-331, 334; and birthday problem, 330, 331-334

Matters of fact, *see* Relations of ideas

Maugham, Somerset, 24

May, Rollo, 312

Mayo, Elton, 33, 44, 66, 101, 102, 117, 132, 137, 307; FJR's first meeting with, 27; impact on FJR of, 29-31, 60, 106, 243; *The Human Problems of an Industrial Civilization,* 31, 449; and Committee on Industrial Physiology, 32; and FJR's counseling of students, 34-35; and FJR's discovery of life space, 36; influence of Freud and Janet on, 38-39, 329; relation of, to Hawthorne researches, 46, 48-51, 69, 365; and *Management and the Worker* (FJR), 52, 53, 305; and Lloyd Warner and Yankee City studies, 54-56; and Henderson and Donham, 60-62, 117, 267-269; and Philip Cabot's executive discussion groups, 87; FJR's relationship with, 90, 91; classroom style of, 107; retirement of, 115, 280; and human relations, 222, 308, 309, 316; and soft data, 238; and clinical method of observation, 304; criticisms of, 305, 306, 310; and Max Weber, 318; and philosophical

questions, 338; *The Social Problems of an Industrial Civilization,* 344; and turbulent sixties, 345-346; on development of skill, 351, 352, 355, 359

MBA program, 287, 288-289, 296; changes in curriculum of, 257-258; aim of, 292-293

Mencken, H. L., 24

Meredith, James, 254

Meriam, Richard S., 109, 291

Merton, Robert K., 183, 265, 318

Metaphysics, 36

Middle Management Program, 296

Model(s): makers or builders, 390-391; natural and artificial systems, 469-473. *See also* Systems

Morley, Christopher, 24

Motivation, in counseling relationship, 214-215

Motivation, Productivity, and Satisfaction of Workers, The (A. Zaleznik, R. Christensen, FJR, and G. Homans), 245, 247, 248, 426

Mouquin, Henri, 11

Mulhearn, Frances (later Mrs. Stephen Fuller), 120

Multi-dimensionality, problem of, 221

Murray, Henry A., 36, 116, 453

Mussolini, Benito, 317

Nathan, George Jean, 24

National Education Association, 222

National Training Laboratories, 218, 222, 309. *See also* Bethel, Maine, Group Dynamics program at

Needs (of individuals): contrasted with organizational purpose, 138, 152; and external and internal systems, 377-382. *See also* Rewarding relations

New York World, 24

Newcomb, Theodore M., 316

Newton, Sir Isaac, 213, 394, 439

Nondirective interviewing method: used with executives, 78; defined, 135-136; in case method teaching, 313

North Atlantic Defense Treaty, 195

Obsessive thinking: FJR's paper on the "Nature of," 40; Janet's view of, 41; and skill, 139

O.D. (organizational design), 321

Office of Production Management (OPM), 87

Ogden, Charles K., *The Meaning of Meaning* (with I. A. Richards), 72

Ohio University, 117

O'Neill, Eugene, 24, 146

Oppenheimer, Robert, 195

Organization(s): relations in, 143-167; technical, 145-148; rational conception of, 182-184; social system conception of, 184-188, 191-192; distinction between formal and informal, 375-376, 377. *See also* Systems

Organizational Behavior, 5, 298-299; early development of area of, 273-279, 285; use of words, in place of "Human Relations," 279, 316; group, FJR as informal leader of, 279-282; FJR's chairmanship of, 297; reading seminar in, 302-304; and management sciences, 429

Organizational theory, state of, in 1960s, 336-339

Orth, Charles D., 281

Packard, Fabyan, 34

Paradigm, concept of a, 344, 385; 395-397

Pareto, Vilfredo, 132, 138, 304, 317, 414, 462; *Sociologie Générale,* 60, 62; and L. J. Henderson, 61, 62-65, 66, 269, 307; triangle of, 130-131; on residue and derivation, 131, 158, 417; on logical-nonlogical, 153

Parsons, Talcott, 116

Paul VI, Pope, 255

Pearl Harbor, 59, 90

Pennock, Mr. (Western Electric), 48

Perrow, Charles, 320

Personal space, *see* Life space

Personnel and Management Controls (course), 110

Phenomena: notion of correspondence to, 37; social, and social skill, 361-367; classification of, 369-373

Philosophy, traditional subdivisions of, 36

Piaget, Jean, 30, 71, 304, 352

Poincaré, Henri, 70

Policy, *see* Business Policy

Poseidon, 152-154, 158

Practitioners: first and second level defined, 217-218: training of, 221, as aim of MBA program, 292-293

Prediction study, 241-247

Preoccupation(s), 45; FJR's control regained over, 35-36; FJR's observations of uniformities in students', 39-44. *See also* Life space

Proactivity, 213, 453-455; defined, 453; of managers and workers, 455-456; and trainer-client relation, 457-458. *See also* Reactivity

Production, course in, 257-260, 262, 270; and administrative point of view, 288-289

Program for Management Development (PMD), 296

Properties, logical, of reflexiveness, symmetry, transitivity, and their opposites, 144; 406-411

Propositions: analytical and synthetic, 37; used in the prediction study, 245; scientific, 385-386; general, 389-390, 391-392, 393-395; empirical, 391-392, 394

Psychologists, clinical, humanistic, and existential, 312-315

Public Relations and Responsibilities (course), 259-260, 263; introduction of, 257; different names for, 264-265

Purpose, organizational: at Spring Lake Ranch, 91-92; 97-102; defined, 152-155; and external and internal systems, 377-382

Purposive space, 336, 415, 419-420, 438-439; definition of, 402-406; logical properties of, 408-409, 411; rationality and ideals of, 412-413; relation of, to concrete systems, 416-418; ordering of, according to some criterion of value, 421-423; ordering of, empirically, 424-426; affinities between technological space and, 426-428; relation of, in concrete systems, 464

Pusey, Nathan, 195, 299

Putnam, Mark L. ("Put"), 49, 57

Radcliffe-Brown, A. R., 29, 54, 138, 304, 371

Radcliffe College, see Harvard-Radcliffe Program in Business Administration

Raiffa, Howard, 330, 334-335

Rationality, machine, 146-147; bounded, 323

Reactivity, 213, 453-455; defined, 453;

of managers and workers, 455-456. See also Proactivity

Reductionism, 393-394

Reflexiveness, property of: in organizational relations, 143-144; in the four spaces, 406-411. See also Properties

Relations of ideas and matters of fact, 36-37; 137; 144

Research Center for Group Dynamics, 309. See also National Training Laboratories

Researchers: and teachers, training of, as aim of Doctoral program, 292-293; and theorists, small-group, 315-316

Residue, 131-132, 158, 417; defined, 131

Restriction-of-output syndrome, 167, 471

Revolutions, varieties of, 5-6

Rewarding relations (satisfaction), 155-158

Ricardo, David, 21

Rice, A. Kenneth, 320

Richards, I. A., *The Meaning of Meaning* (with C. K. Ogden), 72

Richon, Jules, 11

Rights, universalistic versus particularistic, 448-449

Roberts, Mrs. Ragnhild J., 108

Rockefeller Foundation, 32, 52, 115

Roethlisberger, Fritz J., his purposes and concerns in writing the book, vii-viii, 1-2; birth of, 11; childhood and adolescence of, 12-18; early attitude toward science of, 15-16, 17-18; education of, 15, 16, 18-22, 24-27; early attitude toward religion of, 17; early employment of, 22-23; marriage of, to Margaret Dixon, 27-28; joins Harvard Business School, 29. See also throughout index

Roethlisberger, Isa (sister of FJR), 12, 13, 15, 16, 20

Roethlisberger, Jean Richon (daughter of FJR), 92

Roethlisberger, Margaret (Dixon) (wife of FJR), 27-28, 92, 297

Roethlisberger, Robert (uncle of FJR), 11, 15

Rogers, Carl R., 298, 312; *Counseling and Psychotherapy,* 135, 209, 314; *Client-Centered Therapy,* 209, 314; nondirective approach of, 313; *On Becoming a Person,* 314

Role(s): administrative and therapeutic, 100-101; occupational, differences between in modern and primitive societies, 445-449; administrator's, 468-473

Ronken, Harriet (later Mrs. Rolf Lynton), 112, 120; *Training for Human Relations* (with FJR and George Lombard), 221-222

Roosevelt, Franklin Delano, 85, 105, 107

Rousseau, Jean Jacques, 316

Royce, Josiah, 24

Russell, Bertrand, 25, 29, 137; analytic philosophy of, 37; and logic and mathematics, 72, 73, 74

Santayana, George, 24

Sarcka, Wayne and Elizabeth, 90-92; and organization of Spring Lake Ranch, 93-97; and problems of administration, leadership, and therapy at Spring Lake Ranch, 97-101

Satellites, launching of first, 253-54

Satisfaction, *see* Rewarding relations

Sayles, Leonard R., 309, 320

Scientific point of view (SPV), and administrative point of view (APV), 293-294, 301-304

Scientists and actors, misunderstandings between, 453-455; summarized, 464-465

Seiler, John A., 281

Selekman, Benjamin M., 107, 265-266

Selznick, Philip, 183

Semantics, Korzybski and general, 71-74

Sentiments, logic of, *see* Logic

Shaw, Clifford, 33

Sheffer, H. M., 25-26

Shepard, Alan, 254

Simon, Herbert A., 147, 322, 323

Sinclair, Upton, 21

Skill: contrasted to obsessive thinking, 139; of a carpenter, 163-164; contexts for learning human relations, 219-220; nature of, 349-353; development of, 353-354; distinction between technical and social, 354-355, 357, 358, 359, 361-362; nature of social, 354-359; and relation between theory and practice, 359-361; social, and social phenomena, 361-367; of administrators, 468-473

Skinner, B. F., 34, 127

Slichter, Sumner H., 265, 266

Sloan, Alfred P., 80, 81, 86

Small-group researchers and theorists, 315-316

Smith, Adam, 21

Social classes; 55-56, 76, 77, 84, 85, 130. *See also* Social space; Warner, W. Lloyd

Social Psychology of Organizations, 298

Social Relations (social relations): Department of, at Harvard University, 116, 121; spatial, temporal, and, 143-145. *See also* Social space, social system(s)

Social reality: as defined by disadvantaged, 448-449; and A-relations and B-relations, 465-466; complementarity and role of administrators, 468

Social space, 64, 115, 327, 336, 438-439; FJR's discovery of, 2, 45; definition of, 402-406, 419; logical properties of, 409, 411; rationality and ideals of, 413-415; relation of, to concrete systems, 416-418; social systems, concrete systems, and, 419-420; ordering of, according to some criterion of value, 421-423; ordering of, empirically, 424-426; affinities between life space and, 426-428; relation of, in abstracted systems, 464; *See also* Social system(s)

Social system(s): conception of organization, 184-188, 191-192; natural, 369-373; social space, concrete systems, and, 419-420. *See also* Conceptual scheme(s); Social space

Society for Applied Anthropology, 309

Society, modern, problems in, 449-451

Sociologists, bureaucratic, 316-319

Sociology, Henderson's course on concrete, 65-67

Sofer, Cyril, 320

Sorokin, Pitirim, 62

Spaces, 401; pure, of mathematics, 327-328, 330, 405; empirical sample, 328-329; four kinds of, 402-406; logical properties of, 406-411; rationality and ideals of, 412-415; and concrete systems, 415-418; ordering of, according to some criterion of value, 421-423; ordering of, empirically, 424-426; affinities among, 426-428. *See also* Life space; Purposive space; Social space; Technological space

Spatial, temporal, and social relations, 143-145

Spring Lake Ranch: FJR's stay at, 90-102; organization of, 92-97; problems of administration, leadership, and therapy at, 97-101

Staff-line relationships, 200-201

Stalin, Joseph, 195

Stalker, G. M. 320

Starcher, George, 120

Staten Island Academy, FJR's attendance at, 15, 16, 18

Status relations, 148-149

Steadman, Edith, 108

Stein, Gertrude, 235

Stevenson, Adlai, 255

Stoll, Clarence, 53, 86

Stouffer, Samuel A., 303

Stratton, Gerald B., 112-113

Straus, Jack, 86

Subject matter, FJR's: concerns about, 5, 121-122; 195-196; 249-250; defined, 142-168 *passim*; revisited, 401-432 *passim*

Superior-subordinate relations, 149-152; application of counseling in, 199-200

Surface, James R., 281

Syndrome: man-in-the-middle, 167. *See also* Clinical findings

Synergy, 51

Systems: external and internal, 99, 375-381; technical in organizations, 145-148; socio-technical, 319-321; natural and abstract, 371-372; conceptualization of, 381-382; theory, 382; deductive, 386; varieties of, 405, 406; abstracted and concrete, 406, 464-465; social space, concrete systems, and social, 419-420; natural and artificial systems, 426-428; battles in the business schools, 429-431. *See also* Concrete systems; Model(s); Organization(s); Social system(s)

Symmetry, property of: in organizational relations, 143-144; in the four spaces, 406-411. *See also* Properties

Tannenbaum, Robert, 309

Taussig, F. W., 21

Tavistock Institute of Human Relations, 308-309, 320

Taxonomies, 369-371

Teachers and researchers, training of, as aim of Doctoral program, 292-293

Technical organization, 145-148

Technological space, 336, 415, 438-439; definition of, 402-406; logical properties of, 407, 408, 411; rationality and ideals of, 412-413; relation of, to concrete systems, 416-418; ordering of, according to some criterion of value, 421-423; ordering of, empirically, 424-426; affinities between purposive space and, 426-428; relation of, in concrete systems, 464

Teele, Stanley F., 283, 296

Temporal, spatial, and social relations, 143-145

T-groups, 298, 321; FJR's experience in, at Group Dynamics program (Bethel, Maine), 222-229 *passim*; emphasis on, in 1960 version of human relations, 310, 313, 314-315; and organizational design, 321; distinction between external and internal systems in, 376

Transitivity, property of: in organizational relations, 143-144; in the four spaces, 406-411

Thaten, Carl (stepbrother of FJR), 13

Thaten, Max (stepbrother of FJR), 13

Thaten, Max (stepfather of FJR), 13-14, 15, 17

Thaten, Wilma (Dede, stepsister of FJR), 13

Theories X and Y, *see under* McGregor, Douglas

Theorists, descriptive and prescriptive, 454-455

Theory and practice, relation between, 353, 359-361

Thompson, James D., 320

Titchener, Edward B., 36

Tonnies, Ferdinand, 138

Tosdal, Harry R., 291

Trade Union Program (TUP), 121, 296

Trainer-client relation, 457-458

Training for Human Relations (FJR, George Lombard, and Harriet Ronken), 221-222, 244

Training Within Industry (TWI), 87-88

Trist, Eric L., 320

Truman, Harry, 105

Truth, FJR's three notions of, 37-38

Turner, Arthur N., 198, 281

Turner, C. E., 48

Ulrich, David, 112

United Automobile Workers, strike by (1945-1946), 105

United Nations, 105, 255

United Steel Workers, strike by (1946), 105

University of California at Los Angeles, 470

University of Kansas, 117

University of Michigan, 308

Value(s): humanistic and scientific, 298; criterion for ordering the spaces, 421-426; shared, 437-438

Vatter, Paul, 329, 334

Veblen, Thorstein, 21

Vietnam War, 254

Visiting Firemen Program, 117, 119-120, 121

Walker, Ross G., 109, 291

War Industry Retraining program, 110-113, 121

War Production Board (WPB), 87

Warner, W. Lloyd, 155; and Hawthorne researches, 48-49; and Yankee City studies, 54-57; differences between Mayo and, 56; on social classes, 76, 77, 84, 85. See also Social classes

Weber, Max, 154, 163, 324; and bureaucratic sociology, 316-319; *The Protestant Ethic and the Spirit of Capitalism,* 319

Wells, H. G., 24

Western Electric Company, 52, 53, 55, 75, 76, 83; Hawthorne plant of, 46, 57; counseling program at, 57-59, 198; employee cooperation and efficiency at, 98; status relations at, 149; goals of, 152

Wheeler, William Morton, 32

White, Robert W., 312

Whitehead, Alfred North, 25-26, 29, 107, 138; analytic philosophy of, 37; and logic and mathematics, 72, 73, 74; influence on FJR and Homans of, 243; on Descartes, 270; on Hegelian cycle in educational process, 301-302

Whitehead, Thomas North, 49, 107-108; *The Industrial Worker,* 52

Whyte, William F., 308, 311, 320

Woodward, Joan, 320

Worcester, Alfred, 33, 90

World War II, 105

Wright, Harold A. (Hal), 49, 52, 57

Wundt, Wilhelm, 36

Yankee City studies, Lloyd Warner and, 54-57

Zaleznik, Abe, 298, 426; and prediction study, 242, 245-246, 247, 248; and Human Relations course, 278; and Organizational Behavior group, 281

Zander, Alvin, 316